Unholy War

RANDALL PRICE

HARVEST HOUSE PUBLISHERS
Eugene, Oregon 97402

Cover by Terry Dugan Design, Minneapolis, Minnesota

UNHOLY WAR
Copyright © 2001 by Randall Price
Published by Harvest House Publishers
Eugene, Oregon 97402

Library of Congress Cataloging-in-Publication Data
  Price, Randall.
    Unholy War / Randall Price.
      p. cm.
    Includes bibliographical references (p.).
    ISBN 0-7369-0823-4
      1. Jerusalem—International status. 2. Arab-Israeli conflict—1993-
    3. Jerusalem in Judaism. 4. Jerusalem in Chistianity. 5. Jerusalem in Islam.
    I. Title.

DS109.95 .P75 2002

956.94'42—dc21   2001039810

Printed in the United States of America.

06 07 / BP-MS / 10 9 8

Dedicated to

Dr. George Harry Leafe

and

Dr. Stephen Paul Sullivan

Professors,
Pastors,
Prayer Partners,
Mentors,
WBM Board Members
and above all,
Friends

*Thanks, Harry and Steve, for
your faithfulness, fellowship,
and love for the Land God loves.*

Acknowledgments

I am increasingly grateful to more and more people with each new book I write, and beside the purpose of writing itself, the benefit of making new friends in the process has made this effort worthwhile. Thanks must be given first to Harvest House Publishers, president Bob Hawkins, Jr., vice president of editorial Carolyn McCready, and the publisher's committee for accepting and encouraging my writing of this work, a work which was initially completed before the September 11 attack on America and then rushed into rewrite! Thanks is also extended to my editor Steve Miller for his many suggestions throughout the writing and editing stages, as well as the Harvest House production team of Matt Shoemaker, Corey Fisher, and Gary Lineburg, who worked on the layout and photos. And special thanks go to the entire Harvest House team for its efforts to put this book on the fast track without sacrificing its quality.

In Israel my thanks goes to Shmuel Smadja and David Katz of Sar-el Travel for provisions while in Jerusalem, and Binyamin Lalaizou and Dr. Carl DeRouen II for their assistance with the photographs. I am also grateful to the following who shared their time in Jerusalem for my questions: former prime minister Benjamin Netanyahu; Amir Tadmor, former spokesman to Yitzhak Rabin; Yochanan Ramati, director of the Jerusalem Institute for Western Defense; Rabbi Chaim Richman of the Temple Institute; Gershon Salomon, director of the Temple Mount Faithful Movement; and Sheikh Ikrima Sabri, Palestinian Mufti of Jerusalem. I am especially grateful for the assistance with research on the teachings of Islam and Palestinian revisionism provided by David Foster, a SIM missionary to Muslims in Durban, South Africa, Mansour Boutros, and Walid, a former Palestinian activist and fundamentalist Muslim who is now a Christian believer and apologist to Muslims. Thanks also goes to Alexander Schick of Sylt, Germany for valuable research assistance and for the use of his photographic archive.

I am also especially grateful for my mother Maurine Price, who provided a place to write a portion of this book and helped with newspaper research; for my son-in-law, Eric Ream, who typed the Recommended Reading list; and Ken Stanford, who assisted in preparing the index. Appreciation goes as well to my friends Gordon Franz and Bob Handley, who sent articles used in my research. And, my greatest thanks must be reserved for my wife, Beverlee, and my children at home (Eleisha, Erin, Jonathan, and Emilee) who were once again patient with a writing husband and father. They have prayed for this book to bring understanding to those who seek the reason for the war and misunderstand the roles of Israel and Islam. I pray that their petition would be answered in the lives of each of my readers.

Contents

The Day the World Changed 7

1. Why Are We at War? 17

2. What's Israel Got to Do with It? 35

3. What Are Jews and Arabs Fighting About? 55

4. Why Should Their Fight Matter to Me? 69

5. Why Is Jerusalem So Important? 85

6. How Did the Conflict Begin? 105

7. Who Are the Palestinians? 131

8. What Is the Palestinian Claim to the Land? 145

9. What Is the Palestinian Right to Return? 161

10. What Is Islam's Role in the Conflict? 177

11. What Makes a Muslim Militant? 199

12. Why Can't They Share Jerusalem? 223

13. What Is the Trouble with the Temple Mount? 241

14. What Is the Truth About the Temple Mount? 259

15. What Is Happening on the Temple Mount? 279

16. Does Prophecy Affect Politics? 301

17. Why Can't They All Just Get Along? 323

18. Will There Be Another War? 341

19. Will There Ever Be Peace? 361

20. What Should We Do? 375

   Chronology of the Middle-East Conflict 391

   Glossary 401

   Recommended Reading 418

   Notes 422

   Person Index 439

   Subject Index 440

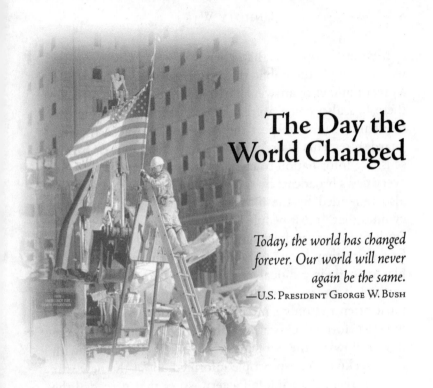

The Day the World Changed

Today, the world has changed forever. Our world will never again be the same.
—U.S. President George W. Bush

Everyone remembers where they were on the morning of September 11, 2001, the day the world changed. I was in a hotel lobby in Atlanta, perusing my notes while waiting to present a conference entitled "The Battle for Jerusalem." Never could I have imagined that before I left that lobby the very war about which I was to speak would come to my own country! I did not give that message that morning, but instead I opened the floor for questions from the anxious audience. And the questions came with passion: Why are we at war? Who's to blame? Why would Muslims do this? What does this have to do with the Middle East conflict? As I attempted to provide answers for these several hundred people, I was aware that millions all across America and in other countries were asking the same questions as well.

My initial hope was that a newly motivated news media would provide the public the answers it needed. Yet while a great number of answers have subsequently been offered, there has also come a great deal of obfuscation. On the one hand, I must respect the news sources' need to safeguard statements in order to not excite the public or betray sensitive information to enemies (who can watch any and every news broadcast by satellite). On the other hand, I am also reminded by the fifth-century Greek historian Thucydides that "most people will not take pains to get at the truth of things, and are much more inclined to accept the first story they hear." Whether or not the news media is biased in their political reporting, or hampered by their sources, its story is usually the first story people hear, and most often the only source by which most people's opinions are formed concerning the Middle East. While the days following the September 11 attack were filled with news seeking to keep people informed about the new war on terrorism, the Middle Eastern issues that preceded the attack have largely been avoided in the press.

Some of this, of course, is to be expected. Reporters report only what they deem newsworthy, and even when the media does touch on the root causes of events, the selected scenes we see on the television rarely reveal the true or full context of the situation to viewers. In addition, because the war on terrorism will take place mostly through covert operations, propaganda and disinformation are acceptable tools of warfare. Such tools have long been employed in reports that originate in the Middle East, and in the case of Israel in particular, there have been attempts to rewrite the history of the region, casting aside historical realities in order to create a national catastrophe around which the Islamic world can rally. But, if this is a war, and we are being asked to fight, then we must have accurate facts. This book seeks to counter this historical revisionism and bring out the truth behind the headlines.

Unholy War—the World's New War

It is also imperative that we understand the nature of this new war. While the United States has strenuously objected to any notion of this war being a religious war, the enemy has never called it anything else. Osama bin Laden, rejecting the American statement that this is a "war on terrorism," has declared, "They came out to fight Islam with the name of fighting terrorism....I say these events [the American-led bombing of Kabal, Afghanistan on October 7, 2001] have split the whole world into two camps: the camp of belief [Muslims] and disbelief [non-Muslims]."[1] In like manner, a Pakistani website posted on its homepage in full-color graphics the words "World War III—America against Islam!"[2] Furthermore, the Islamic suicide squads that attacked the World Trade Center and the Pentagon spoke of their actions as fulfilling the Qur'anic command of *jihad* ("holy war"). Until September 11, most Americans seldom saw or heard the Arabic word *jihad*, but now it has become an unwelcomed part of the nation's everyday vocabulary.

This war, however, is anything but a holy war. Its treacherous tactics and ungodly goal to subjugate the non-Muslim world have made even moderate Muslims decry it as a violation of the Qur'an. It is, rather, an unholy war, waged by despots who cloak their wanton personal ethics in a guise of fundamentalist Islam. In this war they are using the suffering of their poverty-stricken people, caused by their own repressive policies, and the cause of the Palestinians, oppressed by their own corrupt terrorist leaders, to enlist the allegiance of millions of uninformed Muslims the world over. This book is an attempt to expose the façade of injustice claimed by radical Islam against America and Israel and reveal the unholy character of the conflict.

The Israel Factor—Key to the Present Conflict

Because of a deliberate diversion by the U.S. presidential administration away from what it believed would directly affect the success of its war against terrorism, the issue of the Israeli-Palestinian conflict has been sidelined by the media. Yet this is an ongoing and ever-escalating war between a Western culture (Israel) and a terrorist organization (the PLO/Palestinian Authority) that precipitated and controls the outcome of this new unholy war. It is this very issue that is foremost to the Islamic terrorists themselves, and which they claim brought about the unprecedented attack of September 11 (see chapter 1). It is this issue that threatened the building of the American-led coalition against terrorism, and still threatens its fragile formation. It is this issue, in light of the present need to wage a war in cooperation with Israel's enemies, that has accelerated U.S. pressure on Israel for the establishment of an independent Palestinian state and thereby has affected the course of U.S.-Israel relations in the future.

But in pressing for a Palestinian state while waging a war against terrorism, the United States must also contend with the fact that the Palestinian agenda against Israel is both controlled and supported by Islamic terrorist organizations. Whatever path the United States decides to pursue in other countries to root out terrorism, it will be impossible to fully eradicate terrorism so long as the conflict between the Israelis and Palestinians remains unresolved. Because of the connection between this conflict and the U.S.-led war on terrorism, it is imperative that we examine this issue that will not only not go away but may draw our nation, and other nations, into a global confrontation. That's what we will be doing in this book.

Islamic Ignorance—a Warning to the West

The West has long been ignorant of the Eastern mindset. The religion of Islam, which shapes the worldview of the majority of those who live in the Middle East, has for the most part been foreign to our culture and consequently to our concern. In our free democratic society, where we are able to choose our futures as we would a suit of clothes, we cannot fathom what drives Palestinian parents to willingly sacrifice their children as suicide bombers. However, now that Islamic militants have menacingly imposed their religion in our public life, we need an education. Professor Louis Rene Beres of the Department of Political Science at Purdue University has explained the Israeli-Palestinian conflict in this way:

> Jewish supporters of the Oslo "Peace Process" still do not understand the true sources of terrorism against Israel. Projecting their own very generic conceptions of Western history upon the contemporary Middle East, they naively identify these sources within the standard theoretical frameworks of economic disenchantment and rising expectations. Palestinian terrorism is a conscious expression of blood sacrifice, including the blood of "the Jews," and violence against "the Jews" is always an expression of what is sacred. For Palestinian terrorists, violence and the sacred are inseparable.[3]

Such statements may surprise many readers, and this feeling of surprise should serve as a warning that we must know more in order to understand this new enemy. That's what this book is also about—the worldview of Islam and the fanatical followers that embrace radical Islam. And we will learn about Islam from its own sources, the experts who have studied this world, and also from those who have lived in this world.

The Christian Connection

This war has not only targeted Israel and America, but "Christian" America. The terrorists who champion *jihad* have recognized that the American president is a Christian and believe that America's retaliation against terrorism is in fact a Christian crusade against Islam. However misguided this conviction may be, Christians—of all people— must become aware of how and why they are perceived as the enemy by radical Muslims. In particular, Christians need to understand the Israeli-Palestinian conflict in light of their mandate to be witnesses of their worldview. In this light, as a Christian, I was disturbed by one of Kirschen's "Dry Bones" cartoons that regularly appear in the *Jerusalem Post*. The solitary figure in the cartoon addressed the audience with these words: "The Christians of the world kept their *silence* when the Palestinians wrecked *Christian* Lebanon. So why should we expect them to speak out *now*, as the Palestinians target the *Jewish* state?"[4] I am sure that Kirschen believed that a Jewish audience would find this irony amusing, since from their perspective the Christian world barely raised its voice in protest at the Palestinian massacre of Lebanese Christians, yet these same Christians have loudly denounced Israel's actions against the Palestinians. My first reaction to Kirschen's charge was that the Lebanese Christian massacre was not publicized by the international media to the Christians of the world as the Israeli-Palestinian conflict has been. On reflection, however, I am equally troubled that this greater publicity has not provoked a greater Christian concern.

One of the reasons for this lack of concern may be that Christians, like most people, are confused over the fundamental issues that comprise the conflict. Images of Palestinian youths caught in crossfire, such as 12-year-old Palestinian Mohammed al-Durras, killed ostensibly by Israeli fire while seeking shelter behind his father Jamal, tear at the hearts of Christians and non-Christians alike, making them sympathetic to the Palestinian charge of excessive Israeli force. There have indeed been cases of Israeli abuse, but the Israelis have their own images of Palestinian terrorism—such as the two young Israelis who, seeking refuge from a Palestinian mob, entered a Palestinian police station only to be stabbed, thrown from the police station window, and then burned by the unrestrained mob. Or the Israeli baby who was hit by Palestinian gunfire while at home in her stroller. Or the mutilated bodies of two Israeli boys who skipped school one day and were brutally murdered by a Palestinian simply *because they were Jews*. Or the body parts of five Israeli shoppers scattered by a bomb at a mall in Netanya, or the 18 Israeli teens slaughtered at a Tel Aviv discotheque. Or the crowd of Israeli civilians who were exiting a public bus when they were mowed down by machine-gun fire from a Palestinian disguised as an Israeli soldier. All of these images—which are multiplied daily—have also turned the public's heart against terrorism and the Palestinians who inflict it. Yet we cannot let our opinions be shaped solely upon our emotional response to such scenes. Rather, we need to seek to understand the causes of the conflict and its consequences for our lives—especially now that America has taken a much more active role in the Middle East.

It's also vital to realize that the Muslim worldview cannot conceive of religion divorced from politics. This means the political decisions of the day are usually made in view of the religious prophecies of tomorrow. There are certainly apocalyptic overtones to this conflict, for its stage is the Land of the Bible, where the history that shaped civilization began, and where it is destined to end. Foreshadowing the time of the end is the city of Jerusalem, symbolic of the struggle for the Middle East and now tied politically by the terrorists to their war with the West. At the heart of the terrorist demands is the sacred space at the heart of this city, known to Jews and Christians as the Temple Mount and to Muslims as Al-Aqsa or the *Haram al-Sharif*. This hallowed ground has continually been the scene of riots and violence and is assured of still more in times to come. In this book we will look at what has placed this city and its holy site at the center of the religious rivalry between the Arabs and Israelis.

A Wake-up Call from Hell

When former Prime Minister Benjamin Netanyahu met with the United States' Government Reform Committee on September 20, 2001, he called the event of September 11 "a wake-up call from hell." This event not only awakened America from a state of national indifference, but also to a state of unholy war, and although we do not know what lies ahead, the unintended consequences of new foreign policy decisions may move our world collectively toward the apocalyptic future we fear. In 1860, the French scientist Pierre Berchelt made a startling prediction: "Within a hundred years of physical and chemical science, man will know what the atom is. It is my belief that when science reaches this stage, God will come down with His big ring of keys and will say to humanity: 'Gentlemen, it's closing time.'"[5]

Today, man has conquered the atom, and with it conquered other men. And today, nuclear and other weapons of mass destruction are in the hands of terrorist regimes in the Middle East, which have issued a warning to the West. Even so, closing time has not yet arrived. But it might be close! If we are those who number our days, then perhaps it is time to start counting. The Middle East conflict, with the powder keg of Jerusalem at its core, is set to explode! But we still have time. And if we use that time to learn the truth about what is happening—and what is going to happen—we have a chance to secure our souls. May this book be a guide to getting you to that truth and getting you home before closing time.

—Randall Price
Jerusalem, 2001

CHAPTER I

Why Are We at War?

*My Muslim brothers of the world: Your
brothers in Palestine and in the land of the
two Holy Places [Saudi Arabia] are calling
upon your help and asking you to take part
in fighting against the enemy—your enemy
and their enemy—the Americans and the
Israelis. They are asking you to do whatever
you can, with one means and ability, to expel
the enemy, humiliated and defeated,
out of the sanctities of Islam.[1]*
—OSAMA BIN LADEN

*There is a new generation that is willing to
fight America, and this is something
that America cannot stop.*
—PALESTINIAN SHEIKH KHALIL AL ALAMI,
OFFICIAL OF THE AL-AQSA MOSQUE

The day after the terrorist attack on the World Trade
Center, the Pentagon, and the failed attempt on the White
House, newspapers across the country ran the banner
headline: "We Are at War!" President Bush stated this as
the inevitable consequence forced upon the nation
because "a war was declared on America on September
11." In other words, we are at war because the attack of
that day has been interpreted as an act of war. Like the

bombing of Pearl Harbor on December 7, 1941, the crash of the airliner into the Pentagon was an attack on the U.S. military. By contrast, the destruction of the World Trade Center twin towers was an attack on the civilian population and the American way of life (represented by the businesses in the buildings). In contrast, too, was the identification of the attackers. On December 7 the Japanese Zeros were present for all to see, but on September 11 it was American aircraft in alien hands that delivered disaster.

In the days that followed, both government and military leaders stated that America was not at war against a religion, race, or country, but against terrorism, and that the enemy is a "global menace." And in the early days of searching for evidence that would confirm the identity of the enemy, the president stated that "this enemy is hard to see, hard to find," and he made repeated reference to this enemy as "evil," "evil ones," "evildoers," and "people motivated by evil." Having so identified this target, our objective has been declared to be "to root out evil," "defeat evil," "to not let evil stand," and "to bring evildoers to justice."[2] It didn't take long to find out that one of the names of the "evildoers" is Osama bin Laden, and his Al-Qaeda organization, along with lists of other individual accomplices and groups. And early on, President Bush stated that the United States "would make no distinction between those who committed these acts of terror and those *states* that harbor them." It's at this point that the picture can easily become more complex because we're talking not only about the direct perpetrators, but those who in some way support them or have ties with them. That leads us to ask the question, Who are the guilty parties? Or, more specifically, Who's to blame? Throughout the world a number of different candidates have been suggested, and in arriving at an answer, it is necessary to consider and critique each view.

Who's to Blame for the War?

By my count at least five different groups have been blamed for the terrorist attack: Americans, Israelis, Jews, Christians, and radical Muslims (Usamah bin Muhammad bin Laden a.k.a. Osama bin Laden and his Al-Qaeda organization and Iraqi dictator Saddam Hussein). The U.S. government has assigned the blame to individual terrorists who operate terrorist cells as part of terrorist networks throughout the world. Although all of the individuals who were involved in the highjacking of the four jetliners on September 11 or were part of the preparations to do so were Muslims, the United States has been careful to not ascribe any culpability to the religion of Islam, but in fact has gone out of its way to affirm that these individuals acted contrary to the beliefs of Islam. It even changed the original name for its war campaign from "Operation Infinite Justice" to "Operation Enduring Freedom" in order to not offend Muslim sensibilities.

While the State Department has long maintained a list of terrorist organizations known to have instigated destructive activities, it has shied away from taking action against or blaming any of these except Osama bin Laden's Al-Qaeda organization. Furthermore, in its attempt to keep the focus on individual terrorists, the department has reversed its original statement that those punished would include "those states that harbor [terrorists]" and declared that it will not attack any Arab state. In its desire to build a coalition of Islamic partners, which requires Israel to exercise restraint and keep its distance (see next chapter), the United States even considered removing Syria (which sponsors 11 terrorist organizations, including the Palestinian terrorist groups Hamas, Hizbullah, and Islamic Jihad) from its list of countries that sponsor terrorism. Although it did not do so, Syria ended up being elected to the U.N. Security Council by other member states. Its new function in helping ensure world security in the war against terrorism may shelter it for a time from the United States' plan to attack countries that sponsor terrorism, although Washington stated it would "continue to express its concerns regarding terrorism with the Syrian government."[3] Iraq's Saddam Hussein has also been implicated in the September 11 attack by the Israelis as well as by other nations.

Bin Laden has denied any personal complicity in the attack or for his organization Al-Qaeda, but, not surprisingly, has blamed America for the attack. Specifically he accuses American Jews and Christians of causing the disaster as part of a conspiracy against the Muslim religion. In an Urdu language newspaper, the Karachi daily *Ummat*, bin Laden was reported to have blamed Florida's Jewish community because it has not forgiven President Bush for his controversial state victory in the U.S. election. In a separate statement, bin Laden referred to the U.S. declaration of war as a "Jewish-Christian crusade against Islam," a charge that carries implications of continuing the bloody massacres of Muslims (but also Jews!) from the eleventh through thirteenth centuries. President Bush did refer to the American plan to strike back at terrorism as a "crusade,"[4] but apparently only as a synonym for "campaign." Yet Palestinian Sheikh Khalil Al Alami, the official cleric of the Al-Aqsa Mosque in Jerusalem, declared, "When the president of the most powerful country in the world says this is a 'crusade,' this is no mistake....They want to establish a clash of civilizations."[5]

Bin Laden likewise turned his accusations on American Christians as the imagined heirs of the Crusaders when he said, "The attackers could be anybody, people who are part of the American system, yet rebel against it, or some group that wants to make this century a century of confrontation between Islam and Christianity."[6] Christianity, of course, has no calling to wage war with Islam, even though Christians are brutally tortured, enslaved, and murdered throughout the Muslim world. Yes, a *political* form of Christianity once waged war on Islam (and Judaism) through the Crusades and the Inquisition, but there is an essential difference between these "Christian" acts of terrorism and those of Islam. Jesus clearly stated at His trial before the Roman governor Pilate that "My kingdom is not of this world. If My kingdom were of this world, then My servants would be fighting, that I might not be delivered up..." (John 18:36). By contrast, Muhammad said, "Fight and slay the pagans wherever you find them and seize them, beleaguer them, and lie in wait for them in every strategem [of war]" (Sura 9:5), and "Fight those who believe not in God nor the Last Day...nor acknowledge the religion of truth, [even if they are] of the people of the Book [Jews and Christians], until they pay *jizya* [tribute taxes] with willing submission, and feel themselves subdued" (Sura 9:29).

Here, then, is the essential difference: "Christians" committed acts of terror in *disobedience* to the word of Christ, whereas Muslims commit acts of terror in *obedience* to the word of Muhammad. Therefore, every war waged in the name of Christianity must be viewed by true followers of Christ as *unholy*, whereas every *jihad* waged in the name of Allah must be viewed by true followers of Islam as *holy*. If the leaders of radical Islam understood Christianity, they would realize it could never be blamed for a war with Islam. What's more, most Christians distinguish between individual retaliation and national defense. The same Bible that commands the individual believer, "Love your enemies, do good to those who hate you...whoever strikes you on the cheek, offer him the other also" (Luke 6:27,29) says to citizens of a national entity under attack, "Fight for your brothers, your sons, your daughters, your wives and your houses" (Nehemiah 4:14b). Therefore a president, even though a Christian, must act in his country's defense, as must its soldiers (who may be Christians), because to do otherwise would dishonor the institution of human government as established by God (Genesis 9:6; Romans 13:1-2,4-5). Yet, even though the United States is *not* a "Christian nation" sending sainted soldiers on a holy crusade against Islam, this is what the radical Muslim terrorists believe. A recent statement by Osama bin Laden's Al-Qaeda organization reads, "Those who support this crusade must know the truth which is clear: it is a crusade against Islam and Muslims."[7]

Strangely enough, some Christian leaders in America, rightly concerned about declining moral values, have also implicated America, though indirectly, by charging that the nation's immoral culture has brought it to judgment. Indeed the Bible says, "...if a calamity occurs in a city has not the LORD done it?" (Amos 3:6). Did not the Lord use evil empires such as Assyria and Babylon as rods of His anger to punish Israel? Yes, but America is not Israel (contrary to what some say); it is not the Chosen Nation, but simply one of the nations. And unlike Israel, America does not have a covenant made with God (the just basis for His judgments), but a constitution made by and for man. Therefore, one cannot claim any biblical passage conditioning God's response to our cultural corruption. However, the Scripture does reveal the character of God, and in contrast to the strict deity of justice depicted in the Qur'an, the biblical God is a God of mercy. Let us reason together: If God would have spared the wicked city of Sodom for a mere ten righteous men (Genesis 18:32), would He destroy America, where it is estimated that some 100 million born-again Christians reside? Maybe America did deserve a cultural wake-up call, and perhaps God will have used this evil for good (Genesis 50:20;

Romans 8:28). But can we believe that these immoral men whose terrorist cells have slaughtered men, women, and children—both in their own countries and now in the United States—attacked to carry out God's judgment on the nation's immorality? Can we ever justly discern the judgment of God in the wanton murder of nearly 5,000 men and women whose only sin on September 11 was to go to work (some 600 in the defense of their nation)?

The most popular object of blame is Israel and the "Zionist Jews," who are either said to have directly masterminded the attack (in order to divert attention so they could finish off the Palestinians), or to be indirectly responsible because American support for Israel financed "Zionist aggression" against the Palestinians and angered the Islamic world. Saad Hattar reported in the *Jordan Times* that Raed Hijazi, charged with belonging to Osama bin Laden's Al-Qaeda network, and who has received the death penalty in absentia for planning bomb attacks on Christian, Jewish, and U.S. targets in Jordan, accused Prime Minister Ariel Sharon of perpetrating the attacks on the United States.[8] As evidence, he cited a statistic claiming that nearly 4,000 Jews who worked at the twin towers did not report to work on that day. For him, the only way to explain their absence was that they had been forewarned by the "Zionist state" of its planned attack. Never mind that hundreds of Jews and Israelis died in the attack; it only "proved" to Hijazi that the Israeli "terrorists" would accept "collateral damage." In like manner, the spiritual leader of the militant organization Hamas, Sheikh Ahmad Yassin, told a crowd of 3,000 at the Islamic University in Gaza City, "We should worry about Israel because they say all Muslims are the enemy. They are behind what happened in America."[9]

With respect to the Israel-Palestinian conflict, Egyptian president Hosni Mubarak asserted that "Israel encouraged terrorism by her actions and the United States should re-assess its policy toward Israel."[10] King Abdullah of Jordan likewise insisted that the United States not ignore this aspect, and Sheikh Yussuf Al-Qaradhawi, the spiritual leader of the Muslim Brotherhood, declared, "There is no doubt that the one who benefits from this crime is the Zionist entity, which has exploited it in the media, mili-tarily, and politically...."[11]

Outside the Muslim world similar accusations were made. The Italian Premier Silvio Barlisconi said that "the Israeli policy committed against the Palestinians caused hostility against the U.S.A. for supporting Israel." The French foreign ambassador to Israel said much the same. Daniel Plesh of the Royal United Services Institute in London stated on BBC News Online that "U.S. foreign policy [toward Israel] since George W. Bush became presi-dent has led to a climate where such attacks became more likely."[12] Following suit, the *Canberra Sunday Times,* a leading Australian newspaper, also warned that the U.S. policy on the Israeli-Palestinian conflict "appears to be the central issue in the pattern of events leading to the destruc-tion of the World Trade Center."[13] A week after the com-bined American-British strikes on the Taliban, Osama bin Laden's Al-Qaeda organization issued a statement in which it again linked terrorist attacks with America's sup-port of Israel:

> We say to Bush the father, son, former president Clinton, Blair and Israeli Prime Minister Ariel Sharon, who are at the head of the Zionist criminals and cru-saders, who have committed the worst crimes against millions of Muslims...that we will avenge them....The truth is that Bush is an agent of Israel, he sacrifices his people and his economy for them, the Israelis, and helps them occupy the land of Muslims....The storm will not calm, especially as long as you, the United States and Britain, do not end your support for the

Jews in Palestine....We tell and recommend Muslims
in the United States and Britain, and those who reject
the American polices, not to take airplanes and not to
live in towers and high buildings.[14]

In view of such accusations and threats of further
attacks, Israel has justifiably tried to argue against its policies with the Palestinians being a provocation for the terrorists. It does not want a backlash of public opinion
contending that if the United States had long ago changed
its foreign policy toward Israel the events of September 11
would not have happened. Unfortunately, this has already
occurred, although a recent U.S. poll showed only 20 percent of Americans blamed American support for Israel as
the reason for the attacks.[15] However, to curtail such opinions, Israeli politicians have tried to reverse the blame and
argue that America's problems are not because of Israel,
but rather, Israel's problems are because of America,
because "it has been depicted by most Muslim regimes as
the loyal Mideast outpost of the Great U.S. Satan."[16]

It is true that Islamic militantism existed long before the
establishment of the State of Israel, and even if the Jewish
state did not exist America would have *eventually* been
targeted by Muslim terrorists. It is true that Muslim
extremists the world over have attacked people of all
nationalities and religions (including fellow Muslims), and
as an example, the Taliban imprisoned eight social-aid
workers, including two American women, for spreading
Christianity. Still, we cannot dismiss the explicit assertions
by the terrorists themselves that America was targeted
specifically on September 11 because it is considered the
chief ally of Israel and is implicated in the "occupation" of
Palestine.

At the same time, Muslim attempts to depict America as
a victim of its support for Israel while claiming that the
Arab world has no inherent anti-American bias is surely

wrong. The Palestinian Authority has taught their people for years, even in elementary school history textbooks, that "the Palestinian conflict with Israel and America are two branches in the general total global war of Islam against the West and all other religions."[17]

With Whom or What Are We at War?

Officially we are at war with terrorism. *Terrorism* may be defined as "the unlawful use or threatened use of force or violence by a person or an organized group against people or property with the intention of intimidating or coercing societies or governments, often for ideological or political reasons." Based on this definition, it is apparent that terrorism is a *tactic* used by an enemy and not the enemy itself. If so, then who or what is the enemy?

When we examine terrorism, we discover that one-half of all terrorist organizations in the world are united by the religion of Islam. The other half are divided between numerous ethnic, political, and religious groups. During the past two decades, Muslim terrorists have attacked and murdered thousands of people, and bombed and destroyed buildings, planes, and vehicles. Their terrorism has literally covered the globe: Kenya, Algeria, Indonesia, Tanzania, Egypt, Iran, Sudan, Libya, Yemen, Afghanistan, Syria, Lebanon, Israel, Jordan, France, South America, and America. The terrorists the United States first attacked in Kabul, Afghanistan were Muslim terrorists. This raises a question: Are terrorism and Islam connected in some way? While the American government, in its response to the September 11 attacks, has stated we should separate Islam from terrorism itself, we still need to recognize that the religion of Islam is the common denominator for all of the terrorists groups with which we are at war. While terrorism can certainly be separated from Islam, there is reason to question whether Islam can be separated from terrorism (see chapters 2 and 11).

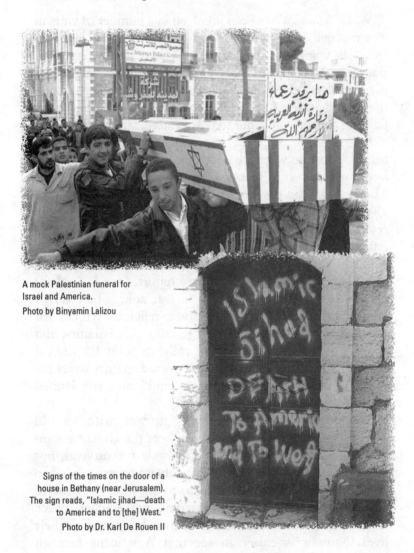

A mock Palestinian funeral for
Israel and America.
Photo by Binyamin Lalizou

Signs of the times on the door of a
house in Bethany (near Jerusalem).
The sign reads, "Islamic jihad—death
to America and to [the] West."
Photo by Dr. Karl De Rouen II

Is Terrorism a New Enemy
to America?

While America has been involved in a number of wars in its existence, in most cases (and especially in the last century), the war has always been "over there," on foreign soil. But the attack on September 11 changed all that—suddenly making war and its consequences very real to the people in the United States. At first thought it might seem that we're fighting a new enemy, but that's not necessarily the case.

For decades, America has watched—with hope—the negotiations between the Israelis and Palestinians. The hope has been that one day, true peace will come to the Middle East. But the seemingly slow "steps forward" have always been followed by steps backwards. And more recently, after almost a decade of deliberation, those negotiations ended unresolved, moving the Middle East from conflict to crisis. This crisis has centered on a single city— Jerusalem, recently described by a reporter for *U.S. News & World Report* magazine as "a war zone where terror comes with territory."[18] This city, a religious symbol for the three monotheistic faiths of Judaism, Christianity, and Islam, has especially become a rallying point for radical Islamic factions as they pronounce *jihad* against Israel for their "occupation of Palestinian land" and the United States for its support of Israel.

Therefore, America is actually at war with an old enemy—one that has, for decades, kept the Israelis entangled in security concerns and a struggle for survival, but for America has been a faraway problem others needed to resolve. It was easy for Americans to question the Israelis' and Palestinians' sincerity regarding peace when peace was all Americans have known in their homeland all their lives. Now it is easier to see that Americans face an intractable foe with which peace is impossible, by our definition. And despite the U.S. government's desperate attempt to distance itself from a connection with Israel and a conflict with Islam, the adversary has not accepted its assurances. Sheikh Hassan Nasrallah, head of the Shi'ite Muslim group, declared to a meeting of Arab and Muslim politicians in Beirut, "The target of this war is the Arab and Islamic world in the first instance, and Arabs and Muslims anywhere on earth!"[19] He added, "These reassurances are like a tiny drop in an ocean of hatred and systematic incitement....U.S. officials and media rushed to accuse Arabs and Muslims of terrorism after the attacks."[20]

I believe that the Muslim world is right: We are at war with Islam, or to be more specific, a radical element in Islam whose goal is the establishment of the *Khilafah* (an Islamic state where the religion reigns supreme and controls every aspect of society and government). If such a terrorist state like the Taliban is allowed to be maintained, it would spread by design to control other countries, such as nearby Pakistan, which possesses nuclear capabilities. Since the Islamic ideal of the *Khilafah* is a united global empire, it would continue its conquest armed with the power and the ambition to destroy every vestige of Western civilization. While some terrorist organizations may be using the guise of Islam as an excuse for exploitation and hegemony, moving to wrest control where democratic regimes have established a presence in their "lands" (such as Yasser Arafat's PLO), they still act in the name of and for the cause of Islam and are followed by masses of Muslims and supported by Muslim countries. Therefore, regardless of the name we call the enemy, if the enemy is Islamic, it is Islam that is being attacked.

Why Do They Hate Us?

I was watching on television the demonstrations in Pakistan against U.S. air strikes in Afghanistan when a sign in

English caught my eye. It read, "Americans, think! Why does the whole world hate you?" Of course this demonstrator exaggerated the point—it's not the "whole world" that hates us, only "his world." Nevertheless, it is a question we need to answer. To be sure, Americans who were born after World War II, many of whom have never felt unloved or even disrespected as Americans, may be puzzled that such a hatred of their country—the economic and technological envy of the world—could spew upon its shores. We pride ourselves as a multicultural, pluralistic, ethnically tolerant, freedom-loving society. Why would anyone hate *us*? Interestingly, it's the very things we pride ourselves on that instigate the hatred.

As one who has lived and traveled frequently throughout the Middle East, I have felt the stigma attached to being an American. The patriotism we wear with pride is viewed in some countries as a shameful symbol of arrogant decadence. In others, it is a reminder that the limitations they suffer, which prevent many from ever traveling outside the cities of their birth, is somehow the fault of the star-spangled savior who not only ignores their oppression but may finance their oppressors.

A key reason for this hatred is U.S. foreign policy in the Middle East, which has for decades propped up anti-democratic regimes, inadvertently lending support to radical Islam, such as when it helped install the Shah of Iran, and later, when it equipped a young Saddam Hussein in Iraq or aided Afghan rebels (including Osama bin Laden) against the Soviets. Even though such policies may have been justified at the time, they produced unintended consequences, such as the rise of Iran's Ayatollah Khomeini (who first branded America "the Great Satan"), and began a revolution of Islamic fundamentalism. They also created a "misunderstanding" that led Saddam Hussein to believe (even today) that the United States told him it would not oppose Iraq's invasion of Kuwait, and even aided the rise of Afghanistan's Taliban regime.

In like manner, U.S. foreign policy today continues to protect American access to oil by supporting repressive rulers in the Persian Gulf states and aids the despotic president of Algeria, Abdelaziz Bouteflika, in his civil war in order to contain the spread of radical Islam. To the radicals, such foreign policies, aside from being viewed as arrogant meddling in the first place, appear hypocritical and have contributed to the impression that America wants to rule the world.

In addition, the hatred of America by Muslim radicals must be viewed in the context of the radicals' religion of Islam, which views political actions as part and parcel of a divine order. In this light, the cause of hatred toward the United States stems from two unpardonable sins: 1) the superpower status wielded by America, whose presence in the world, much less the Middle East, is an affront to the superior status owed to Muslims and to their mandate to subjugate the non-Muslim world to Islam; and 2) U.S. support for the State of Israel, that tiny spot on the map that has challenged Allah's followers after 1,300 years (give or take 200 years of Crusader control) of Muslim dominance.

In regard to America's superpower status, to radical Muslims, colonialism and Western modernism, especially in Europe, ended a millennia of Islamic culture and imposed the corruption of the infidel. Today the presence of 7,000 U.S. troops in Saudi Arabia, which hosts the two most sacred mosques to Islam in Mecca and Medina, even though stationed there at the request of the Saudi government, is tantamount to a pagan invasion and decadent defilement of Muhammad's own homeland. And America's attack on Iraq, an Islamic country, and its subsequent sanctions against it, are deemed intolerable expressions of American imperialism over Muslims.

In regard to the U.S. support of Israel both monetarily ($840 million annually in economic aid and $3 billion in military aid) and militarily (in past wars against Arab states and today—American F-16 fighter jets and missiles are used against the Palestinians), this support has been interpreted (however wrongly) not only as a bias toward Israel, but as a pro-Jewish position against Arabs in particular and Islam in general. For radical Muslims, aside from their belief that Israel is an oppressor of Arab rights, the Jewish state is viewed as an alien intrusion into the Islamic world. And Muslims believe that Jewish sovereignty over the Temple Mount in Jerusalem, the site of Islam's other two sacred shrines—the Al-Aqsa Mosque and the Dome of the Rock—is a sacrilege that must be reversed.

We may want to argue for other reasons for the hatred, such as the still-unavenged stain of the "Christian" Crusades or our enjoyment of an open and free society. But if it is the Crusades or Western civilization and culture that are the culprits, why not target their places of origin in Europe, and especially Great Britain, the home of the knight-errant and the "mother" of America? But these countries, while also hated (such as Britain for joining the attack on Afghanistan), are not at the top of the political food chain, neither have they supported Israel from her birth or nurtured her through her wars with Arab Muslims (such as turning the tide of battle in favor of Israel in the 1973 Yom Kippur War). No, America was and is the first and foremost target because it has always appeared the most impregnable. For that reason, in the wake of the September 11 attack, terrorists like Osama bin Laden are now regarded as heroes because they are believed to have shattered America's strength, crippled its economy, and panicked its public. And having "wounded" the Great Satan, anything is now possible.

But the U.S. was also a first and foremost target because it has been a refuge to the Jewish people (some 6 million), with which it shares the Judeo-Christian heritage and hope. To the Islamic terrorists, whose religion accepts no rivals, America's and Israel's *existence* is sufficient cause for hatred.

Now that we understand the cause of the enemy's hatred and we see that the enemy is not new, let's go overseas to Israel and see if we can get an even clearer picture of how the pieces of the puzzle fit together.

CHAPTER 2

What's Israel Got to Do with It?

To all Mujahideen, your brothers in Palestine are waiting for you...it's time to penetrate America and Israel and hit them where it hurts the most....
Slay the United States and Israel![1]
—OSAMA BIN LADEN

The United States and Israel want to destroy Islam, but Islam will destroy them first![2]
—DEFECTOR FROM OSAMA BIN LADEN'S CAMP

It is important to remember this evening [start of U.S. bombing of Afghanistan] that the war against terrorism was, and continues to be, the State of Israel's war.[3]
—ISRAELI PRIME MINISTER ARIEL SHARON

As horrified Israelis watched the events of September 11 unfold, several were quick to observe, "Now Americans will understand what *we* have been going through!" Israelis have indeed been living with terror on a daily basis, but when former prime minister Benjamin Netanyahu had an opportunity to address the U.S. Congress, he decided it was better for Israel to identify with the U.S. plight and so declared, "Today we are all Americans!" However one cares to join the experience of these countries, America and Israel have been connected in many ways for many years. In demonstrations throughout the Muslim world, protestors have burned Israeli and American flags simultaneously while Muslim leaders have linked America and Israel together respectively as "the Great Satan" and "the Little Satan." Therefore it is correct to say that Americans, of all people, should now empathize more with Israel's standing war with terrorism. On September 11, 2001, Americans suffered their first major attack by radical Islam, yet Israel has suffered through the same kind of unrelenting attacks for over 50 years!

Since 1993, when the peace process began, Palestinian terrorist organizations such as Islamic Jihad and Hamas have launched more than 100 suicide attacks. Since the Palestinians initiated the Al-Aqsa Intifada in September 2000, there have been over 6,000 attacks on Israeli military facilities, Jewish communities, public places, and private vehicles. Even the attack on the World Trade Center in New York had a connection with Israel. Back in 1986, one of the terrorist pilots who crashed into the World Trade Center was arrested by the Israelis for blowing up a bus. He was tried and imprisoned in Israel, but under the Oslo Accord, Israel had to release "political prisoners." Even though the Israelis refused to release this man, because he "had blood on his hands," Washington forced the release—and as the result of "peace" the United States experienced war!

Since the failure of the Oslo peace process in 2000, more than 400 Israelis have been killed by suicide bombers, drive-by shootings, lynching, or other acts of terrorism. By proportion with the population of the United States, this is the equivalent of 24,000 deaths. And while there is no question that more than 5,000 deaths in one day is an enormous loss of life to the American people, we must weigh, as one rabbi has reminded, that "5,000 deaths is only *one-half* the amount of Jews who were murdered *each day* in Auschwitz."[4]

America is at war; Israel is at war; both are at war with the same enemy. There's an old saying that states, "The enemy of my enemy is my friend." Israel, of course, is the best friend (and perhaps the only true friend) America has in the Middle East. It is the only democratic country with a Western civilization and culture, and the only one with a population in which a large percentage of people have dual foreign and American citizenship. In like manner, the number of American Jews living in the United States (six million) equals the number living in all of the State of Israel.

Furthermore, Israel's intelligence-gathering capabilities are strategic to U.S. interests in the Middle East and vital to its overall security. Though denied by U.S. government officials, it was reported in the *Los Angeles Times* (based on an intelligence report from a British source) that the Israeli Mossad (Israeli Intelligence Agency) had forewarned their counterparts in the CIA and FBI a month before the terrorist attack that as many as 200 suspected terrorists had slipped into America and that "large-scale terrorist attacks on highly visible targets were imminent."[5] It is also said they linked the terrorist plot with Osama bin Laden's Al-Qaeda organization.[6] Whether or not such a warning *was* issued from the Israelis, it should be noted that it *could* have been. However, in spite of the importance of Israel as an ally in the war on terrorism, the events of September 11 and their aftermath have pushed the Israeli-Palestinian conflict off the front pages, and Israel seems to have been forgotten by the United States.

Why Has America Forgotten Israel?

Immediately after the terrorist attack on the United States, many people, especially Jewish people and Israelis,

believed that Americans would more readily identify with
the terrorism in Israel and lend more support, if not
greater sympathy, to its struggles with radical Muslims.
Israeli prime minister Ariel Sharon believed that America
would invite Israel to head its coalition against terrorism
because Israel has had the most experience in fighting terrorism in the Middle East. Sharon also recommended to
President Bush to exclude from this coalition any country
that had a history with terrorism. However, just the opposite occurred. The U.S. administration needed to build its
coalition with Islamic states, and every Islamic state—even
the two who have peace treaties with Israel (Egypt and
Jordan), support the Palestinian cause against Israel.
When the U.S. government saw that the Israeli-Palestinian
conflict was an obstacle to building a coalition, and it
wanted to avoid isolating and angering the Israelis, it at
first attempted to simply forget them. The reason for this
was apparent: all the previous attempts at restraint and
resolution (the Mitchell Report, the Tenet Plan, and a 48-
hour cease fire) had been unsuccessful, and the Israelis and
Arabs viewed themselves more than ever as enemies in war
rather than partners in peace. With the bridges to peace all
broken and the breakout of a regional war that involved
America, it appears the U.S. government hoped the world
would forget Israel and concentrate on fighting terrorism.
For a while the focus on finding the terrorists responsible
for the September 11 attack and then fighting them in
Afghanistan diverted attention away from the anxious
Israelis and the escalating conflict with the Palestinians.
But alas, the diversion was not to last, for the enemy identified with the terrorism on American shores went public
with a statement and changed everything.

Osama bin Laden began his address with great praise
for the attacks in America—without admitting responsibility for them. Then, in a few words, he frustrated the

strenuous U.S. diplomatic efforts to leave Israel on the sidelines so as to woo the Arab world into America's coalition alliance against terror. No sooner did President Bush and Secretary of State Colin Powell decree that Israel was firmly outside the anti-terrorist coalition than bin Laden declared that the objectives of his war included "Israel disappearing" and "the Palestinian people and the Al-Aqsa Mosque being saved from the 'non-believers,'" meaning, of course, the Jews and the Christians. Underscoring the strong U.S.-Israel link, he declared, "America has announced its total support of the Zionist entity...a stupid policy." He went on to vow, "America will not live in peace before peace reigns in Palestine." The objectives bin Laden set himself were clearly laid out: The war on "the infidels" would go on, and no American could dream of security before "we have it in Palestine" and "all the infidel armies leave the land of Muhammad."[7]

With these statements, the curtain that had been pulled over the Israelis and Palestinians was rapidly raised and their problem was elevated to *the* problem of the war against terrorism. Nevertheless, such linkage of the United States with Israel in guilt for the "occupation" of Palestine was not a recent invention (though perhaps a recent emphasis). In a 1998 *fatwah* (Islamic legal "decree") urging *jihad* and signed by bin Laden, Ayman al-Zawahiri (leader of the Jihad group in Egypt), Abu-Yasir Rifa'l Ahmad Taha (a leader of the Islamic Group), Sheikh Mir Hamzah (secretary of the Jamiat-ul-Ulema-e-Pakistan), and Fazlul Rahman (leader of the Jihad movement in Bangladesh), we read: "The ruling to kill the Americans and their allies—civilian and military—is an individual duty for every Muslim who can do it in any country in which it is possible to do it, in order to liberate the Al-Aqsa Mosque and the holy mosque [the Ka'aba in Mecca] from their grip...."[8] This call for terrorist attacks against Americans was primarily for the purpose of removing Israeli sovereignty from the Temple Mount in Jerusalem, as well as the American military presence stationed in Saudi Arabia, where Mecca is located. Bin Laden had also put Jerusalem at the center of his agenda when he read a poem about the oppression of the city at the marriage ceremony of his daughter and the son of Mullah Mohammed Omar (the leader of the Taliban), who has been chosen as his successor. He said he composed the poem "because Jerusalem's wounds are fresh in my mind."[9]

As a result of Osama bin Laden's statements, which have been received with ecstatic revelry by crowds in most Arab Muslim countries, Arab and Islamic leaders began meeting with President Bush and insisting they would not join or continue in the coalition so long as Israel was allowed to pursue its present course with the Palestinians. For example, Foreign Minister Abdul-Illah Khatib of Jordan stated, "It will be difficult for the Bush administration to line up Arab support without a commitment to solving the Israeli-Palestinian dispute once and for all. People need to be convinced that Israel is not taking advantage of the situation to demonize the Palestinian cause by comparing it to terrorism."[10] Foreign leaders such as Prime Ministers Tony Blair of Great Britain and Lionel Jospin of France added their voices and advised President Bush to use U.S. influence to force Israel to make peace. Mr. Blair was particularly candid: "The Israeli-Palestinian conflict is one of the main causes of resentment in the Muslim world towards the U.S., which has long backed Israel. The U.S. and Britain are both anxious to reduce the tension caused by the Israeli-Palestinian conflict and to blunt the message of Osama bin Laden, who in a video-taped statement identified himself with the Palestinian cause."[11] The Prime Minister further said he supported the U.N. resolutions on the Israeli-Palestinian conflict, which call for Israel to leave the "occupied" territories, the West Bank, and Gaza. As a consequence of this foreign pressure, the United States pressured Israel to meet with Yasser Arafat, even without a cease fire, in order to renew peace talks under the U.S. Mitchell Plan.

However, from the beginning, Israel refused to be side-lined or pressured to act against its security concerns. Despite the statements of Osama bin Laden to the contrary, Israel has maintained the position that its war with the Palestinians could not have influenced the terrorist actions. Shimon Perez, speaking in the context of the amount of territorial concessions still to be negotiated, declared, "The difference between us and the Palestinians is only three or four percent, and bin Laden has no cause to murder Americans for three or four percent."[12] Next, Israeli prime minister Ariel Sharon addressed the United States in a press conference, saying, "Do not repeat the dreadful mistake of 1938, when enlightened European democracies decided to sacrifice Czechoslovakia for a 'convenient temporary solution.' Do not try to appease the Arabs at our expense—this is unacceptable to us."[13] In response, the U.S. administration returned an unprecedented harsh reply: "We find the Israeli prime minister's statement as unacceptable." This was followed the next week by the announcement that U.S. foreign policy officially supported the establishment of a Palestinian state. President Bush stated, "The idea of a Palestinian state has always been part of a vision," adding, however, the all-important condition: "so long as the Palestinian state recognizes the right of Israel to exist and will treat Israel with respect and will be peaceful on her borders."[14] These statements have pulled the Israeli-Palestinian conflict out of consigned oblivion and back to a place where it has become unavoidably the key to the present conflict.

Why Is Israel the Key to the Conflict?

The United Kingdom has declared that peace in the Middle East between Israel and the Palestinians is "the key to the coalition." Now that the conflict with Islam has spread beyond Israel and the Middle East to threaten the world, the imperative of peace between Israel and the Palestinians has become the determining factor as to which way the war will go. King Fahd Ibn Abdul Aziz of Saudi Arabia, one of the United States' most essential coalition partners, added a sense of urgency to this conclusion. He called upon the world community and Arab leaders to reach a concerted position on the risks facing all nations as a result of the escalating Israeli-Palestinian conflict. Describing the Israeli violence against the Palestinians as unprecedented in history, the king said, "The deteriorating situation resulting from this aggression requires the concentrated attention of the world community in general to curb Israel's extremist approach and force it to act within the framework of the world community's peace-related resolutions aimed at bringing about a fair and comprehensive peace in the Middle East." In addition, he called for "Arab and Muslim countries to unify ranks and exert efforts in support of the Palestinian struggle until they liberate their land and establish their independent state with *Al Quds* [Jerusalem] as its capital and until the Palestinian refugees return home."[15]

Based on this call from the custodian of the two holy mosques (Mecca and Medina), every Arab Muslim state has felt an obligation to exploit their status as potential or actual coalition partners to pressure the United States (which they believe can "control" Israel) to resolve their longstanding problem with the Jewish state. In this regard they have demanded that the United States not attack any Arab state, and that it recognize every "Palestinian" terrorist organization on its official list of terrorists as "legitimate freedom fighters" struggling against occupation. Such a declaration was made at a meeting of the foreign ministers of the member states of the Organization of Islamic Conference on October 10, 2001. Inaugurating the meeting, the Amir of Qatar, His Highness Sheikh Hama bin Khalifa Al Thani, addressed the Muslim world, asking it not to allow the fight against terrorism to have "a double standard." He then stressed "the rejection of any linkage between terrorism and Muslim and Arab people, the Palestinian and Lebanese peoples' right to self-determination, self-defense, sovereignty, and resistance against Israeli and foreign occupation," adding (without fear of contradiction), "the international community should not ignore its responsibilities vis-à-vis the state terrorism practiced by the Israeli government." He also requested the U.N. Security Council and sponsors of the Middle East peace process to "exert the utmost effort to force Israel to lift its blockade, stop its savage practices, provide international protection to the Palestinian people, and end the Israeli occupation of all Palestinian and other Arab territories occupied in 1967."[16]

The Arab states have also joined together to demand that the United States pressure Israel to make all necessary concessions to make peace (including dividing Jerusalem, removing the settlements, giving up the entire West Bank, and allowing for the unconditional right of return of all Palestinian refugees). Thus, far from fulfilling the Bush administration's mandate to the Islamic states to "root out terrorism" in their countries, the Arab position has signaled terrorist organizations that they now have a "green light" to continue their attacks under the banner of "liberating Palestine."

This, of course, put the Israelis in the dilemma of trusting the United States' assurances that their security concerns would not be compromised or that Palestinians would take advantage of their reopening Israeli borders to Palestinian workers (as suicide bombers have done) or their withdrawal from cities like Hebron (as terrorists did after the Israel Defense Forces withdrew from other cities in the West Bank and Lebanon). An even greater dilemma is that of allowing a Palestinian state to redivide Jerusalem, dismantle the Israeli settlements, and permit the massive immigration of millions of Palestinian "refugees." For that to happen would threaten the very survival of the Jewish state. Ariel Sharon has stated, "We are not fighting the Palestinian people; we are fighting terror and those who perpetrate it....I cannot be pressured and I do not intend to make any compromise on issues which endanger the security of Israel."[17] Such a statement tests President Bush's declaration, "We will make no distinction between the terrorists and those who harbor them. Countries will not be able to play it both ways: You're either with us or against us!"[18]

The identification of those against us should be obvious, since the terrorist enemy has been identified with radical Islam, and the beginning of radical Arab nationalism and its warfare with the West can be traced back to the Arab war against Israel in 1948. As Tarwq Y. Ismael puts it:

> So traumatic to the Arab masses was the loss of Palestine and the alien cleavage of the Arab homeland that it fostered a transformation of Arab nationalism. This transformation shifted the emphasis from the glories of the past to the failures—particularly the failure in Palestine—of the present....The Palestine defeat, then, sounded the death-knell of liberal nationalism in the Arab world, and with it has come the growing rejection of Western models of government. The Palestine defeat sparked the reevaluation of Arab society; and from this has arisen what may be called radical Arab nationalism—a nationalism dedicated to fundamental social change to achieve the objectives of freedom and unity.[19]

It was only natural that radical Arab nationalism would embrace radical Islam as the religious complement to its political objectives. It was only natural, in turn, that radical Islam would champion the cause of radical Arab nationalism as a means of unifying the Muslim world for the ultimate goal of *jihad*. And it was only natural that their common hatred of Israel and the West would induce terrorists to attack both. The United States is not ignorant of these facts, nor of the possibility that the Arab states it seeks to appease today may seek to attack America tomorrow. Therefore, while the United States has attempted to make Israel a marginal issue in the midst of dealing with Afghanistan and Iraq, it remains aware that its long-term war with terrorism may end up including confronting countries that border the Jewish state, such as Syria and Lebanon.

Why Is Israel Essential to the U.S.-led War?

Israel is essential to America's war because, as U.S. ambassador Daniel Kurtzer has observed, "the struggle that Israel has been fighting for many years will now take on global dimensions."[20] Not only is Israel the expert in fighting terror in all its forms in the Middle East, but as Eugene Narret, author of *Israel Awakened: A Chronicle of the Oslo War*, has pointed out, it has been at the vanguard in protecting the West from the encroachment of radical Islam:

> Americans and Europeans and South Americans too need finally to recognize that Israel is the front line of Western Judeo-Christian culture in confronting Islam and its imperatives for war on and conversion of the infidel. Israel should be encouraged to fight and be helped in its fight until victory is achieved. Muslims understand only strength. To them, as to other dictators, concessions are a sign of weakness to be exploited.

> Peace will come only through strength. The sooner this lesson is learned, the sooner the blood of those thousands murdered September 11 will be redeemed.[21]

Americans must also realize that the same Palestinian terrorist groups with which Israel is at war are also at war with the United States. Some were certainly involved in the events of September 11 as well as in other attacks on America. Israel alone has the experience and intelligence information—from their long conflict with Palestinian terrorism—that can clearly help the United States. According to General Mousa Arafat, the Palestinian Authority Chief of Military Intelligence, such a fight is imminent:

> There is no difference between Zionism and any U.S. administration, because U.S. administrations are elected primarily by the Zionist body operating in the United States....The state of anger boiling in the Arab world not only threatens U.S. interests but those of other nations. The United States must understand that [because of its bias toward Israel] it is risking its interest; the anger of the Arab world is similar to a fire hidden under the ashes. It is only a matter of time.[22]

This time will come because both Iraq and Syria, which have ties with Osama bin Laden and actively aid Palestinian terrorist operations, will inevitably be targeted in American sights. This time will also come because radical Islam views the United States and Israel as the main obstacles in their path of spreading Islamic fundamentalism to the more moderate Muslim countries and unifying and controlling the entire Middle East. As writer Marc Berley has noted, "The Jihad wants American influence out of the Middle East, and it wants Israel gone. It seeks to divide the United States and Israel, and thus to conquer both....By shunning Israel we betray ourselves. We'll never fight a real war against terrorism until we can have a coalition that includes Israel."[23]

Although Israel sits like an island in the vast sea of Islam, it is an island of resistance in harmony with the West. The United States will clearly need this island Israel when its sea of Islamic coalition partners have deserted to the enemy camp to join in the new "mother of all battles."

How Does the Issue Regarding Jerusalem Fit in this War?

At the center of the conflict—not only between the Israelis and Palestinians, but also with the greater Muslim world—is the issue of Jerusalem. What will happen to Jerusalem the Golden, the holy city of peace, of which the psalmist intoned, "Beautiful in elevation, the joy of the whole earth..." (Psalm 48:2)? At present this place that has been the fulfillment of dreams has become the stuff of nightmares. In February 2001, an unprecedented meeting took place called "The Jerusalem Conference." It was held twice—once in Beirut, Lebanon, and again in the Iranian capital of Tehran. In attendance were some 400 participants from the world's most extreme terrorist groups, such as Osama bin Laden's Al-Qaeda, the Palestinian Hamas and Islamic Jihad factions, the Lebanese Hizbullah, as well as militants from Egypt, Pakistan, Jordan, Qatar, Yemen, Sudan, and Algeria. These usually uncooperative groups met in an effort to set aside philosophical differences and unite in a new holy war against the United States and Israel. A document was drafted called "The Jerusalem Project," in which all of the participants pledged to unite behind the Palestinians in order to achieve total Arab Muslim control over Jerusalem. The document, in part, states, "The only decisive option to achieve this strategy is the option of *jihad* in all its forms," and, "America today is a second Israel."[24] (The Jerusalem Project is headquartered in Beirut and headed by Hamas leader Musa Abu Marzouq and Ramadham Abdullah Shallah of the Islamic

Jihad.) The latter has two sons who served in Osama bin Laden's Mujahideen unit during the Soviet-Afghan war.

In like manner, the foreign ministers that attended an emergency meeting of the Organization of the Islamic Conference in Doha, Qatar on October 10, 2001 placed "the liberation of Jerusalem from military occupation as a top priority."[25] The American Muslims for Jerusalem also sent a letter to the foreign ministers at this meeting, urging the ministers to remain committed to this goal irrespective of the political requirements of the day, such as any joint efforts with the Americans to combat terrorism. Thus, despite the United States' best efforts to keep a coalition together by forcing a peace between Israel and the Palestinians, the struggle over Jerusalem could bring the coalition to an end. As The Jerusalem Project has made clear, Jerusalem is considered central to the plans of the terrorists who are against both the United States and Israel. Any U.S. plan that includes this city must also consider the greater threat of *jihad* to the Jewish state and to the United States as well. Indeed, the struggle over Jerusalem is the principal reason the Palestinians have raged against every American proposal that has attempted to retain Israel's rights to Jerusalem's Temple Mount.

Will an American-Brokered Peace Be Effective?

One wonders why the Palestinians consider America an enemy when, in fact, America has done more than any other non-Arab country to help the Palestinians achieve their stated ambitions. Did not the U.S. government give the Palestinian Authority some 50 billion dollars as an incentive to make peace? Did not the Clinton administration work tirelessly to bring about a resolution that favored the Palestinians?

Not only do the Palestinians not want to accept American intervention, the Israelis feel the same way. When Ariel

Sharon appeared to accept an American proposal for peace, hundreds of Sharon's own Likud members signed a petition stating that "the party opposes a Palestinian state west of the Jordan [and views] the Palestinian Authority as an enemy conducting a war of terror against the Jewish nation and the State of Israel."[26] In like manner, speaking of the United States' Mideast peace plan that calls for the establishment of a Palestinian state with a foothold in Jerusalem, Israeli Cabinet Minister Dan Naveh said, "Israel staunchly opposes ideas which have at their core the establishment of a Palestinian state with Jerusalem as its capital....what's being said by the American government these days is a program that Israel cannot accept....All history shows that when the Americans put a plan on the table, like the famous Reagan plan, the programs did not achieve their aims."[27]

However, if history is proved wrong in this case and the United States is able to persuade Israel to make possible the establishment of an independent Palestinian state, the evidence is that doing such will not end the Palestinian conflict with Israel. That's what radical Palestinian groups explicitly stated when they met recently in the Syrian capital of Damascus.[28] Abu Musa, the leader of Fatah-Intifada, denounced peace efforts as "a farce and a waste of time" and promised the Intifada would intensify. Ahmad Jibril, the secretary-general of the Popular Front for the Liberation of Palestine—General Command, said, "The uprising will continue and get stronger, despite U.S. attempts to bring calm to the Middle East region....armed struggle will continue and such meetings which are held according to Zionist will and under American orders, will be of no avail."[29] Khaled Mishaal, head of the Hamas political bureau, revealed that one reason peace can never be achieved with Israel is because of the Islamic obligation of vengeance: "Israel will pay for its crimes." Hamas, in fact, issued a communiqué to "our *Mujahid*" (warrior) Palestinian people that stated:

> 1) All forces of our people backed by our Arab and Islamic nation are determined on persisting and escalating the Intifada until eradication of occupation from all our usurped land; 2) we urge the Palestinian Authority to break away from the so-called peace process once and for all, adopt the resistance program, refuse all forms of coordination and negotiation and security meetings with the enemy, not to be deceived by American promises...; 3) we ask our people in the diaspora (those living outside Arab lands) to display more interaction with our people's Intifada in the occupied homeland and share with them in the duty of resisting occupation.[30]

This last statement is a call for Palestinians abroad to participate in *jihad*, an ominous thought considering there are some 30,000 Palestinians living in New Jersey alone! Furthermore, a poll of Palestinians conducted in the West Bank and Gaza Strip by the Studies Program at Birzeit University on October 4-6, 2001 concluded that even if the U.S. moves against Israel and helps "resolve the Palestinian issue" it would have only a minor impact (15.7 percent) on the overwhelming Arab opposition to the U.S.-led international coalition on terrorism. This would mean that all of the effort the U.S. might expend in pressuring Israel would be, as the radical Palestinians just quoted said, "wasted effort."

However, there are more serious factors to consider. For example, at the World Council against Racism held August 31–September 7, 2001 in Durban, South Africa, the Arab states and the Palestinians collectively called for a declaration of "Zionism as racism."[31] The United States boycotted the conference because of the inclusion of this statement, which reveals that, according to the Arabs, peace with Israel is unacceptable.

What's more, the ultimate aim of the Palestinian leadership is not an independent Palestinian state, but an independent Palestine, devoid of Jews and a Jewish state. As the PLO Declaration states: "The struggle with the Zionist enemy is not a struggle about Israel's borders, but about Israel's existence."[32] Paul Eidelberg, professor at Israel's Bar Illan University and director of the Foundation for Constitutional Democracy, explains: "Islamic autocrats have foisted on the United States the fiction that the 'Palestinian problem' is the 'core' of the Middle East conflict....Not the 'Palestinian problem' but the 'Jewish problem' is the core of the Middle East conflict." This was once affirmed by none other than U.N. Secretary-General and 2001 Noble Peace Prize recipient Boutros-Boutros-Gali: "The Jews must give up their status as a nation and Israel as a state, and assimilate as a community in the Arab world."[33] "For Islam there is but one 'Final Solution' to this problem, which is why all Moslem states support the PLO Covenant calling for Israel's destruction."[34]

It is this universal hatred of the Jews that is the one unifying element among the otherwise splintered Islamic states. And to believe that giving the Palestinian people their own state, or even homeland, will end the Middle East conflict and allow Israel to exist in peace and security is like believing that killing Osama bin Laden and Saddam Hussein will end terrorism and bring world peace.

What About the Plight of the Palestinians?

In reading this, some may feel that I am being unfairly biased in favor of the Israelis. After all, what about the suffering of the Palestinians? What about the "occupation" of their land? What about the "acts of terror" committed against them by Israel? Indeed, almost the entire Arab world claims that Israel is a terrorist state, that Israelis are terrorists, and that Palestinian suicide bombers and the organizations that train and support them are legitimate freedom fighters defending their homeland from Zionist invaders. Much of the world press thinks this way as well. For example, the *Boston Globe's* Derrick Jackson wrote in a column on September 21, 2001: "If Americans really want to understand why Americans are being targeted for catastrophe in New York and Washington, we can no longer ignore the fact that we are helping the Israeli police and military to outkill Palestinians by more than a 3-to-1 ratio."[35] And on September 19, 2001, BBC's Teheran correspondent Jim Muir stated, in a report entitled, "Explaining Arab Anger," "Many people in and from the region had a deep gut feeling that decades of accumulated poison somehow found expression on 11 September 2001. The poison stems from Israel's conduct toward the Palestinians since its creation in 1948."[36] The Arab group of U.N. member nations, chaired by Libya's U.N. ambassador Abuzed Omar Dorda, made a similar statement. They pledged to eradicate terrorism but demanded "independence for Palestinians," whom they called "victims of modern terrorism practiced by Israeli occupation forces."[37]

These feelings and accusations are real and widespread—so much so that they are in the majority opinion. However, what these feelings lack are facts, and for that reason, in the chapters that follow, I will attempt to give equal time to the minority report. That this survey favors Israel is the result of facing the facts. It is important for all of those with "feelings" to remember that nearly 100 percent of the violence in the present Intifada has been initiated by the Palestinians, not the Israelis. It was not the Israelis who massacred Olympic athletes in Munich, or highjacked Americans on an airliner and held them hostage at Entebbe, or threw a crippled man to his death in the sea on the Achille Lauro, but the Palestinians. It is not the Israelis going to installations and checkpoints to riot and shoot, but the Palestinians. It is not the Israelis' religious leaders who say in their sermons, "Wherever you are, kill the Jews [and] the Americans, who are like them,"[38] or, "O Allah, destroy America, for she is ruled by Zionist Jews!"[39] Those words came from a Palestinian Muslim cleric at the Gaza mosque and the Palestinian Authority Mufti of Jerusalem.

It is not the Israelis who cooperate with terrorist organizations on the United States' list of terrorists, some of which are linked directly with Osama bin Laden, but the Palestinians. It was not the Israelis who joined with Saddam Hussein in the Gulf War against America and who still revere the Iraqi dictator as a hero, but the Palestinians. It is not the Israelis indiscriminately murdering men, women, and children in their cars, it is the Palestinians. It is not the Israelis who hold mass rallies condemning the United States, burning American flags, staging mock murders of Jews, and setting fire to models of the Jewish Temple to cheering crowds, it is the Palestinians. It is not the Israelis who train young men by the hundreds to become suicide bombers and send them into cities to blow up buses, cafes, shopping malls, and supermarkets, it is the Palestinians. It is not Israelis who danced with joy in their streets at the news of the attack on America and cheered for bin Laden, it is the Palestinians.

It will not do to say that terrorism is the only means the poor Palestinians have at their disposal to resist the Israeli military might. As we will see later, Yasser Arafat commands an army of 40,000 to 50,000 well-armed and well-trained soldiers, and has the support—if not arms and supplies—of all the surrounding Arab states, as well as a pledge from Saddam Hussein of a six-million-man "Jerusalem Liberation Army."

It will not do to say that terrorism is the only way the oppressed Palestinians can free themselves and get a state, for they could have had one from the United Nations in 1947. At that time the Arabs owned a mere three percent of the land, but U.N. Resolution 181 offered to create an Arab state in Palestine that gave the people 82 percent of the land. They rejected it and attacked the Jews because the remaining 18 percent of the land was offered to the Jewish people for a Jewish state. Amazingly, at the Camp David II Summit in 2000, Israel made the most sweeping and generous concessions ever made to date—concessions that would have enabled the establishment of a Palestinian state. But Yasser Arafat rejected it and renewed the attacks on Israel.

Neither will it do to say that Israel alone is responsible for the plight of the Palestinians, for their sufferings have been caused as much, if not more, by Arab Muslim states and the jihadic Muslim organizations that have assumed their cause. The 21 Arab states that could easily have absorbed the original 650,000 Palestinian refugees in 1948 refused to do so, even though their combined land mass was 700 times greater than that possessed by Israel. By contrast, the Jewish population of the new state was only 600,000, yet Israel willingly absorbed some 820,000 Jewish refugees from Europe.

Most people are not aware of these facts—especially Palestinians. And to get to this "truth behind the head-lines," you must read on...

CHAPTER 3

What Are Jews and Arabs Fighting About?

They want peace and security, and they want to occupy our land. It's impossible.[1]
—LEBANESE PRIME MINISTER RAFIQ HARIRI

Jerusalem today is a detonating device with no fail-safe, a loaded pistol at a poker dispute, a driverless coach careening toward a blind curve. No other item on the entire Middle East peace agenda forebodes such potential mayhem as the city's future status.[2]
—JOHN LYONS

I was sitting cross-legged in a small room in Austin, Texas in front of a pop singer named Barry McGuire. Like the rest of the flower-power kids who had come to the concert, I smiled and tapped my toes in rhythm as he sang words about "the eastern world exploding," and "the Jordan river having bodies floating." His song concluded with the question, "Don't you believe we're on the eve of destruction?" On that mellow night some 30 years ago I never would have imagined that those words would come true. Especially not in the new millennium, by which time, as another song of the time had promised, peace would rule the planets.

McGuire's song, "Eve of Destruction," was first recorded in 1965 during a time when rising tensions in the Middle East were feared as a prelude to war. The Six-Day War did indeed erupt two years later, and the outcome of the conflict left Israel in control of the entire city of Jerusalem and the hallowed Temple Mount. Yet, despite local conflicts through the years between Jews and Arabs, nothing about the Middle East conflict appeared to pose the threat to peace that "Eve of Destruction" had suggested.

Nevertheless, during that war the seeds were sown for a final showdown over the city and its most sacred site. And today, those seeds, watered by nearly 40 years of unfulfilled ambitions (for both Jews and Arabs), have fatally flowered. Planted in the middle of a war field in which the United States and the Muslim world have collided, its scent seductively beckons to both warriors of *jihad* and the forces of the free world alike. Now as the specter of a regional war moves toward Israel, the world wonders if this ancient battleground will become the new Ground Zero.

Though McGuire's tune is long outdated, his prophetic lyrics indeed describe the headlines of the hour, for as the eastern world continues to explode with violence, many wonder if we are not indeed on the "eve of destruction." Confirming the feelings of the moment, conservative columnist Cal Thomas has written,

> Suddenly the ancient prophecies that foretell Armageddon do not seem so strange and beyond comprehension, even to secular minds. The murder of 17 Americans in Yemen and two Israeli soldiers in Ramallah again reveal the futility of politicians and "leaders" trying to make peace between people whose theology, politics and objectives are irreconcilable.

For those who reject prophecy, how about Oscar Hammerstein, who wrote in a completely different context: "But it's coming, by G-d. You can feel it come; you can feel it in your heart; you can see it in the ground; you can see it in the trees; you can smell it in the breeze. Look around, look around, look around." War is bustin' out all over.[3]

Now that the Middle East is again becoming engulfed in war, we need to ask: What events have taken it there? As we have stated, it is the Israeli-Palestinian conflict that lies at the center of the present war and will continue to attract the focus and forces of the world. But what has caused this conflict and especially the latest Palestinian uprising that has provoked the Islamic attack on America?

What Caused the New Palestinian "Uprising"?

It was Friday, September 29, 2000, and crowds of Israelis were praying at the Western Wall, Judaism's most

The Western Wall, with the Dome of the Rock on the Temple Mount in the background.

Photo by Randall Price

Israeli prime minister Ariel Sharon, whose visit to the Temple Mount in September 2000 was blamed for the Al-Aqsa Intifada.

Photo by Binyamin Lalizou

holy point of contact with the ancient Temple that once stood on the platform overlooking Jerusalem. Most prayers were centered on the Jewish New Year, which would begin that evening at the start of the Sabbath. But many prayers no doubt professed fears about the growing Palestinian threat to the place where they prayed—fears that cast a dark shadow on the prospects of peace in the coming year.

One of those threats had been experienced only the day before as Israeli Knesset member Ariel Sharon and a six-member Likud delegation had entered the Temple Mount through the nearby Mughrabi Gate. The team's purpose was to investigate the building of a Muslim mosque at the site and reports that underground construction work had destroyed archaeological remains.

As the entourage made its entrance, no one at the Wall could help but notice the security escort of some 1,000 Israeli police officers, a precaution made necessary by the growing conflict with the Palestinians over administration of the site and the potential for a Palestinian demonstration. In fact, from the time these members of the Israeli government had voiced their intention to visit the site, threats of violent reaction had been issued by Palestinian Mufti Ikrama Sabri and officials of the Waqf, the Muslim Supreme Council that maintains jurisdiction over the Islamic mosques.

The Sharon team, which was accompanied by Waqf representatives, did not attempt to enter the mosques; rather, they simply surveyed the construction work at the area known as Solomon's Stables. However, when Sharon stated to reporters that "the Temple Mount is in our hands and will remain in our hands. It is the holiest site in Judaism and it is the right of every Jew to visit the Temple Mount," violence erupted. A group of 1,000 demonstrators tried to attack the Israelis and threw stones at the police, wounding

30 policemen and four Palestinians. More disturbing were the broadcasts on Palestinian radio and television some few hours later, which accused Sharon and the Israeli delegation of "defiling the mosques." On the "Voice of Palestine" radio program, Yasser Arafat declared the Sharon visit to be "a serious step against the Muslim holy places," and called all Arabs and Muslims throughout the world to unite and "move immediately to stop these aggressions and Israeli practices against holy Jerusalem."

The next day, as Jews prayed at the Western Wall below, Muslims were observing their holy day in the mosques up on the Temple Mount. In a fiery sermon delivered by the Palestinian Mufti, the Mufti accused the Israeli government of desecrating the Al-Aqsa Mosque (a term used by Muslims not only for the large mosque on the platform but also for the entire Temple Mount area) and called for *jihad* ("holy war") "to eliminate the Jews from Palestine." Whipped into a frenzy by the Mufti's message, the congregation—numbering in the hundreds—rushed onto the Temple Mount to apply the sermon. Some Palestinians wrestled with police guarding the Mughrabi Gate, which leads to the Jewish Western Wall, while others hurled stones from above down upon the Jews at prayer at the Wall. As though a bomb had exploded, the once prayerful crowds scattered in panic, some crying in fear or pain and others in anger, like the Orthodox man who shouted, "Death to the Arabs!"[4]

Within a week the violence begun at the Temple Mount had spread throughout the country, with a rising death toll reported minute by minute by CNN. By week's end, another Jewish holy site, Joseph's Tomb in Nablus (biblical Shechem) had been attacked and torched by a Palestinian mob and 12-year-old Mohammed al-Durras had been killed in an Israeli-Palestinian firefight. The "battle for Jerusalem" had begun.

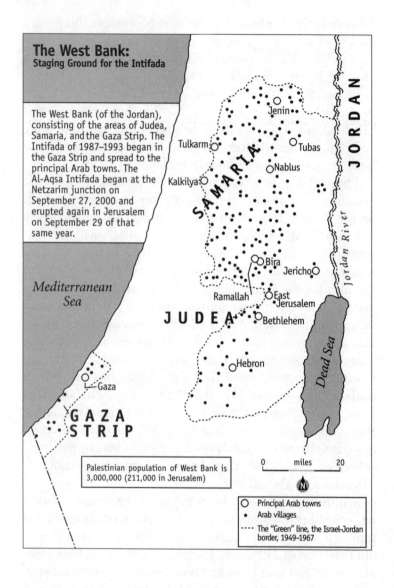

The West Bank:
Staging Ground for the Intifada

The West Bank (of the Jordan), consisting of the areas of Judea, Samaria, and the Gaza Strip. The Intifada of 1987–1993 began in the Gaza Strip and spread to the principal Arab towns. The Al-Aqsa Intifada began at the Netzarim junction on September 27, 2000 and erupted again in Jerusalem on September 29 of that same year.

JORDAN

Jenin

Tulkarm
Tubas

S A M A R I A

Nablus

Kalkilya

Jordan River

Mediterranean
Sea

Bira
Jericho

Ramallah
East
Jerusalem

J U D E A
Bethlehem

Dead Sea

Hebron

Gaza

G A Z A
S T R I P

Palestinian population of West Bank is
3,000,000 (211,000 in Jerusalem)

0   miles   20

N

○   Principal Arab towns

•   Arab villages

- - - - The "Green" line, the Israel-Jordan
       border, 1949–1967

Who Is to Be Blamed for the Violence?

The new "uprising" (Arabic, *Intifada*) was immediately dubbed the "Al-Aqsa Intifada" on the basis of the Palestinian claim that Sharon desecrated an Islamic holy place and, that as a result, this site needs protection from the Israeli government. U.S. media reports of the incident led most people to believe that Sharon's visit was the sole cause of this conflict. The media clearly accused Israel with statements such as "the incitement" of the Palestinians by "the provocative visit" of Ariel Sharon to the Temple Mount "must be blamed" for the violence that ensued throughout the West Bank. In the end, the United Nations passed a resolution condemning Israel for the incident.

What was not mentioned in those reports was the fact that Israel has maintained sovereignty over the Temple Mount since 1967, and Sharon's visit as a representative of the Israeli government was perfectly legal and not an intrusion of another religion's sacred space. By contrast, Palestinian-Arabs in Israel have always had uncontested access to any part of Israel, including Jewish holy sites. The media also failed to note the important point that Sharon *did not approach any mosque*. Even though Muslims asserted later that day, and continue to state today, that the Israelis had done so, Israel's Channel 2 filmed the delegation the entire time and provided evidence to the contrary.

Nevertheless, the media promoted the Palestinian position and failed to mention that months of Palestinian anti-Israel violence, beginning immediately after the Camp David Summit, had preceded Sharon's visit. In fact, at a PLO rally in Ein Hilwe refugee camp in South Lebanon on March 2, 2001, Palestinian Authority Communications Minister Imad Faluji said that the then five-month-old Intifada was not a spontaneous reaction to Sharon's visit, but had been planned after the failure of the peace talks in

July.[5] The media also left out the fact that Muslim clerics and Yasser Arafat had stoked the flames of the faithful's passions with their sermons and speeches calling for all Arabs "to join the battle for Al-Aqsa." Nor did they explain that for the past 34 years, the Israeli government and its police have guarded Islam's solitary supervision of the Temple Mount, while forbidding their own Jewish people religious access to Judaism's most sacred spot.

Furthermore, the media never reported the legal rulings of the Israeli Supreme Court, which protected the Muslim officials and workers on the Temple Mount even while they illegally destroyed ancient Jewish artifacts and constructed a new Muslim mosque on the site! To be sure, there were those in the archaeological community and among Orthodox Jewry who protested this change in the status quo on the Temple Mount, but the government of Israel did not take any action to reverse it.

Given Israel's toleration of such violations, how can the Israelis be indicted of "provoking the violence"? Were they the actual cause of the uprising?

What Was the Actual Cause of the Uprising?

The actual cause for the new uprising was clearly the collapse of the peace process at the American-brokered Camp David II Summit three months before Sharon's visit. For many years leading up to these final-status negotiations, Yasser Arafat had publicly warned that if the Palestinians' demands were not fully met, "Israel would again be taught the lesson of the Intifada!" At the summit, Israeli Prime Minister Ehud Barak took huge political risks by offering unprecedented concessions related to Israeli borders and settlements and permitting hundreds of thousands of Palestinian refugees to return to autonomous regions under the Palestinian Authority. His proposed transfer of 90 to 91 percent of the West Bank to the Palestinian Authority would have put him into a civil dispute with the 40,000 Jewish settlers in the territories who, forced to evacuate, might turn against the government. Arafat, however, believed leaving *any* territories in Israeli hands would be viewed as a compromise, and demanded a *full* right of return for all Palestinian refugees (estimated at five million people).

The paramount issue in the talks was Jerusalem and the sovereignty of the holy places on the *Haram*/Temple Mount. Barak was willing to share sovereignty in portions of Jerusalem; however, on the vital issue of the Temple Mount, both sides came to the summit with no room for compromise—exclusive sovereignty or nothing. Then-president Bill Clinton pressured Barak to adopt a shared sovereignty arrangement (between Islam and the international community), and Barak agreed to make the unprecedented concession, but only in exchange for a signed commitment by Arafat to end the conflict.

This Arafat could not agree to, since his PLO charter, as well as his Muslim faith, allowed no cessation of the struggle (*jihad*) for Palestine and especially Jerusalem, until they were completely under Arab-Muslim control. So Jerusalem, which has symbolized this control in Arab-Muslim history, became a point of impasse, and the prospect for peace walked away with Arafat. As a result, Barak declared that all of his concessions were "invalid," and Clinton placed the blame for failure directly on Arafat.

There is no doubt that Arafat's acceptance of Barak's offer would have been viewed by the Arab world as a weakness and probably would have led to his assassination (he has already survived four periods of exile and several attempts on his life). Yet Barak's concession would have targeted Barak for the same fate, just as the late prime minister Yitzhak Rabin's concessions led to his being gunned down by a nationalist religious Jew.

Would peace have come about if Arafat had agreed to Barak's concessions? Most likely not, for through the years that the Israelis and Arabs have carried on peace negotiations, Arafat has continuously stated that the Palestinians and the Arab world were ready to war against Israel. Recognizing this, Barak stated two months after the resumption of the Intifada that even if he had given Arafat sovereignty at the Temple Mount, new violence would still have erupted.

When Did the Violence Actually Begin?

The actual start of this uprising dates to September 27 (two days before Sharon's visit), at the Netzarim Junction, where violence was initiated by the Palestinians. There, rocks and firebombs were thrown at Israeli military positions and an Israeli soldier was killed by a roadside bomb. Such acts continued even to the very day of Sharon's visit. On that day, an Israeli police officer was murdered by a Palestinian policeman who had served with him on joint patrol.

The "incident" of the Sharon visit, which was not an incident in itself, was used by the Palestinians as an excuse to unleash the next intended stage of hostility against Israel, a local war of attrition that, as part of a phased plan, would lead to a regional war with the Arab states for the "liberation of Palestine." Knowing well that any call by Muslims "to defend their holy places" would fuel the undying fires of *jihad*, Arafat capitalized upon the isolation of the Islamic Waqf (the Muslim custodians of the Temple Mount) with the Israeli government. This isolation had deepened since the 1995 opening of an exit to the Western Wall Tunnel, authorized by Prime Minister Benjamin Netanyahu, and Arafat's unwarranted call to defend the holy places—a call that precipitated a week-long riot that took 58 lives (see chapter 14). Needing momentum to move beyond random shootings and bombings (which had been going on throughout the peace process), he needed a "cause" that would galvanize the Arab world as well as the Palestinian people. Because the pursuit of an independent Palestinian state is a nationalistic ambition separate from the Muslim world from the beginning, Arafat has sought to champion the cause of liberating Jerusalem, a cause that unites all Muslims (as demonstrated by Saddam Hussein's attack on Israel for this same cause during the Gulf War and the statements of Osama bin Laden in his call for *jihad* on the West).

Before 1967 it was only the western part of Jerusalem (held by Israel) that Arafat and his PLO sought to "liberate" (since the eastern part was already in Jordanian-Arab hands). Since 1967, it has been the eastern part (lost to Arabs and restored to Israel in the Six-Day War) that Arafat has claimed for his capital. However, as we shall see, Arafat's ultimate goal is all of Jerusalem and all of Israel. But the Palestinians cannot take on Israel alone, and they are using Jerusalem as a point of contention in the hopes of bringing the Arab world into the fray.

The Al-Aqsa Intifada, therefore, was simply a pretext for a premeditated campaign of violence, visible in the fact that the violence had never really abated during the Oslo peace process. In fact, the violence escalated while cease fires were being called in the wake of September 11 and the hope of renewed peace talks.

What Is the Purpose of the Intifada? Why All the Acts of Violence?

The Intifada is a means to an end. The officially stated goals of the Palestinian National Authority and the National and Islamic Forces (goals that all factions of the PLO have yet to agree to) are as follows: 1) The cessation of Sharon's escalating aggression that aims to impose the

Zionist security perception; 2) the removal of settlers and settlements; 3) the withdrawal of Israeli forces from all occupied territories including East Jerusalem; 4) the return of refugees to their homes; and 5) the actualization of national independence and the establishment of a sovereign state, with Jerusalem as its capital.

While local Arab reactions to a Jewish presence, especially at the holy places in Jerusalem, go back to the beginning of the previous century, the first modern Intifada, among those distinguishing themselves as Palestinians, began in 1987. Over the years, during this Intifada, as I lived in and visited Israel, I have witnessed how the incessant violence has slowly drained Israeli morale, the tourism industry, and the economy. Well do I remember driving through roads cordoned with high fences of wire mesh, bomb checks on public buses, and Arafat's call for sudden and sustained closures of West Bank businesses, especially in the Old City of Jerusalem. This was deemed so intolerable to Israeli society and international opinion that in 1993, the Israeli government felt compelled to meet secretly with the Palestinian leadership (something previously rejected) to discuss a peace process meeting in Oslo, Norway.

This Oslo Accord led to the signing of the Declaration of Principles between Israeli and Palestinian leaders at the U.S. White House on September 13 of that year. With the failure of Oslo, the renewed Intifada is worse by far, and has been staged to force Israel to concede Jerusalem, to return to the borders drawn by the 1947 U.N. commission for the partition of Palestine, and to accept the return of the descendants of the 600,000 Palestinians who left Israel in 1948-49. Adding another five million Arabs to the one million now declaring war within the Jewish state would be both demographic and strategic suicide.

It is clear from Arafat's demand for a Palestinian "right of return" that what is desired is the elimination of Israel itself. This was stated by Hassan Nasrallah, the leader of the terrorist organization Hizbullah, which supports the Palestinian cause: "There can be no peace until the Jews return to their countries of origin." Further championing the cause of the Palestinians are the Lebanese, who have grown more aggressive since Israel's withdrawal from Lebanese territory in May, 2001; the Egyptians, whose Cairo Al-Azhar University student body has called for *jihad* against Israel; Iran, whose troops have been positioning themselves closer to Israel in recent days; and Iraq, whose nefarious leader Saddam Hussein has again sworn to lead the Arab world in war against the Jews.

A key purpose of the Intifada has been to gain international sympathy from the non-Muslim world and political (and military) support for the Palestinian people and their "plight" from the Muslim world. Playing on the celebrity status he has enjoyed with the politically left-wing media, Arafat has made it appear that the Palestinians are outcasts who have received unfair treatment from Israel. There is no question that Palestinians have suffered greatly as a result of their conflict with the Israelis, yet all along, as Israel offered concessions at the peace talks, Arafat exacerbated the situation by allowing violence to be enacted against Israelis, which, in turn, called for reprisals against the Palestinians.

By this method Arafat's goal has been to gain the upper hand in future negotiations, whereby international pressure and the threat of an all-out war with the Arab league nations will force Israel to sue for peace on his terms. This goal, with the U.S.-led war on terrorism, has come close to realization. When Arafat began the Intifada, he believed that the Israeli government did not have the will to fight. He believed Israel would soon buckle and return to the negotiating table (as Shimon Peres has attempted repeatedly to do), allowing him to begin increasing his demands from where Camp David II Summit left off—with Barak's exceptional concessions.

Defense analyst Ze'ev Schiff made the assessment that, "among the Arabs there is an increasing feeling that they have hit on the formula for bringing Israel to its knees." How? "Ongoing, low-level war that combines massive terrorism, guerrilla warfare and the international media....This strategy will expose Israel's Achilles' heel; an extreme sensitivity to loss of life and the kidnapping of its soldiers."[7] To this end the PLO has recently revived its military action groups such as the Fatah Hawks, the Kassam Brigades, the Red Eagle, and others to commit acts of terror and escalate the violence against Israel.

Ariel Sharon, however, has not played into Arafat's expectations. Now facing increased military action by the Israelis with each new attack on Israeli citizens, Arafat has shifted to advance his phased plan and call in favors from the Arab nations in preparation for an expected Israeli invasion of Palestinian-controlled territories for the purpose of removing him and his Palestinian Authority. And remaining at the center of this conflict is Jerusalem and the Temple Mount, the first and foremost provocation for the radical Muslims at war with the West.

Do the sounds of strife that we hear coming from the Middle East mean, as Barry McGuire said, that we're on the eve of destruction? In the chapters that follow, we'll address the issues that may help you arrive at an answer.

Why Should Their Fight Matter to Me?

*Jerusalem is the focal point of the ideals of
all the universe, of the entire history of
Salvation; it is the place that has
witnessed the fusion of all the peoples with
the Jewish people—beloved of God.*[1]
—Cardinal Carlo Maria Martini of Milan

*The right of the Jew not only to life but to
his own life is in a way a symbol of
every man's right. It is in that spirit that
I have sought, and continue
to seek, to champion this right.*[2]
—James G. McDonald
First U.S. ambassador to Israel

It has been said that the best way to get out of a fight is
to never get into one. "Why," you might ask, "after witnessing the constant feuding of a broken family—the
Arabs and Jews—should I want to get involved? The
fighting has gone on for years and nobody's been able to
work out a solution, so why should their fight matter to
me?"

For half a century the U.S. government has been
involved with the "Palestine problem," from casting the

deciding vote for recognition of the independence of the State of Israel to brokering peace treaties between willing Arab states and Israel. Our involvement has put us in the same family with Israel, at least in the eyes of radical Islam, for we and the Zionists together belong to "the Great Satan," as followers of Islam put it. The name of our country joins that of Israel on protest signs, and images of our president are burned in effigy along with those of Israeli leaders. The enemies of Israel have become our enemies, as the war against Islamic terrorism has revealed.

Today, we live at a time in which the fighting in the Middle East has crossed the seas and come into our very homes and Middle Eastern terrorists are at war with the United States. Moving onto center stage in this war is the Israeli-Palestinian conflict, which will require each of us to make critical decisions concerning the issues that have produced this conflict and now have drawn the West to the East for a showdown. And at the center of the Israeli-Palestinian conflict is the city of Jerusalem—a city that we should take time to understand.

Why Should Jerusalem Matter to Me?

No other city on earth commands more attention or has the potential to affect the lives of more people than the holy city of Jerusalem. With over 646,000 people, it is the largest city in Israel. An understanding of its central role in the conflict that currently embroils the Middle East and could soon engulf the world is vital to every person today. Especially significant is the *spiritual* aspect of the city—Jerusalem has been at the heart of civilized thought and spiritual aspiration since the days of the Bible. Writers, poets, artists, and composers (remember George Frederick Handel's "Messiah"?) have joined with Orthodox and Hasidic Jewry in dreaming of a glorified Jerusalem at the end of days. The hope of Jerusalem still touches our secularized society just as it does Jews in the secular State of Israel. In fact, the average secular Israeli, whose public education system still teaches the Bible (it's their history text), and who observes national religious holidays filled with prophecies concerning Jerusalem, has more of a share in this hope than is generally recognized.

Israel's secular leaders also have a respect for the biblical traditions. For example, the first prime minister of Israel, David Ben-Gurion, was not considered a religious man, nevertheless he attended a weekly Bible circle in Jerusalem and enjoyed debating disputed points with rabbinic scholars. Ben-Gurion was typical of the secular Jew of his generation for whom, as Joan Comay notes, "the biblical past was coming alive in the present. For him the Nation of Israel had returned to its beginnings, as the Lord had promised in the days of long ago."[3] In his book *The Rebirth and Destiny of Israel*, Ben-Gurion reveals his belief that the founding of the State of Israel was a fulfillment of the prophetic promises made by the Hebrew prophets:

> "I will surely assemble, O Jacob, all of thee; I will surely gather the remnant of Israel." In our sight and in our days the scattered people is homing from every corner of the globe and every point of the compass, out of all the nations among which it was cast away, and is coursing over the Land, over Israel redeemed.... We live and die for the messianic ideal, the advance-guard of universal redemption....Through generations untold we, and no other people, believed in the vision of the last days. It cannot be that a vision which for so long inspired a people's faith, its hope and patient expectancy will disappoint it now of all times, when the miracle which is the State of Israel has come to pass....Today, as we renew our independence, our first concern is to build up the Land, to foster the economy, its security and international status. But these are the

whereby, not the end. The end is a State fulfilling prophecy, bringing salvation, to be guide and exemplar to all men. In the words of the Prophet is for us a truth perpetual: "I will give thee for a light to the Gentiles, that thou mayest be my salvation unto the end of the earth...." Yes, Israel is a secular state with all the economic and political and social problems that beset others. It has, however, a history and a memory and a tradition like no other. Here we are told that no word of the Lord returns void unless it shall have accomplished that which He intended. Thus we as Jews and Zionists and with the help of America shall resolutely maintain our courage and our faith and our conviction that great moral, spiritual, and ethical truths are going to come from this land in the days that lie ahead.[4]

Therefore, as people who care about the future, we should care about Jerusalem, for it, above all other cities in this world, has a future. We have no guarantee that our nation's capital, Washington D.C., will last forever. The great capitals in London, Moscow, Rome, and Paris will all one day crumble to dust. But it is written of Jerusalem that the city is eternal, and so with it alone we know there is a future. According to the Bible, God has chosen it, yet, there are some schooled in theological matters who contend that what was true of Jerusalem is no longer the case. They say that Jerusalem is no longer God's city.

View of the Temple Mount from Mount of Olives, with Jerusalem in the background.
Photo by Paul Streber

Is Jerusalem Still God's City Today?

Jerusalem has had what no other city has had—written confirmation from the highest Authority that it is a "chosen" city (1 Kings 8:48; 11:13; Psalm 132:13-14). But is that choice still in effect today?

The renown biographer of Rome's decline and fall, Edward Gibbon, dogmatically declared that it was not: "the Jews, their nation and their worship" have been "forever banished" from Jerusalem and its environs.[5] Jerusalem, therefore, is no longer the "holy city," and it does not have any continuing theological significance. This view has been shared and stated throughout church history by such notables as Eusebius Pamphilus, the third/fourth-century bishop of Caesarea and ecclesiastical voice of the pre-Constantinian era, and Martin Luther, the sixteenth-century father of the German Reformation, from which Protestant Christianity developed. Their views were largely based on the theological interpretations of the Roman Catholic Church or the physical realities of Jerusalem at the time they were alive.[6]

When Eusebius formulated his statement toward the end of the third century, Jerusalem's Temple Mount was in ruins, and a Hadrianic edict had forbidden Jews from entering or even setting eyes on the city, thus leaving it, for a time, without any Jewish population.[7] To the Roman Church and Eusebius, this was not only proof of Jesus' prophecies of the city's destruction, which had focused on the Temple (Luke 13:34-35), but a proof that Christianity had superseded Judaism and the Jews were being punished for killing Christ (Luke 19:43-44). That Christianity had superseded Judaism meant that the old earthly Jerusalem had been replaced by the new heavenly Jerusalem in the plan of God. Therefore, to reverence the physical city was to look backwards, and act more like a Jew than a Christian.[8]

For Luther, who was trained in what's now known as replacement theology, the Jews had not yet repented and embraced their Messiah, so they were, by their continued rejection, clearly beyond redemption.[9] In his mind, the last days were being fulfilled in his day by the unruly political power and religious apostasy manifested by the Roman Pontiff. He saw no place for the earthly Jerusalem in God's plan.

By contrast, there are scholars who do not interpret the prophetic promises to Israel symbolically, but maintain that the literal second coming of Christ to the earth could not occur until the Jews returned to a literal Jerusalem. For example, the scholarly heirs of the Reformation known as the Puritans took up the study of Hebrew, and even the Talmud, in an effort to better grasp the long-neglected teachings of the Old Testament.[10] One of their premiere divines, the Reverend John Owen, whose works of seventeen volumes are still in print today, stated as his view, which was representative of most of his colleagues, that "the Jews shall be gathered from all parts of the earth where they are now scattered, and brought home into their homeland before the end of all things prophesied by St. Peter can occur."[11]

This literal interpretation influenced many people in Europe. For example, it is recorded that on April 20, 1799, Napoleon Bonaparte declared that he would issue a proclamation giving "Palestine" to the Jews as a national homeland. This offer, probably motivated more by political savvy than religious conviction, was contingent upon Napoleon's conquest of the city and Jews from Africa and Asia responding to his call to his army "for the restoration of Jerusalem." Although Napoleon did not take Jerusalem, and the proclamation was lost, the historian Salo W. Baron noted that it "symbolized Europe's acknowledgement of Jewish rights in Palestine."[12]

The further awakening in the evangelical Christian world in the nineteenth century to the Old Testament prophecies concerning Jerusalem promoted a sympathy in religious and political circles toward the Zionist movement, which began in 1897. Christian leaders joined with Jewish leaders in gaining public support for the formation of a homeland for the Jews in what was then called "Palestine." Among them were Lord Shaftesbury and Lord Alfred James Balflour, both outstanding British Christian social reformers and statesmen of the nineteenth century, who, influenced by the biblical prophecies, worked in their respective spheres of influence to help achieve Zionist objectives.

The sentiments felt in Britain were stirring in the United States as well. Author David Larsen notes one expression of this when he records that "M.M. Noah, an American Jewish lawyer and American Consul in Tunis, became burdened for the Jews and shared his views with James Madison, Thomas Jefferson, and John Quincy Adams, who wrote in 1825, 'I really wish the Jews again in Judea, an independent nation.'"[13] Such views were necessary to counter an entrenched anti-Semitism in the United States as well as political tides that were bent on washing away the hope for a Jewish homeland. One such tide was directed by President Woodrow Wilson, who, on August 28, 1919 presented the King-Crane Report that proposed merging "Palestine" with Syria and putting all the holy places under international and interdenominational (but not Jewish) guardianship. Fortunately, the view of Jewish restoration prevailed, even in the face of Arab threats, and President Harry S Truman, who had led the American people in support of the creation of a Jewish nation, led the United States in 1948 to become the first nation to recognize the newly reborn State of Israel.[14]

Today, there is a demonstrative Christian Zionism among evangelical Christians, uniquely testifying to the modern Israeli government that a segment of American

Christianity believes that Jerusalem (Zion) still has a future. Among the many Bible prophecies that speak of a return to Zion are those of the prophet Isaiah, who states in the strongest terms the unconditional character of God's purposes for Jerusalem: "But Zion said, 'The LORD has forsaken me, and the Lord has forgotten me.' Can a mother forget her nursing child and have no compassion on the son of her womb? Even these she may forget, but I will not forget you. Behold, I have inscribed you on the palms of My hands; your walls are continually before Me....For a brief moment I forsook you, but with great compassion I will gather you" (Isaiah 49:14-16; 54:7). James G. McDonald, the first ambassador from the United States to Israel, expressed this idea of the fulfillment of Isaiah's prophecy when, in his published account of his mission in Israel, he entitled a chapter "Isaiah Fulfilled" and cited Isaiah 27:12-13 concerning the ingathering of the exiles as evidence.[15]

The Bible not only states that God had not forgotten His people, but that He had also constituted them to be a "kingdom of priests" (Exodus 19:6). How could this purpose ever be realized if the Jewish nation did not possess the holy city and the Temple Mount where the priesthood functioned? Indeed, the very road to restored Zion was called "the Highway of Holiness" (Isaiah 35:8) and Mount Zion "My holy mountain" (Joel 3:17). Looking toward the fulfillment of this future, Jewish prayers in both homes and synagogues have daily entreated God for the restoration of Jerusalem. For instance, the *Mussaf*, a service that follows the Sabbath-day liturgy, petitions the Almighty for renewed worship in a restored Zion. The 13 benedictions of the *Amidah*, recited daily, includes a request to rebuild the Temple, and a Sabbath benediction prays, "Have pity on Zion, which is the home of our life...."

Israeli soldiers at the newly captured Western Wall.
Photo by Wilfred Bullinger

Israeli Defense Forces chaplain Rabbi Shlomo Goren blows the shofar at the liberated Western Wall, which was finally back in Israeli hands after 2,000 years.
Photo courtesy of Israel Government Press Office

Israeli soldiers pray at the narrow area of the Western Wall after capturing it on June 7, 1967.
Photo by Wilfred Bullinger

On June 7, 1967, when Jewish control of Jerusalem was restored with the capture of the Old City and the city's reunification (with the annexation of East Jerusalem), secular Jews the world over were united in an experience of spiritual euphoria. The promise of the prophets appeared to be coming to pass as young and old played, danced, and sang once again in the streets of old Jerusalem and thronged to the Wailing Wall.

It was the conviction that prophecy was being fulfilled that led the government of Israel, in 1980, to officially declare Jerusalem to be the indivisible capital of the Jewish nation even though most countries (including the United States) continued to recognize it as an international city. The united status of the city under Jewish sovereignty has been fervently maintained by every political party in the Israeli government and throughout all of the negotiations with the Palestinians. All who question this uncompromising Israeli position must first understand the intensity of Jewish feelings for this city, now restored after 2,000 years

Israel General Motta Gur at command post on the Mount of Olives as he gives the order to attack the Temple Mount on June 7, 1967.

Photo courtesy of Israel Government Press Office

of Jewish exile. Can this return to Jerusalem, now over three decades old, simply be dismissed as a historical accident or as a socio-political consequence of the Holocaust with no scriptural significance? Many prophecies in the Bible expected such an event to occur. Although the great end-time regathering and spiritual return has not yet taken place, the prophets made it clear that when it does occur, it will only happen in Jerusalem (Isaiah 2:2-4; Zechariah 12:10–14:4).

At the conclusion of the Six-Day War on June 7, 1967, the Israeli soldiers that had taken the Old City of Jerusalem assembled together at the Western Wall. This was the first time in 2,000 years that the Wall was in Israeli control. Using a shofar (a ram's-horn trumpet), Israeli Defense Forces chaplain Rabbi Shlomo Goren sounded a call to prayer at this historic site. The men stood in reverent silence as Rabbi Goren recited the first Jewish prayers heard at the Wall in almost two decades. Then he declared, "We have taken the City of God. We are entering the Messianic era for the Jewish people." A month later, Rabbi Goren was forced to relinquish the Temple Mount to Arab jurisdiction, but he did not change his mind about Jerusalem being the City of God. Rather, he criticized the secularist Jews for "missing their moment."

It would be equally tragic if we, too, "missed the moment" by failing to recognize that Jerusalem has a significant future. We would do well to remember what one of Israel's prophets said: "I am very angry with the nations who are at ease [have dominion]; for while I was only a little angry [with Israel], they [the nations] furthered the disaster [retribution]. Therefore thus says the LORD, 'I will return to Jerusalem with compassion; My house will be rebuilt in it,' declares the LORD of hosts" (Zechariah 1:15-16).

The current crisis in Jerusalem should matter to us not only because the present united city has a future, but also because it is battling for its survival as the political capital of the Jewish state.

Why Should Jerusalem's Present Conflict Matter?

Jerusalem has attracted its enemies by virtue of its unique identification as the capital of God's chosen people, the Jews. As a symbol of political and spiritual power, Jerusalem was a highly desirable prize among conquerors. During the 2,545 years that separate the loss of the city to the Babylonians in 587 B.C. to its recovery by the Israelis in 1967, more than 20 conquerors from different empires have ruled over Jerusalem. These rulers, however, came from their own countries with their own capital cities.

Only for the Jews alone—for more than 650 years during the First and Second Commonwealths, and for the State of Israel since 1948, has Jerusalem served as a capital city. While the Crusaders attempted to make Jerusalem the capital of their Latin kingdom for the 87 years that they held the city (beginning in A.D. 1099), they were not a national entity, so technically it could not have been their capital. And despite the Muslim dominance over the city for 1,122 years, and the insistence today that it is the third holiest site in Islam (after Mecca and Medina), it was never in all of this history ever made the capital of any Arab government. By contrast, it has been the only capital of the Jewish people, the central point of their prayers, the subject of their songs, and their most sacred spot on earth. With the fiftieth anniversary of Israel's independence in 1998, Jerusalem passed the half-century mark as a city that has been partly or entirely under Jewish sovereignty as Israel's capital.

Today the historic Jewish right to Jerusalem has become a source of strife. The Palestinians claim it as the capital of their proposed Palestinian state. However, like the Crusaders, the Palestinians are not a nation and cannot claim a national right to the city (even in the "Arab eastern part"). Most of the world's nations join the Palestinians and Arab states in rejecting Israel's annexation of East Jerusalem and its unification as the capital of the Jewish state. Other nations, including the Vatican, oppose *both* Jewish and Arab control, believing Jerusalem (because of its holy places) should be an international city—a city for the entire world. That shouldn't surprise us, for the Gentile world has, for most of its history, persecuted the Jewish people, and is largely at odds with Israel today. Furthermore, according to the Bible, the nations of the world will one day come against Jerusalem in a war (Zechariah 12:1-2; 14:1).

What's especially tragic is that the world doesn't realize the tremendous dangers facing Israel today, given that it is surrounded by hostile nations. When Israel attempts to defend itself, its actions are often seen as acts of aggression. We in America have not faced a threat from a neighboring nation since 1916, when the Mexican general Pancho Villa lead 1,500 men into New Mexico and killed 17 U.S. citizens. The U.S. government immediately reacted by sending an army of 6,000 men into Mexico to capture Villa. Israel has repeatedly suffered far greater losses and indignities since the beginning of the present Intifada, yet the United States, as well as other nations, has instructed it to refrain from excessive retaliation and has repeatedly condemned military incursions into the West Bank or Gaza Strip to punish or prevent terrorist attacks.

We need to take note of the comments of Edwin Locke, who is the Dean's Professor of Leadership and Motivation at the R.H. Smith School of Business at the University of Maryland at College Park:

The two sides are not morally equivalent. The Palestinians are not seeking to gain their freedom; they are unequivocal enemies of freedom. They, along with the rest of the Arab world, reject the whole concept of rights. Virtually every Arab country is a monarchy, theocracy, or military dictatorship. Freedom of speech, property rights, free elections, and the separation of church and state are almost nonexistent. Speaking out against the rulers or against the Moslem religion leads to imprisonment or death. All attempts to start competing political parties are ruthlessly crushed. Israel is the sole country in that entire region that recognizes individual rights. It is the only Mideast country in which people are free to voice their opinions. The nonviolent, non-PLO-supporting Arab who lives in Israel enjoys far greater freedom than he would in an Arab nation. It is an utter perversion for the collectivized, tribalist Palestinians to claim that they are acting in defense of rights when their aim is to obliterate rights—the rights of Israelis as well as of Arabs.

The fundamental goal of the Palestinians is destruction. They want their terrorist attacks to lead to retaliation, so that more of their people will become terrorists, so that more killing takes place, and so on, in an endless cycle of violence, resulting in death—death to as many people as possible. Why such seething nihilism? Consider that when the Jews came to Palestine, it was a desert. People were living in the same primitive manner as they had been since the time of Moses. The Jews brought Western knowledge and values to the Middle East. They turned an almost-barren land into a modern, industrial civilization. They raised cities where there had been only dirt; they developed irrigated farms where there had been only dry sand; they built cars and trucks and planes where there had been mainly pack animals. They produced wealth where there had been only poverty. They brought freedom and individual rights to a land where these ideas were unknown.[16]

Jerusalem should matter to us all, if not for the reasons above, then because it is a miraculous entity, symbolizing the Jewish people that have been preserved in ancient days through invasions, destructions, and holocausts, and in modern times through five wars, Iraqi Scud missiles, and terrorist attacks. It is a testimony to survival and to a watching world that such ideals, such a destiny, cannot be destroyed and will not die. Despite the threat of the present hour with the Arab Muslims of the Middle East uniting against them, and little support from the West, Israelis are determined that if the world is against them, then they will have to be against the world! But in the end, in spite of the odds, it is Israel who is destined to win!

Rabbi Chaim Richman of Jerusalem's Temple Institute recently proclaimed, "As the Jewish heritage of Jerusalem is challenged before our very eyes, this is the traditional Jewish answer to those that would rise up against Israel in every generation: 'But the more they afflicted them, the more they multiplied and grew' (Exodus 1:12). We will not disappear, but go further, accomplish more, and be strengthened in our faith."[17] The writer Peretz Smolenskin demonstrated a similar trust when he declared: "This shall be our revenge: we shall restore what they kill, and raise up what they fell....This is the banner of vengeance which we shall set up, and its name is—Jerusalem!"[18]

Such sentiments lead us to ask: Why is Jerusalem so significant to the Jews? And why is it so important to the Palestinians who contend for it? This we will explore in the next chapter.

CHAPTER 5

Why Is Jerusalem So Important?

And to Jerusalem Your city return in compassion, and dwell within her as You have spoken, and rebuild her soon, in our days, as an everlasting structure....
—THE AMIDAH (DAILY JEWISH PRAYER)

He who comes to Jerusalem is forgiven by Allah for all his sins; whoever fasts one day in Jerusalem is saved from the Fire of Hell.
—THE HADITH

On the evening of Monday, January 8, 2001, the largest protest rally ever held in Israel's history was staged outside the Jaffa Gate of the historic Old City of Jerusalem. While news media variously reported attendance to be between 100,000-300,000, other estimates placed the number at half a million. The rally, which included Jerusalem Mayor Ehud Olmert and other notables, consisted of a cross-section of Israelis (Palmah veterans, new immigrants, Russian, Ethiopian, secular, Orthodox, ultra-Orthodox) from every part of the country, as well as Diaspora Jews and Christians from many countries.

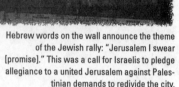

Hebrew words on the wall announce the theme of the Jewish rally: "Jerusalem I swear [promise]." This was a call for Israelis to pledge allegiance to a united Jerusalem against Palestinian demands to redivide the city.

Photo courtesy of Israel Government Press Office

Largest protest rally for a united Jewish Jerusalem draws 300,000+ Israelis to the walls of the Old City. The protest took place in response to former Prime Minister Barak's rumored concession of Jerusalem at the Camp David II Summit.

Photo courtesy of Israel Government Press Office

The purpose of the demonstration was to show solidarity in the support for a united Jerusalem and to protest any plan that challenged Israeli sovereignty over all of Jerusalem and threatened to redivide the holy city. Many banners read, "The Temple Mount Is Ours," reflecting the Jewish resolution to regain Jewish control over the site of the ancient Temples and proposed site of the future Third Temple. It was also a protest against Muslim attempts to de-Judaize the site, turning it into an Islamic mosque and forbidding all non-Muslim access (which had occurred four months earlier). Those present remarked that they had never experienced any demonstration in Jerusalem in the past 34 years that had such unity or intensity. As Gerald Steinberg, director of the Program on Conflict Management and Negotiation at Bar-Ilan University, observed, "The number and broad spectrum of participants demonstrated that this outpouring was a reaffirmation of the national consensus on the sanctity of Jerusalem and of fundamental Jewish rights....It also reminded Israelis and the Jewish people of the strength inherent in 3,000 years of history and revitalized the core values of the return to Zion.... Those who gathered around Jerusalem's walls recognized that they were part of a historic event, and the importance of that moment has been growing since then."[1]

Moshe Landau, former Supreme Court president and the rally's first speaker, proclaimed: "The State of Israel is not just a country of those who dwell in it. It belongs to all Jews of the world. Just as we received the Temple Mount—the very heart of the Jewish people—we must pass it on to the generations that are to come after us."[2] Mayor Olmert put the urgency of the present crises in perspective when he declared to the rally participants,

> You have come from all corners of the Land and even from abroad to say we are here and we will remain here because this city is the basis of our very existence in this Land....no other nation in the world wants peace as much as Israel does, but no nation in the world was ever asked to give up its holiest treasures to placate another nation. We will not give up the most precious treasures of Jewish history [the Temple Mount and Western Wall].[3]

Such words spoken at the time of such a monumental outpouring of spirit concerning Jerusalem raises a key question:

Why Is Jerusalem Important to the Jews?

Jerusalem has been revered for 3,000 years by the Jewish people as a holy city above all other cities on earth. The Jewish Babylonian Talmud boasts that "of the ten measures of beauty that came down to the world, Jerusalem took nine" (*Kidushin* 49b), and that "whoever has not seen Jerusalem in its splendor has never seen a beautiful city" (*Succah* 51b). To Jews,

Jerusalem is the apple of God's eye (Zechariah 2:8), the place above all others chosen for His habitation (Psalm 132:13-14). It is the throne of the Lord (Jeremiah 3:17), the mountain of the house of the Lord (Isaiah 2:2), the Holy Mountain, the City of Truth (Zechariah 8:3)— Zion, the eternal and indivisible capital of the nation of Israel. Those born in Jerusalem are said to be counted by God with a special distinction (Psalm 87:5-6). Jerusalem was given this strategic position by God Himself: "This is Jerusalem; I have set her at the center of the nations, with lands around her" (Ezekiel 5:5). The Babylonian Talmud declared that Jerusalem's centrality extended beyond its Middle Eastern location to all of the world: "Israel lies at the center of the earth, and Jerusalem lies at the center of the Land of Israel" (*Tanhuma* 106). This belief was embellished on the maps of medieval cartographers, where Jerusalem appears as the hub from which all of the other continents proceed like spokes on a wheel.

It was to Jerusalem and its Mount Moriah that Abraham, the father of the Jewish people, came bearing his son as an intended offering (Genesis 22:2-14). It was to Jerusalem that King David brought the Ark of the Covenant (2 Samuel 6:12-17), and the place in which David's son Solomon built the First Temple, where God's presence dwelt (1 Kings 8:10-13). It will be to Jerusalem that the Jewish Messiah will one day come to wage war against all nations (Zechariah 14:2-4), ruling from Zion (Psalm 109:2) and establishing the city as the rallying point for the worship of the world (Isaiah 2:2-3). Only in Jerusalem can the Jewish mandate to be a "light of the nations" (Isaiah 49:6) be fulfilled. Thus, a Jewish midrash states: "Jerusalem is destined to become a beacon lighting the way for the nations" (*Yalkut Shimoni*, midrash on Isaiah 49:9). And Jewish tradition teaches that "Jerusalem below" lies in line with "Jerusalem above"—the New Jerusalem—where God Himself dwells in glory.

To the Jew, then, Jerusalem, both the real and the ideal, is at the very core of all conscious hopes and aspirations. As Chaim Hazaz observes,

> Jerusalem was the stuff of our growing up in our homes, from the cradle on, accompanying us all along our way through life....so close, so intimate, heart of our heart, an integral part of both our sacred and secular time, the essence of our study, the very substance of our thrice-daily prayers, the culminating benediction over our meals, the stuff of all our emotions, feelings and longings. Jerusalem of the prophets, Jerusalem the destroyed, Jerusalem of the Time-to-Come. There is not a single city in the world...not Athens, not Rome, nor any other city...on which has been lavished so much love, so much poesy, so much heavenly rhetoric, so many so-human words of the Living God. And there is not another city in the world that has been so elegized as Jerusalem."[4]

Retracing Jewish history as presented in the Bible, we find that when Jerusalem became a part of Israel, it gained a unique status as the place of blessing for all peoples of the Land. At the time of the dedication of the First Temple in Jerusalem, these words were spoken: "Now My eyes will be open and My ears attentive to the prayer offered in this place. For now I have chosen and consecrated this house that My name may be there forever, and My eyes and My heart will be there perpetually...to listen to the prayer which Your servant shall pray toward this place" (2 Chronicles 7:15-16; 1 Kings 8:29).

Based on this passage, religious Jews, wherever they may be on earth, pray three times a day facing the direction of Jerusalem. When the Jewish kingdom was divided and sent into exile in foreign lands, it was to Jerusalem that the exiles directed their prayers and to which they expected a return as evidence of God's restoration. Such were the prayers of the prophet Daniel, who three times daily interceded with the Lord for Jerusalem (Daniel 6:10). Though in ruins and under the domination of Gentile powers, Jerusalem, for Daniel, was still God's city (Daniel 9:16) and "the holy mountain" (Daniel 9:20). For Daniel's fellow Jews in exile it was the same, and the psalmist records the vow they took to remain faithful to the city: "If I forget you, O Jerusalem, may my right hand forget her skill. May my tongue cleave to the roof of my mouth if I do not remember you, if I do not exalt Jerusalem above my chief joy" (Psalm 137:5-6).

And Jerusalem *has* remained so for the Jewish people for the past two millennia, even though it has suffered destruction some 18 times and they were scattered throughout the globe while the city came under the control of others. Even in Israel's darkest days Jews believed they had a hope, for they knew God's promise to never forsake Jerusalem. This hope was epitomized by Rabbi Hayyim of Volozhin, who said, "Whoever mourns for Jerusalem merits to see it in its rejoicing."

When the State of Israel was on the verge of being established, the issue of Jewish sovereignty over Jerusalem was a central concern. This can be observed in Menachem Mendel Ussishkin's statement made in 1947: "The Land of Israel, without Jerusalem, is merely Palestine. Down through the generations the Jews have been saying not 'Next year in the Land of Israel,' but 'Next year in Jerusalem.'...One can create Tel Aviv out of Jaffa, but one cannot create a second Jerusalem. Zion lies within the walls, not outside them."[5]

The modern-day return of Jews to Jerusalem and the return of the city to the Jews since 1967 have been viewed by Israel's leadership as the fulfillment of ancient promises made by God to the ancient forefathers. Prime Minister

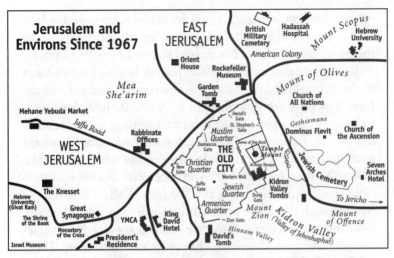

Ariel Sharon expressed this sentiment when he opened an address to members of the United States Congress, saying, "I bring you greetings from Jerusalem, the eternal capital of the Jewish people for the past 3,000 years and of the State of Israel for the past 52 years and forever. Jerusalem belongs to all the Jewish people—we in Israel are only custodians of the city....Jerusalem will remain united under the sovereignty of Israel forever!"[6] An Israeli supporter of Sharon's Jerusalem agenda echoed those sentiments in more direct terms:

> We were here, in unified Jerusalem, the eternal capital of the Jewish people. Although the Temple has not yet been rebuilt, it was clear to all of us that the State of Israel constituted the foundation for the Third Temple—the beginning of the Redemption; the exile ended—the people of Israel returned to its land and established its state in the inheritance of its fathers.... We, the generation that after two thousand years of exile had the merit of establishing our capital in the whole Jerusalem, will not allow anyone to harm its wholeness and integrity![7]

For the Jew, situated again in the place where his biblical destiny will be fulfilled, only a Jewish Jerusalem holds the promised prospect for peace (Psalm 122:6-9; 128:5-6).

Jerusalem also embodies the Jewish hope of restoration to the Promised Land. Since the destruction and exile of the Jewish people from Jerusalem in A.D. 70, Jewish prayers have included a petition to return to Jerusalem and rebuild the Jewish Temple. At Passover, Jews throughout the world end their commemoration of the exodus with the prayer, "Next Year in Jerusalem!" And whenever access was possible throughout the ages, the Western Wall of the Temple Mount was the chief center for pilgrimage and worship. No other city in Israel commemorates a special day of celebration over its liberation. Every year, "Jerusalem Day" celebrates the unification of the city, which occurred in 1967.

Regardless of the religious affectations of Jewish people, there is a universal recognition and affirmation that Jerusalem remains the historic capital of Israel and the place from which the peace promised to the Jewish people and all mankind will be realized. This realization is epitomized in many places around the city, where one can see inscriptions of the familiar verse from the Psalms: "Pray for the peace of Jerusalem."

However, for all that Jerusalem has meant and means to the Jewish people, it is still a contested city. The rivals for its affection are Palestinian Muslims and the global Islamic community, who claim that it is one of the religious centers of their faith. This leads us to ask:

Why Is Jerusalem Important to the Muslims?

In the Bible, we read that Abraham made a journey to Jerusalem to sacrifice his son Isaac. The Qur'an, however, has Abraham and his son Ishmael building the Great Mosque (*Ka'aba* in Mecca) and Abraham offering Ishmael (rather than Isaac) in the environs of Mecca (Sura 2:127; 37:99-110). Arab Muslim interest in Jerusalem is said to have originated with the Night Journey (Arabic, *isra'*) of Islam's founder Muhammad. This has been interpreted by Islam to refer to the place today containing the Al-Aqsa Mosque, which Muslims call the *Haram al-Sharif* ("Noble Sanctuary"), the same site as the Jewish Temple Mount.

According to the first verse of Sura 17 in the Qur'an, Muhammad was sleeping near the *Ka'aba* stone in Mecca when the angel Gabriel brought to him a winged horse bearing a human head, named *al-Buraq* ("the bright one"). This creature carried him from *al-Masjid al-Haram* (the mosque in Mecca) to *al-Masjid al-Aqsa* ("the Outer" or "Farther Mosque"), and from there to heaven ("Ascent to Paradise"). Though some moderate Islamic scholars have interpreted this as a dream, the majority position of fundamentalist Islam is that it was a literal journey the prophet experienced while he was awake.[8] In like manner, while historically the "Farther Mosque" has been interpreted to be heaven, or the mosque in Medina, the accepted tradition today is that it was the *Haram* (Temple Mount) in Jerusalem.

Nevertheless, Jerusalem is not mentioned by name in the entire Qur'an, although the aforementioned reference to "Al-Aqsa" was later taken to refer to the city. But as David Bar-Illan explains: "While the Qur'an does mention a place called Al-Aqsa, which merely means 'the endmost, the farthest,' the reference has absolutely nothing to do with Jerusalem. [The media] also repeats the canard that the Temple Mount is 'Islam's third-holiest shrine.' In fact, Iraq, Iran, Turkey, and Syria also claim to have 'Islam's third-holiest shrine' on their soil."[5] Yet, the modern objection by Muslims to Jewish sovereignty over Jerusalem and the Temple Mount is based on the Muslim contention that since *Al-Quds* (the Muslim name for Jerusalem) is a holy

Aerial veiw of the Temple Mount with Al-Aqsa Mosque in the foreground and the Dome of the Rock in the background.
Photo courtesy of Israel Government Press Office

Poster depicting the night journey of Muhammad to Al-Aqsa from Mecca (the Ka'aba) on his human-headed horse Al-Buraq.
Photo by Randall Price

place for Muslims, they cannot accept rule by non-Muslims, which would amount to a betrayal of Islam. Professor Abdul Hadi Palazzi explains why this objection is both incorrect and unnecessary. Although some of his comments are repetitive for us, such a rare opinion by a leading Muslim cleric needs to be heard in full:

> As is well known, the inclusion of Jerusalem among Islamic holy places derives from al-Miraj, the Ascension of the Prophet Muhammad to heaven. The Ascension began at the Rock, usually identified by Moslem scholars as the Foundation Stone of the Jewish Temple in Jerusalem referred to in Jewish sources. Recalling this link requires us to admit that there is no connection between *al-Miraj* [the Ascension] and Moslem sovereign rights over Jerusalem

since, in the time that *al-Miraj* took place, the City was not under Islamic, but under Byzantine administration. Moreover, the Koran expressly recognizes that Jerusalem plays for Jews the same role that Mecca does for Moslems. We read [in the Koran]: "...They would not follow thy direction of prayer (*qiblah*), nor art thou to follow their direction of prayer; nor indeed will they follow each other's direction of prayer..." (Koran 2:145). Koranic commentators explain that "thy *qiblah*" [direction of prayer for Moslems] is clearly the Ka'bah of Mecca, while "their *qiblah*" [direction of prayer for Jews] refers to the Temple Mount in Jerusalem. To quote only one of the most important Moslem commentators, we read in Qadn Baydawn's Commentary: "Verily, in their prayers Jews orientate themselves toward the Rock (*sakhrah*), while Christians orientate themselves eastwards..." (M. Shaykh Zadeh, *Hashiyyah 'ali Tafsir al-Qadn al-Baydawn*, Istanbul 1979, Vol. 1, p. 456). In complete opposition to what "Islamic" fundamentalists continuously claim, the Book of Islam [the Koran]—as we have just now seen—recognizes Jerusalem as the Jewish direction of prayer. After reviewing the relevant Koranic passages concerning this matter, I conclude that, as no one denies Moslems complete sovereignty over Mecca, from an Islamic point of view—despite opposing, groundless claims—there is no reason for Moslems to deny the State of Israel— which is a *Jewish* state—complete sovereignty over Jerusalem.[9]

In spite of such reasoning, Muslims did eventually refer to the city as *Al-Quds* ("the Holy"), and now declare that "one prayer in Jerusalem is worth 25,000 elsewhere," although prayers in Medina are worth "twice as much," and prayers in Mecca "four times as much."[10] However, under Muslim rule (whether Arab or non-Arab), Jerusalem was never made a political capital of a state or even a province. The Umayyad Caliph Suleiman (A.D. 715-717) ordered that Damascus remain the capital of his empire and built Ramla as the administrative center of the district to which Jerusalem belonged. Even though some Muslim clerics have contended that the reason Jerusalem was not made a political capital was because of its sanctity as a holy city, like Mecca, the lack of spiritual regard for the city throughout the period of Islamic rule argues against this. As historian Shelomo Dov Goitein observes, "most of the traditions about Jerusalem and its sanctuary were local and largely of foreign origin and had no foundation in old Mohammedan stock."[11]

Even so, the religious status of Jerusalem, for the Muslim, ranks only third after the Great Mosque in Mecca and the mosque built upon the house of Muhammad in Medina.[12] The demotion of Jerusalem in Muslim eyes may even be seen as late as 1949–1967, when the city was under Jordanian rule. The governor of Jerusalem, Abdullah al-Tall, complained that Jordan's King Abdullah was deliberately downgrading Jerusalem. Main government offices were in Amman as were the Religious Court of Appeals, and even the Supreme Muslim Council was abolished. Jordan's attitude toward Jerusalem during this time was reflected in this report by the British counsel in Jerusalem to its foreign office in London: "...we are not prepared to allow them to treat the Old City of Jerusalem as though it were nothing more than a provincial townlet in Jordan, without history or importance."[13] Likewise, Palestinians in East Jerusalem whined, "Look at the palaces which are being built in Amman and not in Jerusalem, erected after 1948 on Palestinian shoulders. They [should have been] built in Jerusalem but were removed from there so it would stay like a village!"[14]

One explanation for this devotion could have been because Jerusalem was a center of Palestinian nationalism (which threatened Jordanian dominance), and so Abdullah reduced its power and prestige. Even though Jordan lost sovereignty over East Jerusalem in 1967, it continued to exercise its claim to the city and jurisdiction over the holy sites. This changed in 1988 when Jordan, along with other Arab states, agreed to support Palestinian control. Therefore, today the eastern section of the city is under the control of Palestinian nationalists, along with the Al-Aqsa Mosque (on the southern end of the *Haram*) and the Dome of the Rock (at its western side). For this reason, Palestinians today assert that any kind of agreement with Israel that does not meet the full demands of Palestinian political sovereignty in Jerusalem and Palestinian Muslims over the site of the *Haram* is an unacceptable agreement.

How Have the Palestinians Acted upon Their Claim to Jerusalem?

Until the summer of 2001, the Palestinian Authority in East Jerusalem had been illegally operating a rival government out of an old hotel owned by Faisal Husseini, known as The Orient House. This was in violation of the Declaration of Principles, which forbids a *de facto* government being set up in the city. Nevertheless, the Palestinian Authority still runs schools, clinics, police services, Al-Quds University, a tourism bureau, a prisoner support organization, and even maintains a "national" insurance plan for Arab residents. The Orient House formerly served as the administrative offices for the Palestinians based on their claim that *Al-Quds* (Jerusalem) is the capital of their intended state.

The Palestinian Authority has also installed a Palestinian Mufti (Islamic cleric) for Jerusalem (whose office is on the Temple Mount) for the purpose of controlling all Islamic institutions in the city. In the area of transportation, the Palestinian Authority operates orange-colored passenger vans and collects license fees, another illegal act of government. In addition, the Palestinian Authority has its own judicial system as well. Journalist Nadav Shragai writes that judges "are routinely dispatched from the Orient House in order to broker civil and criminal cases. The most amazing innovation is the takeover of the *Sharia* [Islamic religious] court...by the Authority. Over the past few months, the entrance has been guarded by plain-clothes Palestinian Authority policemen."[15]

This illegal establishment of a Jerusalem-based government during peace negotiations and long before any discussion on the status of Jerusalem reveals the intention of the Palestinian Authority to thwart Israeli sovereignty over East Jerusalem and assume control without Israeli consent. This is exactly what Arafat has always stated: "The sun of freedom, independence, and sovereignty will rise in the sky of independent Palestine with Holy Jerusalem as its capital whether they [Israel] like it or not" (Arafat's Independence Anniversary Speech, November 14, 1999).

Given that Jerusalem is a holy city to the followers of both Judaism and Islam (not to mention Christianity), and that control of the city's holy places are deemed essential to both the Israelis and Palestinians, it might be assumed that these two groups could find a way to make peace, especially in the City of Peace. However, it is clear that not all parties want to make peace (as we will see in later chapters), which keeps Jerusalem at the center of ongoing conflict. This leads to the next question many people ask: Why has this one city been singled out as the key factor for the success or failure of the peace process, which, in turn, affects the Arab-Muslim coalition necessary to the U.S.-led war on terrorism?

Why Is Jerusalem Important in the Present Conflict?

To the Palestinian Muslims, the Temple Mount is viewed as a Zionist invention to Judaize a historically Islamic site. By acquiring sovereignty over the site and excluding Jews, Palestinians will control Israel's high ground politically and prove the Islamic supercession of Judaism religiously.

In A.D. 638, when Islam captured Jerusalem from the Byzantine Christian empire, it wanted to demonstrate its status as military conqueror of Christianity, that Muhammad was a greater prophet than Jesus, and that Islam superseded Christianity. Therefore, the Al-Aqsa Mosque was built over the site of the Byzantine basillica of St. Mary on the site of Solomon's Porch, where the early church was born on the day of Pentecost (Acts 3:11; 5:12). The Dome of the Rock was built over the site of the Holy of Holies that had once been within the Jewish Temple and had been turned into a refuse heap by Byzantine Christianity. Although early Islam recognized it as a Jewish site, its construction was not done out of respect for the beliefs of Judaism or in light of the history of the Jews, but because in the Qur'an both David and Solomon (who built the Temple) were considered Muslims. The clearing of garbage and excrement from the Rock (A.D. 687) and the later erection (A.D. 691) of the *qiblah* "dome" over it not only demonstrated Islam's regard for its own beliefs, but reversed the defilement of a holy site committed by Byzantine Christianity.

A similar practice was effected within the Dome of the Rock. Inscribed inside the gold dome are polemical verses from the Qur'an that tell Muslims that Christianity is false, stating that "God had no son" and "Allah is the One God." In addition, one can see verses of Qur'anic teaching that state that it was Ishmael (Abraham's son claimed as the Arab progenitor), not Isaac (Abraham's son through whom the Jewish people came), who was offered as a prospective sacrifice on the rock that's now within the dome.

The Muslim attempt to show Islam's superiority over Judaism is also seen when we consider the Jewish concept of Jerusalem being "the City of Peace." In the Qur'an, "the City of Peace" is Mecca, not Jerusalem, since the one replaced the other as the new center of faith. This replacement is revealed in the commentary on this passage in the Qur'an by Abdullah Yusuf Ali: "The same root [salama] occurs in the latter part of the name Jerusalem, the Jewish City of Peace. When the day of Jerusalem passed, Mecca became the 'New Jerusalem'—or rather the old and original City of Peace restored and made universal."[16] Therefore, to Muslims, apart from the polemical purpose of demonstrating the superiority of Islam, Jerusalem holds no real religious significance. As Shmuel Katz has observed, "Without Jerusalem, not an iota would be changed in the texture of Islam, or in the personal life of the Arabs or any other Muslim. He would continue to pray in the direction of Mecca, as he has always done."[17]

There is yet another reason that Jerusalem has become so important in the present conflict: It is territory that has come under the control of Islam but which has been "occupied" by non-Muslims (the Jews). According to Islamic law, once a place has been conquered by Allah through Islam, it must remain Allah's property in perpetuity. Otherwise, the command of Allah to conquer the world would be negated and the Muslim religion would be repudiated as inferior. Therefore, regardless of the city's *spiritual* significance, it has now become Islamic property that cannot be relinquished to the infidel or *dhimmi* without the honor of Allah being affected.

That's precisely what concerned Muslims in 1967 when Israeli forces retook East Jerusalem and the Temple Mount. The Qur'an depicts the Jews (and Christians) as *dhimmis* (inferiors), so for the Jews to control life in the city and govern Muslim access to their mosques on the *Haram* (which has happened when Muslim riots have threatened) is an affront to Islam. For this reason Yasser Arafat has said, "I will continue to liberate all Islamic and Muslim holy places. If not [pointing to himself] another one will come along to liberate it."[18] For this reason, too, the issue of sovereignty over the city and its holy places did not simply emerge at the final stage of the negotiations, but has been a central issue in the negotiations all along. When Israel signed a peace accord in 1994 with Jordan, Jordan's King Hussein did so with the proviso that "Jerusalem is the essence of peace between us."[19] The Palestinian terrorist organization Hamas likewise demanded at the beginning of negotiations with the Israelis that the talks deal with Jerusalem first:

Sheik Isma'il Al-Nawahdah, in a sermon at the Al-Aqsa Mosque on Friday, April 3, 1998, stated,

> Jerusalem is at the top of cities sacred to Islam. No city equals its holiness, except for Al-Madina and Mecca....Jerusalem is ours and not yours; this city is more important to us than it is to you....Jerusalem is the key to both war and peace [but] if the Jews think that force will allow them [to keep] both the land and the peace, they delude themselves.[20]

The Israeli position concerning Jerusalem, of course, has never been open to change. Israeli prime minister Yitzhak Rabin, who initiated the negotiations with Jordan and the Palestinians, *never* considered Jerusalem negotiable. He stated from the outset that "Jerusalem is a different issue for us. For us it's *the* symbol....Jerusalem is a living city, but also the heart, the soul of the Jewish people and the state of Israel."[21] Jerusalem's mayor, Ehud Olmert, has affirmed this, adding his own statement concerning the indivisibility of the city: "Now we are in Jerusalem, never to be divided, never to split again, never to pull out from the most ancient and sacred place in Jewish history. Jerusalem is a commitment to our history. Jerusalem is also a commitment to our future."[22]

Rabin's successor, Benjamin Netanyahu, was elected into the prime minister's office primarily on his commitment to never negotiate on Jerusalem. He stated, "If we give in on Jerusalem, then we give in on everything. If we stand on Jerusalem, we'll be able to achieve the peace that we've always dreamed of." The preservation of Jerusalem's unity under Israeli sovereignty has continued to be the test of electability for every politician since. Netanyahu lost to Barak primarily because he gave up Hebron (Judaism's second holy place), and Barak lost to Sharon because the former dared to offer a shared sovereignty over Jerusalem to Arafat. In like manner, any Arab leader who attempts to moderate Islam's position on the sovereignty of Jerusalem will find himself not only out of office, but also assassinated as a traitor to Islam. Both Abdullah I, grandfather of the late King Hussein of Jordan, and President Anwar Sadat of Egypt were assassinated because of their negotiations with Israel.

However even if secular Israeli politicians attempt to compromise on Israeli sovereignty over Jerusalem, such a compromise would have to gain approval of the Knesset (which has an Orthodox religious contingent), the Chief Rabbinate, and Israeli society, whose number-one song for 30 years has been *Yerushalyim shel zahav* ("Jerusalem of Gold"). As for the rabbis, they long ago established three types of remembrances after the destruction of the Temple: the remembrance of *'Eretz Yisrael*, the remembrance of Jerusalem, and the remembrance of the Temple. These three pillars—*'Eretz Yisrael*, Jerusalem, and the Temple— they contend, are the three mainstays of Judaism. And whoever desires to attack Judaism and the Jewish existence in the Jewish state will first attack all three of these pillars. That's why any threat to Jerusalem's status as a united city or to its sanctity as a holy city is considered by Israelis as tantamount to war.

Israelis also remember that when the eastern section of the city (which comprises 60 percent of the city's territory) was in Arab hands (from 1948–1967), Israeli security was constantly threatened. Arab Legion snipers positioned at the Old City's walls would shoot at Jews passing by in the Jewish western section of the city, and concrete walls had to be erected to protect people from being shot. Fifty-eight Jewish synagogues in the Jewish Quarter were completely destroyed, and Jewish graves were desecrated on the Mount of Olives. Jewish gravestones were used to build roads, to line the latrines of the Jordanian army, and in other ways in private houses. Jews were banned from visiting the Jewish holy places and archaeological sites during this period of Arab control of the city despite an explicit promise in the armistice agreement that allowed Jewish access to the Western Wall. In fact, Jews were not allowed in any territory under Jordanian authority. Jews could not live in the Jewish Quarter of the Old City, nor in other Old City quarters where Jews had lived for 19 centuries and up through the British conquest of the holy city in 1917. Nor could Jews live in Jordanian-ruled Jerusalem outside the Old City. The *Shimon ha-Tsadiq, Nahalat Yits'haq,* and *Nahalat Shimon* neighborhoods (north of Orient House and the American Colony Hotel), which were Jewish up to 1948, were off-limits to Jews, as was the adjacent tomb of Simon the Just, a focus of Jewish pilgrimage before 1948. In spite of all this, Jordan is considered a moderate Islamic state. Imagine what would happen if the radical Muslim element in the Palestine Authority were to gain sovereignty in the city!

In light of all this, is it any wonder that Jerusalem is so important to the Israelis, who have now had relative security in Jerusalem for over three decades?

As for the future, Jerusalem has demonstrated to both the Arab world and the international community that the status quo of a united Jerusalem will not be altered without a fight. In the end, whatever plan politicians may pressure parties in the Middle East to adopt, it will be the people of

Israel who will decide if it can be implemented—and it appears that on the issue of Jerusalem the people of Israel have already spoken!

Having seen the historical reasons why the city of Jerusalem is at the center of conflict, it is now time for us to understand how the larger conflict between Jews and Arabs began and how it escalated into the present-day war.

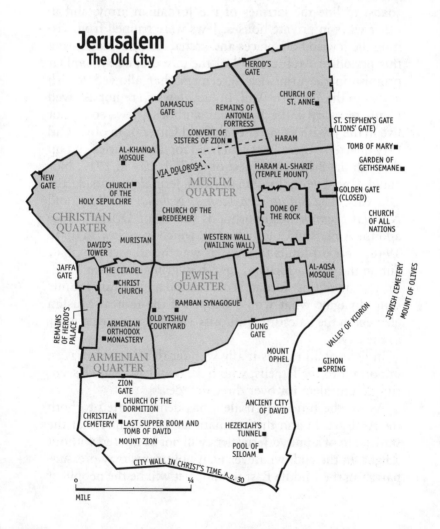

Jerusalem
The Old City

HEROD'S GATE

CHURCH OF ST. ANNE■

DAMASCUS GATE

REMAINS OF ANTONIA FORTRESS

ST. STEPHEN'S GATE (LIONS' GATE)

CONVENT OF SISTERS OF ZION ■

HARAM

TOMB OF MARY ■

AL-KHANQA MOSQUE

GARDEN OF GETHSEMANE ■

VIA DOLOROSA

NEW GATE

MUSLIM QUARTER

HARAM AL-SHARIF (TEMPLE MOUNT)

CHURCH ■ OF THE HOLY SEPULCHRE

GOLDEN GATE (CLOSED)

CHRISTIAN QUARTER

CHURCH OF THE ■REDEEMER

DOME OF THE ROCK

CHURCH OF ALL NATIONS

DAVID'S TOWER

MURISTAN

WESTERN WALL (WAILING WALL)

JAFFA GATE

THE CITADEL

JEWISH QUARTER

AL-AQSA MOSQUE

■CHRIST CHURCH

■ RAMBAN SYNAGOGUE

REMAINS OF HEROD'S PALACE

OLD YISHUV COURTYARD

DUNG GATE

JEWISH CEMETERY
MOUNT OF OLIVES

ARMENIAN ORTHODOX ■MONASTERY

ARMENIAN QUARTER

MOUNT OPHEL

VALLEY OF KIDRON

GIHON ■SPRING

ZION GATE

■ CHURCH OF THE DORMITION

ANCIENT CITY OF DAVID

CHRISTIAN CEMETERY

■LAST SUPPER ROOM AND TOMB OF DAVID

HEZEKIAH'S TUNNEL■

MOUNT ZION

POOL OF SILOAM ■

CITY WALL IN CHRIST'S TIME, A.D. 30

0   ¼
MILE

How Did the Conflict Begin?

"Those who cannot remember the past
are condemned to repeat it."
—GEORGE SANTAYANA, AMERICAN PHILOSOPHER

A British officer seeking to settle the conflict in Palestine once stated, "No other problem of our time is rooted so deeply in the past." That officer rightly understood what we need to recognize about the conflict in the Middle East: The answer to the present conflict must first be sought in past problems. In this chapter we'll consider the historical questions that provide a background for the battle at hand—and discover answers that will enable us to navigate through the troubled waters of political rhetoric and historical revisionism that have today become a part of the conflict itself. Let's begin by looking at the history of this conflict.

How Old Is the Middle East Conflict?

The media has led many people to believe that the Middle East conflict began with Israel's "invasion and occupation of Palestinian land." However, the conflict in the Middle East has persisted for thousands of years and has involved many nations.

The Land of Israel, originally called the Land of Canaan, is a land bridge situated in the middle of the fertile crescent between the continents of Europe, Asia, and Africa to the west, and the lands of Mesopotamia and the Orient to the east. As such, it served not only as a trade route but also as a natural corridor for invading armies. For this reason, Israel has been invaded some 30 times from ancient to modern times. For example, concerning Israel's capital, a Jewish proverb says, "Of ten measures of suffering sent by God upon the world, nine fell on Jerusalem."

In A.D. 70 the Roman army destroyed the city of Jerusalem, and in subsequent years Jews were banned from entering the city. Although a Jewish population remained in Israel (as well as in Egypt and Persia), Jewish people began to settle in other countries throughout the world. Over the next millennia (beginning in the seventh century), Islam came to the former Land of Israel and spread by conquest throughout the lands of the east. At the same time, in Europe, Jewish people prospered in the midst of periodic persecution and became the leaders of industry. Little did they know that come the twentieth century, a holocaust greater than that in A.D. 70 would befall them and decimate Jewish communities throughout Europe.

By the time the free world finally awakened to the Nazi genocide, six million Jews had been horribly murdered—more Jews than had inhabited Jerusalem through all of the ages. Those who had survived the Nazi death camps or who had been forced from their homes turned to their historic homeland, the Land of Israel, and especially to Jerusalem, in hopes of finding a safe refuge. Fighting the cruel seas in overcrowded boats and a British repression that denied them entrance, they eventually joined the long-established Jewish communities in the Land to work toward the dream of reviving Jewish statehood. This brings us to the modern-day era of the conflict.

How Did the Middle East Conflict Begin?

The popular reference to the Middle East conflict has its origin in the events that surround the modern-day creation of the State of Israel and the five wars Israel has had with neighboring Arab states since. The events that lead up to the establishment of the Jewish state begin with Jewish immigration to what was then known as Palestine—an immigration prompted by the Zionist movement begun in 1897. While the waves of persecution and expulsion that came upon European Jews led them to move to Palestine to live alongside Arabs (then under Turkish rule), a resident Jewish population always existed in the Land throughout the past nineteen centuries. These resident Jews have long endured oppressive conditions, just as Jewish communities today still exist in Arab Muslim countries hostile to them (such as in Egypt, Iraq, and Syria).

By the 1920s a growing Arab nationalism (from Turkish rule) was destined for a conflict with the growing Jewish population and its nationalistic (Zionist) ambitions. As early as 1905, Neguib Azoury, in a French publication entitled *Le Reveil de la Nation Arabe* ("The Revival of the Arab Nation"), had foreseen this: "The reawakening of the Arab nation, and the growing Jewish efforts at rebuilding the ancient monarchy of Israel on a very large scale—these two movements are destined to fight each other continually, until one of them triumphs over the other."

During the next few decades, tensions escalated between Arabs and Jews, resulting in frequent riots, primarily over access to holy places. In 1929, a riot, which began in Jerusalem at the Western Wall, spread to Hebron's Arabs, who murdered 67 Jewish men, women, and children and burned their synagogues. Great Britain, which had been granted mandatory jurisdiction over the country by the League of Nations (1922) after their conquest of the Turks (1918), sought a solution to this mounting conflict. The British "solution," which violated both the terms of their own Mandate and the Balfour Declaration (which had called for the establishment of a Jewish homeland in all or any part of Palestine), was to divide the country between the Arab and Jewish populations. On May 14, 1946 the British gave the eastern four-fifths of the Land (known then as Transjordan) to the Arabs and the rule of the Hashemite Bedouin tribe. This created the Hashemite Kingdom of Jordan. Thus, the new state of Israel was left to "occupy" only 23 percent of Palestine (not 100 percent, as anti-Zionist propaganda portrays), while the Arabs received the greatest portion (77 percent) of the land.

Now, the League of Nations had originally intended this territory for the resettlement of Palestinan Arabs, not the development of an independent Arab state,[1] yet it was thereafter identified by its Arab occupiers as "the nation of Palestine." Even as late as 1968, King Hussein of Jordan was still saying, "Jordan is Palestine and Palestine is Jordan."[2] Incidentally, in 1974, Yasser Arafat said much the same thing: "What you call Jordan is actually Palestine."[3] How different is the perception and rhetoric today! Today, *Israel* is called Palestine and Jordan is viewed as a distinct Arab nation, like Saudi Arabia.

The British solution, however, failed to resolve the mounting crisis between Arabs and Jews in the 23 percent of Palestine given to the Jewish people. Thus in 1947 the United Nations stepped in and established a temporary "peace" by partitioning this 23 percent of Palestine into

Jewish and Arab states. At this time the term *Palestinian* (the Anglicized form of the Latin name of Israel's ancient enemies, the Philistines), was applied *equally* to both the Jewish and Arab populations. For example, the well-known English language newspaper *The Jerusalem Post* was then called *The Palestine Post.*[4] However, this peace was short-lived, for when the United Nations narrowly voted to recognize the Jewish declaration of the independent State of Israel on May 14, 1948, the "Palestinian" Arabs, along with the Arab world, went to war against the "Palestinian" Jews (now "Israelis").

Failing to overrun infant Israel, the attacking Arabs occupied what land they could. In 1950 Jordan annexed the biblical territories of Judea and Samaria to the west of the Jordan River (the original dividing line between Israel and Jordan) and created the modern term for their area, "the West Bank." Egypt took the Gaza Strip on the coastal plain north of their country. But the 1948 Israeli victory had left displaced the Palestinian Arab population who had fled Israel's borders under Arab command and fear of Jewish reprisals, and had been promised that upon the defeat of the Jewish enemy they would reclaim their homes, as well as those abandoned by the Jews. However, this did not happen, and thus a "refugee" Palestinian population was created (see chapter 9).

Any of the Arab countries surrounding Israel could have easily absorbed their Palestinian brethren, but all (but Jordan) refused. On the one hand they did not want the economic and social burden of caring for an indigent people, while on the other they wanted to create a future problem for Israel, and they knew the refugees would become an instrument for international criticism and eventual intervention.

Most of the displaced Palestinian Arabs took up residence in "the Palestinian nation" of Jordan in the Jordanian-occupied area of the West Bank, while others chose

PALESTINE—THE JEWISH NATIONAL HOME

43.075 square miles

Beirut

LEBANON

(FRENCH MANDATE)

Damascus

SYRIA

IRAQ (British Mandate)

Tyre

Kuneitra

Safed

Sea of Galilee

Haifa

Tiberias

Mediterranean Sea

Jenin

Irbid

Nablus

Saft

Tel Aviv-Yafa

Jerusalem

Jordan River

Amman

PALESTINE (1919)

ERETZ ISRAEL

Gaza

Hebron

Dead Sea

Port-Said

Beersheba

Kerak

SAUDI

Kantara

El-Arish

JEWISH NATIONAL HOME

ARABIA

Ismailia

BRITISH MANDATE

Suez

(since 1920)

Sinai

Ma'an

Desert

TRANSJORDAN

(1922-)

Eilat

Aqaba

Mudawwara

Gulf of Suez

Gulf of Eilat

Mt. Sinai ▲

EGYPT

Sharm el-Sheikh

Red Sea

The whole country on both sides of the Jordan was destined to be the Jewish National Home, according to the Balfour Declaration of 1917 and the negotiations of the Paris Peace Conference in 1919 and the Palestine Mandate to Britain in 1920. In 1922 Britain redivided the Jewish National Home and gave 77 percent of the Mandate to the Arabs as Transjordan. The area to the left of the Jordan River is the portion that was allocated to the Jewish people.

N

Area given to the Jewish people

Area given to the Arabs

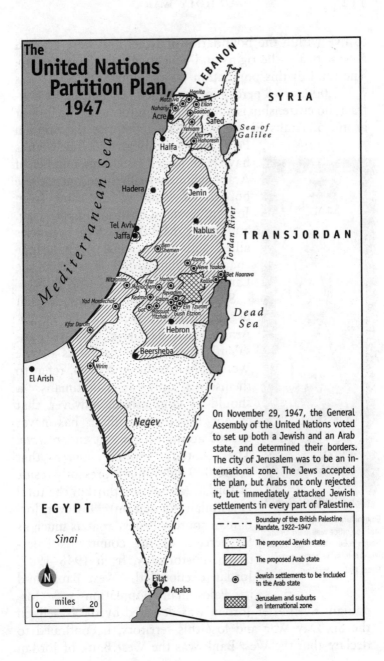

The United Nations Partition Plan, 1947

On November 29, 1947, the General Assembly of the United Nations voted to set up both a Jewish and an Arab state, and determined their borders. The city of Jerusalem was to be an international zone. The Jews accepted the plan, but Arabs not only rejected it, but immediately attacked Jewish settlements in every part of Palestine.

- - - - Boundary of the British Palestine Mandate, 1922–1947

The proposed Jewish state

The proposed Arab state

⊙ Jewish settlements to be included in the Arab state

Jerusalem and suburbs an international zone

to live within the boundaries of Israel and were granted automatically the rights and benefits of Israeli citizenship. The total of this population (as of September 2001) was 1,215,000, or 18 percent of the Israeli population (by contrast, no citizenship is allowed Jews in Jordan). The former group of Arabs in the West Bank comprise the original

Palestinians, although today their ranks have been joined by a large number of Arabs who originally lived outside the borders of Israel. These came from Jordan, Syria, Lebanon, Egypt, Iraq, and other Middle Eastern countries allied with the original Arab League charter to remove all Jews from the Land.

Since the Palestinian Intifada that began in 1987, most of the Israeli-Arabs (such as those of East Jerusalem) have joined the ranks of the West Bank Arabs and now refer to themselves only as Palestinians. It should be emphasized, however, that except for Jordan, there has never existed at any time a Palestinian *state*. The United Nations figures that 1,600,000 Palestinians presently reside in Jordan (about one-third of the total Palestinian population). However, Jordanian sources believe that as much as 50 percent of the country is Palestinian. Historically, from 1948–1967, Jordan occupied the West Bank, and its Palestinian population was Jordanian. Even after Jordan was defeated by the Israelis in the Six-Day War and lost this territory, it continued to declare that the West Bank was the West Bank of Jordan

Embroidered map of Palestinian state on office wall in the Orient House in East Jerusalem (note: Israel is missing from the map!).
Photo by Paul Streber

and demanded that it be returned by the Israelis. However, a year after the Palestinians began their Intifada in 1987, the Arab League (of which Jordan is a part) decided to give the PLO the right to negotiate the status of the West Bank and Gaza Strip. Even so, when Israel entered into a peace agreement with Jordan in 1994, it recognized only Jordan as the protector of the Islamic holy sites on the Temple Mount, a responsibility accepted by Jordan and actualized in 1995 by the installation of a Jordanian Mufti in Jerusalem and the commencement of a restoration project on the Dome of the Rock. However, before the restoration project was completed, Arafat installed his own Palestinian Mufti, who ordered Palestinians to ignore the dictates of the Jordanian Mufti.

It wasn't until 1998 that King Hussein of Jordan "officially announced" that he supported the Palestinian cause to establish a Palestinian State in the West Bank. Today, the Palestinian Authority has established its administrative headquarters in Gaza, but it has also created (in violation of the Oslo Accord) a diplomatic headquarters in Jerusalem, which is tantamount to making it their *de facto* capital. The Palestinian Mufti, Ikrama Sabri (who is virulently anti-Semitic and anti-American), has complete control of the Temple Mount and has banned Israelis from entering the site. This has enraged the Israeli public and set the stage for violent conflict in the near future.

Isn't the Middle East Conflict over Land?

Media reports today present the Middle East conflict as an issue over who owns the Land. However, this is a major misconception; the Middle East conflict is *not* primarily a dispute over land. The struggle over who owns the land, of course, is popularly presented as the main obstacle, with the Palestinians calling for a complete Israeli withdrawal

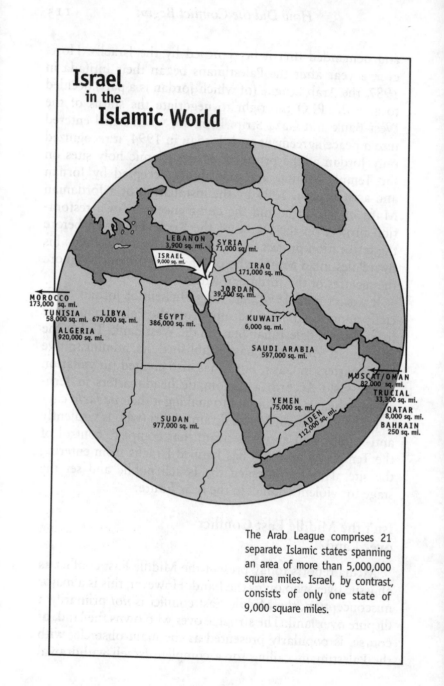

Israel
in the Islamic World

LEBANON
3,900 sq. mi.

SYRIA
71,000 sq. mi.

ISRAEL
9,000 sq. mi.

IRAQ
171,000 sq. mi.

JORDAN
39,500 sq. mi.

MOROCCO
173,000 sq. mi.

TUNISIA
58,000 sq. mi.

LIBYA
679,000 sq. mi.

EGYPT
386,000 sq. mi.

KUWAIT
6,000 sq. mi.

ALGERIA
920,000 sq. mi.

SAUDI ARABIA
597,000 sq. mi.

MUSCAT/OMAN
82,000 sq. mi.

TRUCIAL
33,300 sq. mi.

YEMEN
75,000 sq. mi.

QATAR
8,000 sq. mi.

BAHRAIN
250 sq. mi.

SUDAN
977,000 sq. mi.

ADEN
112,000 sq. mi.

The Arab League comprises 21 separate Islamic states spanning an area of more than 5,000,000 square miles. Israel, by contrast, consists of only one state of 9,000 square miles.

from "occupied" territory (which, according to the PLO charter and Palestinian maps, is *all* of the land!), and Israel arguing that the same territory is their ancient and hard-won homeland given to their fathers by God (see Genesis 12:7; 13:15-17; 15:18-21; 17:8; 22:17). Seeking to distort history in their favor, Palestinians today claim they are descendants of the ancient inhabitants of Canaan in an attempt to prove they predate the Israeli presence in the Land![5] (See next chapter.)

When it comes to talking about land, we need to recognize that the Arab lands total more than 5,000,000 square miles, while Israeli land (including the West Bank) adds up to only about 9,000 square miles. Israel is content to live within this small amount of territory, even though the original covenant with Abraham promised much more land (about 200,000 square miles). However, the surrounding Arab nations refuse to recognize the right of Israel to exist independently in any area, and, despite the Oslo Accord to the contrary, the Palestinian Authority continues to agree with its Arab brethren.

The real reason for the Arab-Israeli conflict is not political, but religious. The problem is Islam, which controls the Arab world and believes that it must subjugate the non-Muslim world to its religion, and that all lands (such as Israel) once in Muslim possession must never be relinquished or returned. In addition, the Qur'an proclaims Israel is wretched and condemned and that Jews are the friends of Satan, worthy only of contempt and punishment. The Qur'an also teaches that Islam superseded both Judaism and Christianity, and therefore Islam cannot tolerate another state or religion sharing equal access or privileges with itself (such as at holy sites),[6] or worse, maintaining political rule over Muslims. To Muslims, it is impossible to negotiate a lasting peace with a perpetual enemy, for the very existence of a sovereign

Jewish state is an affront to Allah and the superior status granted Muslims in the Qur'an. Many Muslims also teach that the Jews of today (and especially European Jews) are really non-Semitic descendants of the middle-age Khazar dynasty, thus they are not Jews at all and have no right to claim any inheritance based on the Bible. It is irreconcilable religious differences, then, that make peace impossible in the Middle East and has now threatened the peace of America and the West.

What's happening in the Middle East is this: Israel is being robbed of its political, historic, and geographic legitimacy while seeming to rob the Palestinians of a nation it never had. What this means is that this newly formed conglomerate of Palestinian-Arabs has sought to create what has never before existed by electing a president, adopting a flag, forming an army, setting up a governmental presence in East Jerusalem, and, with Jordan's agreement, declaring a state—all in violation of the stipulations agreed upon in the Oslo Accord, which precluded any recognition of a Palestinian state. Therefore, the issue is not that of land ownership, but of an Arab-nationalist movement and the religious aims of Islam attempting to eradicate a Jewish presence from the map of the Middle East.

How Did the Conflict over the Temple Mount Begin?

In 1929, Arab violence that began at the Western Wall of the Temple Mount grew into the Arab pogrom in the city of Hebron and the massacre of its ancient Jewish community. When Israeli forces captured East Jerusalem on June 7, 1967, the world watched in wonder. What would happen next? Would Israel annex East Jerusalem, demolish the Muslim mosques and rebuild the Temple? Would the surrounding Arab nations retaliate and stage a massive invasion of Jerusalem to retrieve control of their holy places? Israel did indeed later annex East Jerusalem, but Israel also immediately returned jurisdiction of the Temple Mount to the Muslims and denied any government-approved intention to rebuild the Temple. Thus, at least for the time, a war was averted with the Muslim countries, and the Israeli authorities would protect the multiplicity of religions that now had access to Israel's most holy site. Yet the predominant Jewish expectation on that day in 1967 was that Israel would gain permanent possession of the Temple Mount. The comments of General Mordecai Gur, commander of the Reserve Paratroop Brigade which captured the Old City, on the day that Israel took the Temple Mount, represents the feelings of a deprived generation:

> I feel at home here. The object of all the yearnings. The Temple Mount! Mount Moriah. Abraham and Isaac. The Temple. The Zealots, the Maccabees, Bar-Kochba, Romans, and Greeks. A confusion of thoughts. But there is one feeling that is firmer and deeper than everything. We're on the Temple Mount! The Temple Mount is ours!...We are in Jerusalem to stay.[7]

Similar sentiments were voiced by General Moshe Dayan, the commander of the Israeli forces, who joined General Gur's paratroopers at the newly won Western Wall: "We have united Jerusalem, the divided capital of Israel. We have returned to our holiest of holy places, never to part from it again...."[8] Dayan went on to assure Muslims and Christians that the Israelis would safeguard the holy places and grant free access to them because no one imagined at that time that they would ever again be controlled by anyone other than Israel.

Yet Dayan, who had led in the capture of the Temple Mount while believing Israel must retain political sovereignty over the site, felt Israel could not justify preventing Muslim jurisdiction in view of the greater threat from the

Arab Muslim world and the belief of the Jewish rabbinate that the site was off limits to Jews (owing to its sanctity).

While Dayan believed the West Bank and Sinai, which had also been captured in the war, should be held for the purpose of future bargaining with the Muslims for peace, he knew that Jerusalem, and especially the Temple Mount, held a unique religious status for Muslims, who would go to war again if Jews asserted their religious rights there. Dayan's opinion was expressed within hours of the first day of conquest when he ordered the Israeli flag to be taken down from the Dome of the Rock.

In the days that followed, Israel Defense Forces Chief Rabbi Shlomo Goren opened a synagogue on the Temple Mount itself and Dayan heard of religious Jews (later, Rabbi Goren was included!) who wanted to destroy the Dome of the Rock.

To divert attention from the Temple Mount—a sure recipe for disaster with the Muslim world—Teddy Kollek, Jerusalem's Jewish mayor, gave orders to bulldoze the Arab houses and buildings in the Moghrabi Quarter so that Jews could visit the Western Wall en masse. Meanwhile, Dayan, fearful of Muslim hostilities, decided to take a controversial action of his own. Just ten days after Jews had recovered control of their Temple Mount for the first time in 2,000 years, he entered the Al-Aqsa Mosque and sat on the Muslim prayer carpets in stocking feet to meet with the Waqf (the Islamic trust responsible for managing the religious places on the Temple Mount).

In a move that surely surprised the Waqf, he returned complete control of the entire site to their authority. When I interviewed Rabbi Goren in 1994, he told me that Dayan had acted on his own authority, but that no one in the government dared to oppose his action. As Dayan ordered Rabbi Goren to remove the Jewish prayer books from the Temple Mount, Goren reminded Dayan of the gravity of his deed: "You gave away the Holiest of the Holies to the

Palestinians rally for a Palestinian state with Jerusalem as its capital (note the T-shirt of the man at the front row, which reads, in English, "Jerusalem").

Photo courtesy of Israel Government Press Office

Burning the Palestinian flag in protest of PLO attacks on Israelis. The sign beneath the flames reads "Murderers" and depicts Arafat.

Photo courtesy of Israel Government Press Office

Palestinians burn mock Oslo Accords in a symbolic rejection of the peace process.

Photo courtesy of Israel Government Press Office

Jewish students rally for a Jewish Temple Mount and against Oslo peace process outside the Jaffa Gate of the Old City.

Photo courtesy of Israel Government Press Office

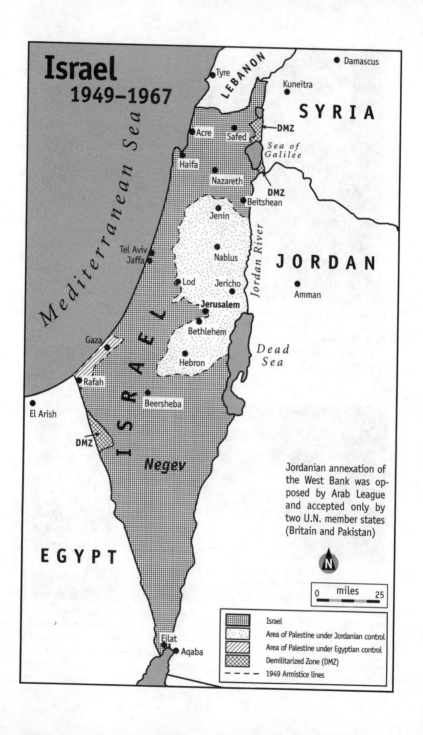

Israel
1949–1967

LEBANON
Tyre
Acre Safed ◄ DMZ
Haifa
Nazareth
DMZ
Beitshean
Jenin
Tel Aviv
Jaffa Nablus
Lod Jericho
Jerusalem
Bethlehem
Gaza
Hebron
Rafah
El Arish
Beersheba
DMZ
Negev
Eilat
Aqaba

Damascus
Kuneitra
SYRIA
Sea of Galilee
JORDAN
Jordan River
Amman
Dead Sea

Mediterranean Sea

ISRAEL

EGYPT

Jordanian annexation of the West Bank was opposed by Arab League and accepted only by two U.N. member states (Britain and Pakistan)

N

0 ——— miles ——— 25

	Israel
	Area of Palestine under Jordanian control
	Area of Palestine under Egyptian control
	Demilitarized Zone (DMZ)
– – –	1949 Armistice lines

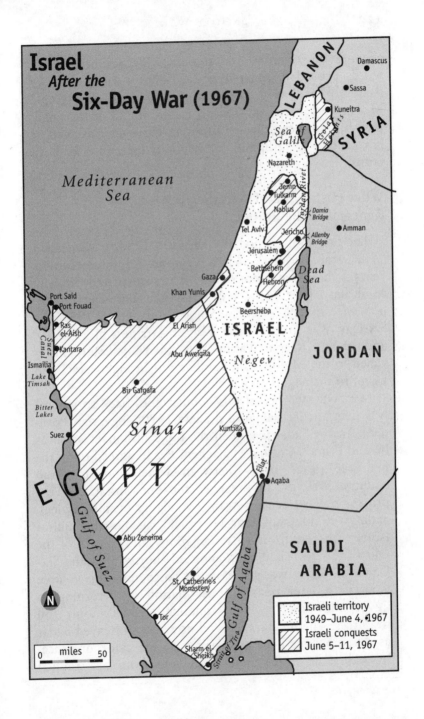

enemies of yesterday and tomorrow!" In time Goren's words proved true; Lawrence Wright, a writer for *The New Yorker*, has pointed out "since then, the Temple Mount has been an Islamic island in an increasingly Jewish, and increasingly Orthodox city—and, as such, it has become a flashpoint for religious extremists of both faiths."[9]

What History Led Up to the Renewal of the Intifada?

The first Intifada actually began in 1936. It was called "The Arab Revolt," and it went on for three fruitless years. It has been succeeded by many since, and the only result has been tragedy. Five wars later (The War of Independence in 1948-49, The Sinai Campaign in 1956, the Six-Day War in 1967, the War of Attrition in 1969-70, and the Yom Kippur War in 1973), the United States intervened in the Middle East conflict and brought Israel and Egypt to the negotiating table.

My own memory of this conflict goes back to when I was living in Jerusalem in the late 1970s. Egyptian President Anwar Sadat was then the topic of conversation as he and Prime Minister Menachem Began agreed upon the first-ever peace treaty between Israel and an Arab country. Well do I remember the one obstacle in the process toward peace—Arab sovereignty over Jerusalem. Sadat was adamant that no peace was possible unless Israel withdrew from its "occupation" and control of the Old City, which had been annexed shortly after the Six-Day War. Began was successful at postponing this volatile issue to a later phase of negotiation by returning to Egypt the Sinai, which contained Israel's only oil resources. The media, then and now, has portrayed Sadat as a courageous hero and martyr to the cause of peace. In reality, he never moved one iota from his staunch

Islamic position, as reflected in these words from a speech on April 25, 1972:

> The most splendid thing the prophet Muhammad... did was to evict them [the Jews] from the entire Arabian peninsula....I pledge to you that we will celebrate on the next anniversary, God willing, and in this place, with God's help, not only the liberation of our land but also the defeat of the Israeli conceit and arrogance so that they may once again return to the condition decreed in our holy book: "Humiliation and abasement has been stamped on them."...we will not renounce this.[10]

Sadat made good on his pledge the next year, launching a surprise attack on Israel during its highest holiday of *Yom Kippur* ("Day of Atonement"), when the military reservists were all at their homes on leave. And it was with this never-renounced pledge in view that Sadat negotiated with Began and came to Israel in 1978. The "paper peace" that has since existed between Egypt and Israel, as well as Israel's current "peace-partner," Egyptian President Hosni Mubarak, who also spouts anti-Israel rhetoric and supports the Palestinian Intifada, reveal that the desire to fulfill Sadat's pledge still continues in Egyptian plans.

Almost a decade later, the PLO, which had been operating as a terrorist organization out of Jordan, Syria, Lebanon, and Tunisia, began an Intifada in 1987 in the Gaza Strip that spread throughout the Jewish areas of Judea and Samaria (West Bank). At the head of the PLO was Egyptian-born Yasser Arafat. His real name is Abdul Rauf el-Chodbi el-Husseini, the name *Arafat* being the name of a hill near Mecca mentioned in the Qur'an (The Cow 194). He is a member of the Husseini family, who produced the Grand Mufti of Palestine, Hag Amin el-Husseini, who organized the anti-Jewish riots of 1921-22, 1929, 1936, and 1938, befriended Adolf Hitler and worked with the Nazis to plan a "final solution" for the "Jewish problem" in Palestine (1943-45). Arafat was not only related, but one of the mufti's students.

Among Arafat's many terrorist activities was the masterminding of the 1972 murder of the Israeli Olympic team in Munich, the 1974 murder of schoolchildren at Ma'alot, the murder of infirmed Jewish passengers on the Achille Lauro cruise ship, the murder of a U.S. ambassador in Sudan, and the bombing that killed 265 U.S. Marines. He is also a friend of Saddam Hussein and Osama bin Laden. Tellingly, Arafat's "minister of war" (later killed in Tunisia) was called Abu Jihad ("Father of the Holy War").

When it comes to the peace process, the Israeli government could not sanction a public meeting with such a terrorist as Arafat to resolve the Intifada, so meetings between leaders took place in secret in Oslo, Norway and were brokered by the United States and Soviet Union. The "peace partners" this time were Israeli Prime Minister Yitzhak Rabin and PLO Chairman Yasser Arafat. Negotiations were initiated in Madrid, Spain, but were soon (again) deadlocked over the issue of Jerusalem. The Arabs would *no longer* put off negotiating a final status agreement on the city, but it was impossible for such an agreement to be reached at that time between a commander of the Six-Day War (Rabin) and a recognized terrorist (Arafat). Therefore, written into the Declaration of Principles the leaders finally signed in Washington, D.C. on September 13, 1993 was a deadline that committed both sides to resolving the matter after their fifth year anniversary together as "peace partners," a date that unexpectedly coincided with (and collided with) the 3,000-year anniversary of Jerusalem as the capital of Israel. It was hoped that through Israel's willingness to follow the formula of "trading land for peace," a relationship of trust could be developed with the Palestinian and Arab worlds that would enable the leaders to resolve the sticky point of Jerusalem. Yet, such was not to be.

What Brought an End to the Oslo Peace Process?

From the beginning of the Oslo peace process, there were radical elements on both sides that believed any kind of agreement was treason, and they attempted to force the talks to a stop by acts of terror. However, in the end, the efforts failed on account of the continued acts of violence and threats of *jihad* from the Palestinian negotiators themselves. Despite the assassination of original peace partner Yitzhak Rabin (by an Orthodox Jew), Israel continued to make unprecedented concessions of land to the Palestinians and made efforts to freeze settlement expansion (claimed as a major obstacle to peace for the Palestinians). Israel gave the Palestinian Authority local autonomy over certain areas of the West Bank and Gaza Strip, and in spite of the risk to Israeli security, permitted them to have weapons and armed forces for the purpose of policing their territories and controlling terrorism within their borders. However, not only was terrorism not contained, but the ranks of the Palestinian police were made up of terrorists that had been jailed by the Israelis and released as part of the peace negotiations! And despite Arafat's denial of cooperation with such terrorist organizations as Hamas, Islamic Jihad, and Hizbullah, it became clear that every act of terrorism that struck Israel through these organizations during the peace process had been ordered or approved by him.

Ultimately, the peace process was doomed from the start because of irreconcilable positions over the status of Jerusalem. Palestinians wanted to redivide the city, return it to its pre-1967 boundaries, establish their capital in East Jerusalem, and have exclusive sovereignty over the *Haram al-Sharif* (Temple Mount). Furthermore, the Palestinians made it clear that only a resolution in their favor could prevent war. Meanwhile, Israelis in their elections, revealed time and again that they would elect only a political hard-liner who would not concede on dividing Jerusalem or giving up sovereignty of the Temple Mount. Therefore, when the issue of Jerusalem finally arose at the negotiating table, the partners were more enemies than friends, and Oslo was clearly on the way out.

As described in chapter 1, the end came at the Camp David II Summit when Arafat rejected an Israeli offer based on an American plan and walked away from the last-ditch effort at peace. According to an interview with Prime Minister Barak,[11] who had represented Israel at the Summit, the offer would have kept the Jewish neighborhoods of East Jerusalem under Israeli control, while the Arab neighborhoods would have gone under Palestinian control. The Temple Mount would have been under a shared sovereignty, but with the Palestinians in custodial control. Arafat bolted at these proposals, stating, "I cannot take these ideas as a basis for negotiation. And I demand the right of return and full sovereignty over the Temple Mount."[12]

Although the Palestinians wanted more from the summit, they had been offered much more than the initiator of the peace process, Yitzhak Rabin, had ever envisioned or intended. He had stated from the outset of Oslo that the Israeli position was against the formation of an independent Palestinian state, but only "to share land with its neighbors." Had Arafat agreed to the Israeli-American terms, the Camp David II Summit would have resulted in the establishment of a Palestinian state. Later, Barak confessed: "Once Oslo's assumptions collapsed, it cast a disturbing shadow in retrospect on what has happened since 1996. Maybe Arafat cheated all of us....It was an end to what Arafat had done for years—namely, talk in English about his readiness to make peace and in Arabic about eliminating Israel in stages....My feeling is that we won't have a peace agreement with Arafat."[13]

Today, the conflict has risen to a crisis stage, with the Palestinians engaged with Israel in a local war, the Arab Muslim states demanding resolution, and the Western powers exerting pressure on Israel to continue negotiations in light of the war on terrorism.

Therefore, a half century after the founding of the Jewish state as the safe haven for the Jews of the Diaspora, the same anti-Semitism that spawned the Nazi Holocaust has provoked an Islamic *jihad*, an Arab-Islamic call to liberate Jerusalem and destroy the Zionist entity. After the February 2001 election of Ariel Sharon as prime minister of Israel, Arab newspaper headlines proclaimed, "Israel Votes for War!" For the Palestinians, their Intifada can continue indefinitely, but Israel will not endure another "war of attrition," and so its military has had to move in to resecure "hot spots" in the West Bank and to prevent further terrorist acts from being perpetrated against its civilian population.

Even though Israel has withdrawn under pressure from most of these areas, it has declared it will not compromise its security for the sake of the United States building an Arab coalition that opposes its existence! Also, Israel sees terrorist acts, such as the assissination of Israeli tourism minister Rehavam Ze'evi (a cabinet position) in Jerusalem (October 2001), as attempts to set off a regional war in order to wreck the Western coalition and unify the Arab world in an all-out assault against Israel. In order to understand what might happen next, it is necessary to understand the key players in the conflict—especially the Palestinians, whose origins bear contradictory claims.

Causes and Contributing Factors to the Middle East Conflict

Religious

ISLAM—Unifies Arabs, promotes *jihad* against Jews

JUDAISM—Isolates Jews, promotes return to Land

Political

Greater Arab Emirate

Zionism

Pledges of other Nations

Pogroms & Holocaust against Jews, creating need for homeland and immigration

Economic
(and security issues)

ARABS—Petroleum wealth, renewed influence and power, nuclear capability/ threat to West

ISRAELIS—Only democracy in Middle East, surveillance and intelligence, nuclear arsenal

Sociological

"Palestinian Problem"

Creation of a refugee people

Demand for statehood

Revisionist history

"Settlement Problem"

Increased Jewish immigration

Settlement in West Bank areas (permitted under British Mandate)

Important Dates in the History
of the Middle East Conflict

B.C. 2000	Abraham—Beginning of Jewish and Arab Lines
1406	Jews enter Canaan Israel
1000-925	Kingdom Established, First Temple Built (Jerusalem)
63	Roman Occupation of Israel
A.D. 70	Jerusalem Temple Destroyed by Romans
135	Jewish Nationalism Ends, Jewish Exile
613	Mohammed Forms Religion of Islam
638	Muslim Conquest of Holy Land, Al-Aqsa Mosque Built
691	Dome of the Rock Built in Jerusalem on Temple Mount
1897	First Zionist Congress
1916	Tripartite (Sykes-picot) Agreement—Creates Borders of Modern Middle East
1918	British Mandate over Palestine Begins
1922	Britain Creates Transjordan (for Arabs)
1929	Arab Riots in Palestine
1933-1947	Jewish Flight from Persecution
1937	Peel Partition Plan of Palestine
1939	British White Papers Restrict Jewish Immigration
1947	United Nations Partition Plan
1948	Declaration of Jewish State, Arab-Israeli War Begins
1950	Jewish Law of Return Enacted, Jordan Cedes West Bank
1956	Sinai War
1973	Yom Kippur War
1979	Egyptian-Israel Peace Agreement (Camp David)
1987	Intifada Begins
1989	Mass Exodus of Soviet Jewry Begins
1991	Gulf War (Alliance of Iraq, Jordan, and PLO against Israel)
1993-2000	Oslo Accords (peace negotiations between Israel and Palestinians)
1994	Peace Treaty with Jordan
2001	Intifada Renewed ("Battle of Al-Aqsa")
	Terrorist Attack on America
	America and Allies Launch War on Terrorism

Terrorist Organizations

Location	Name	Facts
Founded in Kuwait. Bases in Tunisia, Lebanon, West Bank, and Gaza Strip. Most important group within PLO.	**Fatah**	Headed by Yasser Arafat. Name means "conquest." Contains special units: Tanzim, Force 17, Hawari Special Operations Group.
The West Bank and Gaza Strip.	**Hamas**	Palestinian outgrowth of the Muslim Brotherhood; targets Israeli civilians and military.
Beirut, south Lebanon; with cells in Africa, Asia, Europe, the Americas.	**Hizbullah**	Opposes peace negotiations, anti-Israel, anti-West, allied with Syria and Iran.
Israel, Jordan, Lebanon; head-quartered in Syria.	**Palestine Islamic Jihad**	Seeks destruction of Israel, anti-U.S., opposed to moderate Arab governments.
Based in Iraq; supported by Iraq and Libya.	**Palestine Liberation Front**	Split into pro-PLO, pro-Syrian, and pro-Libyan factions. PLO faction led by Muhammad Abbas.
Supported by Syria and Libya. Operate in Syria, Lebanon, Israel, West Bank.	**Popular Front for the Liberation of Palestine**	Founded by Jerusalem businessman George Habash. Cooperates with Hamas and Islamic Jihad. Attacks Israelis and moderate Arabs.
Headquartered in Damascus, Syria, with bases in Lebanon, ties with Iran.	**Popular Front for the Liberation of Palestine— General Command**	Founded by Ahmed Jibril, a former Syrian army captain. Guerrilla operations in southern Lebanon, attacks in Israel.
Global reach, operates out of Afghanistan under the Taliban regime, where training camps are maintained.	**Al-Qaeda**	Founded by Osama bin Laden, seeks to destroy Israel and U.S., establish global caliphate (theocratic state under Islamic law) through offensive *jihad*.
Cairo, with cells in Yemen, Afghanistan, Pakistan, Sudan, and Lebanon.	**Al-Jihad**	Close partner with bin Laden; seeks to overthrow Egyptian government; anti-U.S. and Israel.

Who Are the Palestinians?

The Palestinian peoples' historical roots can be traced back to the distant past of recorded history. The name Palestine came from Philistia, the land of the biblical Philistines, or "Peoples of the Sea."
—PALESTINE INFORMATION SERVICES

From the end of the Jewish state in antiquity to the beginning of the British rule, the area now designated by the name of Palestine was not a country and had no frontiers, only administrative boundaries.
—BERNARD LEWIS, PROFESSOR OF HISTORY, PRINCETON UNIVERSITY

According to a recent census released by the Palestinian Central Bureau of Statistics, nearly three million Palestinians live in the West Bank, Jerusalem, and Gaza.[1] These Palestinians claim to be the descendants of the ancient natives of Palestine. Furthermore, they declare that they and millions more of their Palestinian descendants, scattered as refugees throughout the Middle East and living in other countries of the world (including the United States), are engaged in a national struggle for sovereignty in their historic homeland. In addition, the radical Islamic terrorists have championed this same cause and declared that there will be no peace for the West until the Palestinians achieve their objectives. But what are the facts behind these claims? What is the actual origin of this people who have gained such prominence that their demand for national recognition and right of return is said to be at the center of the Middle East conflict and the deciding factor in the war on terrorism?

What Is the Origin of the Name *Palestinian?*

The term *Palestinian* is thought to have been derived from the Greek and Latin words for one of the chief enemies of the Israelites—the Philistines (Greek *Palaistine*, Latin *Palaestina*, for Hebrew, *Pleshtim*). The Philistine kingdom of Philistia (Hebrew, *'Eretz Pleshet*) occupied the narrow strip of coastal plain between modern Gaza and Joppa from the thirteenth to seventh centuries B.C. Indeed, the word *Palestine* appears in the King James version of the Bible with reference to this region (Joel 3:4). However, more modern versions use the term *Philistia*.

David Jacobson, an instructor at the University College of London on Jews and the classical world, believes that *Palestine* may have originated as a Greek pun on the translations of "Israel" and the "land of the Philistines."[2] He observes that the Greek and Latin terms frequently appear in ancient literature with reference not to the land of the Philistines, but to the Land of Israel. For example, Herodotus (circa 450 B.C.), reputed to be the father of history, recorded that the people of Palestine were circumcised, a distinction of Israelites, not Philistines (who were uncircumcised). Likewise, Aristotle (fourth century B.C.) observed in his writings that the Dead Sea was in Palestine (a geographical setting in Israel far to the east of Philistine territory). And Philo of Alexandria (first century A.D.) identified *Palaistinei* with biblical Canaan and remarked that "Palestinian Syria was occupied by the populous nation of the Jews."

Furthermore, if Palestine was derived from *Philistine*, the Greek translation of the Hebrew Bible, known as the Septuagint (circa 250 B.C.), should have translated the Hebrew word *Pleshtim* ("Philistine") by the well-known Greek term *Palaistinoi* ("Palestine"). However, the translators chose the Greek transliteration *Philistieim* (revealing by the plural ending *im* a term of Hebrew origin). Jacobson argues that the Greek word *Palaistine* ("Palestine") is quite close to the Greek word *palaistes*, which means "wrestler," "rival," or "adversary." This is the very meaning of the Hebrew word *Yisra'el* ("Israel"), based on Genesis 32:25-27, in which Jacob received the name Israel because he "wrestled" (Hebrew *sarita*) with "God" (Hebrew *El*).

To the Greeks, who liked to use wordplays, the word *Palestine* would have sounded both like the people of Israel, who were thought to be the descendants of a hero who wrestled with a god, and the Philistines, who lived on the adjacent coast. The first-century Jewish historian Flavius Josephus, who wrote in Greek, supports this general usage by referring to both the land of the Philistines and the much larger Land of Israel as "Palestine." However, he also distinguished the Land of Israel by this term when he wrote of "the events that befell us Jews in Egypt, in Syria, and in Palestine."[3]

The use of the term *Palestine* in identification with the Land of Israel officially took root when the Roman emperor Hadrian renamed the country *Syria Palaestina*. It is often thought that Hadrian did this to punish the Jews for their revolt against Roman rule (the Bar-Kokhba Revolt of A.D. 132–135), for by removing their name for their country, the historic connection with their homeland would be severed. However, since the first-century Jewish writers Philo and Josephus had already used this term in

Greek for Israel, and Roman writers had continued this practice, Hadrian may have simply codified the ancient and accepted usage. Nevertheless, the designation *Palaestina* appears to have been applied particularly to Judea, at the center of which was the capital city of Jerusalem. Hadrian's attack was clearly leveled against Jerusalem, which he considered the heart of the rebellion. It was from this city he expelled the Jewish population and renamed it *Aelia Capitolina* (in honor of his own family name *Aelia* and the gods on Rome's Capitol Hill). To obscure the Jewish religious character of the city, he plowed under the site of the Temple Mount and erected within it pagan temples and shrines. In this way Hadrian symbolically sought to remove the Jewish past and build a new and revised Roman future.

Even though the Romans attempted to sever a connection between Palestine and the Jewish people, Palestine remained identified with Israel as the place of promise "so that in later times the words Judea and Palestine were synonymous."[4] Therefore, in a general sense, the name *Palestine* has more of a historical link with the Land and people of Israel—the Jews—and in a restricted sense, also with the Philistines. In addition, the later application to Judea and Jerusalem may well have arisen from an attempt by the Roman enemies of the Jews to revise their historic origins.

Who in Palestine Was Called a Palestinian?

Greek and Roman writers used the terms *Palestine* and *Palestinian* to refer to the Land of Israel and its Jewish inhabitants. As we have seen, early secular writers such as Herodotus and Aristotle had used these terms in this way, as had first-century Jewish writers such as Philo and Josephus. In the early first century A.D. the Roman poet Ovid described Jewish Sabbath observance with the words "the seventh-day feast that the Syrian of Palestine observes."[5] Other Latin authors, such as the poet Statius and the historian Dio Chrysostom, also spoke of the Jews as Palestinians and the Jewish homeland as Palestine.[6] Likewise, in talmudic literature (third century A.D.), Palestine is used as the name of a Roman province adjoining the provinces of Phoenicia and Arabia (i.e., the Land of Israel).

In the fourth century A.D. the three provinces into which the Land of Israel had been divided were referred to as first, second, and third Palestine. But the term *Palestine* seems to have disappeared completely in the Land after the Muslim conquest of A.D. 638. In fact, *Palestine* never appears in the Qur'an, which refers to the area as simply "the holy land" (*Al-Arad Al-Muqaddash*). In like manner, Jerusalem is not mentioned in the Qur'an, and Arab historians variously referred to it as *Iliya* (adapted from the Latin *Aelia*), *Bayt Maqdis* (adapted from the Hebrew *Beit Hamiqdash*, "the Holy House" or "the Temple"), and finally as *Al-Quds* ("the Holy One").

The Crusaders renewed the use of the three Palestines, however, after the fall of the Crusader kingdom, the name Palestine was no longer used officially, but was preserved only by Christian cartographers in maps drawn in their native lands. From the establishment of Islamic rule over the Land until the late nineteenth century, inhabitants of the region between the Jordan River and the Mediterranean appear to have referred to themselves primarily with respect to their religions (Mohammedan, Christians, and Jews).

The first modern use of the term *Palestinian* appears during the time of the British Mandate (1917–1948). To the classically trained British mind the Land of Israel had ceased to exist in ancient times; and Palestine had endured in the classical literature as the designation of the Jewish homeland and heritage. This may be seen, for example, in *The Jewish Encyclopedia* (published in London in 1905), which states that Palestine is "the portion of Syria that was formerly the possession of the Israelites."[7] Given the British penchant for historical accuracy, the term is applied with reference to the *Jewish* residents of the country. Therefore, the standard British reference for defining terms, the *Oxford English Dictionary*, defines the term Palestinian as 1) "the Jews who returned to Israel from Moscow," and 2) "Jews from Israel who volunteered to the British Army to fight Germany." In fact, Jewish soldiers serving with the Allies during World War II had the word *Palestine* inscribed on their shoulder badges.

In addition, under the British Mandate, the Jewish-owned newspaper *The Jerusalem Post* was known as *The Palestine Post* and the Israel Philharmonic Orchestra was called the Palestine Philharmonic Orchestra, and postage stamps were issued bearing the appellation "Palestine—EI," the abbreviation EI meaning '*Eretz Israel* (Hebrew for "the Land of Israel").

These usages make it clear that even though the term *Palestinian* could have also been applied to Arabs or many other ethnic groups (such as the Armenians, Greeks, Syrians, and Ethiopians of Jerusalem's Old City or the German Templars of its New City), under British rule, the term was especially understood to refer to a Jew from Palestine.

When Was the Name *Palestinian* Applied to the Arabs?

Palestine was under Arab-Muslim control for only a brief period of time even though after the Muslim conquest Arabic became the language of most of the population. Noted scholar David George Hogarth made this point back in 1877: "When we look back at the history of the early Caliphate, we find the period of genuine Arab empire extraordinarily short....Arabs governed Arabs, though Arabs on an imperial scale for much less than a century, just the Umayyad Damascus period and no more."[8] This becomes evident when we examine the 1,174-year rule of conquerors: Umayyids (112 years), Abbassids (163 years), Egyptians (157 years), Christian Crusaders (103 years), and Turks (743 years). Only the Umayyid and Abbassid dynasties can be identified as "Arab."

What's more, Hogarth acknowledged that sovereign Arab rule lasted "for much less than a century."[9] In like manner, the Muslim chairman of the Syrian delegation to the Paris Peace Conference in 1919 stated that "the only Arab domination since the Conquest in A.D. 635 hardly lasted, as such, 22 years."[10] Furthermore, throughout the entire period of rule, the terms *Palestine* and *Palestinian* were not used for any Muslim peoples, Arab or otherwise, although before the Crusader rule Arabs used the term *Filastin* for the Roman division of "first Palestine" (which included Judea and Samaria), and distinguished it from *Urdunn* ("Jordan"). Otherwise, the Arabs generally referred to provinces by the names of their capital cities.

At the beginning of the twentieth century, Arabs rejected the term *Palestinian* because it was thought to refer to the Jews. This was evident when the 1917 Balfour Declaration referred to the land of Palestine as the place for a "national home for the Jewish people." The Arabs reacted to the document, stating that there was no such thing as Palestine except in reference to the southern part of Greater Syria. Under the British Mandate, the name Palestine was practically restricted to the land on the western side of the Jordan River, because the British had established on the eastern side the emirate of Transjordan.

In 1950 this emirate annexed the western Arab-inhabited part of western Palestine and changed its name to the Hashemite kingdom of Jordan. However, during the Mandate period, the Arab political representation, headed by the Mufti of Jerusalem, was not called the "Palestinian Committee" as it is today, but merely "The Arab Higher Committee." And finally, when the Anglo-American Committee of Inquiry convened in Jerusalem in 1946, the distinguished Arab historian Professor Philip Hitti testified: "There is no such thing as Palestine in [Arab] history, absolutely not."[11] He likewise opposed the use of the name Palestine on area maps because it was "associated in the mind of the average American, and perhaps the Englishman too, with the Jews."[12]

The use of the term *Palestinian* with application to the Western Arab population of Palestine cannot be found in any dictionary, encyclopedia, or history book until after the State of Israel started to become a reality. The use of the term *Palestinian* for the country's Arabs began in the early 1960s as Arab leaders sought to create a unified identity. However, it does not appear that there was any serious nationalistic movement until after the Six-Day War of 1967. Even then the primary goal of the Arabs was terrorism aimed at the destruction of Israel rather than the recovery of a homeland, since the territories captured by the Israelis in that conflict were not theirs but those of Egypt (Gaza Strip), Syria (Golan Heights), and Jordan (West Bank).

The term *Palestinian(s)* does not appear in the foundational documents related to resolving the Arab-Israeli conflicts of the 1967 Six-Day War and the 1973 Yom Kippur War (Security Council Resolutions 242 and 338). Such an omission tells us that at that time, the Arabs described in these resolutions were not thought of as Palestinians. The usage of the term became more prominent in the mid

1970s when it became politically expedient for the PLO to apply the term *Palestinian* to the Arab population in exclusion of the Jews. The PLO leadership realized that it would be much better to describe their effort to destroy Israel as a struggle for freedom rather than as a pan-Arabic effort. Since the formation of the Palestinian Authority in 1993, the Israeli-Arabs, in a show of solidarity, have also changed their identity and adopted the name Palestinians. Since that time, the term has been used to refer exclusively to the Arab residents of the West Bank (and their descendants in the *Diaspora*) and has become commonly accepted through its use by the international media.

What Is the Origin of the Modern Palestinians?

The Palestine of modern history began in the late nineteenth century, in the dying years of the Ottoman Empire, which had ruled the region for some 400 years as part of Greater Syria. The Ottomans had not sought to colonize the country; rather, they had focused their attention only on Jerusalem for bureaucratic purposes, abandoning the rest of the land to desolation. The feudal system that had existed for hundreds of years maintained agricultural farms along the fertile Coastal Plain, employing poor tenant farmers or imported workers.

Starting about 1878, harsh conditions forced many groups to immigrate into Palestine, where work was available. According to historical surveys, these migrant workers, from which the Palestinians of today are descended, came from many nationalities: "Balkans, Greeks, Syrians, Latins, Egyptians, Turks, Armenians, Italians, Persians, Kurds, Germans, Afghans, Druzes, Turks, Circassians, Bosnians, Sudaneese, Samaritans, Algerians, Motawila, Tartars, Hungarians, Scots, Navarese, Bretons, English, Franks, Ruthenians, Bohemians, Bulgarians, Georgians, Persian Nestorians, Indians, Copts, Maronites, and many others."[13] Of the 141,000 mostly Turkish Muslims settled in the Land in 1882, at least 25 percent (35,280) were newcomers.[14] This local element (mostly from non-Arab countries) working for the foreign-based landowners constituted the "Palestinian" population.

Palestinian nationalism, or the desire for a government and an independent Palestinian state, was nonexistent. Even though Palestine had been under Islamic rule intermittently for 1,174 years, no feelings or bent toward nationalism had ever been recorded on the part of its Arab population. On the contrary, Muslim Arabs felt more united with their co-religionists in other countries than with the Jewish and Christian inhabitants of the Land they occupied. The religious centers of Islam lay far to the east in Mecca and Medina, and while Muslims had early sought to reduce the formidable influence of Christian culture, no attempt had been made to erase the ancient and national Jewish connections with the Land, and especially with Jerusalem. In fact, Jews were recognized as the ancient inhabitants of the Land, in keeping with the accounts of biblical history found in the Qur'an.

This continued to be the case largely throughout the entire period of Muslim domination. But, in the last half of the nineteenth century, with the opening of the Middle East to Western travelers and Christian missionaries as well as Europe's intellectual and cultural influence upon younger Arabs, a minority of these people began to seek educational, economic, and national independence. However, this independence was sought not from "Zionist occupiers," but from the Ottoman Turkish Muslim overlords!

This nationalistic ideology raised questions about what constitutes a nation and its boundaries. In the debates that ensued, there is no evidence that these Arabs seeking national independence ever thought of themselves as

Palestinians. In fact, Daniel Pipes, a writer for the Middle East Forum, says this:

> Some said the residents of the Levant are a nation; others said Eastern Arabic speakers; or all Arabic speakers; or all Moslems. But no one suggested "Palestinians," and for good reason. Palestine, then a secular way of saying '*Eretz Yisra'el* or *Terra Sancta*, embodied a purely Jewish and Christian concept, one utterly foreign to Moslems, even repugnant to them....Instead, Moslems west of the Jordan directed their allegiance to Damascus, where the great-great-uncle of Jordan's King Abdullah II was then ruling; they identified themselves as Southern Syrians.[15]

At the March 1919 Paris Peace Conference an agreement that promoted the development of a Jewish homeland was signed between Zionist leader Chaim Weizman and Arab leader Emir Faisal. The language of this document spoke of "the Arab state and Palestine," clearly reflecting the understanding that Palestine was that part of the Middle East designated for the Jewish homeland and separate from that part claimed by the Arabs. However, a different opinion had been expressed a month earlier in February, before the conference convened in Paris. At the First Congress of Muslim-Christian Association, which had met in Jerusalem to choose its representatives for the peace conference, the following resolution was adopted: "We consider Palestine as part of Arab Syria, as it has never been separated from it at any time. We are connected with it by national, religious, linguistic, natural, economic, and geographical bonds."[16] Nevertheless, both opinions indicate that Arabs did not view Palestine as having an *independent* Arab status.

This thinking changed the next year when the British began to delineate Palestine and the French overthrew the Hashemite king Amin Husseini, thereby abolishing the notion of a Southern Syria. Isolated by these events, the Muslims of Palestine had to make the best of a bad situation. A prominent Jerusalemite declared at that time, "After the recent events in Damascus, we have to effect a complete change in our plans here. Southern Syria no longer exists. We must defend Palestine." To what extent this thinking may have been shared by other Arabs is unclear, but when the Peel Commission in 1936 proposed the partition of Palestine, another local Arab leader, Auni Bey Abdul-Hadi, told the commission, "There is no such country [as Palestine]! Palestine is a term the Zionist invented! There is no Palestine in the Bible. Palestine is alien to us; it is the Zionists who introduced it. Our country was for centuries part of Syria."[17]

Despite such denials, a non-Jewish "Palestine" did exist at that time, having been created by the British in 1922 when they separated the land east of the Jordan (which now comprises the present-day country of Jordan). Indeed, a majority of Jordan's population and army are Palestinian, and most of the Palestinian Arabs in the West Bank hold Jordanian passports. Even though this "Palestine" has been said to have ceased to exist as a political entity when the State of Israel and the Hashemite kingdom of Jordan were established, there had remained among Arabs a recognition that Jordan was the Palestinian state. For example, in interviews with the Arab press in 1981 and 1984, the late King Hussein (grandson of Abdullah) stated, "The truth is that Jordan is Palestine and Palestine is Jordan."[18] Yasser Arafat has stated the same thing: "What you call Jordan is actually Palestine."[19] Also, the war between Arafat's PLO (when resident in Jordan) and the Jordanian government was considered a "civil war."

Today, however, the Palestinian demand for international recognition as a distinct people who can receive foreign diplomats, fly the Palestinian flag, elect Yasser Arafat as president, and claim Jerusalem as its capital—all actions of an independent state—have served to create a "fact" from fiction. This Arab nationalism began only in the early twentieth century, and then only in reaction to the dominant Turkish rule, not Jewish immigration. It wasn't until the establishment of the State of Israel (and increasingly so since the 1967 Six-Day War and the Oslo Agreement of 1993) that Palestinian-Arabs have claimed the Land as their historic homeland and themselves as a people distinct from other Arab peoples. Researcher Roger David Carasso is to the point when he explains the purpose of such Palestinian revisionism:

> The Arabs learned their disinformation tactic from the Nazis: if you repeat the lie long enough, and loud enough, people will actually believe you. As a result, most people now believe there is something called the "Palestinian" people, a total fabrication, complete with a phony history and a phony culture. There is only one truth here, that there are 1.75 million people, a hodgepodge of Arabs and Turks, intentionally or maybe unwittingly, masquerading as a "people," and made into a "people" by the PLO and many in the world community who relished attacking the Jews in yet another novel way.[20]

Having seen the historic use of the term *Palestine* with a primary reference to the Land of Israel and a modern application to the nation of Jordan, let's now turn our attention to the basis for the Palestinian claim to the Land today.

CHAPTER 8

What Is the Palestinian Claim to the Land?

The ancestors of today's Palestinians appeared along the southeastern Mediterranean coast more than five millennia ago and settled down to a life of fishing, farming and herding.[1]
—TAD SZULC

The Arabs of Palestine are the indigenous inhabitants of the country, who have been in occupation of it since the beginning of history.[2]
—THE CASE FOR PALESTINE

The modern nationalism expressed by the Palestinians has led most people to assume that they have had a long and ancient history in the Land, disrupted only by the "Zionist invasion and occupation" since the Second World War. Indeed, the term *Palestinian,* in reference to the ancient Land of Palestine, gives the impression that these people are natives or natural descendants of the original inhabitants of the area and that a Palestinian civilization and culture once flourished in the Land.

Yasser Arafat once asserted in a speech to the United Nations in 1947 that Palestine's "Arab people were engaged in farming and building, spreading culture throughout the land for thousands of years, setting an example in the practice of religious tolerance and freedom of worship, acting as faithful guardians of the holy places of all religions." Such declarations have been codified by a new wave of Palestinian revisionism and distributed by such organizations as the Palestinian Academic Society for the Study of International Affairs to journalists, politicians, and other influential members of society.

As examples of the Palestinian-Arab history they promote, consider these statements made in their publication *The Land, Its People and History:*

> In the middle of the Third Millennium (3000 B.C.), after the wave of drought and desiccation that struck the Arabian Peninsula, the Canaanites, tribes of Arab Semites, came to and settled in the territories east of the Mediterranean Sea that consist of present-day Syria, Lebanon, Jordan and Palestine....About the year 4,000 B.C., the Jebusites, a Canaanite subgroup, founded Jebus—Jerusalem.[3]

Along with such declarations are others, such as, "The Philistines gave Palestine its name" and, "Palestinian-Arabs are descendants of the Philistines, who were Arabs themselves." No less a figure than the late Egyptian President Anwar Sadat once stated, "The assassinations of Arab brethren like [the Philistine] Goliath, by Jewish sheep herders like David, is the sort of shameful ignomimy that we must yet set aright in the domain of the occupied Palestinian homeland."[4] This Palestinian interpretation of history teaches that the Jews were simply one of many peoples who passed through the land originally inhabited by the ancient Palestinians, and had little or no impact on it. Such views have been influential in turning modern

Middle-Eastern Christians against Israel. For example, in June of 1998 the Middle East Council of Churches, joined by a body called "the Arab Working Group on Christian-Muslim Dialogue," held a conference in Beirut, Lebanon and issued a statement it called "The Jerusalem Appeal." In this document we read, "Jerusalem is its people. Its people are Palestinians, who, ever since Jerusalem existed and for countless generations, have lived within it. They... know of no other place as their capital...."[5]

Another Palestinian claim is based on the Qur'anic teaching that the Arabs are descendants of Abraham through his son Ishmael. Thus, they have claimed a right to Abraham's land of Canaan (today the country they call Palestine) through this Semitic heritage.

What are the historical facts behind such assertions? Can the Palestinians claim a legal inheritance to the Land through Abraham? Or through the early inhabitants of Canaan? Let's find out by looking first at the issue of ancestry.

Do Palestinians Have a Right to the Land Through Abraham?

As a Semitic people descended from Abraham, the Palestinian people believe they have a legitimate claim to the Land promised by God to this patriarch. Are they right? We should first note that the term *Semitic* was coined by the German scholar A.L. Schloezer in 1781 to group closely related languages that, by his time, had come to include at least 70 distinct forms divided into Northwest Semitic (for example, Hebrew, Ugaritic, Aramaic), East Semitic (for example, Akkadian, Babylonian), and South Semitic (Arabic) languages. Although Schloezer did not include Canaanite (the language of Canaan), in his groupings, nor the languages of the Arab tribes, archaeological inscriptions have since confirmed Hebrew in usage in Canaan before the arrival of the Israelites (also confirmed in the Bible, which calls Hebrew *Sephath Kena'an*, "the language of Canaan") and Arabic dialects as belonging to the South Semitic family. Perhaps his reluctance to do this was because Canaan was a descendant of Ham (Genesis 10:6), not Shem, which would make Hebrew "Hamitic" rather than Semitic. However, the term *Hebrew* is thought to have come from Eber, who was a descendant of Shem (Genesis 10:21,25).

Originally the term *Semitic* only had a linguistic meaning, but nineteenth-century romantic notions that grouped together language, land, and nation imbued it with racial qualities that produced the modern concept of "the Semitic race." Even though there is no scientific basis for the belief that peoples who spoke a Semitic language had a common *racial* origin, the term today has come to be used with reference to "those peoples who speak the Semitic languages, the Semites." Therefore, since language does not determine ethnic relationship, the Jews and Arabs cannot be related on this basis.

However, are not Jews and Arabs cousins through Abraham's two sons Isaac (through Sarah) and Ishmael (through Hagar)? If this were so, as the Qur'an states and as Arab Muslims claim, could they not also claim Palestine as their land? After all, did not the Old Testament promise the Land to Abraham and his seed? They reason that since Ishmael is Abraham's seed (not to mention his firstborn child), Palestinians, as Ishmael's seed, have a right to the Land promised to Abraham. This reasoning makes the common assumption that Isaac was the father of the Israelites and Ishmael was the father of the Arabs.

However, nowhere does the Bible explicitly state that Ishmael was the forefather of the Arab people. We must be careful to recognize that the proper noun *Ishmael* later became used as a common noun to describe desert tribes in general, such as the Midianites (Judges 8:24, cf. 7:12), whose lineage is traced to a different son of Abraham through his second wife Keturah (Genesis 25:2). In addition, even though the "sons of Ishmael" listed in Genesis 25:12-17 can be traced to Arabian desert tribes, many scholars continue to argue that this is a general expression for bedouinlike existence and is not meant to indicate an ethnic relation to the patriarch Ishmael.

Furthermore, the term *Arabian,* used in the Old and New Testaments, indicates an inhabitant of Arabia, and is not necessarily synonymous with *Arabs.* Even so, some scholars have recognized a linguistic affinity between the Hebrew word *Yisma'il* ("Ishmael") and the word *Sumu'il,* a term appearing in Assyrian inscriptions of the eighth-seventh centuries B.C. for an Arab tribal confederacy extending over the whole of north Arabia in the first half of the first millennium B.C.[6] If this identification, though debated, is accepted and further linked with the 12 tribal chieftains mentioned in Genesis 25, Ishmaelite descendants may include the Bedouin people known as the Qedarites, who were succeeded by the Nabateans, whose capital was at Petra in Edomite territory.[7] Since the latest Nabatean Aramaic inscription is dated to A.D. 356, there is no clear picture of what happened to this people, although conversions to Christianity are recorded in the early Byzantine period, and hellenized bishops were active at Petra in the fourth century A.D. It is uncertain, therefore, whether Muhammad's claimed connection with Ishmael was on the basis of a preserved tradition, or on account of taking over traditions in Judaism (as done in other aspects of Islam).

Even if we could find a distant "cousin" connection between the Israelites and the Arabs, and could apply this to the Palestinians (who come from various nationalities), it does not warrant any descendant of Ishmael having a right to the Promised Land. The reason for this is simply because the Land was not promised to *them*. This is clearly stated in the blessing of Ishmael in Genesis 17:20-21. Ishmael's descendants are indeed promised to become a "great nation" (fulfilled in his twelve sons, Genesis 25:12-17). However, the text goes on to emphasize that God's covenant will be "establish[ed] with *Isaac*." This means that the Abrahamic Covenant, and the land promise contained within it (Genesis 15:18-21), is exclusive to the Jewish people as the sole descendants of Isaac. Even though Ishmael was Abraham's *seed,* the promise of the Land was made to only one heir, Isaac. This promise, in turn, was selectively passed on to Isaac's son Jacob (Israel) rather than his son Esau (Genesis 28:13-15; 35:12).

The Qur'an argues that Abraham's favored son had to be Ishmael because he was the oldest. While this may agree with the cultural norms in Middle East society, the biblical text is clear that cultural precedent was not followed in these cases (Isaac, Jacob). In fact, the norm was violated in order to demonstrate God's election overruling natural selection (see Romans 9:7-13). Therefore, the covenant of God is with a chosen line, as Psalm 105:8-11 states: "He has remembered His covenant forever, the word which He commanded to a thousand generations, the covenant which He made with Abraham, and His oath to Isaac. Then He confirmed it to Jacob for a statute, to Israel as an everlasting covenant, saying, 'To you I will give the land of Canaan as the portion of your inheritance.'" Even sin on the part of the Jews (contrary to the teaching of the Qur'an) cannot diminish this covenantal promise being fulfilled in the future (see Isaiah 41:8-9; Jeremiah 30:2-3; 31:35-37; Ezekiel 36:18-28).

Interestingly, some rabbis, considering these Old Testament promises of restoration to the Land, argued that the "great nation" blessing promised to Ishmael in Genesis

17:20 was fulfilled with Islam. For example, one rabbi wrote: "2,337 years elapsed before the Arabs, Ishmael's descendants, became a great nation [this would correspond to 624 C.E., two years after the *Hegira* (Muhammad's flight from Mecca to Medina)]."[8] One reason for this identification was that the supposed fulfillment of Ishmael's promise gave the Jews hope of Isaac's promise likewise being fulfilled:

> Throughout this period, Ishmael waited anxiously, hoping, until finally the promise was fulfilled and they dominated the world. Surely, we, descendants of Isaac, for whom fulfillment of the promises made to us is delayed due to our sins...should certainly anticipate the fulfillment of His promises and not despair.[9]

Whether or not Palestinian-Arabs are related to Abraham, who immigrated to Canaan, they claim that they are descendants of the original inhabitants of Canaan—the Canaanites—as well as other ancient peoples who occupied the land *before* the arrival of the Israelites. Is there evidence in the historical and archaeological record to support this claim?

Can the Palestinians Claim an Ancient Heritage in the Land?

Although for thousands of years this same area has been inhabited by Jews, Christians, Druse, and Bedouin, none of these peoples ever claimed that they were the natural owners of the Land. Yet today's Palestinians claim that they are the ancestors of the indigenous population of Canaanites, Jebusites, and Philistines that predated the arrival of the Israelite tribes, and therefore, they are the rightful heirs of the Land. Let's briefly examine their claim.

First, archaeology and history are united in the fact that both the Philistines and the Jebusites were *non-Semitic* peoples. The Philistines were one of the ancient sea peoples of the Aegean, and the Jebusites were most likely of Hurrian origin. Their being listed in the biblical Table of Nations as descendants of Canaan (Genesis 10:16) probably is part of a geographic grouping in this list and simply means they lived in the land of Canaan.[10]

The Bible lists the Arabs as distinct from the Philistines (2 Chronicles 17:11), documenting that these two peoples allied themselves together to attack the Judean King Jehoram (2 Chronicles 21:16), but were defeated by King Uzziah in the eighth century B.C. (2 Chronicles 26:7). The Jebusites were defeated at the time of the Israelite conquest under Joshua, and they were later reduced to a slave remnant under King David. The Jebusites disappeared altogether by the end of the tenth century B.C., and the Philistines vanished from the historical record after being taken into captivity about 600 B.C. by the Babylonian ruler Nebuchadnezzar.[11]

Arab heritage is traceable in secular history to no earlier than references in the Neo-Assyrian annals of the ninth to seventh centuries B.C. The only reference I found along this line was from an Arab historian who explained that Canaan was the father of the Canaanites, who, before the time of the Israelite conquest under Joshua, fled to Africa and became the ancestors of the Berbers. However, Muslim legend also says that Canaan (based on Genesis 9:22-26) was cursed to be the slave of his brothers Shem and Japheth. Palestinians would hardly want to claim this ancestry, for it would make them cursed slaves of the Jews and Greeks![12]

Recently, Palestinians have distanced themselves from their former claim to be descendants of the Philistines. One of the original purposes in this identification was to be able to claim that the Palestinians predated the Israelites in the Land. However, since the Philistines historically arrived at about the same time (if not considerably later) as the Israelites (twelfth century B.C.), such an identification would not support their claim. Therefore, they have abandoned this argumentation.

Palestinians now prefer to claim that they are descendants of the Canaanites through the Muslim invaders of the seventh century, who intermarried with the Canaanite remnant *still living* in the land. The Canaanites were indeed strong survivors; even the biblical commands to expel them from the Land (Exodus 33:2) and exterminate them completely (Deuteronomy 20:17) did not remove their persistent habitation in the period of Israelite settlement. However, it is assumed that the Canaanite remnant was absorbed into the Israelite population in Canaan during the period of the biblical monarchy. While it's true that there are later ethical criticisms of Canaanite religious *practices* among the Israelites by some of the Israelite prophets (Amos 5:21-25), this does not imply that an ethnic *people* still existed.

Some have traced Canaanite artistic traditions (through the Phoenicians) in script, pottery designs, and cultic motifs of the Punic culture in Carthage up to the time that the city fell to the Romans in 149 B.C.[13] But even if we stretch just the preserved *influence* of Canaanite art to this period, we still have another 800 years before the coming of the Islamic Arabian nomads to the land. Furthermore, even if Canaanite descendants still existed, they would have long before intermarried with the non-Arab peoples of the land—Greeks, Romans, and Byzantine Christians— leaving no distinct ethnic heritage.

There is simply no historical documentation whatsoever from this long period of time that indicates any of the Canaanite peoples continued to exist in the Land. Furthermore, the Muslims' own Qur'an does not mention any ancestral connections with the Canaanites (or the Philistines or Jebusites), nor does any Muslim writing from any period after the Muslim conquest make such an allegation. That means there is no historical basis for the Palestinians' claim to an ancient lineage in the Land. Their claims, then, are rooted in nothing more than modern Palestinian revisionist history.

However, when it comes to the matter regarding who owns the Land, there's another question we have to ask concerning "common law" rights through sustained occupation.

Haven't the Palestinians Been in the Land for the Past 1,300 Years?

The Arabs originated as nomadic tribes in the modern Arabian Peninsula and emerged in Palestine only after the Islamic invasion of the Land in the seventh century A.D. On that basis, many believe that the Palestinians, as Arab descendants, have been in control of the land for the past 1,300 years. However, Philip Hitti, a leading Arab historian, has stated that "the invaders from the desert brought with them no tradition of learning, no heritage of culture, to the lands they conquered."[14] This means that there could not have developed a distinct Palestinian-Arab culture based on an Arab heritage, because there was no such heritage to receive. What they inherited was the religion of Islam (a mixture of Arab ethics with those of Judaism and Christianity within a military matrix adapted to Bedouin lifestyle of the seventh century A.D.).

However, as stated in the last chapter, most of the Muslim rulers during the 1,174 years of Islamic dominance were *not* Arab; therefore, they have no ethnic relationship to the Palestinians. Consider the historical succession of Islamic rulers: The Seljuks, whose rule lasted from 1071–1099, were Turkish mercenaries. The Muslim commander Saladin, whose defeat of the Crusaders began the Ayyubid period (1187–1260), was a Kurd. The Mamluks

(1260–1516) were descendants of Turkish and Caucasian slave soldiers from the Caucasus. And Suleiman the Magnificent, whose capture of Jerusalem began the last period of Islamic rule, the Ottoman period (1516–1917), and who rebuilt the walls of the Old City to their modern appearance, was a Turk.

While it is true that the Jews as we know them today did not establish their independence until the twentieth century, that's also true about many of the nations in the Arab League: Saudi Arabia (1913), Lebanon (1920), Iraq (1932), Syria (1941), Jordan (1946), and Kuwait (1961). None of these nations, then, can make a historical claim to certain borders on the basis of antiquity—and certainly neither can Palestinians. Today, in theory, there is only one Arab nation comprised of some 21 Arab countries, including Palestine. Even so, the bonds that join them are linguistic, religious, and cultural, rather than ethnic and political, and for this reason, wars continue between neighboring Muslim states.

Despite these ongoing conflicts, the Palestinian revisionists have been successful in promoting the view that Palestinian-Arabs are one with their Arab brothers, who unilaterally support their national ambitions. Unfortunately, many of the United States' most prestigious and authoritative international news, political, and geographical journals—as well as popular encyclopedias—adopt and promote the revised Palestinian history of Israel and Jerusalem.[15]

Though Palestinians were not in the Land in the last millennia, weren't they, as their historians assert, pastoral farmers who had been cultivating the Land for generations *before* the Jews arrived in modern times?

Weren't the Palestinians Native Farmers in the Land?

Yasser Arafat, in the United Nations speech cited previously, declared that when "the Jewish invasion of Palestine began in 1881....Palestine was then a verdant land, inhabited by an Arab people in the course of building its life and enriching its indigenous culture."[16]

The historical facts, however, do not support this bold assertion. Palestinian-Arabs were *not* in control of the Land in the nineteenth century, which was at that time part of Syria (under Ottoman Turkish rule). The native Arab population consisted of nomadic Bedouin tribes and poor tenant farmers that came to the country to work for the Ottoman landowners. While academics such as Dawoud El-Alami, a lawyer and lecturer in Islamic Studies at the University of Wales, argue that these Palestinian workers were part of the native population employed by the Ottomans in the nineteenth century,[17] former prime minister Benjamin Netanyahu contends that they "came to the country as foreign workers during the British Mandate and to the West Bank just prior to the Six-Day War."[18]

Furthermore, in those days, the land was not "verdant pastoral land," as Arafat claims, but as every historical record of the condition of the country depicts, it was a poor and barren wasteland, barely hospitable to life. As one historian observed: "In the twelve-and-a-half centuries between the Arab conquest in the seventh century and the beginnings of the Jewish return in the 1880s, Palestine was laid waste. Its ancient canal and irrigation systems were destroyed and the wondrous fertility of which the Bible spoke vanished into desert and desolation."[19]

Likewise, a traveler to Palestine in the 1890s describes the whole land as devoid of inhabitants: "I traveled through sad Galilee in the spring, and I found it silent....As elsewhere, as everywhere in Palestine, city and palaces have returned to dust....This melancholy of abandonment...weighs on all the Holy Land."[20] In addition, historian Joan Peters notes that "endemic massacres, disease, famine and wars" continually devastated the population of Palestine.[21] Because of the constantly declining population, Muslim rulers brought in large numbers of non-Arab peoples. The 1911 edition of the *Encyclopedia Britannica* recorded that at the beginning of the twentieth century the divergent nationalities in Palestine spoke no less than 50 different languages. In fact, it was at this time that the majority of Palestinian-Arabs immigrated to the Land on the heels of the Jews.

As the Zionist pioneers began reclaiming swamp land, ridding the country of disease, and building cities, Palestinian-Arabs became attracted by the economic opportunities that had been created. Much of the land bought by Jews was purchased from the Turkish landowners living outside the country. And usually the land the Jews bought was of poor quality (sand dunes and swamps) and undeveloped. This was pointed out by Abdel Razak Kader:

> The nationalists of the states neighboring on Israel, whether they are in the government or in business, whether Palestinian, Syrian or Lebanese, or town dwellers of tribal origin, all know that at the beginning of the century and during the British Mandate the marshy plains and stony hills were sold to the Zionists by their fathers or uncles for gold—the very gold which is often the origin of their own political or commercial careers. The nomadic or semi-nomadic peasants who inhabited the frontier regions know full well what the green plains, the afforested hills and the flowering fields of today's Israel were like before. The Palestinians who are today refugees in the neighboring countries and who were adults at the time of their flight know this, and no anti-Zionist propaganda— pan-Arab or pan-Moslem—can make them forget that their present nationalist exploiters are the worthy sons of their feudal exploiters of yesterday, and that the thorns of their life are of Arab, not Jewish, origin.[22]

As the Jews drained the swamps, cultivated the land, and improved or built roads and buildings, they produced plentiful jobs, a higher standard of living, and increased wages. Between World War I and World War II, Arabs began to gravitate toward Jewish-inhabited areas from neighboring Arab countries because of the jobs that were available and the higher wage scale. In heavily populated Jewish cities such as Jaffa and Ramla, the Arab population grew by an annual rate of 12 percent—four times as much as could be attributed to natural increase. This means that the Palestinians, in most cases, came to the Land as immigrant workers *after* the Jews were already in the Land.

In conclusion, the facts clearly reveal that present-day Palestinians cannot claim at the same time a Semitic heritage (as Arabs) and non-Semitic heritage (as Jebusites or Philistines). It is impossible to trace any ancient heritage for the Palestinians at all, not only because the peoples they claim relation to (such as Canaanites) went into extinction in the distant past, but for the more fundamental reason that there has *never* been a distinct Palestinian ethnicity, culture, language, or nationality. Jewish immigrants, for the most part, preceded the Palestinians and purchased useless and untilled land directly from Turkish or other Arab landowners. After the Jewish immigrants made improvements, the Arabs came as migrant workers and, for the most part, did not have any title to the lands they worked, and have no claim to possession of the land (apart from individual or family plots) based on prior ownership.

By contrast, the Jewish people can document an unbroken presence in the Land for 2,000 years. In the case of Jerusalem, there have always been permanent residents of Jewish descent, except for during two periods of exile (under Byzantine rule from A.D. 135–438 and during the Crusader kingdom from 1099 to 1187) during which time

Muslims were also excluded. Even under oppressive rulers and the most desolate of conditions, Jews remained in the holy city because of the belief that it held their future. In the modern period, from 1820 onward, Jews have constituted the majority of the resident population in the city, including East Jerusalem (except for the 19-year period of

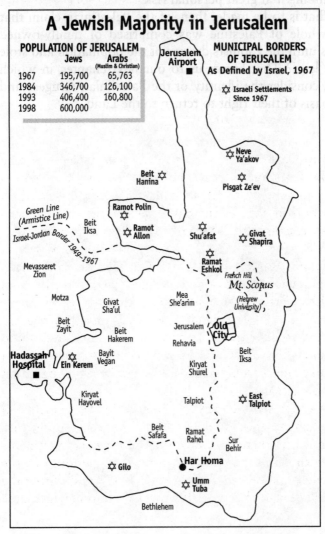

A Jewish Majority in Jerusalem

POPULATION OF JERUSALEM		
	Jews	Arabs (Muslim & Christian)
1967	195,700	65,763
1984	346,700	126,100
1993	406,400	160,800
1998	600,000	

MUNICIPAL BORDERS OF JERUSALEM
As Defined by Israel, 1967

✡ Israeli Settlements Since 1967

Jerusalem Airport ■

Neve Ya'akov ✡

Beit Hanina ✡

Pisgat Ze'ev ✡

Green Line (Armistice Line)
Israel-Jordan Border 1949-1967

Ramot Polin ✡

Beit Iksa

Ramot Allon ✡

Shu'afat ✡

Givat Shapira ✡

Ramat Eshkol ✡

French Hill

Mt. Scopus

Mevasseret Zion

Motza

Givat Sha'ul

Mea She'arim

(Hebrew University)

Beit Zayit

Beit Hakerem

Jerusalem / Old City

Beit Iksa

Rehavia

Hadassah Hospital ■

Ein Kerem ✡

Bayit Vegan

Kiryat Shurel

Kiryat Hayovel

Talpiot

East Talpiot ✡

Beit Safafa

Ramat Rahel

Sur Behir

● Har Homa

✡ Gilo

Umm Tuba ✡

Bethlehem

exile under the Jordanians). Therefore, even though waves of Jewish immigrants entered the Land in the nineteenth century, a Jewish community had already been there for 19 centuries. These resident Jews, and those who came in the nineteenth century as pioneers to Palestine, did so at great financial cost, purchasing undeveloped land and reclaiming it at great personal risk.

What is to be made, then, of the Palestinian claim that the whole of Palestine was comprised of family-owned lands until the Zionists drove out the population and stole their land? That brings us to our next chapter, in which we'll consider the identity of the Palestinian refugees and the basis of their right to return to the Land.

CHAPTER 9

What Is the Palestinian Right to Return?

We have succeeded in convincing much of the world that the right of return is at the heart of the Palestinian issue and that without granting the refugees that right, there can be no enduring peace in the region.[1]
—HUSSAM KHADER, HEAD OF THE COMMITTEE FOR DEFENSE OF THE PALESTINIAN REFUGEE RIGHTS AND MEMBER OF THE PALESTINIAN LEGISLATIVE COUNCIL

The greatest obstacle to peace between the Israelis and Palestinians thus far has been the sovereign status of Jerusalem and its holy places. And the next greatest obstacle has been the question of whether all Palestinian refugees have a right to return to their "homeland." The Palestinians claim that the Jews forcibly exiled millions of native Palestinians from their homes in 1948 and 1967. The Committee for Defense of the Palestinian Refugee Rights has even created an oath that refugee descendants must adhere to. The oath reads, "I swear to God to reaffirm my adherence to the right of return to my locality [in Palestine] from which I was/my parents were evicted by the Zionist invaders. I further declare that I have not delegated anybody to renounce this right and I reject any and every alternative proposal for my resettlement." It is these people, and their descendants today, the Palestinian Authority claims, which, on humanitarian and legal grounds, must be granted "repatriation to Palestine."

The Israelis contend, however, that the refugee problem was the result of wars forced on them by the Arab nations, and that only mediated solutions consistent with international law, accepted legal definitions and precedents, and above all, Israel's security, can be the basis of resolution. The issues involved are complex, and in order to understand them, it is necessary to address the identity of the refugees and to retrace the historical events that caused the refugee problem.

Who Are the Palestinian Refugees?

According to the Ariel Center for Policy Research, the "Palestinian refugees" of 1948 were of questionable origin. The following are excerpts from this agency's findings:

> Many Palestinians are descendants of Egyptian, Sudanese, Syrian and Lebanese migrants, who settled in the current boundaries of Israel during 1830–1945....Migrant workers were imported by the Ottomans and (since 1919) by the British authorities....Illegal Arab laborers were also attracted by the relative boom, stimulated by Jewish immigration, which expanded labor-intensive enterprises (construction, agriculture, etc.).

> ...The (1831–1840) conquest, by Egypt's Mohammed Ali, was solidified by thousands of Egyptians settling empty spaces between Gaza and Tul-Karem up to

the Hula Valley....30,000–36,000 Syrian migrants (Huranis) entered Palestine (in 1934). Syrian rulers have always considered the area as a southern province of Greater Syria. As-ed-Din el-Qassam, the role model of Hamas terrorism, who terrorized Jews in British Mandate Palestine, was a Syrian, as were Said el-A'az, a leader of the 1936–38 anti-Jewish pogroms and Kaukji, the commander in chief of the Arab mercenaries terrorizing Jews in the thirties and forties.

[Western travelers] identified over 15 Arab nationalities who settled in Jaffa. Libyan migrants and refugees settled in Gedera, south of Tel Aviv. Algerian refugees (Mugrabis), escaping the French conquest of 1830, settled in Safed, Tiberias and other parts of the Galilee. Circassian refugees, fleeing Russian oppression (1878), Moslems from Bosnia, Turkomans, Yemenite Arabs (1908) and Bedouin tribes from Jordan (escaping wars and famine) diversified Arab demography there.[2]

When we consider why the Arabs of Palestine left their homes in 1947–48, we discover it was for a variety of reasons. The initial Arab exodus of some 30,000 wealthy Arabs came immediately after the announcement of the U.N. partition resolution. They left in anticipation of the upcoming war, called by the Israelis the War of Independence and by Palestinians *Al-Nakba* ("the Great Catastrophe"). Setting up shop in neighboring Arab countries, these wealthy Arabs planned to wait out the end of the conflict and then return home. Less affluent Arabs from cities with a mixed Arab and Jewish population either followed the money and jobs that went with the wealthy Arabs or moved to all-Arab towns to stay with relatives or friends.

Arab sources of the time reported this exodus and criticized it as an abandonment of the Arab objective. For instance, the Jaffa newspaper *Ash Sha'ab* reported on

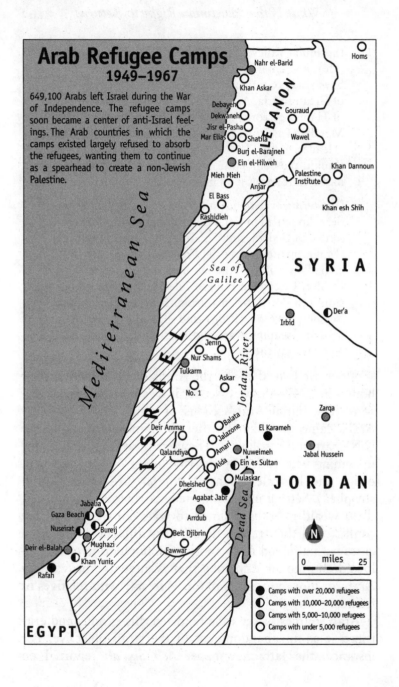

Arab Refugee Camps
1949–1967

649,100 Arabs left Israel during the War of Independence. The refugee camps soon became a center of anti-Israel feelings. The Arab countries in which the camps existed largely refused to absorb the refugees, wanting them to continue as a spearhead to create a non-Jewish Palestine.

Mediterranean Sea

LEBANON

Homs
Nahr el-Barid
Khan Askar
Debayeh
Dekwaneh
Gouraud
Jisr el-Pasha
Mar Elias
Shatila
Wawel
Burj el-Barajneh
Ein el-Hilweh
Khan Dannoun
Mieh Mieh
Palestine Institute
Anjar
El Bass
Khan esh Shih
Rashidieh

Sea of Galilee

SYRIA

Der'a
Irbid

Jenin
Nur Shams
Tulkarm
Askar
No. 1

Jordan River

Zarqa
Deir Ammar
Balata
Jalazone
El Karameh
Qalandiya
Amari
Jabal Hussein
Aida
Nuweimeh
Ein es Sultan
Dheished
Mulaskar
JORDAN
Agabat Jabr
Jabalia
Gaza Beach
Arrdub
Nuseirat
Bureij
Deir el-Balah
Mughazi
Beit Djibrin
Dead Sea
Khan Yunis
Fawwar
Rafah

ISRAEL

N

0 miles 25

EGYPT

Camps with over 20,000 refugees
Camps with 10,000–20,000 refugees
Camps with 5,000–10,000 refugees
Camps with under 5,000 refugees

January 30, 1948, "The first of our fifth column consists of those who abandon their houses and businesses and go to live elsewhere....At the first signs of trouble they take to their heels to escape sharing the burden of struggle." These retreats were also reported in another Jaffa newspaper, *As Sarih* (March 30, 1948), which excoriated Arab villagers near Tel Aviv for "bringing down disgrace on us all by abandoning the villages." However, thousands of other Arabs left because they were heeding Arab leaders' warnings to evacuate before the arrival of their advancing soldiers. According to the Jordanian newspaper *Filastin* (February 19, 1949), "The Arab States encouraged the Palestine Arabs to leave their homes temporarily in order to be out of the way of the Arab invasion armies."

Still other Palestinian Arabs were literally scared away from their homes by rumors of bloody massacres being perpetrated on local Arabs by Jewish gangs. Even if these tales were unfounded, throughout the period that preceded the invasion by the Arab regular armies there were large-scale military engagements, incessant sniping, robberies, and bombings. The chaos and casualties that resulted from this preinvasion violence led many Arabs to legitimately flee out of fear for their lives.

It is also true that the Jewish Haganah employed psychological warfare to encourage the Arabs to abandon some of their villages. Yigal Allon, the commander of the Palmach (the "shock force of the Haganah"), said he had Jews talk to the Arabs in neighboring villages and tell them a large Jewish force was in the Galilee with the intention of burning all the Arab villages in the Lake Huleh region. The Arabs were told to leave while they still could, and they did exactly that. In addition, some were expelled by Jewish troops, as would be expected in a war, but most simply fled to avoid being caught in the crossfire of battle. However, when expulsion did take place, the Jewish forces were usually careful to avoid being accused of confiscation.

For example, when Jewish forces seized Tiberias on April 19, 1948, and the entire Arab population of 6,000 was evacuated under British military supervision, the Jewish Community Council issued this statement: "We did not dispossess them; they themselves chose this course.... Let no citizen touch their property."

Likewise, in both Tiberias and Haifa, the Haganah issued orders that none of the Arabs' possessions should be touched, and warned that anyone who violated the orders would be severely punished. By the end of January 1948, the Arab exodus had grown to such numbers that the Palestine Arab Higher Committee asked neighboring Arab countries to seal off their borders to prevent further flight. (This same thing has happened since the renewed Intifada, with some 150,000 Palestinians moving to Jordan and the Jordanian government closing the borders to all but those with Jordanian citizenship.)

How many Arabs left the country during the war? Although the number has been fiercely debated, a census taken before the war on November 30, 1947, when the United Nations voted for partition, found the number of permanent Arab residents to be 809,100. After the war, a 1949 Israeli census counted 160,000 Arabs living in the country. This means that no more than 649,100 Arabs could have become refugees. A report by the U.N. mediator on Palestine arrived at an even lower figure of 472,000.

A second refugee population was created by the Six-Day War in 1967. Ignoring warnings to stay out of the war, King Hussein of Jordan joined the other Arab states that had attacked Israel and launched his own attack on Jerusalem. The United Nations estimated that during the fighting about 350,000 Palestinians left for the first time and another 175,000 fled for a second time, most of these coming from the West Bank, which was under Jordanian control. About 200,000 moved to Jordan, 115,000 to Syria, and approximately 35,000 left Sinai for Egypt. In both wars that caused the Palestinian exodus, the Arabs who left their homes fully expected to return after an early Arab victory. As Palestinian nationalist Aref el-Aref explained in his history of the 1948 war,

> The Arabs thought they would win in less than the twinkling of an eye and that it would take no more than a day or two from the time the Arab armies crossed the border until all the colonies were conquered and the enemy would throw down his arms and cast himself on their mercy. Their leaders had promised them that the Arab armies would crush the "Zionist gangs" very quickly and that there was no need for panic or fear of a long exile.[3]

As a result of the Arab states (and especially Jordan) losing the Six-Day War, there were a great number of Palestinians who were "displaced"—that is, people who had to leave their homes and move to another place in the *same* country. These "displaced persons" were dealt with by Security Council Resolution 237 of June 4, 1967, which called upon the government of Israel "to facilitate the return of those inhabitants [to the areas where military operations had taken place] who have fled the areas since the outbreak of hostilities." This resolution does not speak of a "right" of return, yet in various agreements, Israel has willingly agreed to their return.

Do the Palestinian Refugees Have a Right to Return?

The Palestinians contend that the refugees and their descendants have a right to return, reclaim their houses and land, and receive compensation from the Israeli government. They have interpreted U.N. Security Council Resolution 194 as granting the refugees the *absolute* right of repatriation and have demanded that Israel accept their interpretation of this ruling. Are they correct? Let's take a closer look at this resolution and the way it is understood by both Palestinians and Israelis.[4]

The most universal provision on the right of return, or right to reenter one's country, is included in the 1966 International Covenant on Civil and Political Rights, which states, "No one shall be arbitrarily deprived of the right to enter his own country." This implies that a relationship must exist between the State and the person who wishes to return—in other words, the right of return is apparently reserved for nationals of the State. Remember that the Palestinians have never had a state of their own, and in many cases they hold citizenship in another country (Jordan). In 1947–48 they left a country under British rule which became Israel, and in 1967 they left the West Bank, which was then within the kingdom of Jordan. Therefore, to what state or country do they have a right to return?

What's more, even the right of nationals is not an absolute one, but may be limited on the condition that the reasons for the denial or limitation are not arbitrary. Moreover, the right of return or the right to enter one's own country—per the 1966 International Covenant—is intended to apply to *individuals* asserting an individual right, not masses of people who have been displaced as a result of war.

As noted previously, the major United Nations resolution that refers to the refugees is Resolution 194 (III), adopted by the General Assembly on December 11, 1948. It is this document that the Arab states initially rejected, but which the Palestinians now accept as the basis for their repatriation. Let's examine it carefully.

First, Paragraph 11 deals with the refugees:

> The General Assembly...resolves that the refugees wishing to return to their homes and live at peace with

their neighbors should be permitted to do so at the earliest practicable date, and that compensation should be paid for the property of those choosing not to return and for loss of or damage to property which, under principles of international law or in equity, should be made good by the Governments or authorities responsible.

Notice that this paragraph does not recognize any "right," but only *recommends* that the refugees "should" be "permitted" to return and that the permission is subject to two conditions: the wish to return, and the wish *to live at peace with his neighbors*. How can the violence that has existed since the beginning of the Intifada and the daily call for war by Palestinians offer any hope of peaceful coexistence with a massive return of refugees? The reference to "principles of international law or in equity" applies only to compensation and does not seem to refer to the permission to return. Finally, it should be noted that the provision concerning the refugees is but one element of the resolution that foresaw "a final settlement of all questions outstanding between" the parties. However, the Palestinians have insisted only on the resolution's implementation (and only in accordance with the interpretation favorable to them) independent of all other matters.

The Arabs claim that Resolution 242 of November 22, 1967 incorporates the solution recommended by General Assembly Resolution 194. In Security Council Resolution 242 the second paragraph states that the council "affirms further the necessity...for achieving a just settlement of the refugee problem." Note, however, that the Council did not propose a specific solution, nor did it limit the provision to Arab refugees, because the right to compensation also applies to Jewish refugees from Arab lands. In fact, the number of Jews that were forced to leave Arab countries and came to Israel in the years following Israel's independence (some 820,000 people) was roughly equal to the number of Arabs that left Palestine. Most of these Jews could take nothing more than the shirts on their backs. Some 586,000 were resettled in Israel at great expense, and without any offer of compensation from the Arab governments who confiscated their possessions.

In the Declaration of Principles on Interim Self-Government Arrangements of 1993, an agreement between Israel and the Palestinians, it was agreed that the issue of refugees should be negotiated in the framework of the permanent status negotiations (Article V,3). The 1995 Israeli-Palestinian Interim Agreement on the West Bank and the Gaza Strip 10 adopted similar provisions (Articles XXXVII,2 and XXXI,5). There was also a relevant provision (Article 8) in the Treaty of Peace between Israel and Jordan in 1994 which considered displaced persons, but also in conjunction with the permanent status negotiations. However, none of the agreements between Israel, Egypt, Jordan, or the Palestinians grants the refugees a right of return into Israel.

Therefore, neither the international conventions, nor the major U.N. resolutions, nor the relevant agreements between the parties state that the Palestinian refugees have a right to return to the Land. The problem of refugees is an unavoidable consequence of war. The Jews of Europe experienced this during World War II, and for this reason the State of Israel came into existence, in the historic homeland of the Jewish people, as a refuge for refugees. And let it be remembered that had the Arabs accepted the United Nations resolution in 1947, there would have been no need for U.N. Resolution 194, for not a single Palestinian would have become a refugee, and an independent Arab state would now exist alongside Israel. However, the Palestinians claim that a major obstacle for peace is the Israeli government's unwillingness to let the refugees return.

Why Have the Israelis Been Unwilling for the Refugees to Return?

Jewish leaders in fact tried to prevent a refugee problem by urging the Arabs to remain in Palestine and become citizens of Israel at the time of the United Nations' vote for partition in the Land. The Assembly of Palestine Jewry issued the following appeal to the Arab community on October 2, 1947: "We will do everything in our power to maintain peace, and establish a cooperation gainful to both [Jews and Arabs]. It is now, here and now, from Jerusalem itself, that a call must go out to the Arab nations to join forces with Jewry and the destined Jewish state and work shoulder to shoulder for our common good, for the peace and progress of sovereign equals."

In addition, David Ben-Gurion sent Golda Meir to Haifa to try to persuade the Arabs to stay, but she was unable to convince them because they feared they would be judged traitors to the Arab cause. Israel repeatedly has offered Israeli citizenship with all of its benefits (including free education and holding public office) to those Palestinians who would live within the State of Israel. However, now, as in the past, the acceptance of such an offer has been considered by nationalists as treasonous. There are, of course, hundreds of thousands of Israeli-Arabs who live within the State of Israel and have Israeli citizenship, but almost all now identify themselves as Palestinians and constantly run the risk of being branded as a collaborator with Israel, a crime that brings the death sentence in Palestinian-controlled areas.

One of the significant obstacles Israel has faced in dealing with the rights of refugees has been the continual redefining of who is eligible to receive refugee status. The UNRWA (The United Nations Relief and Works Agency for Palestine Refugees in the Near East) created a unique definition, defining a refugee as "a person whose normal

residence was Palestine for a minimum of two years immediately preceding the outbreak of the conflict in 1948 and
who, as a result of that conflict, lost both his home and
his means of livelihood...." This less-limited definition also
extends the right of refugee status to Palestinian descendants now living as residents in other countries (not simply
in refugee camps). On this basis, the Palestinian Authority
now claims that the number of refugees who have a right
to return is four to five million!

In the negotiations that have taken place under the Oslo
Accord, the Israeli government has been willing to repatriate and compensate hundreds of thousands of Palestinians who can demonstrate refugee status, but it has
refused to accept the massive population the Palestinian
Authority is attempting to foist upon the country. For
Israel to concede on these terms to a "full return" would
mean demographic suicide for a Jewish nation of 5.2 million Jews (38 percent of the world's Jewish population). As
Barak stated, "This is a euphemism for the elimination of
Israel, and no government will accept it. There is a thin
line between a calculated risk and yielding to terror."[5]

Even if no Palestinian refugees return, demographic
trends indicate a decline in the Israeli population and a rise
in the Arab population that will remove Jews from
majority status within 19 years (by 2020), causing Israel to
crumble from within. The Jewish Agency has estimated
that in order to maintain a Jewish majority in Israel,
50,000 new Jews must immigrate annually. In the year
2000 the Israeli population grew by 152,000 people, with
360 new babies being born daily and 150 immigrants
arriving each day. But if the Intifada continues, no such
immigration numbers will be realized. Evidence of this
was given by Itamar Marcus of Palestinian Media Watch,
who reported the dramatic decline in new Russian immigration after the Tel Aviv terrorist attack. Furthermore,

Marcus noted that the Palestinians are aware of the Israelis' statistical problem: "The Arabs have a demographic plan to, within a few decades, outnumber the Jewish population." While speaking to the Knesset Foreign Affairs and Defense Committee, Arab member Taleb Al-Sana said mockingly, "Just like the Turks were here and they disappeared, and the English were here and they disappeared, so will the Zionists disappear."[6] The Arabs are also trying to hasten the decline by scaring off future immigrants; the official newspaper *Al-Hayat Al-Jadida,* in March 2001, printed an article that called for terrorist attacks against the Russian immigrants: "We must target those who will cause them death and fear."[7]

At a closed meeting of Arab ambassadors in Stockholm, Sweden, where Arafat had gone to receive a peace prize on January 30, 1996, Arafat explained the real reason for his demand for a right of return:

> Within five years we will have six to seven million Arabs living on the West Bank and Jerusalem. All Palestinian Arabs will be welcomed by us. If the Jews can import all kinds of Ethiopians, Russians, Uzbekians, and Ukrainians as Jews, we can import all kinds of Arabs. We plan to eliminate the State of Israel and establish a Palestinian state. We will make life unbearable for Jews by psychological warfare and population explosion. Jews will not want to live among Arabs....They will give up their dwellings and leave for the United States. We Palestinians will take over everything, including all of Jerusalem.[8]

Arafat's statement was nothing new; a similar sentiment was stated at the time of the original Arab exodus: "It is well known and understood that the Arabs, in demanding the return of the refugees to Palestine, mean their return as masters of the Homeland and not as slaves. With a greater clarity, they mean the liquidation of the State of Israel."[9] It was because of these Arab threats that U.N. Security Council Resolution 194 recognized that Israel could not be expected to repatriate a hostile population that might endanger its security and become a fifth column.

The solution to the problem, like all previous refugee problems, would require at least some Palestinians to be resettled in Arab lands. But the Arabs have unanimously rejected this proposal, because since 1948 they have seen that the refugees could be used to gain world sympathy against Israel, and then used in the future as part of a military force to bring about Israel's destruction. In keeping with this ambition, most all of the Arab states have refused to allow the Palestinian refugees to enter their countries. Egypt, when it controlled the Gaza Strip, not only refused to allow the Palestinians into Egypt, but would not let them move elsewhere. Syria, Iraq, Lebanon, and Libya also refused refugees. Likewise, Saudi Arabia, when it faced a severe labor shortage in the late 1970s, rejected unemployed Palestinian refugees and instead hired South Koreans!

Jordan has been the only Arab country willing to accept Palestinians and grant them citizenship. And there's a reason—consider what one writer said about Jordan's actions: "Jordan accepted the refugees as citizens as a matter of self-interest. Jordan wanted to integrate them as Jordanians so they would not have to form a Palestinian government on the West Bank, which would threaten Jordan's rule there."[10]

In August 1958, a former director of UNRWA, Ralph Garroway, said this: "The Arab states do not want to solve the refugee problem. They want to keep it as an open sore, as an affront to the United Nations and as a weapon against Israel. Arab leaders don't give a damn whether the refugees live or die." And later, in the early 1990s when the Gulf War broke out, Kuwait, which had employed large numbers of Palestinians but denied them citizenship, expelled more than 300,000 of them. The Kuwaiti Ambassador to the United States, Saud Nasir Al-Sabah, justified this expulsion in this way: "If people pose a security threat, as a sovereign country we have the right to exclude anyone we don't want."[11] Yet all of the Arab states, even with Israel under attack in the Palestinian Intifada, are demanding the total repatriation of Palestinian refugees who would join in a war to destroy Israel! Given this reality, and the very definite threat to Israel's security, if not its survival, the right of the Israelis to refuse the Palestinian interpretation of a right to return can be understood, even if all of the questions concerning it cannot be answered to the satisfaction of all parties.

Even though Israel is justified in its position concerning limiting Palestinian returnees, since the beginning of the Oslo Accords more than 400,000 Arabs *have entered* the West Bank and Gaza. Coming from Jordan, Egypt, Iraq, and other Arab countries, they have increased the Arab "settlements" in the West Bank (some 261 built since 1967 compared with 144 Jewish "settlements"). These statistics, based on the number of Arab day workers entering from the Allenby Bridge (but not leaving), was published by Israel's Central Bureau for Statistics in 1996–1997. As Winston Churchill observed in 1939, "So far from being persecuted, the Arabs have crowded into the country and multiplied till their population has increased more than even all world Jewry [of the time] could lift up the Jewish population."[12]

Yet, as significant as the threat of a massive Palestinian refugee return would be to Israel's security, an even greater threat to Israel and the West is the religion of Islam, which combines nationalistic aspirations with the terrorist tactics of *jihad*. Let's now consider the role of Islam in the Israeli-Palestinian conflict and the war against terrorism.

CHAPTER 10

What Is Islam's Role in the Conflict?

For the conquering Islam of today, those who do not claim to be Muslims do not have any human rights recognized as such. In an Islamic society, the non-Muslims would return to their former dhimmi status, which is why solving the Middle East conflict by the creation of a federation including Israel within a group of Muslim peoples or states, or in a "Judeo-Islamic" state, is a fantasy and an illusion. From the Muslim point of view, such a thing would be unthinkable.[1]
—JACQUES ELLUL

Jerusalem is a symbol for every Muslim in the world. The claim of the Jews to the right over it is false, and we recognize nothing but an entirely Islamic Jerusalem under Islamic supervision....[2]
—PA MUFTI IKRAMA SABRI

The war that America and Israel are fighting is not simply against terrorists, but against terrorists who are adherents of Islam. The problem in the Middle East is a problem of religion. Recognizing this, the Supreme Islamic

Research Council stated: "The Palestine Question is not a national issue nor is it a political issue. It is first and foremost an Islamic question."[3] If that's true, then it is vital that we have a clear understanding of Islam.

Islam is universally acknowledged as the world's fastest-growing religion. Over the past 50 years alone the total number of followers has grown 500 percent (Christianity, by comparison, grew only 47 percent).[4] With over 1.3 billion followers, Islam is the faith of one-fifth of the world's population. While 85 percent of the world's Muslims are non-Arabic (such as in the Soviet Union with 100 million Muslims and in Indonesia with 200 million Muslims), Islam controls the attitudes and actions of every Arab country in the Middle East and North Africa (about 92 percent of the population in these regions). Its dictates reach far across the globe, encompassing 67 different nations that comprise a seventh of the world's total landmass.

Furthermore, countries with historic Christian cultures are rapidly being won over to Islam. For example, in Western Europe Islam is the second-largest religion and is expected to become the dominant religion in just two decades. In France there are one-and-a-half million Muslims (about six Muslims for every one Christian). England has more than 2,000 mosques, and the United States has an estimated seven million Muslims and some 1,370 mosques. (By comparison, 30 years ago the United States had only 500,000 Muslims and in 1986 there were 598 mosques.) Islamic groups are penetrating deep into every aspect of American society and culture through student activities (such as the Muslim Student Association), local elections, and the media.

Is this worldwide expansion of Islam a global threat? Should we be concerned about the part Islam has played in the attack on America and its influence in the Israeli-Palestinian conflict and throughout the Middle East? To get an answer, we must first understand something of the nature of Islam and its role in the present-day relations between Arabs, Jews, and the Christian West.

What Are the Beliefs of Islam?

It has been popularly claimed that Muhammad, the founder of Islam, never intended to start a new religion that canceled out the earlier monotheistic faiths of Judaism and Christianity. As Karen Armstrong states: "He was convinced that he was simply bringing the old religion of the One God to the Arabs, who had never before been sent a prophet....he and his converts prostrate themselves in prayer in the direction of Jerusalem [because] they were symbolically reaching out toward the Jewish and Christian God, whom they were committed to worshiping, and turning their back on the paganism of Arabia."[5] However, an investigation of Islam at even a cursory level reveals that Muhammad claimed to be the prophet of God's final revelation and that Islam is the only true and eternal religion (Qur'an 3:17). Islam claims that the prophets of Israel and Jesus had proclaimed Islam and predicted the coming of Muhammad, but that Jews and Christians, jealous of the perfection of the new religion, had rejected him and falsified their own Scriptures. Islam's goal is not a pluralistic world where the three great monotheistic religions cooperate with one another in tolerance and share equal access to sacred sites, but a total domination of the world and a universal "submission" (the meaning of *Islam*) to Allah. A state of *jihad* exists permanently between Muslims and non-Muslims until the absolute supremacy of Islam is attained throughout the world.

At the time of Muhammad's birth in Mecca about A.D. 570, Arab tribes in Mecca and throughout the Arabian peninsula were polytheistic, each tribe having its own local deity. A large black meteor found in the desert and believed to have been sent by astral deities was placed in the southeast corner of a cube-shaped structure in Mecca known in Arabic as the *Ka'aba* (stone). In pre-Islamic Arabia it became the central shrine of Hubal, a chief male god among 360 other deities. Among these was *Al-Hajar Al-Aswad*, a nature deity who was symbolized by the black stone. The most prominent Meccan deities besides Hubal were the three sister goddesses *Al-Lat*, *Al-Manat*, and *Al-Uzza*. The Qurash tribe to which Muhammad belonged was in charge of idol worship at the Ka'aba shrine and the chief goddess of Muhammad's tribe was *Al-Uzza*, to whom Muhammad's grandfather almost sacrificed Muhammad's father, had a fortune-teller not counseled him against doing it. The head of this pantheon was *Al-Ilah* or Allah, which corresponds to the Babylonian *Bel*. Today, however, the term *Allah* is translated in Arabic as "God" (in Arabic Old and New Testaments), which gives the impression that the Muslim Allah refers to the same deity as that worshiped by Jews and Christians— a notion that Muhammad declared to be a fact, stating that Noah, Abraham, Moses, and Jesus were all prophets sent by the same Allah who sent him as a prophet and gave the Qur'an.

However, a look at the original concept behind this name *Allah* reveals he is not the same deity that Christians and Jews worship. The word for both *god* and *idol* in Arabic is *ilah*. The name Allah is derived from the Arabic words *al* ("the") and *ilah* ("god") to indicate a *particular* deity ("the god" or "the idol"). It is believed that *Allah* was used in Muhammad's time as the personal name for a vague high god who was one of the astral deities associated with the moon. Muhammad's father's name was *Abd-Allah* ("the slave of *Al-Illah*"), so it is evident that Muhammad was well acquainted with this deity. Early on, Muhammad also worshiped the three Meccan goddesses *Al-Lat*, *Al-Manat*, and *Al-Uzza* as deities because he believed them to be daughters of Allah. This was a plausible conclusion because *Al-Lat* (or *Allat*) is the feminine form of *Allah,* and was probably the female counterpart of Allah.[6] But Muhammad later renounced this worship, declaring his thinking had been corrupted by Satan. Incidentally, the belief that this teaching had been part of an earlier version of the Qur'an (later removed) was the basis of Salman Rushdie's 1989 novel *Satanic Verses.* Its publication led the late Iranian Muslim cleric Ayatollah Khomeni to offer a $3 million bounty (which still stands) for the assassination of the book's author and publisher. In pre-Islamic Arabia, there was also a prescribed annual pilgrimage to Mecca to worship at the *Ka'aba.* Worshipers were taught to turn towards Mecca several times a day, and one month every year—beginning and ending with the crescent phase of the moon—was dedicated to fasting. This was the basis of Muslim prayer five times daily and the month-long fast of Ramadan. These facts indicate Muhammad's religion of Islam was built upon preexisting forms of idol worship and that Allah is simply a pagan deity that has been isolated and made supreme by Muhammad. This idea is still preserved in a basic confession taken by Muslims which forbids the worship of other Meccan deities: "Allah is greater than all the other idols. There is no god but Allah and Muhammad is his prophet." Given this perspective, professor Augustus H. Strong (in his Christian *Systematic Theology*) defined *Islam* as "heathenism in monotheistic form." Therefore, the Allah of Islam is not the same as the one and only God (YHWH) of the biblical faiths of Judaism and Christianity (Exodus 20:3; 1 Corinthians 8:6).

Beginning in A.D. 610, Muhammad claimed to have received angelic revelations that *Al-Illah* (Allah) was the supreme god and had a message of warning.[7] Several years later Muhammad began to speak publicly as a prophet of

the one god Allah but was rejected by the polytheistic
Meccans. The intensity of the persecution against Muhammad and his followers grew through the years and forced
him to flee to Medina in A.D. 622. This event, known as
the *Hijra* ("Migration"), later marked for Muslims the
beginning of the Islamic era. After gaining local favor and
amassing an army, Muhammad returned to Mecca in A.D.
630 and conquered it (killing 600 of the 900 men of his
Qurash tribe and taking a number of the widows for his
wives). He destroyed all of the Meccan idols, except the
black stone, which he made the spiritual center of his new
religion, converting the pagan shrine into a mosque
("place of kneeling").

The sacred texts of Islam are the Qur'an ("Recitation")
and the Hadith. The Hadith contains collected sayings and
deeds of Muhammad, but it is the Qur'an that serves as the
"Bible" of Islam. It claims to be composed of messages
from the angel Gabriel to Muhammad, personal revelations of Muhammad, selected and "corrected" accounts of
Abraham, Joseph, Moses, and David's psalms from the Old
Testament, and the story of Jesus (Arabic, *Isa*) from the
New Testament. These accounts are not the same as those
in the Jewish and Christian Bibles. For example, Abraham
offers his son Ishmael rather than Isaac, and it is not Jesus
who dies on the cross but a substitute (Judas). Furthermore, all of the Jewish patriarchs (such as Abraham) and
heroes (such as King David) are stated in the Qur'an to
have been Muslims (even though they lived thousands of
years before the birth of Muhammad!). [8] In fact, according
to the Qur'an, Abraham and Ishmael built the first
"temple" in history—the Sacred House at Mecca. In addition, many of the stories in the Qur'an reveal a dependence
on Jewish aggadic and rabbinic literature as well as Byzantine Christian legends. Muhammad may have become
acquainted with these sources through his familiarity with

the predominately Christian (but heretical) Najran tribe, which exercised significant influence in northern Arabia. By some accounts, Muhammad was at one time a student of Christianity, and possibly also a student of Judaism. However, Muhammad recognized that his beliefs did not agree with the Jewish and Christian Scriptures, so he claimed that Judaism and Christianity had perverted their Bibles so that they are now corrupted. Therefore Allah rejected Christianity and Judaism, sending Muhammad to replace the corrupted Bible with the pure Qur'an and the cursed religions of Judaism and Christianity with Islam. Christians in particular are said to be guilty of the unpardonable sin of *shirk*, which means to assign partners or companions to Allah. The accusation that Christians worship "three gods" results from the Muslim misunderstanding of the Christian doctrine of the triune nature of the one God (trinitarianism). Islam teaches that the Muslim must observe "five pillars of Islam": 1) recite the creed: "There is no God but Allah"; 2) pray five times a day facing Mecca; 3) give to the poor for the furtherance of Islam; 4) fast for one month each year during the lunar month of Ramadan; and 5) make a pilgrimage to Mecca (Hajj) once in one's life. In addition, a Muslim must repent and purify himself while on earth so he can attain Paradise after death.

What Role Does Islam Play in the Political Situation of the Middle East?

From its inception, Islam stated that its duty is to destroy "infidels" (non-Muslims) and subjugate the *dhimmi* (tolerated minorities under Islamic rule, namely, the people of the Book—Jews and Christians). As a religion of the sword (*Al Harb*), the concept of *jihad* has been mandated by Allah and requires Muslims to completely subdue the earth through military conquest. This can be seen in the following statement in the Hadith: "Allah's apostle was asked, 'What is the best deed?' He replied, 'To believe in Allah and his Apostle.' The questioner then asked, 'What is the next (in goodness)?' He replied, 'To participate in Jihad in Allah's cause'" (Hadith, *Al Bukhari*, vol. 1, no. 25).

What Is the Islamic Concept of *Jihad?*

Islam divides humanity into two camps—the way of *al-jahiliyya* ("heedlessness" or "ignorance") and the way of *al-islam* ("submission"). The former describes the natural state of the non-Muslim world, the latter the followers of Allah, Muhammad, and the Qur'an. However, these "ways" are institutionalized as the Islamic and non-Islamic political entities *Dar al-islam* ("house of Islam") and *Dar al-harb* ("house of the sword"). Since the latter threatens the former and stands as an obstacle to the spread of Islam, the two cannot coexist. The means commanded in the Qur'an to resolve this tension is the duty of *jihad*. So essential is *jihad* to the existence of Islam, that according to many Muslims, it is a *sixth* pillar of the religion.

The Arabic word *jihad* literally means "struggling" or "striving" and generally indicates holy efforts in the cause of Allah, especially the spreading of the faith of Islam, whether by missionary or military means. The popular definition of *jihad* is "holy war," and though some Muslims have criticized this as "Crusader terminology," both Muslim and non-Muslim writers use the phrase. It is important to remember that *jihad* is not simply against non-Muslims, for much of the *jihad* of the past (and present) has been between Muslim states (such as the eight-year-long "holy war" between Iraq and Iran). Fundamentalist Muslims have declared *jihad* on moderate Muslims, whom they view as apostates, and within

Islamic states *jihad* is called to overthrow a political leader who is thought to not follow true Islam. Therefore, secular dictators like Saddam Hussein will build monumental mosques and act overtly religious in order to appear faithful to Islamic law (appearance is what counts most in Arab culture).

Muslim scholars have often stated that Islam teaches that it is unholy to start a war: "Fight in the way of Allah against those who fight against you, but begin not hostilities" (Sura 2:190). Nevertheless, it is always easy to argue that any situation that has the potential to inhibit the spread of Islam is an attack against it. On this basis, the existence of the Jewish state in the midst of Islamic states on land previously conquered by Muslims is an "attack against Islam." On the same basis, Western civilization and culture, including the American nation, which has become a dominant culture, is viewed as a threat to Islam and an attack on its superior status and universal mandate. For this reason radical Muslims contend they are "defending Islam" when they attack American institutions and personnel.

It should also be recognized that *jihad* is not optional but obligatory for all Muslim leaders. As author Jonathan Riley-Smith notes, "The *Bahr* insists that the first duty of a Muslim ruler is to prosecute the *jihad* and bring about the victory of Islam, and if he does not do so and he makes peace with the infidel, that ruler would be better dead than alive, for he would be corrupting the world."[9] Understanding that all Muslim leaders know this warning, one must reconcile it with the cold "peace" that exists between the Muslim rulers of Egypt and Jordan and the enemy State of Israel. Accordingly, such a peace must be qualified by Islamic definition as a "temporary" peace until a permanent peace (through *jihad*) can be effected, where the *Shari'ah* (Islamic law) can be enforced.

The Various Types of *Jihad*

It is also necessary to distinguish between the different forms *jihad* can take. Muslim jurists hold to four types of *jihad*: the war waged by the heart, the tongue, the hand, and the sword. The first three may be distinguished as "greater" or "interior" jihad and the last as "lesser" or "exterior" *jihad*. Interior *jihad* is the struggle of the individual Muslim against spiritual and moral temptations, and lack of faithfulness to the five pillars of Islam, but also includes missionary activity to convert non-Muslims and social and political programs to conform local policy to Islamic ideals. Exterior *jihad* is the traditional armed conflict waged in the name of Allah against the enemies of Allah for "the expansion or protection of Islam."

This warfare may be further distinguished as *offensive* and *defensive*. Offensive *jihad* is a collective duty imposed on the Muslim community in order to extend Muslim territories (*Dar al-Islam*). While not all Muslims may be able to take part in the physical warfare, those who cannot fight are obligated to support the military campaign with money and approbation. Defensive *jihad* is military action against aggressors who have occupied lands formerly held by Muslims. Basic to the tenets of the Qur'an is the idea that once Muslims have conquered a territory, it forever belongs to them. It does not matter whether they ever inhabit it or develop it (as in the case of Jerusalem and "Palestine"); they are never permitted to relinquish it. Therefore, every immigration and settlement of non-Muslims (whether for peaceful purposes or humanitarian purposes—such as to escape persecution) is considered an invasion of Muslim land, and the settlers are considered enemy occupiers. This action requires defensive *jihad,* and it is the duty of every able-bodied Muslim to fight a war to remove the occupying force and restore the land to Islam.

In the case of the Israeli-Palestinian conflict, whether it is Palestinian women and children who throw rocks, use slingshots, and hurl molotov cocktails, or Palestinian teenagers and adults who fire rifles and machine guns, hurl grenades, use rocket launchers, and strap on explosives, their "resistance" against the Zionist "occupiers" is considered to be a *defensive* act and not terrorism. In this regard it is also significant to note that due to the Crusades, Muslim propagandists for the *jihad* in the twelfth and thirteenth centuries stressed the special status of Jerusalem to Islam. They wrote treatises especially devoted to the *fada'il* ("excellences") of Jerusalem in particular and Syria-Palestine in general. However, these attributions derived not from any historical attachment of Islam to the city, but because after the Crusader conquest of 1099 there were no Muslims left in the city and such appeals were necessary to the Muslim world to 1) counter the devotion that had driven the "Christian" Crusaders to "redeem" Jerusalem, and 2) provoke Muslims to *jihad* to reclaim (or later, defend) it.

From the beginning, Islam was spread by exterior *jihad* and especially by the *jihad* of the sword. It is significant that the calendar of Islam does not begin with the birth of Muhammad, nor the onset of his supposed "revelation," nor the assembling of the first Muslim community, nor the flight of Muslim refugees to Abyssinia. Even the 12 years of persecution in Mecca were not considered the start of their new religion. The Muslim calendar began only after Medina was subjugated to Islam through *jihad* and became a political state. Tracing this event historically, it can be seen that the concept of *jihad* was "created" for this very purpose. After fleeing to Medina (the *Hijra*) in A.D. 622, Muhammad summoned his followers to attack and plunder the caravans of Mecca. His followers initially resisted these calls, until Muhammad presented a series of "revelations" commanding *jihad* and permitting the looting of those killed in battle: "Whoever has killed an enemy and has proof of that, will possess his spoils" (Hadith, vol. 4, no. 370). If the booty was not sufficient, Muhammad held captives as hostages until their families paid a large enough ransom for their release. Hostage-taking (as well as enslavement) has continued to be a practice in Islam to this day.

Those who participate in *jihad* are granted a blanket absolution (Sura 8:17) and guaranteed to go straight to Paradise if killed. This is the all-important motivation for *jihad*—the reward promised the Muslim warriors of *jihad*, known as *Mujahideen* ("men who fight in Allah's cause").

The Reward of the Warriors of *Jihad*

In the Islamic theology of *jihad*, warriors and martyrs receive a special place in Paradise with priority status. In fact, this promised reward was so great that Muhammad stated that martyrs would be willing to come back and get killed again! The Qur'an states: "There are two other Gardens....In them will be fair [Companions], good, beautiful...Companions restrained (as to their glances), in (goodly) pavilions....Whom no man or Jinn before them has touched....Reclining on green cushions and rich carpets of beauty. Then which of the favors of your Lord will you deny?" (Sura 55). Many other verses in the Qur'an (see 44:54; 52:20,24; 56:17,22; 74:19) and the Hadith, as well as in traditional Muslim treatises, present graphic statements of the sexual and sensual delights awaiting the warrior or martyr in Paradise. These include weddings, but with wives kept in separate quarters where their husbands visit them discreetly, 72 *houris* (a special type of perpetual virgin who never ages) that exist to grant sexual favors, and the bestowal on the *Mujahideen* of youthful age, increased sexual prowess, and exceptional endurance.

All Muslims who volunteer to fight with radical Islam against the United States and Israel, and especially those who will volunteer to become martyrs, are given this promise by their parents (in the case of youths), the Imams, and jihadic leaders. From their viewpoint they are not committing suicide, but are "sacrificing" themselves for the cause of Allah. Therefore, they are praised, honored, revered, and upheld as examples for others to consider martyrdom.

The obligation of *jihad* has been the chief motivating imperative for young Palestinian suicide bombers who believe "sacrificing" their lives brings them a martyr's reward in Paradise. According to the Qur'an, "those that embraced the Faith [Islam]...and fought Allah's cause... their Lord has promised mercy from himself, and his pleasure and gardens of eternal bliss" (Sura 9:20). "Therein are bashful virgins whom neither man nor jinn will have touched before" (Sura 55:54)—"virgins as fair as corals and rubies" (Sura 55:55). According to Al-Ghazzali, one of Islam's greatest spiritual teachers, "The believer in Paradise will marry 500 *houris* (companions), 4,000 virgins, 8,000 divorced women."[10]

The orthodox Muslim interpretation of Paradise is a literal sexual orgy—just the kind of place adolescent, unmarried men, isolated through their lives from the opposite sex by rigid cultural standards, would die for! The Islamic Jihad terrorist organization is now running camps in Palestinian Authority-controlled Gaza for 8- to 12-year-old children. According to an Israel Channel 2 television report, these so-called "Paradise Camps" train the children in military tactics and weapons operations, and instill into them the significance of being a suicide bomber and dying as a martyr (and going to Paradise). I have personally watched Sesame Street-style children's programs on Palestinian television that show young boys and girls dressed like suicide bombers and chanting and singing songs about their ambition to die as martyrs.[11]

Now, what about moderate Muslims, who condemn such "martyrdom" as acts of terrorism and declare that those who do such things are "not Muslims"? According to the Hadith *(Abu Huraira):* "None will enter Paradise but a Muslim soul, yet Allah may support this religion [Islam] even with an evil soul." Consequently, even though moderate Muslim leaders may agree with U.S. politicians that Osama bin Laden, Al-Qaeda, the high-jackers, and all other terrorists involved with the attack on America are "evildoers," this does not prevent them from believing that such men were used by Allah for the *good* of Islam!

The Muslim Understanding of "Peace" in Light of *Jihad*

When Muslim leaders say that Islam is "a religion of peace," they do not qualify for non-Muslims what this means in their religion. The Arabic word for peace is *salam,* and Islam is the active form of *salam.* Therefore, Muslims see themselves as a "peacemaking force" in the world. However, this for the Muslim means that the peace of the world cannot be fully secure until people come under the protection of Islam. To accomplish this requires *jihad* that extends the territory of Islam (i.e., the protection of Islam) over non-Islamic lands. For this reason, *Islam,* in Arabic, does not mean "peace," but "submission," "surrender," or "subjugation." And this "peace" can be brought about using argument, intrigue, commerce, threats, terrorism, warfare, and every other means possible to secure Islam as the only religion on earth. What's more, the Qur'an teaches that Muslims are not permitted to make peace with non-Muslims or with a non-Muslim country until its inhabitants surrender to Islam. They can agree to a cease fire or a truce for a limited period of time, but never to an unconditional peace. Why, then, would Muslim leaders give the impression that they appear to agree with the non-Muslim definition of peace?

One explanation is that Islam commands Muslims to lie in the cause of *jihad:* "Um Kalthum said, 'I never heard the Prophet Muhammad allowing people to lie except in three cases.' The first case is in the relationship between husbands and wives. The second case is that Muslims can lie to their enemies in the midst of *jihad.* The third case is that a Muslim can lie to another Muslim for reconciliation" (*Book of Ehyae Iloum Il Deen,* vol. 3, p. 137). In addition, a Muslim can lie and deny his faith if doing so will be to his advantage or for the benefit of Islam: Ibn Katheer said in his book *The Beginning and the End* that "when Ammar bin Yaser was under the persecution of the Qurash tribe he was asked to deny his faith in the Prophet. In order to release his suffering, Ammar denied his faith. When they released him, he ran to Prophet Muhammad and told him the story. The Prophet asked him if he denied him from his heart (changed his faith) and Ammar said 'no Prophet of God.' Then the Prophet said, 'even if they come back to you again deny again.' "[12]

As an Egyptian friend who has lived among Muslims in Islamic countries most of his life stated, "Muslims are not permitted to make peace with a non-Muslim country until its inhabitants surrender to Islam. They can agree to a cease fire for a period of time, but never to peace with non-Muslims."[13]

Therefore, the political actions of any Islamic state are bound by the religious rulings of Islam, known as *Shari'ah* ("the way"), which, in turn, are aimed at achieving the destiny of the religion. Although presently no Islamic state other than the Taliban observes this fundamental aspect of the religion, the revival of radical Islam has as its goal to make all moderate Muslim states conform to a purer practice of Islam politically.

For this reason, the Muslim position concerning the State of Israel is that an injustice against the Palestinians (the uprooting of an indigenous Arab Muslim population by "the late-arriving Jews") must be rectified by the removal of the Jews from the region (since, if they were left, they would seek to expand and displace Muslims and Muslim lands). Therefore, the justification for this is not simply political, but religious.

The failure to recognize that religion is the key in the Middle East conflict has caused many people to misunderstand the nature of the conflict and the problems to its resolution. As *Chicago Sun Times* reporter Andrew Greeley observes,

> The Oslo peace process seems to have failed because of its pretense that the conflict is not a religious war. Much of the well-intentioned American "mediation" has assumed that compromises over territory—land for peace—can settle the conflict. Western liberalism with its easy optimism that religion doesn't matter anymore simply cannot comprehend that for most people it still does, especially in the "Holy" Land.[14]

And if the Israeli-Palestinian war is religious in nature, how can it be asserted that the war America is waging with the *same* enemy is not? Furthermore, the religious call for external (offensive) *jihad*, especially against the Jew and the State of Israel, is particularly explicit. Who has not seen the images of both Palestinians and Muslims throughout the Middle East chanting "Death to America and Israel" while burning effigies of their leaders or flags? The reason for this violent compulsion is driven by religion. As we noted earlier, the Qur'an requires that any lands once occupied by Islam must remain completely, not partially, under Muslim sovereignty (*Dar Islam*). One Muslim teacher stated this:

> There can be no peace until all of the stolen area is
> returned back to the rightful owners. It is inconceivable
> for any Muslim to agree to take back the garden shed
> of his illegally occupied house, with the illegal occu-
> pant keeping the rest. Not only is it against logic, and
> all laws known to a civilized world, but more impor-
> tantly, it is not permitted from the Legislator, Allah.[15]

This Islamic law allows no compromise of shared sovereignty over lands or cities, and pronounces that *jihad* is
the only acceptable response until all of the occupied areas
are restored to Muslim control.

How Are the Beliefs of Muslims an Obstacle to Peace?

One radical Muslim organization has this statement on
their website: "Islam is not a religion such as Christianity,
Judaism, Buddhism, Sikhism, or Hinduism, in that it is not
merely a spiritual belief, but a complete way of life, having
its own unique ruling, social, economic, and judicial systems and foreign policy."[16]

In Islam, religion and politics are joined together. Unlike
Zionist Jews, who are at the helm of the government of the
State of Israel, there are no secular Arab leaders in the
Palestinian Authority. Dr. Kamel el Baker, president of Om
Dorman Islamic University in the Sudan, explains:

> Judaism is a "religion" in which the believers follow
> a certain creed. Zionism is the same as Judaism, but
> seeks to achieve the end sought by Judaism through
> political action....This, then, is the essence of the
> Palestinian problem—and religious Jewish state
> founded by Zionists—even though it may appear in
> the form of political implications [dis]guised by the
> successors of the Crusaders in modern garb.[17]

For Dr. Baker, as for the Palestinian Authority, there is no
such thing as a secular Jewish state; the Jews are on a religious quest to destroy Islam (like the Crusaders), and must

Protest poster in the West Bank that proclaims Israelis are murderers and demands they get out of Palestinian territories.

Photo courtesy of Israel Government Press Office

be driven permanently from the Islamic land they occupy. The reason for this, in their minds, is that Islam is destined to rule the world. For this reason the Palestinians cannot but view the secular Zionist state as a religious entity humiliating Allah and violating his command to never let his land be lost to the unbelieving (non-Muslim) world. Islamic law requires that once a place comes under Islamic authority it becomes a part of *Dar Islam* ("the House of Islam"). It is considered Islamic territory forever, no matter who gains control of it. Further, it is a divine requirement of Islam that Islamic territory not under Muslim sovereignty be regained through *jihad*. In radical Islam, this duty is taught to Muslim youths early in life. For example, Aziz Khan in the village of Shakot, Pakistan, says, "In our culture, we give our baby son an unloaded pistol to play with in the cradle so that he becomes acquainted with guns. Every man and boy will defend bin Laden and the Taliban against America. It would be dishonorable not to protect him."[18]

The same mentality exists even in a moderate Islamic country like Jordan. A Jordanian manual for first-grade teachers advises, "It is necessary to implant in the soul of the pupil the rule of Islam that if the enemies occupy even one inch of the Islamic lands, *jihad* becomes the imperative for every Muslim." Therefore, it is the duty of every Muslim from birth to go to war against Israel and the West because they occupy or maintain a presence in Islamic territory.

When Israel was established in 1948, it created a catastrophic problem for the Arab and Muslim Middle East—not a political problem, but a religious one. Hamas spokesman Ismail Abu Shanab said in an interview, "The Israelis should understand that their existence is the only provocation in the area." The religious imperative to remove Israel may be seen in the statement of His Eminence Sheikh Umar Abd-al-Rahman, the spiritual guide of the Islamic Group in Egypt, in his call for the worldwide Islamic society (*ulema*) to issue a *fatwa* (an Islamic ruling binding on all Muslims) on the duty of killing Jews who occupied the land of Muslims and desecrated their holy shrines. Muntasir al-Zayyat, a defense lawyer of the Muslim groups in Egypt, explained it this way: "The problem is that Jews are Jews. God has clarified for us this description of them."[19]

For example, the Qur'an says, "They have incurred anger from their Lord and wretchedness is laid upon them..." (*The Family of Imran,* Sura 112); "Allah will raise against them till the day of Resurrection..." (*The Heights* 1, Sura 167); "for this reason Allah decreed that they should be scattered all over the globe so that no nation would be made out of them. They would rather live as an evil on earth, or like diseases and pests..." (*The Heights,* Sura 168); "this is our enemy, and the disease that plagued our lands. They are cursed like Satan....This enemy is also sent out to launch war on people exactly like Satan....They are the enemy, so beware of them. Allah confound them. How they are perverted" (*The Heights* 4); "in the same way the devil, rallied by his supporters is weak and fragile before the force of faith so are the Jews who may now appear strong by virtue of the support of imperialism. In fact they are weaker than the devil and...Allah has shown us the result of their conflict with us when he said: 'They will not harm you save a trifling hurt, and if they fight against you they will turn and flee...they will not be helped'" (*The Family of Imran*, Sura 111).

Therefore, in Islamic thinking, killing the Jews and eliminating Israel is the only possibility for peace. There are more verses from the Qur'an to this effect: "Allah sent down to him [Muhammad]: 'Fight them so that there be no more seduction...and the religion is Allah's [until no one is worshiped but Allah]'" (Sura 22:39-41; 2:193); "faith in Allah and Jihad is his path" (Sura 61:10).

Muhammad was a terrorist who launched a campaign of conquest against his own people and especially against the Jews. A.B. Davidson, a professor at New College, Edinburgh, wrote of one such instance: "On one day he caused 800 Jews to be beheaded in cold blood, himself standing by and watching the butchery; and in the evening, to efface the unpleasant impression from his mind, and give a more happy turn to his ideas, he took home the wife of one of the murdered chiefs, and added her to his harem."[20]

Hamas poster that proclaims, "Israeli Murder—Army Out of Palestine."
Photo by Binyamin Lalizou

Following Muhammad and the Qur'an, the Palestinian Mufti Ikrima Sabri stated in a sermon at the Al-Aqsa Mosque in the summer of 2001: "It should be clear to all of us that we all should work to re-establish the Islamic *Khilafah* State because it is the most important duty for Muslims today."[21] Sheikh Muhammad Abu Zahra, a member of the Academy of Islamic Research, declared, "*Jihad* will never end, because it will last to the Day of Resurrection. But war can come to a close so far as a particular people are concerned. It is terminated when the war aims are realized...."[22]

One of the principal aims of Islamic holy war is the liquidation of the Jewish people, the total destruction of Israel, and complete sovereignty over *Al-Quds* (the Jerusalem of Islam). The following represents only a small sampling of the statements the Palestinian Authority has made with respect to its designs for all of the Land of Israel:

- We are announcing a war against the sons of apes and pigs [the Jews] which will not end until the flag of Islam is raised in Jerusalem (Hamas leaflet, September 1, 1993).[23]

- We Palestinians will take over everything, including all of Jerusalem....We plan to eliminate the State of Israel and establish a Palestinian state (Yasser Arafat to Arab ambassadors in Stockholm, January 30, 1996).[24]

- The Muslims say to Britain, to France, and to all the infidel nations that Jerusalem is Arab. We shall not respect anyone else's wishes regarding her (Sheikh Ekrima Sabri, Palestinian Mufti of Jerusalem at the Al-Aqsa Mosque, July 11, 1997).[25]

- If Israel persists in not recognizing Palestinian sovereignty in the eastern part of Jerusalem, it is the Palestinian side's right to demand its rights from the [Jordan] river to the [Mediterranean] sea (Faisal Al-Husseini, November 28, 1997). [26]

Islam can never accept a non-Muslim state like Israel in its midst, and the only way Islam could ever accept a "peace" with Jews would be on Islamic terms: Islam must receive and maintain complete domination of the Land of Israel, exercising both political and religious sovereignty, and Jews must accept servitude status as *dhimmi*. From the Islamic viewpoint Jews who practice Judaism are unbelievers (though not infidels) and unfit to have possession of any Muslim land. However, they recognize that the Jewish state is a secular creation and that the majority of Israel's Jewish citizens do not practice any form of Judaism. For this reason Sheikh Hamid Al-Bitawi, chairman of the Palestine Religious Scholars Association and head of the Palestinian Authority's Sharia Court of Appeals in Nablus, has declared, "The existing State of Israel is not worthy of ruling since they know no religion and no God."[27]

Now that we understand the general perspective of those who follow Islam, now let's turn to the distinct beliefs of radical or militant Muslims who today have also championed the cause of *jihad* against America and the West.

CHAPTER 11

What Makes
a Muslim Militant?

The process of the revival of Islam in different parts of the world is real. A final showdown between the Muslim world and the non-Muslim world, which has been captured by the Jews, will take place soon. The Gulf War was just a rehearsal for the coming conflict....Muslims of the world, including those in the U.S.A., prepare yourselves for the coming conflict.[1]
—Dr. Israr Ahmed
Amir of the Tanzeem, Islami of Pakistan

I say these events [the U.S. bombing of Afghanistan] have split the whole world into two camps: the camp of belief and the camp of disbelief. So every Muslim shall support his religion.[2]
—Osama bin Laden

Islam, though unified as a system and allowing no deviations from its "five pillars of faith," is not a monolithic religion. Some 73 minor sects of Islam are known (such as the puritanical offshoot Wahhabites or the Alawites, to which the Assad dynasty of Syrian rulers belongs), although most Muslim countries today are divided according to the major orthodox divisions of Sunni and Shi'ite. Islamic terrorists come from both of these major sects (as well as from some of the minor ones). For example, the Iraqis are Sunnis and the Iranians are Shi'ite, as are the Syrians (and both Iran and Syria were instrumental in the founding of Shi'ite Hizbullah in Lebanon). Saudi Arabians are Sunni as are Afghans and Pakistanis, but Palestinians are both Sunni and Shi'ite (Yasser Arafat is Sunni). In addition to these sectarian distinctions, various other terms have been used by the news media to describe the type of Muslim that advocates and perpetrates terrorist acts. Some of these are fundamentalist Muslims, militant Muslims, fanatical Muslims, extreme Muslims, and radical Muslims.

Now, all of these terms describe those who are followers of Islam regardless of their interpretation of the Qur'an or their practice of its tenet of *jihad*. However, the "politically correct" position today is that the Muslims who host terrorism do not represent the teachings of Islam and are not accepted by the majority of Muslims, who are moderate and interpret *jihad* symbolically as an inner moral struggle. But is the Islam of most Muslims really a different religion than that which the terrorists espouse? And if the radical terrorists are not the product of Islam, from where did they arise? What exactly makes a Muslim *militant?*

Where Did Radical Islam Come From?

From the president to prominent news anchors such as Peter Jennings, a chorus of voices have stated that Islamic terrorists do not represent the religion of Islam. In the previous chapter, we saw that the teachings of the Qur'an and the Hadith are absolute and authoritative and showcase the concept of external *jihad*. For this reason, to claim that the religion of the Islamic terrorists is not that of Islam or that their religion is a perversion of Islam and is vengeful and politically motivated—while the true religion of Islam is peaceful and loving—is not favored by the facts. Throughout the history of Islam, the religion has been spread by conquest and reconquest from the fertile crescent to Western Europe, killing or enslaving those who refused to convert to Islam.

Not all of these conquests were by the sword; during the early period of Islam, Jews and heretical Christians were offered refuge from persecution by the Byzantine (Eastern Orthodox) and Catholic (Western Orthodox) regimes. In some cases the Islamic empire spread by stepping into the political vacuum created by the weakening of other empires, such as that of the Byzantine Empire, which was the main barrier to the spread of Islam into southeast and central Europe, via the Crusades. There are other cases (such as in Serbia) where the higher birthrate of Muslims altered the demographic makeup of the population and permitted Islam to dominate.

Few countries and cultures taken by Islam over the last 1,400 years have ever regained their former land or religion. On occasion, non-Muslims have reconquered lands taken by Islam, although it took half a millennium to expel Muslims from Western Europe, and the Crusades were a rare exception of reconquest in the Holy Land.

After World War I, a fusion of religion and state that had existed as law in Muslim lands since the seventh century A.D. began to become more aggressively advocated in the interest of the purity of Islam. Having a Muslim population governed by a secular government that could be controlled by non-Muslim powers was considered an abomination. The nonviolent spread of Islam through missionaries (the *Da'wah*) was not considered sufficient to accomplish the overthrow of such governments and fulfill the primary mission of Islam in the world, which is to unify all of the Muslim world under pure Islam. What was needed was a revival of revolutionary Islam, of jihadic extremism, to accomplish this unification. Thus a form of Islam that had extended Islam through conquest since the seventh century reappeared as modern radical Islam.

The roots of this militant emphasis can be traced to movements beginning as early as the 1880s, such as the Tablighi Jamaat, which was formed in Pakistan to revive and spread radical Islam. Today, its annual convention, held at Raiwind in Pakistani Punjab, is attended by more than one million Muslims from all over the world. It has been described as the second-largest gathering of Muslims anywhere after the *hajj* in Mecca.

Radical Islam has also grown rapidly since the decline of the Soviet Union from superpower status and due to the wealth obtained from oil revenues over the past few decades. This oil wealth is what enabled radical Islam to become the dominant force in international terrorism.

Osama bin Laden's particular genre of jihadic Islam emerged in Southwest Asia, which has now eclipsed the Middle East as the epicenter of terrorism. This jihadic form of Islam gained prominence after infiltrating Pakistan's theological schools (known as *madrassahs*), which function as the country's main educational system. Pakistani clerics and Muslim missionaries then carried this influence to Muslim communities in the former Soviet bloc and Eastern Europe. As a result, writes Ray Takeyh, a research fellow at the Washington Institute for Near East Policy, "An international *jihad* movement was gestating beyond the glare of the international community that would soon be puzzled by the intensity and scope of the new claimants of radicalism."[3]

One creation of these Pakistani *madrassahs* was the Taliban, a group of theological students who usurped the secular government of Afghanistan and placed the entire country under the strictest interpretation of Islamic law. Following their mentally unstable leader Mullah Mohammed Omar (who suffers brain seizures as the result of a mortar attack during the Russian-Afghan war, and lost one of his eyes in that war), they attempted to establish in the city of Kabul the first truly Islamic state (*Khalifate*) under *Shari'ah* (Islamic law) in a century. This state would serve as the revolutionary model to which every Islamic state would be conformed, either voluntarily or through conquest. As such, the West is not the only civilization under threat from Islamic invasion. For example, much of the Hindu and Buddhist civilization of India was once destroyed by the Muslim Moghul invasion (and we can well remember how the Taliban recently destroyed ancient colossal Buddhist statues in Afghanistan). The appalling poverty experienced in India today is a result of that original Muslim invasion and destruction. And the ongoing conflict in the Middle East, begun in 1948 with the first Israeli-Arab war, has given further impetus to radicals to expand the theme of a global rivalry between a Zionist-Western alliance of new "crusaders" and Islam.

Even with this rapid growth, the expansion of radical Islam has been kept in check in Muslim Third-World countries, Arab states in the Middle East, and even the heart of the Islamic empire—Saudi Arabia—by U.S. foreign policies that influence the secular governments. The adherents of radical Islam have resented this, and still more offensive has been the stationing of U.S. forces in some of these countries. And, the United States' military action against an Islamic country (Iraq) during the Gulf War was considered an act requiring vengeance.

When America was attacked on September 11, then, Uncle Sam had already been in the crosshairs of radical Islamic terrorists. Radical Islamic groups in Libya, Syria,

Yemen, Afghanistan, Sudan, Egypt, Saudi Arabia, Iran, and, of course, Iraq, had already—since the early 1980s—targeted any symbol of American presence on Muslim soil. For example, in the fall of 1983 a Gulf Air 737 jetliner crashed into the Persian Gulf after a bomb exploded in the baggage compartment, and a truck laden with bombs killed 241 marines at U.S. barracks at the Beirut airport. Five years later, a Libyan terrorist planted a suitcase bomb on Pan Am Flight 103, which exploded over Lockerbie, Scotland, killing all 270 aboard. The next year, Americans were among the 171 who died aboard a French UTA DC-10 jetliner bombed by a group known as The Lebanese Islamic Holy War. Then there was the bombing of the World Trade Center in 1993, and in 1998 there were bombings at the U.S. embassies in Kenya and Tanzania. Both were believed to have been orchestrated by Osama bin Laden, and the American death toll from these attacks was 230 people. Then on October 12, 2000, the U.S.S. Cole, a guided-missile destroyer docked in the Yemeni port of Aden, was attacked by two suicide bombers who belonged to a group called the Islamic Army of Aden. Seventeen soldiers were killed and more than 40 seriously maimed or wounded in the blast that cut a 40-foot hole in the ship's side.

All of these assaults on America came from radical Muslims, and some still suspect Islamic connections to other attacks, such as the mysterious loss of TWA Flight 800 off Long Island and the bombing of the Alfred P. Murrah Federal Building in Oklahoma City. In addition, since the beginning of the new millennium, there have been more than 200 attempted terrorist attacks that have been intercepted or thwarted by U.S. intelligence operatives—attempts that have never been reported to the public.

In order to better understand the enormous threat this Islamic expansion through *jihad* poses to Western civilization, let's take a closer look at the beliefs of radical Muslims.

What Do Radical Muslims Believe?

The belief system of radical Islam combines the Islamic call to external *jihad* with the virtues of martyrdom, exegeting Qur'anic texts to justify terrorism and suicide bombings while promising the reward of eternal hedonism. One must remember that the majority of poor Muslims who support radical terrorism are illiterate and cannot read the Qur'an for themselves or understand the meaning of the verses they recite. By contrast, the Taliban is comprised of Pakistanis and Afghanis who are considered the true *Mujahideen* or "holy warriors of Allah." They have established a purely Islamic state that rigidly conforms to the "pious Muslim ideals" outlined and set down by Prophet Muhammad. The radical Muslim believes that the solution for the problem of the *Ummah* (the international Muslim community) is to establish a righteous *Khalifah* (a single state that fuses together religion and politics and is governed by Islamic law) that will unite all Islamic lands and peoples and subjugate the rest of the world (non-Muslims) to Allah. The notion that they are in a permanent struggle against non-Muslims until non-Muslims are converted to Islam, subjected to Islamic authority, or killed comes from the Qur'an. In the previous chapter we examined a number of Qur'anic passages dealing with these matters, so here I'll just give a general summary of the texts with their references: 1) Islamic warning against mixing with non-Muslims (Suras 2:21; 3:28,118; 5:51,144; 9:7,28; 58:23; 60:4); 2) Islamic calls for Muslims to wage war against non-Muslims (Suras 2:191,193; 4:66,84; 5:33; 8:12,15-18,39,59-60,65;   9:2-3,5,14,29,39,73,111,123; 25:52; 37:22-23; 47:4-5; 48:29; 69:30-37); 3) Islam encourages the war against the non-Muslims by glorifying it (Suras 2:216; 9:41; 49:15) or by promising paradise to the *Shaheeds* (martyrs) who die in such a war (Suras 3:142,157-158; 9:20-21); 4) The Islamic promise of the punishment of hell to non-Muslims (Suras 3:85; 4:56; 5:37,72; 8:55; 9:28; 15:2; 21:98-100; 22:19-22,56-57; 25:17-19,55; 29:53-55; 31:13; 66:9; 68:10-13; 72:14-15).

Despite these texts, moderate Muslims contend that Islam does not force people to change their religion. They point to Sura 2:256, which says, "There is no compulsion in religion." However, according to an Islamic scholar, the phrase "no compulsion" is a condemnation of compelling people to do evil, while compelling people in the truth is a religious duty. Does the infidel get killed for anything other than his religion? The prophet Muhammad said, "I have been ordered to fight against the people until they testify that none has the right to be worshiped but Allah." This Hadith is taken from the words of Allah: "Fight them on until there is no more tumult and religion becomes that of Allah" (Sura 2:193).[4]

Radical Muslims believe that they are not terrorists but martyrs. But the difference, as someone has pointed out, is that a martyr says, "I will die for what I believe," and a terrorist says, "*You* will die for what I believe!" Given their attacks on innocent people, they are terrorists plain and simple. What *they* are willing to die for is the promise of 72 *houris* or celestial virgins who call to them from Paradise (*The Rangers* 40:45; *The Tidings* 30; *The Stinters* 20:25). Hadith *Titmzi*, volume 2 (pp. 35-40, 138) gives a description of these ever-young and immortal beings who grant sexual favors to the dead martyrs. What's ironic is that the lifestyle promised to martyrs is anything but pious, yet these radicals consider themselves to be the most devout of Muslims.

Daniel Pipes of the Middle East Forum, an expert on Islam, has examined the past behavior of both Osama bin

Laden and the suicide bombers who attacked America. He observes that "preoccupied with gaining power...they often show more talent at politics than at living by Islam's precepts. In fact, Islamists, for all their ostentatious piety, tend to be severely deficient as believers."[5] The results of his investigation confirm the following: 1) an Islamic bank scandal in which the largest Islamic bank (the Bank of Credit and Commerce), owned by devout Muslims, embezzled billions of dollars from 1.3 million people, mostly Muslims, in over 70 countries; 2) the two suicide bombers who attacked the U.S.S. Cole cheated their Yemeni landlord out of their last month's rental payment because they knew they would not be returning; 3) Rami Yousef, who masterminded the 1993 bombing of the World Trade Center, used to frequent Manila strip joints and karaoke clubs and flirted with women; 4) Rashide Baz, who killed a Hassidic Jewish boy on the Brooklyn Bridge, was described by his father as liking girls, cars, and sports, and having never been to a mosque in his life; 5) Al-Qaeda, Hamas, and Hizbullah terrorist organizations are drawn to pornography and place encrypted information such as maps, photographs, and instructions within pornographic websites; 6) and the Iranian government arrested the head of an Islamic revolutionary court for running a prostitution ring made up of underage runaway girls.

In addition, an Egyptian friend of mine who has lived in Saudi Arabia, Morocco, Algeria, and in the Muslim community of Spain has written:

> We are very familiar with the Arab Muslim culture and morals. Muslims are just as immoral, corrupt, and decadant as Westerners. The only difference is that they commit immoral acts in secret while Westerners do it openly. In Saudi Arabia, for example, Muslim men fly frequently to spend weekends of drunkenness,

adultery, fornication, and debauchery in the night
clubs of Cairo, then return to Saudi Arabia and pre-
tend in public that they do not drink alcohol or use
drugs. Homosexuality, prostitution, and drugs are
rampant in the Saudi Royal family, yet the *Shari'ah* is
strictly applied to anyone among the Saudi people
caught doing these things."[6]

Such behavior, especially on the part of radical Muslims, betrays the true beliefs to which they hold—beliefs
that have generated the most extreme forms of hatred,
prejudice, and disregard of human life.

How Do Radical Muslims View the United States?

Radical Islam believes that the United States, as the
leader of the West, is an enemy of the Muslim world. As
one rabbi put it: "Most Americans don't realize that what
the Moslem fundamentalists think is that Americans are
the evil demented monsters and the terrorists are holy
heroic martyrs who are making the world safe for
mankind under the sanctity of Islam."[7] The West is
depicted as "the Great Satan" who wants to conquer true
believers (Muslims) as did the Crusaders of old and conform the world to infidel idolatry.

The Islamic idea of *Dar Islam* binds all Muslims in a
solidarity that constitutes any attack on a Muslim country
(such as Afghanistan) as an attack on the whole of the
Muslim world. Radical Muslims capitalize on this religious solidarity while, under the guise of social justice,
telling crowds of economically repressed Muslims that
U.S. colonialism and imperialism is responsible for their
poverty. Even the aid given by the United States to Third-
World Muslim countries is said by the radicals to be a
"deception" to lure the weak away from Islam. Thus, as
we have witnessed recently in the case of Afghanistan, the
$177 million the United States gave to this poor country

was used by the radicals to teach their people to hate the hand that feeds them.

To avoid the accusation that the United States has imperialistic intents or is waging a "religious war," the U.S. government has been careful to state that attacks on terrorism are not attacks on Islam and that it intends no attacks on Arab states. However, many analysts—both in America and in other countries—have insisted that Iraq shares the blame for the attacks on September 11 and for the anthrax incidents that followed shortly thereafter. If that's true, then Iraq will surely be a target for attack, but if the United States does expand its targets, the delicate coalition of Muslim countries "partnering" with the United States' attack on Afghanistan will fall apart. What's more, unless the United States is able to get Israel to make progress toward peace with the Palestinians, as the Coalition demands, the Coalition will not survive. Radical Muslims also believe that the United States is allied with Israel against Islam so that it can take over the world and establish a Jewish-Christian kingdom. While such thinking may be far removed from that of the West, it is axiomatic in Islam and therefore assumed for other religions.

Now, what about even some westernized Muslims, who are called "moderates" and who as American citizens decry the acts of terrorism, proclaim their patriotism, and insist that Islam is a religion of peace? Do they hold these same perspectives? In what ways do they differ from radical Muslims?

What Is the Difference between Moderate and Radical Islam?

Before September 11, most Western non-Muslims, if asked about the distinction between fundamentalist and moderate Islam, would have described the former as the provenance of Third-World countries stuck in the twelfth century (with a citizenry that represses women and denounces Western influences such as the automobile, radio, and telephone), and would have described the latter as liberated and receptive to the influences and technology of the modern Western world. However, since September 11, the distinction between fundamentalists and moderates has focused on Islamic beliefs on matters such as *jihad*. We are told by the moderates that "Islam means 'peace,'" that "its teachings are good," and that it is "a religion of love, not hate." It is said by moderate spokesmen that "Islam is a friend of Christianity and Judaism," sharing the same roots in Abraham and the Bible.

Yet even if we accept that Muslims may be our "friends," the Qur'an is not a friendly book. "On the contrary," say these Muslim spokesmen, "those who interpret the Qur'an to justify violence do not understand the spiritual teachings of the prophet Muhammad and are ignorant of Islam." They contend that non-Muslims who try to lump all Muslims together by citing passages from the Qur'an that appear to advocate hatred or violence are Islamophobic and misrepresent the true nature of Islam. In fact, it is claimed that "most of the world's 1.3 billion Muslims do not support the holy war bin Laden is said to be waging against the United States."[8] As *New York Times* columnist Thomas Friedman put it, "Surely Islam, a grand religion that never perpetrated the sort of holocaust against the Jews in its midst that Europe did, is being distorted when it is treated as a guidebook for suicide bombing."[9]

But the facts say otherwise. We have already noted how the Grand Mufti Haj Amin el-Husseini aided and abetted the Third Reich in its genocidal plan against the Jews of Europe for a pledge of Nazi support in a Middle Eastern "Final Solution."

If we're being told to not judge the religion of Islam by the actions of a "fringe group" of terrorists and that there exists a misconception about the nature of Islam itself, then how are we to understand what moderate Islam stands for?

What Does Moderate Islam Stand For?

As I researched this question, an answer presented itself in the form of a three-hour radio talk-show broadcast with Dr. Laura Schlessinger.[10] Her guest was Dr. Hasan Hattut, the official spokesman for the Los Angeles Islamic Center of Southern California and the author of *Reading the Muslim Mind*.

Dr. Hattut described himself as a moderate Muslim who represented the true Islam. His interview comments offer some interesting insights into the moderate Muslim mentality. When Dr. Laura asked about a statement describing Islam's goal as "an apocalyptic struggle against the West to create an Islamic world," he replied, "Laura, I have learned not to believe everything I read." When asked about specific passages in the Qur'an that spoke about "fighting unbelievers" (Sura 9:123; 8:62), "the Jews and Christians" (Sura 5:51), or "infidels" (Sura 2:56; 9:5), in every instance he stated the interpretation was "incorrect" and could only be understood in reference to the time it was written. All such passages, he explained, "were temporary, meant only for that time and situation." They were "never meant to be permanent and continually applied." In other words, the seventh-century Muslim controversies with the Jews and Christians and Muhammad's "defensive" wars against idol-worshiping pagan invaders were the sole focus of Muhammad's statements. He never intended them to be applied to any other persons or eras. According to Dr. Hattut, radical Muslims use these "real words of Muhammad," but "out of context," and so misapply them to this day. A caller then asked how was it that the radical Muslims could make such mistakes with the

Qur'an. Dr. Hattut's reply was that "they are simply uneducated—they do not understand Islam" and "they may be educated, but not in the Qur'an." On this basis, mainstream Islamic scholars have been said to have denounced Osama bin Laden (who trained in civil engineering and underwent no formal theological studies) as "a religious pretender."[11]

But what do these same scholars make of Sheikh Omar Abdel Rahman (presently serving a sentence in the United States for conspiring to destroy the World Trade Center and New York City bridges and tunnels in 1993), who is revered by radical Muslims around the world (including Osama bin Laden) as their spiritual leader? He holds a doctorate from Cairo's al-Azhar University, the world's oldest center of Muslim education, and he received the highest honors in Qur'anic studies. A dedicated student of Islam all of his life, he is at the top of the Islamic ladder—an Islamic cleric who is able to issue *fatwas* (Islamic rulings). Can we believe that the foremost spiritual inspiration for the leaders of radical Islam today is "simply uneducated and does not understand Islam"?

Sensing a problem with Dr. Hattut's answer, a caller then asked why all of the Islamic countries in the Middle East were not using Islam correctly. To this he replied, "It is because they are all under dictatorships." In other words, the tyrannical governments of these countries subvert true Islam by using a form of it in support of their political agendas. But if that were really the case, why is it that these dictators, even in countries where a secular government exists, are subject to the dictates of the Islamic clerics? In fact, in many Islamic countries it is the Muslim clerics that run the country. In fact, the most dictatorial regime, the Taliban government of Afghanistan, is made up entirely of Islamic theological students.

Then there's the matter of the oppressive treatment of women in Islamic countries (such as in Afghanistan under the Taliban government), which is based on Qur'anic passages such as Sura 4:15,16,34, which instructs the husband to beat his wife. Representing moderate Muslims, Dr. Hattut declared, "Men and women are equal in Islam; the problems in other countries are cultural." Yet the Qur'an says, "And women shall have rights similar to the rights against them, according to what is equitable; but men have a degree [of advantage] over them" (Sura 2:228).

Interestingly, the next caller came from Egypt. He stated that as a boy in school he had been taught to hate westerners, and that all his life the mosques he attended every Friday preached hatred against the West. Dr. Hattut, raised in Egypt and once a member of the radical Egyptian Brotherhood, calmly responded, "The Qur'an, the Prophet, all preach love. You find those who teach hate among Jews and Christians, but God does not condone hate." In this context of love, Dr. Laura asked about the much-publicized motivation of the suicide bombers—the sexual reward of 72 virgins in Paradise. In response, Dr. Hattut laughed and said, "This is exotic folklore!" If he's right, then Islamic leaders throughout the Muslim world are knowingly deceiving thousands of Muslim youths (and their parents) by telling them to sacrifice their lives for such "folklore"! This atrocity alone should enrage moderate Muslims to publicly protest such deception. The closest Dr. Hattut would come to a censure was to say, "To kill onself is forbidden in Islam; suicide is against the religion." But does the Qur'an condemn killing oneself in the cause of *jihad*? No suicide bomber thinks he is committing suicide, he is a *Mujahideen*, a warrior of Islam, sacrificing his life in the defense of Islam—the highest calling of the religion. Thus Dr. Hattut's statement is misleading because it does not address the context of *jihad*.

Other misleading statements by Dr. Hattut—supposedly reflecting moderate Islam—were as follows: "Islam has been fighting terrorism for centuries—terrorism is against Islam"; "the U.S. Constitution is the essence of true Islam"; "the principle of freedom is uppermost in Islam—the post-Muhammadean era was a golden age of freedom"; " 'holy war' is coinage from Crusader Europe"; and, "Jews were always welcomed in the Arab world, and when the Inquisition came, Jews fled primarily to Muslim lands." Finally, Dr. Hattut stated that "the terrorists are a very small majority of the [Muslim] people and don't represent Islam at all."

How is it that moderate Muslims can make these assertions? How is it that their brand of Islam, seen mostly in Western countries, is so different from the Islam of the east? One answer, according to a missionary to Muslims who has a Ph.D. in Islamic studies, is that moderates and militants are reading different parts of the Qur'an. The Qur'an, a compilation of Muhammad's teachings after his death, is not in chronological order. When Islamic scholars rearrange the suras (chapters) into chronological order, they are comprised of Mecca and Medina suras. Muhammad had his beginning in Mecca and returned there after conquering his own tribe, so Mecca suras are both early, middle, and late in the Prophet's life. Muhammad's later life was spent in Medina, so those suras represent the latest part of his life. Because Muhammad experienced less opposition in his early life, his earlier suras contain teachings about peace. But because the latter part of his life was filled with warfare, his later suras contain teachings about violence. The many contradictions in the Qur'an, then, arise from the changes in the Prophet's perspective from the earlier Mecca suras to the later Medina suras. According to the missionary, in places where Muslims are in the minority, such as in North America and Europe, the Muslims tend to follow the earlier Mecca suras. In places where Muslims are in the majority, such as in the Middle

East and Southeast Asia, the Muslims tend to follow the later Medina suras. According to this explanation, the difference between moderate and radical Islam is merely a matter of emphasis—accepting or alternately avoiding those suras that accommodate one's experience in society.

Dr. Hattut gave a similar explanation when he pointed to culture and the form of government as factors that influence a Muslim's worldview. Muslim leaders in a free society under a democratic government tend to emphasize the peaceful suras, while Muslim clerics in a closed society under a dictatorial government tend to emphasize the violent suras. Still, this does not explain the number of radical Muslims who are American citizens (as were some of the highjackers on September 11) or the presence of major Islamic terrorist organizations in democratic European countries (such as Germany).

Another concern, to my mind, is that most moderate Muslims aren't taking action to back up their assertions that they are different than radical Muslims. It is well known that the terrorists of September 11 were not exposed, but protected, by the moderate Muslim community among which they lived for years. Since hearing Dr. Hattut's explanation of moderate Islam, I have thought of steps that moderate Muslims can take to prove they are indeed different from their radical counterparts. These steps are fairly simple: Moderate Muslims can 1) publicly separate from the "small majority" of radical Muslims in the Islamic community; 2) desist from supporting all radical Muslim groups and causes (including those in Palestine); 3) label all radical Muslims as apostates (and treat them as such); and 4) immediately undertake an aggressive re-education campaign within Muslim communities throughout the world that have been influenced by radical Islam.

If these things were done, the world would surely see a different face of Islam, and radical Islamic states could be transformed from tyrannical regimes to peaceful, nonviolent countries in harmony with the West (and even the state of Israel). Furthermore, in the United States, doing such would dispel any fear of the Arab or Muslim community being a fifth column in our midst.

However, to my knowledge, no such organized actions have yet been attempted by moderate Muslims. One reason for this may be the problems moderate Muslims would encounter in such a campaign of rehabilitation. First and foremost would be the difficulty of selling fundamentalist Muslims on their liberal, nonliteral, and mostly temporary interpretation of the Qur'an. The moderates would have to prove that the Qur'anic texts obligating Muslims to support the *Umma* (Islamic Brotherhood) do not apply to fundamentalist Muslims. Yet trying to get Muslims who are part of the culture of Islam to consider such a distinction is practically impossible. That's because Muslims in general are not taught to think critically, but to simply memorize the Qur'an and recite back what they are taught (understanding is optional, and actually not encouraged in the Qur'an).

Even more difficult is the possibility that radical Muslims will accuse the moderates of being apostates, which would make the moderates targets for terrorism. Moderates are well aware that radical Muslims have declared *jihad* not only on non-Muslim enemies, but also on *murtads*, those Muslims who support the enemies of Allah. Nevertheless, such a break with others in the Islamic community would probably never occur, even in America. As my Egyptian friend (who is a longtime missionary in many Muslim countries) maintains: "Muslim Americans will always choose loyalty to Islam above any other loyalty, whether to family or country, especially a so-called Christian country."

Just How Moderate Are Moderate Muslims?

Consider two moderate Muslim leaders, Abdurahman Alamoudi, president of the American Muslim Council, and Muzammil Saddiqi, spiritual leader of the Islamic Society of Orange County. These two Muslim clerics were chosen by the U.S. administration to represent moderate Islam to the American masses. They appeared on television flanking President Bush as he repeatedly stated that "Islam is a religion of peace, not hate." Both men joined the president three days after the terrorist attack in a televised memorial service at the National Cathedral in Washington, D.C., where Muzammil Saddiqi was given the honor of offering the opening prayer. Yet these "moderates," who were selected to calm public concern over Islamic terrorism, were later shown on television (in a videotape obtained by Fox News) at a Washington, D.C., rally supporting terrorist organizations and openly denouncing the United States! On the tape, Abdurahman Alamoudi is clearly heard to say, "Hear that, Bill Clinton: We are all supporters of Hamas. *Allahu akbar.* I wish to add that I am also a supporter of Hizbullah. Anybody supports Hizbullah here?"[12] And Muzammil Saddiqi, who helped organize the rally, said on the tape, "The United States of America is directly and indirectly responsible for the plight of the Palestinian people. If you remain on the side of injustice, the wrath of God will come...."[13]

If the statements of these clerics represent moderate Muslims, then how do they differ from radical Muslims? Were not the words *Allahu akbar* the same words uttered by the suicide bombers before crashing the airplanes into the World Trade Center and the Pentagon? Did not Osama bin Laden make the same threat to the United States for its support of Israel? Even Hillary Rodham Clinton, during her New York Senate race in 2000, recognized Abdurahman Alamoudi's ties with terrorism (Hamas) and returned a campaign contribution from him!

How is it that in trying to spread a message of tolerance and peace the White House ended up endorsing as its spokesmen Islamic leaders who were known purveyors of the terrorists' message? Is it possible that there are two faces to moderate Islam? The Qur'an instructs Muslims not to tell the truth to non-Muslims (especially if doing so would cause them to lose face). Deceiving the infidel is a virtue. Since the American perception of Islam at present is a negative one, Americans should expect Islamic leaders to make statements of a positive nature. After all, one of the best-known moderate Muslims, extolled as the paragon of peacemakers, the late King Hussein of Jordan, once urged Muslims to "kill Jews wherever you find them, kill them with your hands, with your nails and teeth."[14]

Despite what we might be told about the differences between moderates and militants, it is radical Islam which today represents the majority of the Muslims outside the Western world. This is evident in the fact that the name most frequently given to newborn male Muslims, after the name Muhammad, is Osama—the hero who wounded the Great Satan. The reason radical Muslim leaders such as Osama bin Laden are so popular in the Muslim world is because, as Professor Paul Eidelberg of Bar Illan University and director of the Foundation for Constitutional Democracy contends, there is really no essential difference between Muslims—whether they profess to be moderate or extreme:

> When people ask me, "But are all Arabs and Moslems like this?" My answer has been that the policy against Arab-Islamic terrorism must not be based on the exceptions, but on the rule, and the rule is that Islam is a militant creed that arouses savagery and the cruel hatred of Jews and "infidels."...What is called "Islamic Fundamentalism" is authentic Islam, and this Islam is at war not only with the Jewish state of Israel, but with Western civilization.[15]

Moderate Muslims may claim that they do not take the Qur'an literally like the fundamentalists, but the Qur'an is taught by moderates and militants alike as the immutable (unchanging) word of Allah, every word of which must be accepted as literally true. Furthermore, according to historian Paul Johnson, "these canonical commands cannot be explained away or softened by modern theological exegesis, because there is no such science in Islam."[16] Rather, as Abdullah Al Araby explains, Muslim activists in the International Islamization Movement have created a new edition of Islam—revised, modified, and abridged—in order to convert Westerners to the religion. Nevertheless, he claims, the religion remains the same—it only *appears* moderate.

In his study of the changes that have taken place to make Islam less offensive to Westerners, Abdullah Al Araby observes that Muslims have adopted the following: 1) *a change of identity,* in which they downplay any literal sense of *jihad*, refrain from referring to non-Muslims as infidels, stress their affinity with Moses and Jesus, boast about patriotism and American values, and use Christian phrases like "God bless you"; 2) *a change in vocabulary,* in which words formally foreign to Islam such as *love, grace, salvation,* and *Sunday school* are now used; 3) *a change in strategy* in religious, social, and political arenas in order to be accepted in the mainstream culture, which includes becoming involved in partisan functions, educational programs, and running for public office.[17]

If these opinions are correct, moderate Islam is merely a deception and it's actually radical Muslims who represent the teachings of Islam. This verdict is a harsh one and is the potentially explosive issue the U.S. administration and media are trying to diffuse.

At the same time, this does not mean people should fear that moderate Muslims might be a "fifth column," for most moderates do indeed oppose the terrorist actions of the fanatics. But it does require a closer examination of the statements made by and about moderate Muslims in light of the unalterable tenets that define their faith, of which external *jihad* is one. It also requires both Muslims and non-Muslims to be more discerning of Muslims in their midst, since one of Osama bin Laden's top aides, Ali Mohammed, told the FBI in 1997 that bin Laden had planted hundreds of terrorist "sleepers" or "submarines" who would lie low for years until they were "activated."[18] In fact, the 19 terrorist hijackers who committed the attack on September 11 had lived and moved among Americans for years. Some had American citizenship, and most had rented good homes, worked out at neighborhood gyms, thrown parties for neighborhood kids, attended colleges, and taken flight lessons. They were, as one writer put it, "the terrorist next door."[19]

In addition, there are more than 75,000 students in American universities and colleges from countries that support terrorism—such as Iraq, Iran, Syria, and Libya. These students receive some two billion dollars in Pell Grants funded by the United States Department of Education. Radical Muslims have also been known to infiltrate Muslim student associations at college campuses for the purpose of recruiting individuals for terrorist cells.

Still, the rank-and-file Muslim is not a threat. He is not a jihadi extremist simply because he has not been taught the Qur'anic passages used by radical Muslims in support of *jihad*. Moderate Islam began in compromise when it became painfully clear that immediate worldwide conquest was not to be. Facing stronger armies than their own, Muslims in countries that were too mighty adopted a peaceful approach and practiced an accommodation to the common culture. The plan was to wait until Islam could grow strong enough to resume the battle, but in the patient process moderate Islam developed distinctions from its extreme beginnings, crystallizing and propagating a diluted form of Islam through moderate *madrassahs*. Therefore, moderate Islam today is not necessarily being deceptive, but has itself been deceived in its understanding of the nature of Islam, and runs the risk that radical Muslims may brand it as traitorous and force its adherents to share the fate of infidels. This fear alone, coupled with the impetus to belong to *Dar Islam*, could compel moderates to move to the radical camp. An additional factor could well be how moderates interpret the war the United States is waging against their fellow Muslims across the globe.

Is the United States Waging a War with Islam?

From the American point of view, the war with terrorism has nothing to do with religion, and it is not a war with Islam. However, from the Islamic viewpoint, it is all about religion, and every radical Muslim spokesman refers to the war as an attack on their religion. As soon as the United States began to respond to the terrorist attacks on the World Trade Center and the Pentagon, numerous Islamic websites on the Internet featured anti-American slogans, such as "World War III: Islam at War with the U.S.A." While the United States has proclaimed the war is on terrorism and not Islam, Osama bin Laden has stated, "They came out to fight Islam with the name of fighting terrorism."[20]

If bin Laden is right and the United States *is* at war with Islam, then so are many other races, religions, and nations around the world. Even while the terrorists were attacking America, radical Muslims in northern Nigeria were killing Christians in the city of Jos after the Nigerian government imposed *Shari'ah* (Islamic law) on its majority Christian population. The violence included three days of mass murders and the burning of churches. Radical Muslims are likewise engaging in a holy war against Coptic Christians in Egypt, Hindus in Kashmir, Baha'is in Iran, Catholics in the southern Philippines, and Christians in East Timor. For the past 18 years, a particularly vivid example of external *jihad* has been demonstrated in Sudan for the entire world to see. The Sudanese government in northern Sudan imposed a genocidal policy of Islamization and Arabization upon the African people in the south part of the country, forcing them convert to Islam or suffer massacres, mutilations, gang rapes, bombing, pillaging, blockades of humanitarian aid, and slavery. For this reason the Coalition for the Defense of Human Rights, an organization supporting those persecuted by militant Islam, states that "radical Islamism is a world ideology, fielding a world-terror army, which oppresses millions with a racist ideology that deems non-Muslims less than fully human."[21]

So, is the United States waging a war with Islam? If it isn't, it should be!

In relation to the attacks on America, we have examined some basic aspects of militant Islam, but there is a pronounced element in radical Islam that we have neglected, and that is the unparalleled hatred against the Jews and the State of Israel. In the next chapter we will seek to understand the nature of this hatred and why Israel and its conflict with the Palestinians has been catapulted by the terrorists themselves into a place of major prominence. In particular, we will focus on the one city—Jerusalem—which represents the nexus of the religious war between Islam and the West.

CHAPTER 12

Why Can't They Share Jerusalem?

*The Promised Land. Promised to whom?
The Jew who came first? Or the Arab,
who came last? These cousins of the
Semitic peoples would say, the both, that
the land is the pledge of their God.
But which God: Jehovah or Allah?
What God hath joined together, let no
man put asunder. But man had,
this to the Jew, that to the Arab.*[1]
—WES GALLAGHER, GENERAL MANAGER
ASSOCIATED PRESS

*Now we are in Jerusalem, never to be
divided, never to be split again, never to
pull out from the most ancient and sacred
place in Jewish history. Jerusalem is a
commitment to our history. Jerusalem is
also a commitment to our future.*[2]
—JERUSALEM MAYOR EHUD OLMERT

*Whoever does not accept the fact
that Jerusalem will be the capital
of a Palestinian State, and only that State,
can go drink from the Dead Sea
[die] and go to hell.*[3]
—YASSER ARAFAT

Sharing is something we teach our offspring to do from infancy. We regard it as bad form if an older child has not learned to share, and refer to him or her as spoiled or selfish. However, what do we do in the case of grownups who number in the millions and have access to arsenals of mass destruction? How do we get them to settle a fierce dispute peacefully?

The approach taken so far in U.S. foreign policy has been to deal with Israel as with an unruly child and force them to share—or else! But Israel has grown up and now, before considering our advice, watches our example to see if we practice what we preach. Could the United States take its own advice to Israel on how to handle its war with terrorism and begin negotiations with Osama bin Laden and Saddam Hussein? Did the United States call for a cease fire with the Taliban and withdraw its troops even while suicide bombers threatened America and their soldiers were under fire?

Yet the United States and its allies, including its Arab Coalition, demand that Israel not only return to the peace plan under these conditions, but get serious about sharing its sovereignty over its most sacred city, Jerusalem. And since this struggle to share now affects the stability of the war, and therefore of the world, the terms are again share—or else!

One proposal for peace suggests this:

> Solutions can be found to all outstanding issues that should be fair and just to both sides and should not undermine the sovereignty of the Palestinian and Israeli states as determined by their respective citizens, and embodying the aspirations to statehood of both peoples, Jewish and Palestinian. This solution should build on the progress made between November 1999 and January 2001.[4]

Such a solution seems reasonable, but is it realistic? Let us consider the roadblocks that have stood and still stand in the path of bringing an end to the Israeli-Palestinian conflict.

Nearly a half-century ago British prime minister Winston Churchill suggested to diplomat Evelyn Shuckburg another approach than sharing. He said, "You ought to let the Jews have Jerusalem; it was they who made it famous." However, if Churchill's statement was appropriate in his time, based on the Jews' historical reputation in the city, the publicity the Palestinians have since commanded in the press appears to entitle them to a share of Jerusalem as well. Indeed, a joint Israeli-Palestinian declaration proposed on July 25, 2001 states in part, "The way forward lies in international legitimacy and the implementation of UNSCR 242 and 338 leading to a 2-State solution based on the 1967 borders, Israel and Palestine living side-by-side, *with their respective capitals in Jerusalem*" (emphasis added). To live side-by-side with capitals in the same city makes it imperative that both share, and have a share.

But a share may not be enough: Consider the warning of Sheikh Muhammad Hussein in his prayer from the Al-Aqsa Mosque, which was broadcast on the official Palestinian Authority radio station *Voice of Palestine*: "Whomever has occupied part of Palestine or Jerusalem faces *jihad* [holy war] until judgment day!"[5] This hardly indicates a willingness to share! Aware of the threat in such statements and that redividing Jerusalem would mean disaster for the Jewish population of the city, prime ministers like Benjamin Netanyahu have publicly sworn, "I will never allow Jerusalem to be divided again. Never! Never! We will keep Jerusalem united and...we will never surrender those ramparts."[6] On another occasion, Netanyahu stated, "Jerusalem has been the capital of Israel for 3,000 years since the time of King David and we don't expect to change that for the next 3,000 years!"[7] Such words leave little room for compromise, as do the polarized positions of the Israelis and Palestinians today. Israeli prime minister Ariel Sharon said Jerusalem "would not be split." In reply, Palestinian leader Yasser Arafat stated that the splitting of Jerusalem is the only key to lasting peace. Sharon said that Israel "will retain full sovereignty over the Temple Mount." By contrast, Arafat and the Arabs demand full sovereignty.

The conflict over Jerusalem, to many people, seems to be a recent phenomena, but for Israelis it is past history—a failed experiment tried before with disastrous consequences. Most people unfamiliar with this past assume that relations between the Jews and Arabs could not always have been as bad as they are now. What are the facts?

Haven't the Arabs Lived in Harmony with the Jews in the Past?

Many people wonder why the proposal to partition Jerusalem into two separate capitals won't work as the Jews and Arabs have lived together in the city for so long. Palestinian writers and ill-informed historians often make the claim that the Jews and Arabs lived in harmony until the advent of political Zionism, which they believe undermined the good relations between the two. However, this claim, like so many others made by the historical revisionist, is a myth. Some non-Arab (Turkish and Kurdish) rulers such as Saladin and Suleiman did lift some of the previous restrictions concerning Jewish access and prayer, but Jews were still regarded as *dhimmi* and had many discriminatory measures imposed against them. Some of these measures (begun in A.D. 717) included the following prohibitions and rules:

- Jews could not ride on horses or camels (and only on donkeys *with a saddle*)

- they could not build synagogues
- their shoes had to be different from those of Muslims
- if struck by a Muslim they could not strike back
- they could not employ Muslims
- their houses and tombs could not be *higher* than those of Muslims (the graves had to be level with the ground so people could walk on them)
- they could not learn or be taught the Qur'an
- their sworn testimony was not admissible in Islamic courts
- Jews had to stand in the presence of any Muslim as a show of respect
- they had to accommodate any Muslim traveler for three days free of charge
- and they had to wear yellow cloth girdles and hats

The Reverend James Parks accurately summarized the facts of Arab and Jewish (and Christian) relations in Jerusalem through the centuries when he wrote, "The legend of favorable treatment of Christians and Jews by Islam out of Koranic tolerance has no support of the last thousand years, apart from the brief period of the Osmalni Sultans. Infidels who strayed into the Arab part of the city were open to abuse and assault. Entry into the compound of the Dome of the Rock was punishable by death."[8]

A historical review of the last thousand years reveals this to be the case—both for Jews and Christians, who shared *dhimmi* status. The Fatimid Caliph (A.D. 996–1020) ordered the destruction of synagogues and churches, and 230 years later both were closed by decree for the duration of the Mameluk period (1250–1516). In 1514, Muslim authorities sealed the gate in the eastern wall of the Temple Mount—also known as the Golden Gate or the Gate of Mercy. This

The Eastern Gate of the Temple Mount, with Muslim-sealed entrance and Muslim cemetery. The Hebrew graffiti on the gate reads, "Come Messiah, Israel is waiting!"

Photo by Paul Streber

was done to prevent Christians from entering by the route Christ supposedly took in His triumphal entry into the city, and also to prevent the coming Jewish Messiah from entering through that same gate. Not only was the gate sealed, but a Muslim cemetery was placed in front of the gate—an act of defilement for a Jewish sacred site and something which Jews are forbidden to enter (or they would incur ritual impurity). From the Mameluk period to the nineteenth century, Jews under Muslim rule were kept in great poverty. Even when the Jewish population came to outnumber that of the Muslims in Jerusalem (as it did from 1818 onward), reports continued to be heard about Muslim injustice. One such report, by Karl Marx (infamous author of *Das Kapital*), which appeared in the *International Herald Tribune* on April 15, 1854, stated this: "The sedentary population of Jerusalem numbers about 15,000 souls, of whom 4,000 are Mus-

Jewish people praying in the narrow area of access at the Western Wall prior to 1967. What is now an open plaza was previously covered with Arab houses and buildings.

Photo by Wilfried Bullinger

lims and 8,000 are Jews. Nothing equals the misery and suffering of the Jews who are the constant object of Muslim oppression and intolerance."

One of the most intense periods of Arab persecution of the Jewish people took place during the British Mandate years (1917–1948). The first anti-Jewish riots in Jerusalem began in 1920, and by 1922, when Jerusalem Mufti Haj Amin el-Husseini took power, he orchestrated continuous Jewish oppression. Husseini, who was the uncle of the late Palestinian Authority Jerusalem administrator Faisal Husseini, and is related to Yasser Arafat (on his mother's side), allied himself with Adolf Hitler and planned with the Nazi SS to head a German-Arab force to exterminate the Jews of Palestine. He also initiated a terrorist campaign against Jewish worship at the Temple Mount—a campaign upon which the Palestinians' present-day conflict is modeled. By 1927, the Muslim attacks on Jews praying at the Western Wall had intensified and turned into widespread rioting by Muslims throughout the country. The riots climaxed with the massacres of the Jewish communities of Hebron and Safed.

In 1930, the British recognized the Muslim claim to sovereignty over the Western Wall (yet allowed Jewish access for prayers) and imposed a list of restrictions on the Jews at the site that might "disturb" Muslims, such as blowing the shofar and wearing striped clothing. In 1936 the establishment of the Arab Higher Committee, under the auspices of the Jerusalem Mufti, incited increased Muslim rioting against the Jews that eventually led in 1939 to an Arab revolt that resulted in the loss of 10,000 lives (500 among the Jewish community). And as the world entered into World War II, the British, wanting to build an Arab alliance against the Axis powers (as in World War I), supported Arab objections against the Jews. This led them to limit Jewish immigration through the notorious White

Papers, thus making it difficult, if not impossible, for Jewish refugees in Europe to escape to Palestine and avoid the Nazi death camps.

In the mid-1940s, when the United Nations presented its partition proposal, which called for the establishment of a Jewish state alongside a larger Arab one, Arabs began an all-out attack on Jews in Jerusalem. During 1947–1948, they blew up apartment buildings and mining roads, ambushed Jewish convoys, and isolated the city of Jerusalem by cutting off access to the Jews. This siege of Jerusalem threatened the entire Jewish population of the city with starvation as well as slaughter. By the end of the siege's first week alone, 105 Jews were killed. Then there was the armistice agreement signed with Jordan after the War of Independence (1948–1949), which the Jordanians violated, banning Jews from access to East Jerusalem, which contained the Jewish sites such as the Western Wall, Hadassah Hospital, the Hebrew University campus, and the Mount of Olives cemetery.

To better understand the history which the present generation of Jews cannot forget and which affects their decision "to share" the city, we must focus on the recent period when Jerusalem was previously partitioned.

How Did Jews and Arabs Get Along When Jerusalem Was Previously Partitioned?

From 1949 to 1967, Jerusalem was divided, and Israeli Jews and Jordanian Arabs lived in separate parts of the city, which were, of course, in separate countries. Still, the animosity of Arabs toward Jews continued unabated. One reason for this is that even though the War of Independence had ended with an armistice, the Jordanians did not honor it and continued to treat Israel as an enemy that had no right to exist. In fact, it is the fallout from this period of

Jerusalem's history that most argues against redividing the city today.

We can gain much insight into the problem by looking in more detail at the events that led up to and included this period of partition. Prior to May 1948, Jerusalem existed as an undivided city, as had always been the case from the beginning of its history. However, in the final days of the British Mandate, the United Nations proposed Resolution 181 to partition the city into two states—one Jewish, and one Arab. This document was to have established Jerusalem as a *corpus separatum*—an international regime to be administered by the United Nations. The Jews of Palestine accepted the terms of the resolution as the price of statehood, but the Arabs rejected it (incidentally, this same proposal resurfaced in modern-day negotiations, but this time *with* Arab support!). The Arab nations then launched "a war of extermination and a momentous massacre," as Azzam Pasha, then secretary-general of the Arab League, expectantly called it. The war began on May 15, 1948, and by May 28, the poorly defended Jewish East Jerusalem had fallen to Jordanian troops.

For the next 19 years the city was divided between east and west. It was dangerous for Jews to be near the dividing line that ran through the city because snipers fired continually at Jews passing by on the Jewish side of the line. In 1954 alone, nine people were killed and 55 wounded by sniper fire. The need for protection forced the Jewish citizens in West Jerusalem to erect unsightly concrete barriers and barbed wire fences along the dividing line. This, of course, made the city look and feel like a prison camp. And, as already mentioned, restrictions reminiscent of those that had previously existed under Muslim rule kept Jews from even visiting the Western Wall, the Jewish cemetery on the Mount of Olives, or any other site in East Jerusalem.

In June 1967, when the Jewish forces recaptured East Jerusalem and returned to the Jewish Quarter, they discovered that everything Jewish had been looted and destroyed. Fifty-eight historic synagogues had been razed to the ground or used as garbage dumps or chicken coops. Jewish graves were found open with bones strewn on the ground (a severe desecration in Judaism) and some 75 percent of the 50,000 gravestones in the ancient Jewish cemetery on the Mount of Olives had been removed and used to build a hotel and to pave a path leading to Jordanian army latrines. What's more, a road had been cut right through the cemetery itself. These acts of desecration to Israeli holy sites are typical of the kinds of things that happened during the previous "Palestinian" occupation during a time of partition.

Is it any wonder, then, that Jews do not believe that things would be any different if they again partitioned the city and relinquished the eastern section (which is more than 60 percent of the city and contains a majority of Jews), with its all-important holy sites and 34 years of Israeli building improvements? An additional reason for not partitioning the city has been the violent attacks by the Palestinians on Jewish areas turned over to Palestinian autonomy as gestures of peace. In each case, synagogues, street signs, Hebrew/Arabic explanatory signs at tourist sites, and anything appearing Jewish has been removed or destroyed. These facts should be weighed carefully before new proposals are made to redivide the city—whether by the Israelis and Palestinians themselves, or by foreign political or religious entities who want to enforce such a division.

Why Do the Palestinians Want a Part of Jerusalem?

The Palestinians contend that the city has always been "divided" because the population of East Jerusalem is and has been Palestinian for centuries. From a practical stand-point, they argue, daily life is completely Arab, and everyone lives and acts as though the Jews and Israel do not exist. This, however, is totally untrue, as any visitor to this part of the city can testify. There is no doubt that an Arab presence is evident, but far from ignoring Israel's existence, the benefits of living in its democratic society are everywhere to be seen. What's more, the majority of the population of East Jerusalem is not Palestinian, but Israeli, and major Israeli institutions dominate this part of the city, such as Hadassah Hospital, one of the largest and most advanced in the Middle East (which treats Palestinians), and the Hebrew University on Mount Scopus, which houses thousands of students. In the Old City itself, only *one* quarter of its four quarters is Arab Muslim (although the Christian quarter also contains Arab Christians).

Too, while the Palestinians are demanding a part of Jerusalem, their ultimate objective is to have *all* of the city! Yasser Arafat declared exactly that on September 19, 1993: "Our first goal is the liberation of all occupied terri-tories...and the establishment of a Palestinian state whose capital is Jerusalem. The agreement we arrived at is not a complete solution....it is only the basis for an interim solu-tion and the forerunner to a final settlement, which must be based on complete withdrawal from all occupied Pales-tinian lands, especially holy Jerusalem."[9] Arafat said that less than a week after the signing of the Declaration of Principles, which launched the now-failed peace process. In effect, Arafat was reassuring the 19 foreign ministers whom he addressed that he was still committed to the original PLO commitment to a complete removal of Israel from the Land. Even though the matter of Jerusalem's status was then to be tabled for the next five years, Arafat continued to contend that peace was not possible unless the Palestinians had complete sovereignty over Jerusalem

The Temple Mount and Western Wall after the 1967 war and return of East Jerusalem to Israel. In the foreground can be seen the newly expanded Western Wall plaza that allows for larger crowds of Jewish worshipers. At this point in time, no Arabs were on the Temple Mount.
Photo courtesy of Israel Government Press Office

and the city was the administrative center of a Palestinian state. One of Arafat's frequent boasts was (and is), "Soon the Palestinian flag will fly on the walls, the minarets, and the cathedrals of Jerusalem." So as to also make clear his intention toward the Temple Mount, Arafat later added, "I will design my own house—not in Jericho, but in Jerusalem. I remember living there with my uncle near the Wailing Wall."[10]

Arafat's memory is apparently tainted with thoughts of vengeance, since his uncle's house, like all Arab homes in the Mograhabi district, was bulldozed by order of Teddy Kollek immediately after the Six-Day War in order to widen the Western Wall plaza so it could accommodate larger numbers of Jewish worshipers. Arafat's ambition to control completely the Temple Mount is likewise evident from the huge photographic mural of the Dome of the Rock that covers the wall behind his office desk or appears in the background of posters displaying his portrait. That the Palestinians want all of Jerusalem is apparent from yet other statements their leaders have made: "Our Palestinian nation will never forget Jerusalem, and will sacrifice half of its number to sanctify the holy name of Allah for the Arab, Palestinian, Islamic, and Christian character of occupied Jerusalem."[11]

"We Palestinians will take over everything, including all of Jerusalem....We plan to eliminate the State of Israel and establish a Palestinian state."[12] "Everything within the Palestinian area [in Jerusalem] will be subject to Palestinian sovereignty, no matter who lives there."[13]

The Palestinian objective of removing Israel from the Land is vividly portrayed by the land boundaries that appear on the logos of all seven major branches of the PLO. At the center of each of these logos is the outline of the Palestinian state, which clearly includes all the territory west of the Jordan River, including all of Israel. The reality of this has been stated by Nayef Hawatmeh, leader of the Democratic Front for the Liberation of Palestine, the third largest PLO organization: "The popular revolution in Palestine will continue the struggle to expel the Zionist occupation from all Palestinian Arab soil, from the [Jordan] River to the [Mediterranean] Sea."[14] On March 30, 2001 Arafat repeated his vision: "Our people will continue the Al-Aqsa uprising until we raise the Palestinian flag in every mosque and church and on the walls of Jerusalem."[15] This objective, in part, was realized for one brief part of a day during the funeral of the Palestinian administrator for Jerusalem, Faisal Husseini. The Damascus Gate was draped with Palestinian flags, as were the walls of Jerusalem, and Palestinians were hysterical with the feeling that their dream had come true—if only for a day!

Yet there is no doubt Arafat intends for the Palestinians to control every Muslim,

Palestinian crowds at the Damascus Gate for the funeral of Faisal Husseini.
Photo courtesy of Netanel Doron, *Nai* magazine (Israel)

Jewish, and Christian aspect of the city. That is one reason the peace negotiations have proven so difficult—without the realization of this goal, no short-term solution will be satisfactory. Interestingly, the Palestinians recognize that, in order to conquer Jerusalem, strategic portions of the rest of the country must first be possessed or controlled. This fact is so basic that it was included in a textbook on Jerusalem prepared by the Board of Jewish Education for use in Jewish schools. This textbook points out the tactics used by the Romans when they captured Jerusalem in A.D. 70:

> The Romans did not proceed directly to the conquest of Jerusalem. On the contrary, they left Jerusalem to the last. First they fought for Galilee and Judea, and only after they had conquered the country was Jerusalem invested. *For it is impossible to hold Jerusalem unless the whole of the country is held*[16] (emphasis added).

This has been the operational objective of the PLO's "phased plan," and the reason the conflict has moved from discussions about the status of Jerusalem to the Al-Aqsa Intifada, which no longer speaks of "dividing Jerusalem" but of "destroying Israel."

Why Do the Israelis Say the City Cannot Be Redivided?

The redivision of Jerusalem and its establishment as the Palestinian capital is a prospect that has been popularly rejected by the majority of Israelis. Jerusalem Mayor Ehud Olmert has gone on record with his reason why Jerusalem can only be significant as a unified city:

> Look, for Arafat, Jerusalem is a negative element. It's a negative driving force. What he wants, he wants to

deny us of certain things. That's what drives him. That's what inspires him. Jerusalem has never been important for the Moslems and the Palestinians as such. It has never been a capital for any Moslem or Arab nation, ever, even though they controlled the city of Jerusalem for 12 centuries. So, it has always been a negative force. It's what he can deny us that drives him; what he can take from us, which inspires him; what he can change against us, which is very important for him in this context. Therefore, the view I hold of Jerusalem is fundamentally different from that of Arafat in the sense that for me it's a positive force, it's a positive place. It's the realization of all the dreams that we have had for 2,000 years. Every single day we have been praying and crying and dreaming and dying for the city of Jerusalem—for the return back to the heart of Jewish existence to the place where we have started our lives as a nation. And, it can't be a divided city. You don't make peace by dividing cities. You don't break cities when you want to make peace you unite cities. You destroy walls you don't build walls. So, for me this is Jerusalem. It is a realization of a dream. It is the focus of everything that we have been aspiring for all our lives. I love the city of Jerusalem. For me, it is a source of great inspiration."[17]

For nationalist and religious Jews the issue is simple. Jerusalem is the place God chose (Psalm 132:13-14). God commanded King David to conquer the city, and there is no such thing as a *partial* conquest. God demanded total victory over Israel's enemies and total possession of all of the Land that He had promised. There was no other way to fulfill His will. What's more, God has promised in the Bible that in the future, Jerusalem and the Temple Mount will be fully controlled by the Jewish people:

> And it shall come about that in the last days, the mountain of the house of the Lord [the Temple

Mount] will be established as the chief of the mountains, and will be raised above the hills; and all the
nations will stream to it and many peoples will come
and say, "Come, let us go up to the mountain of the
house of the lord, to the house of the God of Jacob;
that He may teach us concerning His ways, and that
we may walk in His paths." For the law will go forth
from Zion, and the word of the Lord from Jerusalem
(Isaiah 2:2-3).

From this passage it is evident that the Bible's vision for
the future is quite different than that of the Palestinians—
who want a non-Jewish Jerusalem with an Islamic-
controlled Temple Mount adorned with mosques, from
which "the Qur'an will go forth from *Al-Quds!*"

Why Can't the Israelis and Palestinians Share the Temple Mount?

The possibility of "sharing" the Temple Mount is
unthinkable to the Palestinian Authority, the Islamic Waqf,
and the entire Arab Muslim world. It is likewise opposed
by almost all religious Jews as well as by secular Israelis.
Israel's chief rabbi Yisrael Lau, representing the religious
Jews, has stated, "Nobody in government has the mandate
for concessions on the Temple Mount."[18] In like manner,
Israeli cabinet minister Roni Milo, representing the secular
element, has declared, "The Temple Mount is an asset to
the Jewish people, without which we weaken the basis for
our very right to be here."[19] There have been some who
have wondered why the Israelis and Palestinians can't
solve their problems by allowing a Jewish Temple to be
built on the Temple Mount beside the Al-Aqsa Mosque or
the Dome of the Rock. In fact, such a scenario has been
envisioned by Christian prophecy writers, who suggest
that a shared site will be the ultimate achievement of the
Antichrist, who would use his access to the site to inaugu-

rate the worship of himself as god. There is even a Christian movie that depicts such an outcome.[20] Yet, a number of factors argue against such a scenario ever being realized.

First, Orthodox Jews contend that the Third Temple must occupy the exact same location that the previous Temples occupied. This is because that site alone was consecrated by the presence of the Shekinah glory of God, which, according to rabbinic teaching, never left the spot. If the Al-Aqsa Mosque or the Dome of the Rock stands on that site today, then the structure would have to be removed in order to build the next Temple.

Second, even if it were proved that neither Islamic structures occupied the sacred spot, both Islam and Judaism fervently contend that the *entire* Temple Mount platform (as well as everything beneath it) is sacred to their religions. (This, in fact, was a main point of contention during the Camp David II Summit. Arafat would not concede even the buried remains of the Temple to Israel.) For the Jews, this would mean that before the Temple could be rebuilt anywhere on the platform, the entire Temple Mount would have to be ritually purified. Foreign structures, especially pagan structures like the mosques and shrines of Islam, which are considered abominations in Judaism, would have to be destroyed before the Jewish ceremonial system could function. This same exclusivity of the site is a fundamental tenet in modern Islam. Muslims cannot allow non-Muslims to desecrate their worship by their presence. It is for this reason that no Jewish prayers have ever been permitted on the Temple Mount while the site has been under Islamic jurisdiction.

Third, the sharing of religious holy sites is not a political issue that can be negotiated by two representative leaders, even though that has been attempted up through the Camp David II Summit. This point has been made clear by Palestinian leader Jeris Soudah:

Everybody in Saudi Arabia has a 100 percent right to vote yes or no about what happens on the Temple Mount, and they are not going to vote yes. All the Muslim world is involved here....The Arabs and the Palestinians have no problem with dividing the city [of Jerusalem] between the east and the west. The east was the Arab side and the west was the Israeli side....the Temple Mount is on the east side and that is why we cannot negotiate on this."[21]

The people of Israel can also vote in regard to what happens to the Temple Mount, and they are united in their determination to keep the Temple Mount under Israeli sovereignty.

Because there can be no compromise on the Temple Mount, the only way one of the religions will gain exclusive access is by denying the other and enforcing a *de facto* sovereignty. This is, in fact, what the Islamic Waqf has done under the Palestinian Mufti Ikrama Sabri (see chapter 15). So, even though Israel has never relinquished its sovereign control over the site as part of East Jerusalem (now part of united Jerusalem), it has been careful not to confront the Palestinian Authority about its recent seizure of the site. This bold new assertion of sovereignty by the Palestinians is forcing Israel to a confrontation in the near future, even as America and the West are pressing for a cessation of conflict between them.

And there's still more to consider: To fully understand the issues that affect the question of Jerusalem, we must concentrate on the most contested area of the city, the Temple Mount. In the next several chapters we will do this together, continuing our search for the facts behind the headlines.

CHAPTER 13

What Is the Trouble with the Temple Mount?

I am sounding the alarm against the Jewish scheme, which aims to establish the Solomon Temple in the place of Al-Aqsa Mosque, after removing the mosque....Delivering holy Jerusalem from the monster represented by this continuous and advancing... threat of Judaization is a duty imposed upon all of us by Allah.[1]
—PLO CHAIRMAN YASSER ARAFAT

Al-Aqsa [the Temple Mount] is not bound by any legal or political decision [of the Israelis].[2]
—PALESTINIAN MUFTI IKRAMA SABRI

Muslims all over the world are asked to move as quickly as possible in order to protect their shrine and to support the Palestinian people in their resistance against the Zionist aggression on the Holy site.[3]
—HAMAS, A TERRORIST ORGANIZATION

In the previous chapter we saw that radical Islam has global objectives, and that terrorism is the means used to achieve those objectives. At the heart of all this is the dispute over the Temple Mount in Jerusalem, which has served as one of the greatest catalysts for Islamic *jihad*.

The Temple Mount has today become the centerpiece of the political and religious conflict in the Middle East—a conflict that has forced America to try and force a resolution because of its explosive potential to unite the Islamic world against Israel and all who give it support. Yet the conflicting claims over the site confound not only politicians, but also most people who have little knowledge about its history. How has such an old place created so many new problems? Why is there so much disagreement over the Temple Mount? Let's begin by looking at what the Palestinians are saying.

What Are the Palestinians Saying About the Temple Mount?

As the Camp David Summit negotiations drew near, Yasser Arafat made it clear that the deciding point would be the Temple Mount. In an interview with CNN's Christiane Amanpour at the end of 2000, Arafat stated that peace will come down to what happens with the holy sites in the Old City of Jerusalem, where the Temple Mount is located. Since that interview the Intifada has moved onto the Temple Mount, and both Islamic clerics as well as spokesmen for the Palestinian Authority have repeatedly asserted that the ambition of the Israeli government has always been to destroy the Muslim mosques on the Mount and rebuild the Temple. This assertion is nothing new. Back in 1968, Sheikh Nadim Al-Jisr, a Lebanese member of the Islamic Research Academy, stated, "The Zionist philosophers who thought out the creation of the Jewish state had really deceived themselves when they stressed the appeal of religious propaganda, thought to be most enchanting to every Jew, to whom it was said that he would revive the Kingdom of David and Solomon and re-establish the Temple...."[4] Palestinian revisionists claim that Jewish statements to the contrary are simply Zionist attempts to "Judaize Jerusalem" by creating a fictitious Jewish history in the city. In light of this conviction Hasan Tahboub, head of the PLO-backed Supreme Muslim Council, stated, "We expect the Israelis to give us back these holy places....We believe in freedom of religion, but Jews don't have rights there because these are our places."[5]

Other examples of public statements by Palestinian Authority figures include that of Yasir Abed-Rabbo, a senior aide to Yasser Arafat and one of the leaders of Arafat's team of negotiators with Israel. Abed-Rabbo stated this in an interview with the French newspaper *Le Monde* on September 25, 2000 (as reported in the Israeli daily *Ma'ariv*, September 26, 2000): "There never was a Jewish Temple in Jerusalem." In like manner, the official Palestinian Authority newspaper *Al-Hayat Al-Jadida* reported (August 12, 2000) that at the recent Camp David talks, Arafat told President Clinton, "I will not allow it to be written of me that I confirmed the existence of the so-called Temple underneath the mountain [the Temple Mount]." The Palestinian Authority Ministry of Information said in a December 10, 1997 press release that "there is no tangible evidence of any Jewish traces/remains in the old city of Jerusalem and its immediate vicinity." Palestinian Authority Ministry of Information official Walid Awad said, "Jerusalem is not a Jewish city, despite the biblical myth implanted in some minds....There is no tangible evidence of Jewish existence from the so-called 'Temple Mount Era.'...The location of the Temple Mount is in question...it might be in Jericho or somewhere else" (*Independent Media Review and Analysis*, December 25, 1996).

The worst statement of historical revisionism I have yet read came from an Egyptian study published in a book issued by the Ain Shams University Middle East Research Center. The study said the Islamic Al-Aqsa Mosque in Jerusalem was built 2,000 years *before* Solomon. That's a neat trick, for Islam's founder wasn't born until 1,500 years *after* Solomon; there were no Muslims in Jerusalem until six years *after* Muhammad's death; and history shows that the Caliph Abd El-Wahd built the Al-Aqsa Mosque 80 years *after* that!

Of course, the Palestinian Authority statements apply not only to Jerusalem's Temple Mount, but to all the Jewish holy sites in Israel. Consider, for example, this statement from Arafat: "Abraham was neither Jewish nor a Hebrew, but was simply an Iraqi. The Jews have no right to claim authority of the Tomb of the Patriarchs in Hebron, Abraham's resting-place, as a synagogue. Rather, the whole building should be a mosque"[6] (*Jerusalem Report*, December 26, 1996). Then there was the Palestinian Authority official who said that "Rachel's Tomb in Bethlehem is the traditional tomb of the Cushite servant of Muhammad" (*Ha'aretz*, October 9, 1996).

On February 20, 2001, the Palestinian Authority-appointed Mufti of Jerusalem, Sheikh Ikrama Sabri, issued a religious decree stating that the Western Wall of the Temple Mount is Islamic property that has no connection to Jewish history. "No stone of the Western Wall has any connection to Hebrew history," Sabri asserted in his *fatwa*.[7] To Muslims, the Wall is the western wall of the Al-Aqsa Mosque. As such, he said, it should not be called the Western Wall or the Wailing Wall but the Al-Buraq Wall (the name of Muhammad's mystical horse, which Islamic tradition says was tied to the wall during the Night Journey).

The Palestinian Authority Mufti's view of the Western Wall is not new; Yasser Arafat and his aides have made similar claims in the past. For example, Arafat once declared, "That is not the Western Wall at all, but a Moslem shrine" (*Ma'ariv*, October 11, 1996), and Palestinian Authority Religious Affairs Minister Hassan Tahboob stated, "The Al-Buraq Wall [the Western Wall] is Muslim property and it is part of the Al-Aqsa Mosque, of course" (*Independent Media Review and Analysis*, November 23, 1997). Muslim history books teach that "Jews come to pray at *Al-Buraq* Wall" [the Western or Wailing Wall], which in Islam is associated only with Muhammad. For this reason the vigil of Jews at the Wall 24 hours a day must be confusing to Palestinians. One of those apparently confused Palestinians is the spiritual leader of the Al-Aqsa Mosque, Sheik Muhammad Hussein. When a reporter friend of mine asked why Jews pray at the Western Wall if it isn't a retaining wall of the Temple Mount, he replied: "I don't know. Some people pray to the moon. Some people pray to Jupiter. I don't know why the Jews pray there!"[8]

However, most Palestinians *do* have an answer—the same answer given to most questions about the Temple Mount: The only reason Jews want to pray there is because they want to destroy the Islamic mosques and rebuild the Temple. And for Palestinians, the *Haram* (Temple Mount) and the Al-Buraq Wall (Western Wall) are not up for negotiation. The Palestinian Mufti Ikrama Sabri, speaking before the Camp David II Summit (at which it was rumored the Israelis would trade sovereignty over the Temple Mount if they could retain sovereignty over the Western Wall), stated, "The Al-Buraq Wall is a part of the Al-Aqsa Mosque. The Jews have no relation to it, whether or not a decision to expropriate it was made."

Palestinians also explain away any archaeological remains that Jews identify with the Temple by the process of simple negation. For example, Jeris Soudah, a Palestinian Authority leader who works with Yasser Arafat, said,

It has not been proven that the Temple was ever located there [the Temple Mount]....Do the Jews have proof that this is the site of their holy place?...There are the arches and everything [beneath the Temple Mount], but are these things from a Jewish Temple being there? How do we know that these are not Muslim or Christian constructions?...Maybe there are certain pieces that prove that *something* Jewish was there. But there is no absolute proof that a Jewish Temple ever stood there.[9]

In conversations I've had with Palestinians, the Palestinians have conveniently labeled every archaeological discovery either "Islamic" or "pre-Islamic," thereby avoiding any possible association of the artifacts or structures with a *particular* pre-Islamic (Jewish) culture. Therefore, a Palestinian Authority Information press release could state this as a fact: "The archaeology of Jerusalem is diverse—excavations in the Old City and the areas surrounding it revealed Umayyad Islamic palaces, Roman ruins, Armenian ruins and others, but nothing Jewish. Outside of what is mentioned/written in the Old and New Testaments, there is no tangible evidence of any Jewish traces/remains in the Old City of Jerusalem and its immediate vicinity."[10] Of course this information failed to mention that most every non-Jewish archaeological artifact they mention as uncovered in Jerusalem, including the Islamic ones, was made by and identified by the same Jews who have excavated and published a wealth of *Jewish* discoveries!

Given the Palestinian view of the Temple Mount, it is possible to understand the negative reaction that Palestinian Muslims have when non-Muslims enter into "their" holy site. However, it's important to recognize what the Palestinians are actually saying about these incursions and their relationship to the present uprising and avowed war with the Israeli government and its supporters, including the United States.

What Are the Palestinians Saying About Incursions onto the Temple Mount?

Every incursion onto or around the area of the Al-Aqsa (Temple Mount) by non-Muslims has been interpreted by the Palestinian Authority as part of an orchestrated plot by the Israeli government to destroy the Islamic structures at the site and replace them with a rebuilt Jewish Temple. The first instance of such an accusation by the Waqf came only two years after the Israeli government had granted custody of the site to the Waqf after its capture in the Six-Day War. The first occasion for the charge was when someone intentionally set fire to a wooden pulpit in the Al-Aqsa on August 21, 1969. The perpetrator was an Australian tourist named Dennis Rohan, who was a member of the Worldwide Church of God, an organization founded by Herbert W. Armstrong. This organization, which evangelical Christians considered to be a cult (until some recent changes were made), was active in teaching about Bible prophecy and how it relates to Israel. Rohan had studied Hebrew at an Israeli kibbutz and, after several days in Jerusalem, came to believe he was chosen by God to destroy the Muslim mosques so that the Temple could be rebuilt. Bribing a guard at the Al-Aqsa Mosque, he gained access to the site before opening hours under

The Al-Aqsa Mosque burning from a fire set by a cultist who wanted to see the Temple rebuilt. Muslim officials blamed the Israeli government for the fire, believing that the government wanted to help destroy the mosque so the Temple could be rebuilt.
Photo courtesy of World of the Bible Ministries, Inc.

the pretense of taking a photo. He then set fire to a wooden pulpit brought to Jerusalem by the Turkish monarch Saladin—a pulpit that commemorated his defeat of the Crusaders.

The symbolism was significant: a Christian burning the very object that marked an end of Christian rule over Jerusalem and the Temple Mount would signify the end of Muslim rule.

The unstable Rohan, later judged a paranoid schizophrenic by Israeli judges, had acted out his delusion alone. Nevertheless, despite every protest by the Israeli government that it had nothing to do with the incident and the subsequent sentencing of Rohan to 15 years of imprisonment, the official report of an Arab investigation team still concluded that the act was a "Zionist crime" and that it had been perpetrated by the Israeli government. Their convoluted argument was that since the Israeli government was in charge of the site, no one could have committed such an act without its permission. Because of the lack of democratic structure in the Palestinian Authority (and in Islamic dictatorships), Muslims simply cannot comprehend people or groups acting independently of the government. For example, even while Israeli firemen were fighting the blaze at Al-Aqsa, Muslim leaders met and accused the Jews of spraying gasoline on the flames to hasten the burning and claimed that the Israeli City Hall had ordered the water supply cut off to the site to keep the fire going!

A similar misunderstanding was evidenced when Arab delegates obtained a United Nations censure against the Israeli government for a riot that had taken place at the Temple Mount in October 1990. The riot was instigated by the Temple Mount Faithful organization, headed by an Orthodox Jew named Gershon Salomon. This organization has no connections with the Israeli government. Yet Adnan Husseini, the director of the Waqf, stated that

Palestinians believe there is a connection between so-called "extremists groups" like the Temple Mount Faithful (TMF) and the Israeli government:

> We see no difference between these two groups and the government. We consider the government and these two groups as one body. The government leaves these persons working....What the Jews want there is a pure Jewish country. If they want to fight us, they will have to fight Islam....They [the TMF] want to convert the *Haram* into another place. The stone [cornerstone] symbolizes that they have started to build the Third Temple. The stone is pointing forward to something more, which is the Temple. That is why everybody wanted to protect the *Haram* last year. And the government says, "We are a democracy, we can't shut his [Gershon Salomon's] mouth."[11]

Today, Muslims have become more and more outspoken in claiming that there is a "Zionist conspiracy" behind every incursion of Islamic sacred spaces. For example, on August 20, 2000, to commemorate the Al-Aqsa fire started by Dennis Rohan, the Department of Islamic Relations of the Islamic Resistance Movement (Hamas) made the following statement. Note how they accuse Israel of a plot to destroy the Al-Aqsa Mosque by linking together the acts of Dennis Rohan, Jewish religious nationalists, and the secular Israeli government's negotiations at Camp David (I have left the original wording intact, though it reads awkwardly in places):

> Our souls and blood will be sacrificed for the Aqsa on the 31st Anniversary of burning the Aqsa Mosque. To the Palestinian Authority people: To the Arab and Islamic Nation: Ever since the Zionist Dennis Rohan committed his crime on Thursday 21 August 1969 and Zionist Jewish spite against the Aqsa Mosque was growing and hoping to destroy the whole lot of it after

the fire destroyed most of Salahuddin pulpit, which was installed after liberating Al-Quds from 90 years of Crusader occupation in 1187 A.D. Incidents are accelerating these days and that acceleration bears dangers against the Aqsa Mosque as the Jewish threats and violation of its sanctity increase and as Jewish elevation daily grows to the extent that it is about to assume power in the strongest state on earth. Furthermore, calls are voiced out loud calling for demolishing the Aqsa and building the alleged temple in its place!

Tomorrow falls the anniversary of that ugly crime to remind Muslims with what happened to their Mosque and the possible destruction that could target it, God forbid, in the event silence towards our enemies' conspiracies persisted. During the recent Camp David summit's discussions, the enemy's premier Ehud Barak demanded the establishment of a Jewish synagogue inside the holy Aqsa Mosque's yards....In line with the accelerating campaigns to Judaize the city, mayor of the so-called Jerusalem municipality Ehud Ulmert said on 9 August that after 33 years of preventing Jews to practice their right of prayers in the Aqsa, today work must be done to actualize that right....In a serious development, members of the Temple Mount Trustees accompanied by other fanatic Jews tried to enter the Aqsa Mosque through Bab Al-Maghareba on Thursday 10 August. They marched in tumultuous demonstrations chanting anti-Arab and anti-Muslim slogans. They demanded the construction of their alleged temple in place of the Aqsa Mosque on the anniversary of what they consider the destruction of the two temples, which fell on that same day. They carried the foundation stone of what they called their temple and washed it in Ein Silwan while reiterating, "Bring down the Mosque over their [Muslim] heads!!"

We urge the nation's religious scholars to be at the forefront of the lines in face of the Zionist danger and to spread awareness among the Muslim masses about that enemy's aggressive plots against the Muslims' first *Qibla,* site of our prophet's ascension to the heavens and third mosque that should be visited in Islam....Let the whole world know that wiping out, demolishing or attacking the Aqsa Mosque would only be possible over the skulls and remains of the whole nation. So when the time of the second (Jewish) mischief in the holy land comes, we will send against you our worshipers to inflict on you utter defeat and enter the Mosque (of Al-Aqsa) as they had entered it before and to devastate the Al-Aqsa Intifada was initiated to defend Palestinian Muslim holy sites against the Zionist State whose ambitions, they claim, are to destroy the mosques and rebuild the Jewish Temple. With such impassioned rhetoric and denunciations against the traditional understanding of Israel's central Sanctuary, we must ask what is the truth about the Temple Mount? With utter destruction whatever they [the Jews] have built in their elevation. [12]

These closing words, "whatever they have built in their elevation," refers to whatever structures (including the Temple) the Israelis are able to erect while they exercise sovereignty over the site. One of the most controversial of these "structures" was the opening of an exit to an underground tunnel beneath the Western Wall of the Temple Mount, which has been a major tourist attraction since its official opening in 1991. The plan to create the tunnel was approved by the Muslim authorities at

Exit tunnel connecting to the Western Wall Tunnel. The opening of this exit tunnel in September 1996 led to Palestinian rioting that continued for a week and brought about 58 deaths.

Photo by Paul Streber

the time that Rabin was prime minister. However, with Rabin's death and the change in government, the project was delayed.

On September 25, 1996, prime minister Benjamin Netanyahu ordered the exit to be opened just before the surge of tourism that comes with the Jewish high holidays. In response, Muslim authorities instigated a riot and Yasser Arafat declared to the international media that the Israelis were attacking the mosques in an attempt to destroy them and rebuild the Temple. Even after Jerusalem Mayor Ehud Olmert stated that this was "nonsense" and the government and archaeologists demonstrated that the exit, which was not near the site, could not possibly endanger the mosques, the rioting continued for a week, and more than 58 persons were killed. Muslims continue to believe that the opening of the exit was an attempt by the Israeli government to destroy their mosques and rebuild the Temple. One Islamic website made this remark about an illustration that is in the Western Wall Tunnel: "In that picture there is no record of any Islamic holy sites, and that includes the Al-Aqsa Mosque, clearly reflecting the actual plans to destroy the Al-Aqsa Mosque and to build the 'Temple' in its place."[13] However, the only pictures in the Western Wall Tunnel are those of the Second Temple, which was destroyed over 620 years before any mosque existed on the Temple Mount!

The Palestinian Muslims protest most the incursions carried out by Orthodox Jewish nationalist groups who want to see the Jewish Temple rebuilt. Of these groups, the Temple Mount Faithful is feared above all others. This organization, which receives permission from the government to hold symbolic demonstrations annually outside the gates of the Old City yet near to the Temple Mount, openly denounces the Muslim presence on the Temple Mount and proclaims the soon rebuilding of the Temple on the site. When I interviewed Palestinian Mufti Ikrama Sabri about an Associated Press news release in which Yasser Arafat was shown holding a photo with the Dome of the Rock removed and the Temple in its place, the Mufti replied that he had given Arafat the picture to show the world the incitement of the Jews against the Islamic mosques. He went

Palestinian Mufti of Jerusalem Ikrama Sabri, the chief Muslim cleric in charge of Islam's holy places on the Temple Mount.
Photo by Randall Price

Poster of Jewish Temple in place of the Muslim Dome of the Rock, which Yasser Arafat showed to Mufti Ikrama Sabri and led to Sabri's statement to the media that no Jewish Temple had ever existed on the site.
Photo courtesy of National Diamond Center, Jerusalem

on to explain that since no Temple ever existed there, the Jewish obsession over the Temple Mount is merely an attempt to legitimize the Zionist occupation of Jerusalem.

On July 29, 2001, the Temple Mount Faithful (with government permission) brought a cornerstone for the Third Temple to an outer gate of the Old City in a *Tisha B'Av* ceremony (a national commemoration of the destruction of the Second Temple). Palestinian leaders had warned the Israeli government that the act would provoke clashes similar to those that erupted after Ariel Sharon's visit at the Al-Aqsa Mosque. The Waqf called on their faithful to come to the shrine to protect the mosque compound "with their bodies" if the cornerstone was brought in (which the Israeli authorities had assured them would not happen). Nevertheless, on the day of the event, the Muslim Mufti used the loudspeakers on the Temple Mount to proclaim, *"Allahu akbar!"* ("God is great!"). This incited the Palestinians on the site to throw rocks from the Temple Mount onto the Jews praying at the Western Wall below. Demonstrations also spread across the West Bank, with hundreds of Palestinians in Nablus burning effigies of Sharon and the Temple, and burning Israeli and U.S. flags. (Incidentally, models of the Temple were also burned on the first anniversary of the Al-Aqsa Intifada, September 28, 2001). Although no deaths resulted from the demonstrations, the Arab world condemned the Israeli government in the strongest terms and called on the international community to intercede. Here are some of the reactions that came from Islamic organizations or countries, beginning with the Palestinian Authority:

- An official from Orient House, once the unofficial Palestinian headquarters in Jerusalem, said, "We consider the storming of *Haram al-Sharif* and the occupation of Al-Aqsa Mosque compound a provocative step that will increase tensions in the region."

- Palestinian lawmaker Hanan Ashrawi said the police decision to storm Al-Aqsa was "an act of supreme provocation."

- Yasser Arafat's top aide Nabil Abu Rudeina said the Israeli government bore full responsibility for the "provocations of radical Jews." "They are playing with fire and will only plunge the region into a religious war. It is a pure provocation and a blatant challenge to Arabs, the Muslim world, and the international community."

- In Cairo, Arab League Secretary-General Amr Moussa said, "The developments which the Aqsa Mosque compound is witnessing are serious and indicate the extent of [Israeli] bad intentions. Bad intentions will have serious consequences."

- In Kuwait, the government warned that the Jewish ceremony was a provocation and flagrant challenge to Muslims and called on the international community to "take measures to block such a serious provocative act."

- In Manama, the cabinet condemned "this provocative act, which represents a challenge to the feelings of the Arab and Muslim peoples, and a violation of international law."

- The Bahraini government called on the international community to "protect the sacred place of Al-Quds [Jerusalem]," and "to stop Israel from carrying out its plans."

- In Sanaa, the foreign ministry condemned "this ignoble act which strikes at the sanctuaries of Islam and represents a serious provocation and a flagrant challenge to Arabs and Muslims."

- The official Syrian newspaper *Ath Thawra* (in the city of Damascus) said, "The green light given on Wednesday by Israel's Supreme Court for the ceremony which took place at one of the gates of the Old City" is a "dangerous provocation" of "the feelings of Muslim Arabs, a greater provocation even than Ariel Sharon's." The "laying the cornerstone of the so-called third temple is a blatant violation of international conventions which ban any modification in the structure of the occupied

Palestinians hurl stones at Jews
from atop the Temple Mount.

Photo courtesy of Israel Government
Press Office

Israeli police running for cover
during a Palestinian riot taking
place at the Temple Mount—note
the stones covering the Western
Wall plaza (thrown from the
Temple Mount above at the Jewish
worshipers below) and gas
grenade exploding in the women's
prayer area.

Photo courtesy of Israel
Government Press Office

Israeli police at the Chain Gate entrance prepare to quell a
riot on the Temple Mount.

Photo courtesy of Israel Government Press Office

territories, including historical sites and places of worship," and the ceremony proved "the aggressive intentions of Israel, which wants to intensify its expansionist, racist and terrorist policy by muffling the Arab and Islamic character of the occupied territories, notably Jerusalem."

- The official newspaper of Jordan, *The Jordan Times*, stated that Bahrain, Kuwait, and Yemen were among the nations that joined in the Arab world's denunciation.

Perhaps the most detailed condemnation of the event, and one that again reveals the "conspiracy concept" held by the Muslims, was that issued in a Hamas Islamic Relations Department communique:

Here is the plain statement to men: The Zionist invaders daily prove their suspicious intentions and their devilish plots against the holy Aqsa Mosque. Here they are today laying down what they consider as the foundation stone of their alleged temple in one of the holy city's suburbs, the Maghareba suburb, which is adjacent to the holy Aqsa Mosque. Their project would only be completed with the demolition of the Aqsa Mosque, God forbid....The league of Palestine Ulama has issued a statement addressed to the Arab and Islamic nation denouncing that heinous crime and the flagrant encroachment on Muslims' holy shrines, top amongst them, the holy Aqsa Mosque. The Islamic Resistance movement, Hamas, also issued a statement describing the Zionist decision as a crime that exposes the Jews' scheme to demolish the Aqsa and urged the Arab and Islamic peoples to express their rejection of that notorious plot. We, for our part, appeal to the nation, with its official and popular forces, to rise up in defense of the holy Aqsa Mosque with all possible means...in confrontation with the Zionist enemy.[14]

Throughout this chapter, we've seen what the Palestinians have said about the Jewish Temple and the site of the Temple Mount. We have also looked at how they view what they consider to be incursions into their holy places. Having considered these, let's now examine the historical facts about the Temple Mount so that we can correctly evaluate these sensational assertions.

Chapter 14

What Is the Truth About the Temple Mount?

There is not the smallest indication of the existence of a Jewish temple on this place in the past. In the whole city, there is not even a single stone indicating Jewish history.[1]
—Palestinian Mufti of Jerusalem Sheikh Ikrama Sabri in 2000

This site is one of the oldest in the world. Its sanctity dates from the earliest times. Its identity with the site of Solomon's Temple is beyond dispute.[2]
—Guidebook issued by the Supreme Muslim Council of Jerusalem in 1930

Is the Temple only a myth, as the Palestinian Authority claims? Are Jewish statements to the contrary simply political propaganda aimed at Judaizing Jerusalem so Israel can justify its occupation of Palestinian land? What is the truth about these conflicting claims to the Temple Mount? In order to find the answers, we must consider the historical and religious evidence set forth by both the Israelis and Palestinians.

What Is the Jewish Claim to the Temple Mount?

The Bible attests to the presence of at least two Temples being built on Mount Moriah in Jerusalem. Extrabiblical sources, both Jewish and Gentile, as well as monumental architecture (such as the Arch of Titus' Triumph in Rome), affirm the existence and destruction of the second of these Temples in A.D. 70. For centuries after the Temple's destruction, Jews who had been exiled under Roman and Byzantine edicts would come to the Mount of Olives (which overlooks the Temple Mount) to weep on *Tisha B'Av* over their desolate holy place. And for centuries before the invasion of Islam, Roman, Christian, and pilgrim accounts affirm that this place, and no other, was identified as the site of the Jewish Temple. What's more, Islam itself, when it originally came to this site under the Caliph 'Umar, records that it rediscovered the Rock of Sacrifice that once occupied the Temple's Holy of Holies.

Although no actual traces of the destroyed Temple have been discovered (other than fragments of outer structures in the Temple precinct), such remains are believed to be buried on the eastern side of the Temple Mount, where the Romans threw the bulk of the Temple ruins. Archaeological excavations have verified the location of the Temple Mount. The Mount's topographical setting in relation to David's city and the Ophel agree with the locations cited in ancient literary sources. And nineteenth-century British surveys, explorations, and excavations within the Temple Mount complex identified the location of walls, cisterns, underground tunnels, and other structures that match ancient sources such as Josephus and the Talmud, which describe for us the placements and measurements of the Temple compound.

These explorations established the Western Wall as a retaining wall of the Temple Mount platform. In addition, since 1967 Israeli archaeologists have been able to excavate in the shadow of the Temple Mount and have found abundant material evidence of Israel's presence at the Temple Mount in ancient times. These finds include the remains of the monumental staircase that ascended to the Temple at the southern end of the Temple Mount, the massive colonnaded hallway behind this area (which gave access to the Temple Mount, and which the Muslims have used for centuries), the entrance gates to the Temple Mount, the streets and shops that lined the Second Temple thoroughfare on the western side of the Temple Mount, and numerous pieces of Temple Mount architecture (such as a guard rail atop the Temple walls indicating the place of trumpeting and sections of the *Soreg*, a fence on the Temple Mount that prevented Gentiles from entering the complex). Hebrew inscriptions and reliefs that identify the site as Jewish have also been found (such as depictions of Jewish ritual objects like the Menorah). (For further descriptions and photos, see my book *The Stones Cry Out,* chapter 10: Archaeology and the Temple [Eugene, OR: Harvest House Publishers, 1997].)

These archaeological confirmations of the Jewish presence at the Mount have confirmed without a doubt that the Temple Mount has great significance to Judaism. In this light, Rabbi Pesach Lerner, the executive vice president of the National Council of Young Israel, has asserted, "The Temple Mount is a central Jewish link throughout the ages, throughout the world....Anybody who can say that Jerusalem and the Temple Mount are not the centrality of the Jewish people does not believe in Jewish history."[3] And it might be added: Anybody who does not believe that the Jewish Temple stood on the Temple Mount does not believe in history!

Why Do Muslims Reject Jewish Claims to the Temple Mount?

The Palestinians reject the unambiguous archaeological evidence of the Jewish Temple as simply "pre-Islamic" and "inconclusive." Gaayla Cornfield explains the reasoning behind this when he notes, "Everything lying beneath... [the Dome of the Rock] is...to the Muslim, irrelevant, even the insights of archaeology in the last hundred years, even the results of contemporary excavations being conducted now. Even these, to the descendants of the Moslems who walled up all the historical underground passages and kept infidels and curious away, are unimportant."[4] While that statement may make it seem as if the Palestinians give no consideration to archaeological discoveries, the fact is that they *have* accepted archaeological discoveries when they have been thought to work to their political advantage.

For example, recent Israeli excavations at the City of David have revealed the impressive remains of gates and fortifications that date to an early Canaanite occupation prior to Israel's presence in the Land. As a result, some Israeli archaeologists have revised their former theories concerning Warren's Shaft, believing now that it is of Canaanite, not Israelite, origin. Unfortunately, this evidence has also been used by some of Israel's minimalist archaeologists, who believe that the accounts about biblical kings David and Solomon and the existence of the First Temple are etiological fabrications.[5] The Palestinians have seized such statements and used them to say that "even the Jews admit that their ancestors were never in Jerusalem nor built a Temple."[6] John Mitchell confirms this when he says,

> A radically different view on the matter is held by the Muslim custodians of the sanctuary area. They point out that Solomon and David are mythological figures, recorded only by tradition, and that there is no conclusive evidence that the Jews' Temple stood within the walled enclosure. It could have been elsewhere in the city. It is easy to see and sympathize with one motive behind this attitude, which is to discourage Jewish interest in Islam's most sacred precinct. But the case for the Temple in its traditional location is quite

formidable, and in denying it the Muslim authorities also deny that there is any need for archaeological research in the area.[7]

By preventing any archaeological excavation from taking place on the Temple Mount, the Palestinians protect their contention that there is no archaeological proof that the Temple existed on the Temple Mount. Furthermore, destruction of existing remains by the Palestinians (see next chapter) have also contributed to this conspiracy to conceal evidence. However, the discoveries already made and accepted by the international scholarly community are sufficient to make it undeniable that the Jewish people had a Temple on the site and that they worshiped at that Temple.

The Palestinian denial of the Temple's existence is based on religious and political beliefs. Adnan Husseini, a senior Waqf official, argued from religious conviction when he once declared, "The mosques on the Temple Mount were built by the order of God....Our sovereignty is not subject to compromise." The religious basis for rejection of the Jewish claim became clear when, in a 1998 interview, Palestinian Mufti Ikrama Sabri explained, "The Temple could not have been built on the Temple Mount because the Al-Aqsa Mosque was built there. Allah would never have told them to build it if a Jewish Temple had been there."[8] This kind of blind religious reasoning, as well as the Palestinian political notion that money is the motive for Zionism, is evident in the following excerpt from a Hamas publication. This excerpt is an example of the revisionist history the Palestinians are teaching their people today:

> Historians and archaeologists claim that the temple built by Solomon (peace upon him)—as the Jews claim—has no evidence of ever existing. The most likely of opinions is that the temple that the Jews are

looking for is in fact the blessed Al-Aqsa Mosque. The
Al-Aqsa Mosque in fact has a history predating the
Prophet David (peace upon him). Imam Qurtuby said,
"It is conceivable that it was built by the angels after
finishing with the always attended house with the permission of their Lord Most High. The superficial
meaning of the Hadith indicates this, and Allah knows
best." The Hadith...has been narrated on the
authority of Abu Zarr (s.a.a.w.) [abbreviation for
Arabic phrase *Salla Allah Alaihi Wasallan,* which
means "God prayed and gave peace upon him"], who
said, "I said, 'O Messenger of Allah, which mosque
was placed on the earth first?' He (s.a.a.w.) said, 'The
Sacred Mosque' (that is the Mosque where the *Ka'aba*
is at Mecca. Tr.). Then I said: 'Then which?' He
(s.a.a.w.) said, 'Al-Aqsa Mosque.' Then I said, 'How
much is between them?' He (s.a.a.w.) said, 'Forty
years.'"

The idea of creating a nationalist nation for the Jews
was a dream of many of the most influential Jews and
Jewish thinkers. The suggestion of Palestine as this
nation springs from their religious belief—as they
claim—that this is the promised land, and the temple
of God was in it. However, this belief is no more than
a cover for the bringing together of the Jews. The new
goal for choosing Palestine as a country for the Jews
springs from a strategic and economic objective and
not from a religious objective at all....Palestine forms
the point of concentration of all the world powers,
because it is the strategic centre for controlling
money" (reported in "Hamas, the Historical Roots
and the Pact," p. 16).[9]

Palestinians, as we have seen, likewise contend that the
Western Wall is not Jewish but *Muslim,* and call it Al-
Buraq Wall because they believe that the celestial steed of
Muhammad (Al-Buraq) was tied up there at the time of
the Night Journey from Mecca to Al-Aqsa, which they

interpret as the *Haram* (Temple Mount). However, in the sixteenth century, the Islamic Ottoman Turkish sultan Suleiman the Magnificent, who built the existing walls of the Old City, recognized the Western Wall as the official holy place of the Jews and had his court architect Sinan build an oratory there for the Jews. History records that Suleiman based his recognition on "a long-standing tradition" concerning the Jews and the Wall. For example, the Babylonian Talmud (*Brachot* 32), codified around A.D. 600, teaches that when the Temple was destroyed, all the gates of heaven were closed except for one—the Gate of Tears. Thus the Western Wall is also known as the "Wailing Wall" because of all the tears Jews have shed there through the ages. One of the many pilgrim travelers who observed this was Benjamin of Tudela. He noted in an account written in A.D. 1170 that the Wall was then venerated by the Jews: "All the Jews, each and every one of them, write their names on the Wall." Likewise the traveler Samuel Ben Shimshon of Lunee reported in A.D. 1210 that those beholding the Wall "tore their garments as is proper...and wept a great weeping."

Some scholars have questioned whether the wall mentioned in these pilgrim accounts was in fact the Western Wall, since Jews from the Muslim conquest in A.D. 638 are known to have prayed at the sites of the High Priest's Gate in the *eastern* wall and the Hulda Gates in the *southern* wall. The reason for this was that during their periods of exile from the city, they were only allowed to view the Temple Mount from the Mount of Olives, and these gates were within range for viewing purposes. The change to the Western Wall is thought to have occurred after the fall of the Crusader kingdom, when the size of the city had been reduced, leaving the southern wall outside the city wall and thus outside of protection. The safer choice was the Western Wall within the city, a choice believed to be made official in 1267 when the Jewish settlement was renewed by Nahmanides. Yet even during the early Muslim period (A.D. 638–1099) one of the four gates in the Western Wall—now know as Warren's Gate—served as a place of Jewish prayer. In fact, the internal space of the gate-passage (known as "the Cave"), in proximity to the ancient site of the Holy of Holies, was used as the main synagogue of the Jews. Therefore, there is no reason to doubt that the Western Wall itself had significance to the Jewish community well before the Muslim conquest.

What Is the Truth About the Palestinian Claim to the Temple Mount?

Islam, from the beginning, knew that Jerusalem and the Temple Mount were important to the Jews. The Caliph 'Umar selected a Jew to guide him to the place of the Sacred Rock because he recognized it was connected with Jewish biblical tradition. The first Muslims called Solomon's "great place of prayer" the "City of the Temple," and during the early years of Muhammad's ministry among the Arab tribes, Muhammad attempted to win over the Jews of the Arabian Peninsula by ordering every believer to face Jerusalem in prayer (in accord with Jewish custom). But in A.D. 632, when this produced no Jewish converts, he ordered his believers to turn back toward Mecca, as is recorded in the Qur'an (Sura "The Cow"): "We appointed the *Qiblah* [direction] towards which you did formerly pray only that we might know him who follows the messenger from God from him who turns back on his heels." This is in line with the fact that later, Ka'b al-Ahbar proposed to the Caliph 'Umar (or Omar) that the place of prayer in Jerusalem should be fixed north of the Dome so that Muslims, during their prayers, would turn towards the *Sakhra* ("the Holy Rock"). However, 'Umar is said to have retorted, "You want to adapt yourself to Jewish usage, but we were not told to pray towards the *Sakhra,* but towards the *Ka'aba* [in Mecca] alone." These early testimonies from the Muslim occupants of Jerusalem make it obvious that the later denials of a connection between the site of the *Haram* and Judaism are arising from a deliberate rejection of the mount's pivotal place in Judaism.

One major reason the Muslims focused their building efforts in Jerusalem at this early stage of the city's Islamic history was that the capital of the new and expanding Islamic empire was Damascus (in Syria). The proximity of the two cities meant that Jerusalem was within the orbit of the many activities evolving from the main center of Islam at that time. Although the cradle of Islam was Arabia, and the sacred cities of Mecca and Medina are located there, the whole of Syria and its surroundings eventually came to hold a greater interest for the Muslims. Miriam Ayalon, professor of Islamic Art and Archaeology at the Hebrew University noted these additional factors for the Muslim interest in Jerusalem:

> The first and foremost of these considerations is undoubtedly the religious associations of ideas and events, with the city prevailing among both Jews and Christians. Indeed, the fact that Jerusalem was already important to the two monotheistic faiths from earlier times, and the fact that Islam considered itself as the last of the revelations...made it legitimate for Islam to absorb and identify with former beliefs obtained there. Jerusalem could not be ignored. The Temple area, which had been abandoned after the destruction of the second Temple and turned into the municipal dung center as a deliberate policy of the Byzantines, offered an ideal space to establish the monuments of the new rulers. Moreover, the very fact that some of the preexisting Byzantine buildings remained in Jerusalem and could provoke admiration, or eventually jealousy, required a Muslim response.[10]

This provides us with a motive for the building of the Dome of the Rock just 60 years after the Muslim conquest of Jerusalem. Historical explanations range from a competition with a rival caliph in Mecca to an attempt to replace the *Ka'aba* and divert the *hajj* (Muslim pilgrimage to Mecca) to Jerusalem.[11] Gershon Salomon, an expert in Oriental history, argues:

> The Dome of the Rock was built in an attempt by the ruler of the northern, Omaic part of the Islamic Empire to prevent their people from going to Mecca, which was part of the southern, Abassic part of the empire, and returning with Abassic sympathies while the two parts of the empire were at war. However, when the Abassic ruler died, the people continued to go to Mecca, and the Dome became almost unknown in the Islamic world.[12]

One would think from modern Muslims that as the third holiest place in Islam, the Dome of the Rock would have been erected immediately after the Caliph 'Umar recovered the location of the Night Journey. However, early Muslim sources reveal that such was never in 'Umar's mind. Instead, the Dome of the Rock was designed as a shrine or monument to what had previously existed at the site—"the House of Suleiman" (Temple of Solomon). What's more, caliph 'Abd al-Malik's motive for erecting the shrine may have been political propaganda rather than religious reverence. Islam lacked an established culture and monumental architecture to rival that of centuries-old Byzantine Christianity. This was especially true in Jerusalem, where from the time of Constantine, magnificent churches, basilicas, and monasteries had been erected to the glory of Christ. The historian Muqaddasi, a native of Jerusalem, offers just such an explanation:

> So he ['Abd al-Malik's bin al-Walid] sought to build for the Muslims [in Damascus] a mosque that should

> prevent their admiring these [Christian churches] and should be unique and a wonder to the world. And in like manner, is it not evident how Caliph 'Abd al-Malik, noting the greatness of the Dome of the Holy Sepulchre and its magnificence, was moved lest it should dazzle the minds of Muslims and so erected, above the Rock, the Dome which is now seen there.[13]

What we know of the history of that era supports Muqaddasi's statement. We know that the original primitive wooden structure built to house the Rock was satisfactory to the first generation of Muslims, who were accustomed to the simplicity of Muhammad's mosque in Mecca. However, the splendor of the Christian churches that filled Jerusalem, which were built in close proximity to the Temple Mount, called for a response from second-generation Muslims who had grown up as conquerors. Indeed, the polemical aspect of the Dome of the Rock can be seen to some degree in its Byzantine architecture, but especially in the many Qur'anic inscriptions decorating its walls, which clearly were intended to counter Christian doctrines. This was important to Muslims because although Jesus is regarded as a prophet in Islam, the impressive Christian structures throughout Jerusalem magnified Jesus' *divinity*, which is *shirk* ("heresy") in Islam.

Furthermore, for much of the Muslim period, Jews and Christians were made the object of scorn and derision. For example, during the reign of Caliph Harun al-Rashid (A.D. 786–809), Jews and Christians were stripped of any religious rights and forced to wear colored badges to identify their inferior status. Christians had to wear blue badges and Jews had to wear yellow ones (note that this practice of having Jews wear yellow badges was later brought back during the Holocaust). The Muslims did not want Jews or Christians (who were inferior *dhimmis*) to gain respectability because of their association with a superior architecture or religious history, which would be a grave offense to Allah and his true prophet.

In time, the "need" to prove superiority through prominent Arab structures and attract visitors to Jerusalem may have precipitated the circulation of the stories about Jerusalem being the place of final resurrection and of Muhammad's Night Journey. This is consistent with the rich collection of Islamic folklore and tradition that emerged in response to the Jewish and Christian history associated with the sacred places the Muslims had occupied. Since there was nothing to compare with or explain the significance of this history in the Qur'an, such connections had to be invented over time. This has occurred for most all of the antiquity sites in and around the Temple Mount.[14] That this is the case with the account of Muhammad's Night Journey is obvious from the fact that the name of Jerusalem (the supposed location in later tradition) is not mentioned in the Qur'an. If it was 'Abd al-Malik who built the mosque (some say Caliph Walid built it between A.D. 705–715), he probably used this story to justify his propagandistic campaign and because he needed a mosque to match the beauty of the Dome of the Rock.

The fact that Muslims were attempting to counter Jewish and Christian traditions in Jerusalem is evident by the fact that both the Dome of the Rock and the Al-Aqsa Mosque were built over the ruins of either synagogues or Byzantine churches. Byzantine records reveal that the Christian basilica of Saint Mary, which was built by Emperor Justinian south of the Temple Mount in the sixth-century, had the same dimensions as the Al-Aqsa Mosque built later on this spot. Some sources even state that Saint Mary's Church was simply converted into the Al-Aqsa Mosque. The octagonal shape of the Dome of the Rock, which is foreign to Islamic architecture, shows that 'Abd al-Malik was copying Byzantine architecture in his design.

The absorbing or replacing of Christian tradition by Muslims is also seen in the Hagia Sophia Church in Constantinople (the focus of eastern Christianty), which was turned into a mosque even as the city was renamed Istanbul. And the fourth holiest place in Islam, the Umayyad Mosque in Damascus, built in the city where Jesus' disciples were first called "Christians" (Acts 11:26), was built over the site of the Basilica of St. John the Baptist.

The evidence we have considered up to now reveals that there is no historical basis for the Muslim claim that Jerusalem and the Temple Mount are Islamic holy places. It was not until A.D. 1187, when the Crusaders were finally dislodged by Saladin, that Jerusalem was said to be the third holiest place in Islam (after Mecca and Medina). What's more, even Arabs once recognized Jerusalem's significance to the Jewish people. For example, the Arab geographer Yakut wrote in A.D. 1225 that "the city of Jerusalem was holy to Jews and Christians, *as it has been for 3,000 and 2,000 years respectively*," and noted that "Mecca was holy to Muslims"[15] (emphasis added). This distinction was affirmed again a few decades after Yakut, when one of the most orthodox Islamic thinkers, Taqi a-Din, attempted to purify Islam from foreign influences and came out openly against the idea that Jerusalem or the Temple Mount had any sanctity in Islam.[16]

While Islam has multiple holy places, by contrast, the Temple Mount is the one and only holy place in Judaism, and is backed by at least 3,000 years of recorded history. And despite the fact that Muslims have dominated the Temple Mount for 1,300 years, Jews have continued to direct their daily prayers toward it and to look forward to the day when the Temple can be rebuilt. An example of this can be seen in a thirteenth-century statement by the Jewish sage Nahmanides in a letter to his son:

> What shall I say of this land...the more holy the place, the greater the desolation. Jerusalem is the most desolate of all....there are about two thousand inhabitants...but there are no Jews....People regularly come to Jerusalem, men and women from Damascus and from Aleppo and from all parts of the country, to see the Temple and weep over it. And may He who deemed us worthy to see Jerusalem in her ruins, grant us to see her rebuilt and restored....

Muslim clerics in fact know of the historical claim Jews have to the Temple Mount. Even though their modern historians rewrite history to teach that nothing occupied the site before the beginning of Islam, the Qur'an speaks not only of the Jewish Temple, but of a Jewish return to it. In *Night Journey* 8 we read this: "We sent against you [Israel] our servants to discountenance you, and to enter the Temple, as they entered it the first time, and to destroy utterly that they ascended to. Perchance your Lord will have mercy upon you; but if you return, we shall return...." Some have said that it was because the Muslims knew these facts and believed that the Jews would return to the Temple Mount to rebuild that the Jordanians were able to abandon the Temple Mount without a major conflict in 1967. Furthermore, the early Muslim conquers of Jerusalem knew that the Persian King Kursau II, who held the city from A.D. 614–629, had captured it with the help of 25,000 Jews from the Galilee, and, as a reward, had given them permission to rebuild their Temple on the Temple Mount. Although Kursau later reneged on his pledge to his Jewish allies in order to make peace with the Byzantines, still, all this happened just 25 years *before* Caliph 'Umar rode into Jerusalem and onto the Temple Mount!

What's especially amazing is that confirmation of the existence of the Temple and its identification with the place of the Muslim *Haram al-Sharif* comes from no less an authority than the Supreme Muslim Council in Jerusalem itself! Back in 1930, long before there was a State of Israel or Muslims cared about any political associations with the Temple Mount, this Muslim entity, appointed by the British Government during the Mandate period, issued a nine-page English-language guidebook entitled *A Brief Guide to al-Haram al-Sharif*. This authoritative guide to Muslim holy places states, "This site is one of the oldest in the world. Its sanctity dates from the earliest

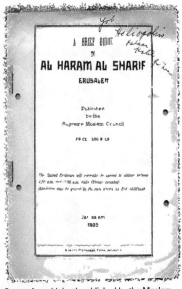

Cover of a guidebook published by the Moslem Supreme Council in 1935. The guidebook states that the site was that of the Jewish Temple.
Photo by Alexander Schick *Bibelausstellung Sylt*

times. Its identity with the site of Solomon's Temple is beyond dispute."[17] Now, this is not the only reference to the Temple in this booklet, but this statement alone is sufficient to show that until Muslims resisted the creation of the Jewish state in 1948 (and until they lost the site to Israeli control in 1967), the very body that said the Temple's association with the *Haram* was "beyond dispute" now *denies* that very fact!

What Are Muslims' True Feelings About the Temple Mount?

While modern Muslims regard the *Haram* and the mosques on it with reverence, Muslims have not historically shown such devotion to the site. For centuries, Muslims have prayed only in the direction of Mecca (the opposite direction of the ancient Jewish Temple toward which Jews

Close-up of Muslims at prayer during Ramadan, facing Mecca (*away* from the Temple area).
Photo by Randall Price

Aerial view of some 300,000 Muslims at prayer on the Temple Mount during Ramadan.
Photo courtesy of Israel Government Press Office

pray). Even today at the major Islamic feast of Ramadan, which is held annually, one can see the area between the Al-Aqsa Mosque and the Dome of the Rock filled with some 300,000 praying Muslims all turned *away from* the Dome of the Rock.

Furthermore, Muslims do not make *hajj* (pilgrimage) to the Al-Aqsa and the Dome of the Rock. In fact, when an acquaintance of mine in Jerusalem sought to specialize in Muslim tours to the city, he had to close up shop because he was unable to get business—partly because other Muslims prevented their brethren from other countries to travel to Israel. Today the Muslims call Jerusalem *Al-Quds* ("Holy One"), but an earlier Arab name for the city was *Iliyia*, derived from the Roman renaming of the city as *Aelia (Capitolina)*. However, in the Islamic period the Arabic name of Jerusalem was *Bayt al Maqdis*, based on the Hebrew *Beit Hamiqdash* ("the Holy House"—i.e., the Temple), revealing the city's Israelite origin. Only later was the name changed to *Al-Quds*. This is supported by professor Abdul Hadi Palestinian Palazzi, Secretary General of the Italian Muslim Association (Rome), an Imam (spiritual teacher) of the Italian Islamic Community who holds a Ph.D. in Islamic Sciences by decree of the Grand Mufti of the Kingdom of Saudi Arabia:

> The Arabic name of Jerusalem *[Al-Quds]* comes from the root *q-d-s,* meaning "holiness." It is an abridged form of *Bayt al-maqdis,* "the sanctified House" or "the House of the Sanctuary," an exact equivalent of the Hebrew *Beth ha-mikdash.* The name originally referred only to the Temple Mount, and was afterward extended to the city as a whole. This extension of meaning became common among Arabs from the tenth century C.E. onwards. Earlier Islamic sources use the name *Iliyia,* an adaptation to Arabic pronunciation of the Roman name *Aelia.*[18]

If some Muslim authorities actually feel this way, why does the Palestinian Authority deny any Jewish claims to the site and continue to make exclusive demands on Jerusalem and the Temple Mount? Karen Armstrong suggests Palestinian reaction has its roots in Israel's regaining control of the city and the Temple Mount in 1967: "In history, a holy city has always become more precious to a people after they have lost it....As Muslims the world over feel that Jerusalem is slipping from their grasp, some espouse an intolerance that is far from the Koranic spirit."[19] Perhaps this also explains the reason for Islam's recent claim to the Western Wall *after* the Israeli Knesset approved a bill in 1997 to change the status of the Wall from a national site to a *religious* site. We have to keep in mind that Muslims view both the city and its holy place from the perspective of Islam's superiority over Judaism and Christianity. As the *Palestinian Encyclopedia* states, "Ever since the destruction of the Temple, the link with

Jews and Christians has been severed. Muslims alone have a right to the Temple."[20] Dr. Sari Nusseibeh, head and founder of the Palestinian Authority Academic Society for the Study of International Affairs and General Secretary of the Council for Higher Education in the West Bank, explains:

> If one looks at Islam as one of three separate religions, and at Muhammad as Islam's prophet, one is bound to see or understand there to be far more sentimental attachment by Jews and Christians to Jerusalem....[That is why we can] understand why the nocturnal journey took place through the divine rock, why this was the *Qiblah* for the first sixteen months of Muhammad's message, and why 'Umar ordered the building of a mosque on the site of the ruined temple. The mosque, on this reading, was itself a revivification of the old Jewish temple, an instantiation of the unity with the Abrahamic message, an embodiment of the new temple yearned for and forecasted. And why should this seem strange when Muhammad himself, according to the Qur'an, was the very prophet expected and described in the "true" Jewish literature? I realize, of course, the political sensitivity of my remarks, especially in a context in which Muslims feel threatened by Jewish zealotry, and where such zealotry and exclusivity posits the Dome of the Rock Mosque as a "usurper" of a Jewish holy site, rather than as a legitimate celebration of that site.[21]

As Dr. Nusseibeh reveals, the Muslim belief that Islam has superseded Judaism and Christianity in its literature and as an institution means that the Dome of the Rock, though originally drawing its significance from both religions' connection with the Temple, has superseded the old Temple and replaced its past significance with a meaning only defined by Islam. This means that Islam should not be viewed as simply usurping a site of Jewish reverence, but "as crowning Islam's purpose as the final and divinely approved revelation of God." This belief transforms both Jerusalem and the Temple Mount into exclusive Muslim domains, accessible in the proper sense only by those of the true (Islamic) faith. Therefore, in political terms, the Temple Mount has become a central object that symbolizes Islam's and the Palestinians' struggle with Israel. Elwood McQuaid, the former executive director of The Friends of Israel, summarizes this fact for us when he says,

> It is a fascinating argument that is brought forth by the Islamic people that the Temple Mount had no prior relationship to the Jewish people and that it is sacred to Islam. The Islamic religion did not come into existence until seven centuries after the Lord Jesus Christ was in the world....For them to make the statement that [the Temple Mount] belongs to them contradicts everything that is biblically given to us, archaeologically verified by us, and as far as history is concerned, testified to on almost every page of the history of the Middle East and certainly the city of Jerusalem. [The Temple Mount] is a flashpoint. I think it is reflective of the whole obsession to control the city of Jerusalem and to control the entire area—to succeed in their thought that they are going to drive Israel into the sea. I think it is just one more place that they can use as a ground for controversy and for possible conflict.[22]

As a result, we must be very careful to search out the truth of any Palestinian statement about the Temple Mount and heed the advice of Morton A. Klein, the national president of the Zionist Organization of America: "Arafat and his aides show no respect for Judaism or Jewish holy sites. Arafat and the Palestinian Authority seem to have learned well from other dictators, who understood that the bigger the lie, and the more frequently it is repeated, the more people will believe it."

Now that we have a clear idea of the truth about the Temple Mount and we've examined the Palestinian efforts to revise that truth, let's look at what is happening today at the Temple Mount and consider the circumstances and actions that are provoking this conflict to a final show-down with both regional and global consequences.

CHAPTER 15

What Is Happening on the Temple Mount?

The ongoing destruction of the remnants of the Jewish past at a site that is the most important in the fabric of life of the Jewish people...combined with a situation that is straight out of the theater of the absurd, namely the prohibition on Jews to visit the site, which no one imagined could come to pass at the Temple Mount... is like a sword plunged into the heart of many Jews.[1]

Imagine if a Jewish group stormed the Al-Aqsa Mosque and began dynamiting it or ramming it with heavy construction equipment. How long would that be tolerated by the Arab world?[2]

No battle was fought. No shots were even fired. But a war has been won. With scarcely a mention in the media, the Palestinian Authority has taken over the Temple Mount, altered the 34-year-old status quo of the site, and denied the law of religious freedom of access. The magnitude of this dramatic change of affairs should not be underestimated. It is nothing less than a total rejection of Israeli sovereignty in 1967, a *de facto* counterdeclaration of Palestinian sovereignty, and replacement of Judaism and Christianity's historical link with the Temple. It is a conquest that has been imposed on Israel without compromise or negotiation, and Jews worldwide are being held hostage. And it is a sample of the challenge radical Islam is issuing to the entire free world of its presently unchallenged dominion.

For those whose emotions are not stirred by this news, may I suggest they visit a small museum in the middle of the Cardo in the Jewish Quarter of the Old City. The museum's exhibition, entitled "The Last Day," is about the Jewish struggle for Jerusalem and features a photographic display that chronicles the year 1948, when the Jews were being expelled from the city by the Arabs. Prominently presented are both "before" and "after" shots so the viewer can get an impression of today's restored Jewish Quarter with its many impressive synagogues, public buildings, and elegant shops, in contrast to its almost total destruction after the Jews were driven out. Yes, things are bad for Israel now, but one look at those photographs reminds us that things could have been much worse had Israel *lost* the war in 1967! However, only a short distance away, on the Temple Mount, those who have charge of the site are acting as though no war was won by Israel in 1967 and have turned the clock back again to 1948. Now, as then, Jews have been expelled from their holiest site in their holy city while the legitimate presence of Israeli government officials at the site has been called a "provocation" and even blamed—before a watching world—for the violence instigated by the Palestinians in the new Intifada. Even Orthodox Jews conducting a religious ceremony in a parking lot *outside* the walls of the Temple Mount have been attacked. Their simple service resulted in Palestinian rioting and universal condemnation from the leaders of

Arab nations (see chapter 13). This Jewish exile from a Jewish site, especially one that technically *still remains* under the sovereign control of the State of Israel, has left many Jews, as well as onlookers from around the world, asking...

What Is Happening on the Temple Mount?

To explain what is happening today, it is necessary, as the museum exhibit does, to make a comparison with the past. Dr. Aaron Lerner, director of Independent Media Review & Analysis, puts the matter in perspective when he writes:

> During the period of Jordanian occupation from 1948 to 1967, all Jews were barred entry into the entire Old City. When the Arabs failed to destroy the Jewish state in 1967 and instead found themselves facing an Israel with lines extending to the Jordan River, the representatives of the Waqf on the Temple Mount prepared for the worst. But Israel didn't pay the Arabs in kind. The city was not cleared of Arabs and, Mordechai Gur's memorable 'The Temple Mount is in our hands' notwithstanding, Moshe Dayan made it clear to the Waqf that the mount remained firmly in its hands. Today Arafat's appointees incite the masses against Israel in their Friday sermons broadcast by the Palestinian media from the Temple Mount, in gross violation of the Oslo Accords.[3]

The desire in 1967 to maintain the status quo, with the custody of the Temple Mount being returned to the Islamic Waqf, was nevertheless made with a condition: *equal access for all religions to the site.* The Muslims agreed but with a proviso: non-Muslims would be allowed to enter only as tourists, but must not engage in religious expression, since that would violate Islamic law. For the next 33 years, the Israeli police officers assigned to the Temple Mount, as well as the Israeli courts, rigorously upheld this ruling and prosecuted every Muslim complaint against those who were accused of offending Islamic sensitivities.

Consequently, every attempt by Jewish individuals or groups to assert their rights as Jews in a Jewish state to pray on the Temple Mount has met with arrests and sometimes even permanent expulsion from the site, as in the cases of Yehuda Etzion, head of Chai V'chaiyam, and Gershon Salomon, director of the Temple Mount Faithful Movement. As Israeli Foreign Minister Shlomo Ben-Ami has said, "Does anybody think that there is a sane person in this country, this government, who wants to harm the sacredness of Islam, who wants to harm Al-Aqsa? We have had sovereignty over the Temple Mount for 30 years, and we have never changed the status quo."[4] Under Israeli sovereignty, there has been freedom: Jews had free access to the Western Wall, and Christians could carry crosses down the Via Dolorosa and pray at the Church of the Holy Sepulchre. And most of all, Muslims could freely worship at their mosques on the Temple Mount. Freedom under Israeli rule was something of which Israel could boast, as Prime Minister Ariel Sharon did recently: "Only under the sovereignty of Israel has Jerusalem been open to all faiths. Jerusalem and the Temple Mount, the holiest site to the Jewish people, is something you should stand up and speak out about."[5] That openness, however, no longer exists because freedom and religious tolerance does not exist in Islam. This is a lesson the world is also learning and

Israeli soldiers and police on the Temple Mount in accordance with sovereignty Israel exercised over the site prior to Al-Aqsa Intifada closure.

Photo courtesy of Israel Government Press Office

why the events happening on the Temple Mount are so critical at this time.

Nevertheless, the Israeli government is supposed to have had political sovereignty over the Temple Mount since 1967—a control that legally requires the Islamic Waqf to make official requests of the Israeli government for anything that might affect the site's status quo. This control was demonstrated, for example, in March 1994 by a closing of the Western Wall (the only remnant of the Temple Mount accessible to Jews) after Arabs threw stones there in response to the Hebron mosque shooting. This was the first-ever attempt by the government to restrict the religious rights of Israelis at the Temple Mount, and this act was viewed by religious Jews as more symbolic than security-oriented. "Why," they wondered, "was the Jewish site *below* the Temple Mount closed, and not the Muslim place *above,* where the violence *originated?*" This closing caused religious Jews to wonder about the government's attitude toward the future of the Temple Mount. Rabbi Benny Alon, the head of a movement attempting to establish a Jewish presence throughout Judea and Samaria, said this in response to the government's action: "We [Israel] do not impose sovereignty over the Temple Mount, and as a result we are afraid of rocks thrown over to the Western Wall. We have already conceded the Temple Mount [to the Palestinians] so the Western Wall also must be evacuated because it is dangerous."[6] If the rabbi felt like that in 1994, imagine how he must feel today, with the Palestinians having imposed their sovereignty over the Temple Mount and regularly threatening Jewish worshipers at the Western Wall!

What Have the Palestinians Done to Change the Status Quo of the Temple Mount?

Up until September 28, 2000, when Ariel Sharon visited the Temple Mount and Palestinians rioted that day and the next, the site was open to all visitors, even though tight security prevailed. Thereafter, the Palestinian Authority announced the beginning of the Al-Aqsa Intifada and the Temple Mount was closed to non-Muslims. Jewish authorities claimed the Waqf had imposed a ban on all visitors, while the Waqf stated that the Israeli government, not they, had shut the site to tourists. What is the truth?

The facts are that the Waqf banned Israelis (including Israeli archaeologists and the Israeli police) from the Temple Mount, not tourists, but stated to the Israeli authorities that they could not guarantee the safety of any non-Muslims. Previously, on April 7, 2000, the Islamic resistance movement (Hamas) had warned Israeli Jews against going to the Temple Mount, "calling Palestinians, Muslims and Arabs to prevent by all means their entrance to the *Haram al-Sharif*."[7] The Israeli government, realizing it was impossible to protect tourists (especially Jewish ones), since its own police could not enter to offer protection from riots, brought the matter to the Israeli Supreme Court, which decided a general ban was required, which the Israeli police would enforce.

In this way the Waqf could change the status quo (which always permitted Jewish access), yet hold the Israelis responsible for the closure to the public. Even so, Israeli Internal Security Minister Uzi Landau termed the barring of Jews, Christians, and archaeologists from the site an anomaly that "runs against all the basic principles of the state."[8] But to understand the real motivation that led to the Waqf's "Jewish ban," we must retrace the Muslim efforts to control the site and conform it exclusively to Islamic religion.

It was after midnight on September 27, 1996, and officials in Israel's Ministry for Religious Affairs were relieved that Israeli engineer Meyer Kusnitz' crew had finally completed a new exit for the Western Wall Tunnel, a major tourist attraction that up to this time, had been booked 24 hours a day due to the fact that only 30 people could be accommodated at a time. This limitation was an insurance requirement imposed on the tunnel for safety reasons, for visitors in the tunnel had to turn around and return the way they had come. "At last," the officials said, "people will be able to go through safely and without restrictions. Even the Palestinians will be pleased, since all the tourists will exit right into their shops in the Christian Quarter!"

Little did they realize that with the morning would come a violent reaction from ungrateful and enraged Palestinians, who would force a closure of the tunnel and the Temple Mount and instigate a riot resulting in 58 deaths (some estimate 80) throughout Jerusalem and the West Bank territories. Palestinians heaved stones from atop the Temple Mount down on Israelis at prayer at the Western Wall below as loudspeakers on the Mount called for Arabs to come and defend the holy places. And Yasser Arafat, who had been out of the political limelight, anxiously addressed the international media and claimed that the newly carved exit tunnel was a deliberate Israeli attempt to destroy the Muslim mosques on the Temple Mount. Even though Arafat knew full well that the exit tunnel was no threat, being located 50 feet underground at the opposite far end of a 2,000-year-old tunnel and an even older Hasmonean water tunnel

Palestinian poster of the Western Wall Tunnel distributed in the Old City, claiming that the Israeli government was attempting to destroy the Muslim mosques and rebuild the Temple.

Photo by Randall Price

some 1,500 feet to the north of the Al-Aqsa Mosque and almost 1,000 feet from the Dome of the Rock. Nevertheless, he called the tunnel "a crime against our religious and holy places...completely against the peace process." Jerusalem mayor Ehud Olmert accurately targeted true intentions as he angrily countered his accusations, stating, "The tunnel has no connection to the mosques—it is far away—this is about who will control Jerusalem!"[9]

The Waqf, who issued Arabic maps of the tunnel showing the tunnel's correct location, still used this event to justify an official rejection of Israeli sovereignty over the Temple Mount. They demonstrated this by acting upon their own authority to cooperate with a massive construction project on the site initiated by Raed Salah, mayor of the Arab city Umm el-Fahm and head of the Islamic Movement. While the Rabin government had given approval for a limited renovation project that would allow use of the Solomon's Stables area for the yearly Ramadan prayers on the *Haram* (which draws about 300,000 Muslims), it had done so in exchange for the Waqf's agreement that the exit tunnel could be opened for the Western Wall tourists! Not only did the Waqf get their renovations, but they used the very terms of the agreement against the Israelis to execute the extensive construction project to build a new underground mosque for 15,000 Muslim worshipers.

This project, which involved hundreds of volunteer laborers, required the conversion of a 2,000-year-old Herodian passageway that used to bring Jewish worshipers onto the Temple Mount from the southern Huldah Gate entrance and the excavation of a tremendous amount of the underground area within and surrounding Solomon's Stables. Tragically, the construction area was known by Israeli archaeologists to have been rich in Temple-period remains (as well as extant underground structures). However, Israeli archaeologists have always been unable to officially investigate the site because of its proximity to the Al-Aqsa Mosque. Even when the Temple Mount was under Israeli control in the early days following the Six-Day War, the Israeli government still prohibited digging through the ruins because of political and religious sensitivities. For this same reason, and to preserve the all-important status quo, Israel made it illegal for Muslims to do any work on the site that might violate this archaeological ban. The Waqf authorities have always been required to submit detailed plans of any repair work or construction activity they wanted to conduct on the Temple Mount—a requirement they have now ignored in their rejection of Israeli sovereignty over the site. Every Israeli archaeologist has dreamed that he or she might one day be able to conduct careful excavations in this ancient place, but because of the destructive construction activity, that opportunity is now gone forever!

The extent of the devastation is great, for the Muslim construction workers used bulldozers, front-end loaders, dump trucks, and mechanical stone cutters to dig in the underground chambers beneath the Al-Aqsa Mosque and carve up the ruins of Solomon's Stables and the Eastern Huldah Gate. The walls and ceiling of the Huldah passageway were once decorated with ornamental designs of the seven holy fruits chiseled in relief sculpture. This artwork, as well as beautiful marble pillars in the middle of the tunnel, were covered over by cement.[10] The plan originally proposed by the Waqf stated that they would merely construct an emergency exit for the al-Marawani Mosque located in Solomon's Stables. Instead they removed more than 6,000 tons of earth, creating a huge pit 200 feet long and 75 feet wide (in flagrant disregard of approved limits). And the "exit" was made into a broad, double-arched entranceway with landings of monumental proportions (measuring 18,000 square feet and up to 36 feet in depth).

Next the underground Marawani Mosque was expanded to form an additional mosque that includes a mosque hall and an emergency hall. Today, a friend of mine who recently visited the site as part of a joint Muslim-Christian peace tour described the entire area behind the east-west length of the southern wall of the Temple Mount as stripped of its ancient remains and transformed into a vast mosque complete with carpeted floors, chandeliers, and furniture.

Following this, the Waqf also constructed buildings within the boundaries of the Temple Mount, adjacent to the northern wall, between the Gate of Forgiveness and the Afel Gate. They removed hundreds of truckloads

Construction debris and trash piled north of the Dome of the Rock on the Temple Mount.

Photo by Binyamin Lalizou, courtesy of Prophecytoday.com

Muslim construction has turned some ares of the Temple Mount into a junkyard, as this path behind the Dome of the Rock reveals.

Photo by Binyamin Lalizou, courtesy of Prophecytoday.com

(some tens of thousands of pounds) of valuable material from the site and dumped it at municipal garbage sites in Azariya, on Mount Scopus, and in the Kidron Valley. These remains, exposed to weather and pillaging by locals, included artifacts from the Byzantine and early Islamic periods as well as relics from both the First and Second Temple periods, including pottery and glassware. Hundreds of broken columns, cut building stones, and large ornamented stones have also been found strewn around the Temple Mount compound, and have been photographed in a dump area behind the Dome of the Rock. Although some archaeological students have been able to sift through the remains and recover some artifacts, the finds are practically worthless without a context that would positively identify their date and relationship to other structures and artifacts.

Rabbi Chaim Richman of the Temple Institute, who has been monitoring the Waqf's construction activities, said, "Several structures that had been preserved underground in their entirety for nearly two millennia had been unearthed, including a water aqueduct from the Holy Temple. These were then completely demolished by the Moslems with exacting precision."[11] Jerusalem archaeologist Ronny Reich, who directed the most recent excavations at the southwestern wall of the Temple Mount, added his voice to the protest, saying, "Information that could have contributed to the current debate over whether Jerusalem was a strategic city in King David's time has also been lost forever with the removal of so much material from the Waqf's excavation."[12] And one Israeli group, trying to convince the Israeli Knesset to stop the illegal proceedings, stated, "There is a full-scale destruction of antiquities underway on the site!"[13]

Still, the destruction and construction continued. The most recent, in February and March of 2001, involved the destruction of an ancient arched structure erected against

The Temple Mount Today

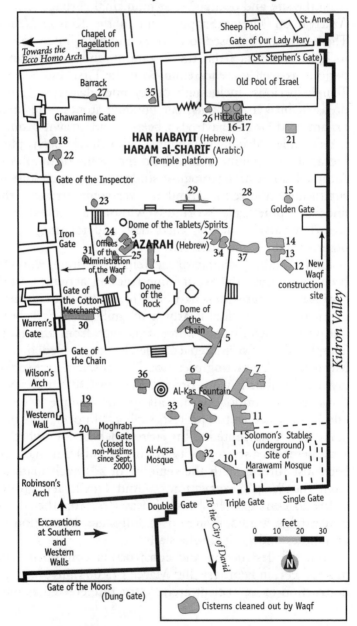

Towards the Ecco Homo Arch ←

Chapel of Flagellation

St. Anne

Sheep Pool
Gate of Our Lady Mary
(St. Stephen's Gate)

Barrack 27 35

Old Pool of Israel

Ghawanime Gate

26 Hitta Gate
16-17

18
22

21

HAR HABAYIT (Hebrew)
HARAM al-SHARIF (Arabic)
(Temple platform)

Gate of the Inspector

23

29 28

15
Golden Gate

Iron Gate

24
31 Offices
of the
Administration
of the Waqf
4

3 O Dome of the Tablets/Spirits
AZARAH (Hebrew)
25 1
34 37

2

14
13
12 New
Waqf
construction
site

Dome of the Rock

Dome of the Chain

5

Gate of the Cotton Merchants
30

Warren's Gate

Gate of the Chain

Wilson's Arch

36

6

7

19

Al-Kas Fountain

Western Wall

33 8

11

20 Moghrabi Gate
(closed to non-Muslims since Sept. 2000)

Al-Aqsa Mosque

9
32 10

Solomon's Stables (underground)
Site of Marawami Mosque

Robinson's Arch

Kidron Valley

Double Gate

Triple Gate

Single Gate

To the City of David

Excavations at Southern and Western Walls →

feet
0 10 20 30

N

Gate of the Moors
(Dung Gate)

Cisterns cleaned out by Waqf

the eastern wall of the Temple Mount, which was destroyed for the purpose of enlarging the emergency gate of yet another new mosque (the fifth on the site). Arab volunteers in Israel also went every weekend to help clean out 37 cisterns found in the mount. The chief of police of the Temple Mount station had ordered the clean-up operations to be stopped after only one or two cisterns had been cleaned, but his orders were ignored. These large underground cisterns, mostly from the Temple period, contained fill dirt that most certainly would have held a treasure house of antiquities. All of this, reports Israeli journalist Nadav Shragai, has been done despite protests from the Israeli government, the city municipality, and the Antiquities Authority.[14] The Waqf does not deny this, but has openly refused Israeli officials and sent away inspectors sent to the site. As Palestinian Mufti Ikrama Sabri boldly asserts, "We don't wait for permission from anybody." As a result, Jerusalem Mayor Ehud Olmert and the Israeli Antiquities Authorities have called for a stop to these illegal acts by the Waqf, and more than 140 Israelis across the political spectrum, including 82 Knesset members, have signed petitions against the excavations. Still, the Barak government refused to interfere while the sensitive political negotiations over the site continued, and Attorney General Elyakim Rubinstein refused to impede the Waqf in any way.

As a result of the Waqf's construction activities on their mosque in the area of Solomon's Stables, the southern retaining wall of the Temple Mount and Al-Aqsa Mosque has a large section bulging out and in danger of collapse. This bulge has existed for some time but apparently has grown since the construction of the Marawani Mosque. One expert said, "The extensive construction being carried out by the establishment of the new underground mosque contributed to the wall's inclination, [and] the presence of tens of thousands of worshipers in the

Mosque, mainly during Ramadan, is pressing on the wall's stones and causing them to deviate."[15] The Waqf has attempted to pour cement between the stones from their side of the wall, a primitive method that Israeli archaeologists say is damaging, in order to buttress the damaged section. According to Avraham Lewin, if a collapse occurs, "such an event would carry a vast potential for destruction extending well beyond Israel proper. The Arab world would probably see the wall's collapse as part of an Israeli plot to destroy the mosques on the Temple Mount and build the Third Temple in their place."[16]

All this time, Israel has been exceedingly patient, endeavoring to maintain peace, while the destruction continues. By contrast how many lives would the Muslims give to defend it? The reason for inaction was the determination that appropriate action would have to be forceful and violent. An Israeli Antiquities Authority official stated that "the construction could easily have been stopped, but at a heavy cost in lives—probably 50 Palestinian rioters and 10 Israeli policemen."[17] Yet, as Nadav Shragai reminds us: "Imagine, however, if a Jewish group stormed the Al-Aqsa Mosque and began dynamiting it or ramming it with heavy construction equipment. How long would that be tolerated by the Arab world?"[18]

What Is the Reason for the Islamic Construction?

The recent construction activity accomplishes two goals: it removes the evidence of Israel's historical connection at the site, and it gives the Temple Mount an exclusive Islamic identity. This is nothing less than what the first Islamic caliphs did when they came to the Temple Mount as conquerors 1,300 years ago. They replaced the Jewish and Christian holy structures with Islamic ones for political purposes, and they also replaced Jewish history with new

Islamic traditions. In previous centuries the Muslims built Islamic prayer platforms, offices, and cupolas all over the Temple Mount in order to make any unoccupied space exclusively Islamic. They closed the Golden Gate and built a cemetery in front of it, and they turned the inside of this gate into an Islamic center and library.

More recently, in the 1980s, the Waqf dug a large trench near the Dome of the Rock to relocate utilities and exposed more than 16 feet of a six-foot-thick wall believed to be from one of the courts of the Second Temple. Rather than allow Israeli archaeologists to study the wall, the Waqf destroyed it and covered the trench. Because of incidences such as this, in 1993 the Israeli Supreme Court found the

View of the newly constructed steps leading to the underground Marawani Mosque.
Photo by Alexander Schick, *Bibelausstellung Sylt*

Huge pit dug by Muslim authorities to expose arched entrance below ground at the site of the Hulldah Gate entrance, which dates from the Second Temple period.
Photo by Zachi Zweig

Piles of building stones stacked in the Solomon's Stables area for construction of the new mosque.
Photo by Binyamin Lalizou

Waqf guilty of 35 violations of the antiquities law that involved irreversible destruction of ancient features on the Temple Mount. Among these were the deliberate removal of a monumental row of stone steps near the Dome of the Rock and the planting of gardens to hide evidences of the Temple's location in the northeastern corner of the Temple Mount, and the plowing up and paving over of a long row of exposed stones in the eastern area. The same is being done today by the new construction projects in order to create a new historical reality for the Palestinians and support their claim that they, not the Jews, are the rightful sovereigns of the sacred site.

By removing all the available remains from the First and Second Temples, the Palestinians will be able to continue denying the Jewishness of the Temple Mount. Arafat's and the Palestinian Authority's actions are deliberate attempts to destroy all historical evidence of a Jewish presence on Temple Mount and thereby discredit Israel's claim to political (and certainly religious) sovereignty over the Mount.

Another recent attempt to "Islamize" the Temple Mount includes the burial and construction of a monumental tomb for Palestinian Authority leader Faisal Husseini, a relative of Arafat and the nephew of Haj Amin al-Husseini, the Grand Mufti who worked with Adolf Hitler on "the Jewish problem." Faisal Husseini was the administrator for governmental affairs for the Palestinian Authority in Jerusalem and one of those most outspoken against Jewish access to the Temple Mount. Husseini's burial on the Temple Mount followed the Islamic practice of burying important Islamic leaders near major mosques, and has served to provide further justification for the Palestinian Authority's claim to the site. However, it has also desecrated a site claimed as holy to the Jews, which Muslims believed would disrupt Jewish plans to rebuild the Temple, since Jewish law forbids the Jewish people to tamper with or move graves. Thus, the Muslims intended to end any Jewish hopes by an act of irreversible defilement.

The ultimate goal, of course, is to completely transform the Temple Mount into one gigantic Islamic mosque. Yasser Arafat revealed this plan when he ordered that the underground halls under the Temple Mount be unified into a single fortified space in order to create one of the largest mosques ever built in the Middle East. The scheme to create this monumental mosque was confirmed in June 2000 by Nadav Shragai, a correspondent for the Israeli newspaper *Ha'aretz*. He revealed that the Waqf's master plan, which had also been given to Israeli prime minister Ehud Barak before the Camp David II Summit, stated that the purpose is to turn the entire *Haram* into a rival of the Great Mosque of the *Ka'aba* in Mecca.

In harmony with the site becoming a Muslim mosque was the banning of non-Muslims from the site. The Waqf has stated that it has no intention of ever lifting this ban, and has sought to enforce it by ordering violent reprisals any time a violation occurs. This, apparently, applies even to religious ceremonies conducted outside, but near, the Temple Mount—ceremonies by nationalist groups such as the Temple Mount Faithful. What's more, Palestinian Mufti Ikrama Sabri has also been attempting to resurrect old British Mandate legislation that restricted Jewish prayers at the Western Wall "from disturbing Muslims."

Such blatant efforts to deny the Jewish people even the most basic rights with respect to worship and access, given Israel's sovereignty over the Mount, seem unbelievable to most Jews: "The ongoing destruction of the remnants of the Jewish past at a site that is the most important in the fabric of life of the Jewish people...combined with a situation that is straight out of the theater of the absurd, namely the prohibition on Jews to visit the site, which no one imagined could come to pass at the Temple Mount...is like a sword plunged into the heart of many Jews."[19]

How Is Israel Responding to What's Happening on the Temple Mount?

While Israeli groups have continually petitioned the Israeli High Court to reverse its ruling and intervene in both the illegal destruction and construction on the Temple Mount and the ban on Israeli entrance to the site, all appeals to date have been rejected. Foreign support to stop the Waqf's activities once came from the United States in the form of the "Temple Mount Preservation Act of 2001" (H.R.2566.IH), introduced with bipartisan support at a press conference at the Sam Rayburn Building in Washington, D.C. on July 19, 2001. This act was introduced by congressman Eric J. Cantor, a Republican from Virginia's seventh district. The bill proposed eliminating all financial aid to the Palestinian Authority until all the unauthorized excavations were ended. Calling the destruction "one of the most unprecedented attacks on religious heritage of our time," Cantor stated that under the current circumstances,

> thousands of years of Judeo-Christian heritage is under siege at this most sacred of sites to Christianity, Judaism, and Islam. Its attempt is to not only eradicate valuable archaeological evidence of construction and events in Christian and Hebrew religious writings, but its corollary denies Americans the validation of needed information to comprehend and enhance their Judeo-Christian heritage.[20]

Unfortunately, with the advent of the war on terrorism, such efforts have been forgotten, and any U.S. support that would impede a peaceful resolution works against U.S. policy and the goals of the war effort. Despite such failures, the Temple Mount Faithful continues to demonstrate several times a year near the Temple Mount, challenging the Muslim future of the site with a cornerstone intended for the Jewish Third Temple. In July 2001, at the annual commemoration of the destruction of the Temple (known as *Tisha B'av*), this group, with the government's approval and protection, celebrated a short ceremony in which they anointed the cornerstone *outside* the walls of the Old City. No sooner had they begun than Muslims inside the compound began throwing rocks, bricks, and bottles down from the Temple Mount platform onto the hundreds of Jews praying at the Western Wall below. About 400 Israeli police officers entered the mosque compound to prevent further violence but were themselves met by a hail of stones. Responding with stun grenades, the police contained the mob, but only after 15 police officers and 10 Palestinians were injured and 28 people were arrested.

No deaths occurred, but the outcry heard from the Muslim press would have led people to think Armageddon had erupted. The Grand Mufti of Lebanon's Sunni Muslims, Sheikh Muhammad Rashid Kabbani, called the demonstration the "beginning of the end for the State of Israel." The Iraqi Foreign Ministry urged the start of a "holy war" to liberate the Islamic site. Such responses hearken back to the past, when, under Muslim domination, any entrance by non-Muslims into the area was punishable by death.

Following the morning ceremony carried out by the Temple Mount Faithful, 80,000 Jews from around the country marched in silence around the walls of the Old City to mourn the destruction of the Temple—not only the historical event, but its continuing destruction under the Palestinian Authority. Rabbi Shalom Gold, a leader of the march, said:

> The lesson is that history is not made in the future, but rather, in the past. History is *not* about telling our grandchildren what we did to prevent the continuing

destruction. History is about our being responsible to our ancestors who set it up in the first place! We *had a Bais Hamikdash* (Temple) and *we let it go!* We had access to the Temple Mount and *we allowed access* to be denied to *us, this year!*...Jews should forget the *idea* of going to the Western Wall. We should replace it with the idea of going to *Har Habayit* (the Temple Mount)![21]

At one time, the rabbi's proposal would have been thought to be extreme, but perhaps no more. The Muslim blockade against Israelis entering the Temple Mount area, and the systematic destruction of areas under the surface of the Mount, have prompted the full rabbinical council of Judea and Samaria, a group that has influence over hundreds of thousands of Jewish people, to reconsider the *halakhic* ban on going to the Temple Mount. One of the key reasons for the turnabout, at least from the national religious rabbis' point of view, is explained by Rabbi Daniel Shilo of Kedumim: "The halakhic argument that has prevented Jews from going to the Mount cannot be decided by violence on the part of the Waqf and the Muslims. There's a danger that the connection between the Jewish people and Temple Mount will be forgotten, if we don't act."[22] Worse still, as Muslim authorities grow accustomed to Jewish exclusion and are able to punish with impunity (but without incurring penalty) any Jews who encroach on their sacred space, they can call for *jihad*, claiming Israel is violating *their* sovereignty!

For this reason, Jerusalem's public security minister Uzi Landau has tried to take steps to reinstitute the Israeli government's sovereignty over the site. When the Waqf submitted an application asking for cement to be delivered to the Temple Mount in order to seal Faisal Husseini's grave, he rejected the request, stating he will not allow further illegal building on Temple Mount until the Waqf agrees to allow inspectors onto the compound. And, in a precedent-setting rule, Landau instructed the Israeli police to raid the Temple Mount if the Western Wall is stoned. He told the officers they were allowed to use clubs and concussion grenades, if necessary, but they cannot use live weapons. Landau also said he is interested in preparing the grounds for his next step: allowing Jews to enter the Temple Mount. He sent a recommendation to Prime Minister Sharon that such a move be carried out in the event of another terrorist attack. However, the Palestinian Authority has warned the prime minister against using armed forces to reopen the site or even protect Jewish nationalists who attempt to pray nearby: "We advise the Israeli government not to respond to the Jewish extremists who are trying to create an unsettled situation and bathe the whole area in an ocean of blood."[23] Adding their own voice as protest the Islamic Resistance Movement (Hamas) issued a call to: "Muslims all over the world to move as quickly as possible to protect their shrine and support the Palestinian people in their resistance against the Zionist aggression on the holy site."[24]

Will the recent happenings at the Temple Mount escalate into the next great conflict in the Middle East, especially in view of the call of radical Muslims to Islamic states, and Saddam Hussein's boast that he can defend them if the Palestinians cannot? Gerald M. Steinberg, analyzing the situation for the *Jerusalem Post*, said this after the *Tisha B'av* commemoration:

> Jerusalem remains a source of major instability, as Muslim and Palestinian officials keep the Temple Mount closed, and construction continues in secret, fueling reports of gross destruction of Jewish sites. Every action in Jerusalem eventually has an equal and opposite reaction, and the current situation is extremely explosive. Yesterday's events may have been

contained, but as long as the situation remains unchanged, the tension will grow.[25]

Or, as one commentator suggested: "Perhaps Israel is waiting for what some view as the inevitability of renewed war in the Middle East before asserting its military authority over the most sacred ground in Jerusalem."[26] Whatever happens, it will surely ignite a religious showdown between Orthodox Jews and fundamentalist Muslims over the Temple Mount.

In the next chapter we will explore how the prophetic beliefs of these groups set Jerusalem as a stage for the final conflict and, at the same time, affect the present one.

CHAPTER 16

Does Prophecy
Affect Politics?

*Today, as we renew our independence,
our first concern is to build up the Land,
to foster the economy, its security and
international status. But these are the
whereby not the end. The end is a
State fulfilling prophecy....*[1]
—DAVID BEN-GURION,
FIRST PRIME MINISTER OF ISRAEL

*Great conflicts are insoluble because they
involve absolutist principles and uncompromising visions. In wars of religion,
no peace can be made between true
faith and idolatry. And so wars
continue, endlessly and insolubly.*[2]
—ARTHUR HERTZBERG

For most modern secular Jews, prophecy plays no part
in present-day politics. Even the divine threats of future
penalties for past failures, so much a part of the Jewish
prophets, do not trouble the average person. After a history in which Jews spent 400 years as slaves of the Egyptians, 173 years exiled and captive to the Assyrians and
Babylonians, and 2,000 years scattered throughout the
globe and persecuted by many—including the perpetrators

of the Nazi Holocaust, which claimed more than six million Jewish lives—what threat could the future hold? As
one student of Jewish tradition stated, "We have had
World War I and World War II and the Cold War and the
fulfillment of all the worst prophecies in the Bible. Why
would we expect more?"

The answer Gershom Gorenberg (a journalist with *The
Jerusalem Report*) gives in his book *The End of Days:
Fundamentalism and the Struggle for the Temple Mount* is
that expected or not, the end will be forced on us all
because of zealous interpreters of prophecy who see it as
fulfilled literally in the future. According to Gorenberg
(himself an observant Jew), fundamentalist Jews, Muslims,
and Christians may well create the very scenarios they
haphazardly predict. Gorenberg's warning, however, did
not deter Hasidic rabbi Pinchas Winston from penning a
novel exploring Jewish prophecies in light of current
events in the Middle East. His title, *Not Just Another Scenario: A Scenario for the End of Days*, makes it clear that
he believes what Gorenberg shuns: that the present political situation has sufficient signs to sound a warning that
the end is near. What Gorenberg fails to observe, however,
is that even the secular movement of Zionism that created
the State of Israel saw itself in prophetic terms. Secularists
who early advanced Zionism in the political realm, often
interpreted it as fulfilling prophecy. This can be seen, for
example, in Joseph Heller's (1888–1957) book *The
Zionist Idea* (1947):

> The aim of Zionism is not merely the establishment of
> a Jewish Commonwealth in the Land of Israel, but to
> pave the way for a rebirth of the spirit of the prophets
> and for a revival of Judaism....The highest value of
> Zionism lies, however, not in the material and polit-
> ical sphere, but in its spiritual meaning for Jews and
> for the world. It is this moral and spiritual effect of the

development of a free Jewish community in the land
of the prophets which paves the way for the final settlement of the Jewish question....Zionists believe that
the land of Israel will again become a source of spiritual life for the Jews and for the non-Jewish world
alike.[3]

By contrast, on the Muslim side, the prophecies of the
Qur'an are universally believed to reveal what will
happen in the future. The proliferation of Islamic books
on prophecy since the beginning of the Intifada in 1987
demonstrates that Muslims today are also thinking a lot
like Rabbi Winston.

In addition, we must consider Christianity's views on
the future, since America is believed by both Jews and
Muslims to be a "Christian country" and radical Islam
views the war on terrorism to be a religious war with a
"new army of Christian crusaders." Indeed, President
George W. Bush professes to be an evangelical Christian
and that his life is guided by the Bible. Whether or not his
beliefs affect his political decisions, it is necessary to compare Christianity's views on prophecy with those of
Judaism and Islam, since all three religions are represented
in this unholy war.

With that in mind, let's examine what Judaism, Christianity, and Islam have to say about the prophetic outcome
of today's political conflict, with special consideration
given to Jerusalem, which has a central role of prophetic
fulfillment in each of these three religions. (For a specific
comparison of these views, see the chart at the end of this
chapter.)

What Does Judaism Teach About the Future of Jerusalem?

According to the Bible, God made this promise to King
David in regard to Jerusalem and the Temple Mount: "I

will also appoint a place for My people Israel and will plant them....He shall build a house for my name, and I will establish the throne of his kingdom forever" (2 Samuel 7:10,13). Later, when David's descendant King Hezekiah was besieged by a foreign foe, God promised, "I will defend this city [Jerusalem] to save it for My own sake and for My servant David's sake" (2 Kings 20:6; Isaiah 37:35). The Jews have always relied upon such promises of divine election and protection in their relationship with Jerusalem. Furthermore, Jerusalem is not simply a city in which Jewish people live, but it is a destiny to which the Jewish people belong. The Jewish Midrash states, "Jerusalem is destined to become a beacon lighting the way for all nations" (*Yalkut Shimoni*, Isaiah 499). With the establishment of the Jewish state, this destiny seemed once again assured, as Jerusalem's status was being restored in line with the prophetic predictions. Although Israel's first prime minister, David Ben-Gurion, was a secular Jew, he nevertheless believed the Bible, studied and debated the Talmud, and attended weekly Bible classes. His understanding of the prophetic path that would end in Jerusalem was in mind when he declared:

> The Jewish people, after two thousand years and tribulation in every part of the globe, having arrived at the first step of renewed sovereignty in the Land of their origin, will not abandon their historic vision and great spiritual heritage—the aspiration to combine their national redemption with universal redemption for all the people of the world. Even the greatest tragedy ever wrought by man against a people did not dim the profound faith of the Jews, including those who went to their death in the ovens of Europe, in their national redemption and in that of mankind. Unlike other ancient people, ours did not look backward to a legendary Golden Age in the past, which has gone never to return, but turn their gaze to the

future—to the Latter Days, in which the earth will be filled with the knowledge [of the Lord] as the waters cover the sea, when nations will "beat their swords into plowshares...and nation will not lift up sword against nation, or learn war anymore."[4]

According to the *Tanakh* (the Jewish Bible), the non-Jewish nations of the world will be defeated by God and gather in Jerusalem after the final battle to pay tribute and learn the Torah from the Jews. With that event the Jewish destiny "to be a light to the nations" (Isaiah 42:6) will finally be fulfilled. One prophetic Bible text that treats this subject of the end time is the book of Zechariah. In chapter 14 of Zechariah we read, "Then it will come about that any who are left of all the nations that went against Jerusalem will go up from year to year to worship the King, the Lord of hosts, and to celebrate the Feast of Tabernacles" (verse 16). This statement is part of the conclusion to a section of Zechariah (chapters 12–14) that details a future Gentile invasion of Jerusalem. In the immediate context (chapter 14), a summary of events is unfolded: the advent of Messiah (verses 3-4), the rescue and restoration of the Jewish remnant (verse 5; cf. Luke 21:27-28), the experience of heaven-sent light and living water (verses 7-8), the recognition of God as the universal King (verse 9), the transformation of Jerusalem (verse 10), and the gathering of the wealth of the Gentile nations (verse 14).

Those who are addressed in verse 14 as being obligated to observe the Feast of Tabernacles are the remnants of the Gentile nations who were previously allied together in the war against the Holy City (Zechariah 12:3,9; 14:2,12; cf. Psalm 2:1-3). Representatives of these nations will be required to demonstrate their allegiance to God as King by bringing tribute and material offerings annually to Jerusalem. This requirement is in accordance with an ancient association of the Feast of Tabernacles with the recognition of the king as God's son, an act alluded to in Psalm 2:10-11: "Now therefore, O kings, show discernment; take warning, O judges of the earth. Worship the LORD with reverence and rejoice with trembling. Do homage to the Son, that He not become angry, and you perish in the way." The ancient observance of the feast was also followed by a ceremony of covenant renewal (Nehemiah 9:1-38), in which a national allegiance to the Lord was reaffirmed (Nehemiah 10:29).

Zechariah 14 also gives a warning to national representatives who fail to observe the Feast of Tabernacles (verses 17-19), which would be tantamount to an act of spiritual and national rebellion. Since the Feast of Tabernacles was celebrated in anticipation of receiving rain, one punishment that will be meted out to the nations that fail to appear annually in Jerusalem will be a withholding of rain, the very provision that makes possible the gifts they are to bring to the city.

Therefore, Judaism views Jewish sovereignty over Jerusalem as essential for the fulfillment of its ultimate destiny toward God and toward the Gentile nations.

What Does Christianity Teach About the Future of Jerusalem?

Christianity, like Judaism, has complex interpretations of its prophetic texts. By this is meant there are various schools of interpretation that view prophecy as more literal or more symbolic. This is especially true with regard to the city of Jerusalem, which has historically been a prophetic point of departure between Christians and Jews, with Jews seeing the future of the city as more literal and Christians seeing it as more symbolic. Since Jesus was crucified in Jerusalem and predicted its destruction by the Roman armies, the more symbolic school of Christianity has seen the old, earthly Jerusalem as having no future while the New Jerusalem is the future home of the church, the bride of Christ. However, whenever Christianity has recognized its Jewish roots and the Old Testament as the context out of which the New Testament developed, and interpreted the New Testament in light of the Old Testament, its interpretation has been more literal than symbolic. Even the symbolic school has confessed that the earliest church seen in the New Testament (which had a strong Jewish element for the first three centuries) had a hope in the literal return of Jesus and saw Jerusalem as being restored (following the repentance of the Jews). Today, evangelical and Charismatic Christianity have secured majority positions in Christendom by virtue of commanding the highest profile through preaching, publications, and their use of the media. Even though within these camps there is a diversity of interpretation, the most widely held view of Jerusalem's future coincides in most points with that of Judaism. This would be expected, since both are using the Bible and both are interpreting its prophetic texts more literally.

According to this viewpoint, represented foremost by the premillennial school of thought, Jerusalem is destined to become once again the city of God on earth and the place to which the Jewish people return in the last days (Isaiah 2:2-3; 11:11-12; Ezekiel 36:18-36; Matthew 24: 15-16; Romans 11:25-27). Jerusalem is where the Jewish Temple will be rebuilt and where the Antichrist will effect the "abomination of desolation" (Daniel 9:27; Mark 13:14; 2 Thessalonians 2:4; Revelation 11:1-2). Jerusalem is also where the Two Witnesses will die and be resurrected (Revelation 11:3-12) and the site of the final battle of Armageddon, in which nations that follow the Antichrist will attack the Jews (Zechariah 14:2; Revelation 19:11-16). At the climax of this battle, Christ will return to the

Mount of Olives (Zechariah 14:3; Acts 1:11), defeat the Antichrist, and rescue the Jews who repent and receive Him as Messiah (Zechariah 12:9-14; Matthew 23:39; Luke 21:25-28; Romans 11:25-27). Afterward, Christ will judge the nations that went against Jerusalem (Zechariah 14:9; Matthew 25:31-46) and set up His millennial kingdom (Revelation 20:1-6), which will include ceremonial worship in an ideal Temple (Ezekiel 40–48), and during which time the predictions concerning Jewish national restoration will be realized (Isaiah 60:1-20; 62:1-7; Jeremiah 31:31-34; Micah 4:1-8; Zechariah 8:1-23). There may also be at this time the New Jerusalem positioned above the earthly Jerusalem and some relationship between the two (Revelation 21:9–22:7). Dr. Harold Foos, professor of Bible and theology at Moody Bible Institute, wrote a doctoral dissertation about Jerusalem in prophecy and provides a succinct summary of the millennial Jerusalem from the premillennial perspective:

> Spiritually, the city will be the holy city, the city of righteousness. It will be the city of Jehovah, for there once again the visible manifestation of His presence will be seen as Christ rules. It will be the city of worship, not only for Israel, but for the nations. Politically, it [Jerusalem] will be the center of the whole earth, for the Messiah King-Priest will reign from Jerusalem over the nations. With no fear of an invader, Jerusalem will be the city of unconditional peace and joy, and with no lack of wealth, the glorious city will be the world's most prominent. Physically, Jerusalem will be exalted above the surrounding area, enlarged greatly, beautified by the waters from the temple, and illuminated by the effulgent glory of the triune god.[5]

At the end of the thousand-year millennium, Satan will attack Jerusalem and then be defeated (Revelation 20:7-9), and after the creation of a new heaven and earth, Jerusalem will continue into eternity (2 Chronicles 33:4; Psalm 48:8; Joel 3:20; Micah 4:7).

These views, however, find a rival in Islam, whose teachings we must likewise consider to understand how prophetic interpretation affects the Muslims' response in the present-day political conflict.

What Does Islam Teach About the Future of Jerusalem?

Islamic apocalyptic treatises such as *A Note on the Status of the Dead and Final Matters* have become increasingly familiar to Palestinians engaged in what they believe may be the final battle with the Jews—a battle predicted in the Qur'an. The Qur'an, however, though devoting considerable attention to eschatological events, never specifically locates those events in a particular place. Despite this fact, and despite the absence of any reference to Jerusalem by name, Islamic tradition (based in large measure on Jewish and Christian prophetic interpretation) says that the stage for the final drama is the Holy City and its environs. Some Muslim traditions even say that the *Ka'aba* stone in Mecca will transport itself to Jerusalem at the time of the end!

At the hour of resurrection, the angel *Israfil* will sound a trumpet three times, and all men will assemble at a purified place on the Mount of Olives. From there and all the way across the valley to the Temple Mount will be stretched a slippery bridge narrower than a hair, sharper than a sword, and blacker than night, over which men will cross in judgment. Stopping at seven arches, they will be questioned concerning their deeds before appearing before the scales of justice, which are hung, it is said, from a pillared structure on the eastern side of the Temple Mount platform. That is one reason high-ranking Muslim officials and spiritual leaders are buried on the Mount of Olives or on or near the Temple Mount—so they can be among the first to rise on resurrection day.

Islam also has its own version of the Battle of Gog and Magog, known as the War of Yajuj and Majuj. Muslims believe this battle will be fought in Jerusalem. This battle is one of ten signs that, according to Islam, signal the approaching end and day of resurrection. Another sign is a beast that will arise out of a place near Mecca—this beast will have the head of a bull, and will also have a tail and beard. There will also arise 30 or more imposters and *al-Masih al-Dajjal* or *al-Dajjal*, a false messiah who claims to be Allah, much like the Armilus of Jewish legend and Antichrist of the New Testament (see 2 Thessalonians 2:3-4). *Al-Dajjal*, who is a follower of Asbahan Judaism, will ride at the head of an army of Jews and, with a plague, will conquer the whole world. Only three cities will be spared: Mecca, Medina, and Jerusalem.

Then, with spear in hand, Jesus (*Isa*) will return to over-throw *al-Dajjal* in a battle at a place in Greater Syria called 'Aqabat Afiq. However, according to another account, this will happen at the Lud gate in Jerusalem. After this defeat, Jesus will kill all pigs and break all crosses, confirming Islam as the only true religion and causing non-Muslims to believe. Then Allah will destroy all nations except Islamic ones. After establishing a rule of justice for 40 years, during which there will be peace on earth, children will play with snakes and wolves will live with sheep (as in the Jewish and Christian prophecies of the millennium, see Isaiah 11:6-8; Revelation 20:4-6). After this time Jesus will die, have a funeral in Medina, and be buried beside Muhammad. There is also another figure in Shiite Islam known as *al-Mahdi*, a divinely guided messianic Imam who acts as the Savior of Islam and appears with Jesus in Jerusalem at the final hour.

How Does the Belief in Prophecy
Affect the Current Conflict?

Beliefs have always determined behavior. For both Orthodox Jews and Christians or fundamentalist Muslims, the present struggle for sovereignty over Jerusalem and the Temple Mount—places so richly depicted in religious texts and traditions—cannot help but be interpreted in terms of an apocalyptic scenario. Consequently, the actions and reactions of true believers will follow suit. With that in mind, let's consider how prophetic interpretation affects Christian political practice and look at some statements that Israelis and Palestinians have proclaimed in verbalizing a call to action against the enemy based on their beliefs.

Gershon Salomon, a tenth-generation Jerusalemite who saw action on the Temple Mount as an officer in the Israel Defense Forces in 1967, directs one of the largest activist organizations in Israel, the Temple Mount and Land of Israel Faithful movement. He exemplifies the thinking of many nationalist religious Jews who believe the current conflict is ushering us toward a biblical battle of apocalyptic proportions:

> The terrorist Arafat has stated that this war will not stop until he comes to Jerusalem. The Arab countries have decided to stand behind Arafat in his war against Israel. Violent attacks against Jews are occurring in many other areas. On the border with Lebanon, the Hizb'allah terror organization has launched attacks. Other so-called "Palestinian" terror organizations are holding violent demonstrations, burning Israeli flags and figurines representing Israeli figures. They intend to destroy and burn the State of Israel and occupy Jerusalem. Many violent anti-Semitic demonstrations have again started to appear all over the world. In

London a Jew was attacked and stabbed on a bus. Synagogues have been burned and anti-Semitic graffiti written on the walls. The tomb of Joseph in Shechem was destroyed, and the ancient synagogue in Jericho was burned. Many other holy Israeli places were desecrated. The same thing has been done on the Temple Mount with the remains of the First and Second Temples....What is the meaning of this that is taking place? There is no doubt that these are the first steps in what the G-d of Israel called the end-time Gog and Magog war."[6]

Salomon then went on to explain the Temple Mount's connection to this prophecy of end-time war:

The war against Israel is focused more and more on the Temple Mount and Jerusalem, just as prophesied (Ezekiel 39 and Zechariah 12 and 14). It appears that this is the beginning of the war that Ezekiel called the Gog and Magog war. It is no accident that it started when Ariel Sharon, the current prime minister of Israel, visited the Temple Mount in September 2000 to demonstrate Israeli sovereignty on the holy hill of Israel. The so-called "Palestinian" enemies started their war and called it the El-Aqsa Intifada. (El-Aqsa is the name of the mosque that the Moslems built on the Temple Mount.) It is no accident that the Temple Mount and Jerusalem have become the focus for their violence. It is no accident that the Camp David negotiations between Barak, Clinton, and Arafat collapsed when Barak was unwilling to give the Temple Mount to Palestinian sovereignty because, as Barak stated, our Temple exists on this hill. The enemies of Israel still cannot understand the major part played by the Temple Mount in G-d's end-time plans with Israel.... There will never be peace in Israel until the Temple Mount is liberated, G-d's enemies are removed from Jerusalem, the hill of G-d is purified from the pagan Moslem presence, and the house of G-d is rebuilt.

G-d is determined for Israel to rebuild the Temple in the same location as that of the First and Second Temples on the Temple Mount, and then He will send Mashiach ben David to Jerusalem to be the king of Israel.

The people of Israel are strong and are coming closer and closer to G-d with a determination to defeat all the enemies of G-d. Together with G-d we shall win this difficult battle....Since 1967 we have said that the Temple Mount will save the people and land of Israel from all their enemies and that the destiny of Israel will be decided on the Temple Mount. As a result of this campaign the leader of the opposition in Israel, Ariel Sharon, went up on the Temple Mount, not only to visit the G-d of Israel at a critical time, but also to declare Israel's sovereignty over the holy Temple Mount. The Arabs, Arafat, and the "Palestinian Authority" used this to initiate violence against Israel. As we mentioned earlier, it is no accident that the Temple Mount and Jerusalem are at the focus of this war. G-d will never again accept any pagan presence of the enemies of Israel on the Temple Mount. Thousands of years ago the Temple Mount, Jerusalem, and the land of Israel were dedicated by G-d for His purpose. In G-d's end-time plans there is no place for the cruel enemies of G-d. The terrorist Arafat, and his "Palestinian Authority," will not succeed with their war. We do not fear them or their violence. The great event of the redemption of Israel cannot be stopped. Who can stop the G-d of Israel?"[7]

This interpretation of prophecy has produced strong evangelical and Charismatic Christian support for the State of Israel and especially for its sovereignty over the city of Jerusalem. This influence is demonstrated in the political realm by Christian organizations that lobby for Israel or travel to Israel to show their solidarity (such as at the annual Christian Feast of Tabernacles conference in

Jerusalem), or where Christians in public office have championed religious causes, such as that of the Temple Mount (see the previous chapter). Of course, this literal, fundamentalist interpretation has produced in unbalanced individuals an apocalyptic fear, causing them to interpret every menacing event as a sign of the end. But those Christians who are consistent in other matters of their theology have kept a balance between an imminent hope and a careful caution in how they view current events. Even so, events that affect the future of Israel, including the war on terrorism, will be seriously studied and motivate political action in light of the accepted prophetic scenario outlined by the Old and New Testament prophets.

The Muslims also depend upon the prophetic script outlined in the Qur'an and the Hadith to direct their actions in response to Israel's presence in the Land and the present conflict. According to Muslim clerics,

> The final hour will not arrive until the Jews are gathered together from all over the world to Palestine. There they are predicted to grow rich and powerful, increase in great numbers and be well prepared [for battle]. Then all Muslims will wage a great war with the Jews and defeat them. The prophet Muhammad's description of this is given in different versions of the Hadith as transmitted by several authorities. A synopsis of these accounts would read as follows: "The hour will not arrive until the Muslims fight the Jews. The former will be given power over the latter and kill them. The Jews will hide behind the rock and tree, but the rock or tree will say, 'O Muslim! O Servant of Allah. There are Jews behind me. Come and kill them!' "[8]

According to some Muslim interpreters, Allah will bring all the Jews to Palestine and give them great wealth so that it can be turned against them and they can all be destroyed.

For example, Sheikh Nadim Al-Jisr, a Lebanese member of the Islamic Research Academy, states: "It is understood, according to another version of the Hadith, that the Jews would fight against Muslims, which means that they would establish a state and wield power; and thereby would be encouraged to start aggression."[9]

This Muslim scholar goes on to argue that this prophecy from Muhammad must be genuine because when it was given, the Jews were a scattered and powerless people, and no one would have imagined that they could again be gathered and assemble an army sufficient to fight the Muslims. He further states that the fulfillment of this prophecy must have been future and that the present state of Israel established in 1948 in part fulfills it. He argues that Muslims do not recognize an independent Jewish state to have existed in either the Hejaz or the Arabian Peninsula before the advent of Islam, and after the advent of Islam, Jews lacked the ability to wage war against Muslims. The only way Israel could have established a state is through the will of Allah, and that will, as the prophecy shows, makes possible Islam's final destruction of Israel.

This Muslim scholar also argues that Muhammad's prophecy could not have been understood until the present time: "The answer to the question [of the meaning of this prophecy] has remained concealed behind the veil of the unseen for fourteen centuries, until the creation of the modern State of Israel, which Bukhari and Muslim [two Muslim compilers of Islamic traditions known as *sahih*] had never thought of, or imagined...in the third century of the *Hijrah* (ninth century A.D.)."

That the State of Israel was established in the center of the Holy Land is deemed significant in Islam, for that is where the prophecies place the final battle and Day of Resurrection: "It is in the heart of the Arab and Muslim land, where the clash with the Jews has become an actual issue.

Nay, it has been created in the core of the Holy Land where the struggle has come to be inevitably pursued...."[10] Muslims believe it is important that they maintain a state of war with the Jewish state, since this will lead to the victory spoken of in Muhammad's prophecy. To them, relinquishing the fight against Israel is tantamount to unbelief and the renunciation of Islam.

Muslims also believe that when this battle is won, the victory will serve as an undeniable proof of the power and rightness of Islam: "Thus, has come to be true the miraculous prophetic tradition that had announced the occurrence of such a struggle. More of its authenticity would inevitably be realized when this war comes to a successful end by the expulsion of the Jewish aggressors, if God will. We will see when the day be ours."[11]

In summary, Muslims interpret the Jewish return to the Land and the Palestinian uprising as partly fulfilling Muhammad's prophecy and setting the stage for the final battle between Muslims and Jews. All Muslims are exhorted to occupy themselves with this goal, since it serves to make Islam a universal faith. To this end Sheikh Nadim Al-Jisr states: "We hope that our victory would soon materialize through the co-operation and mutual support of the present rulers of the Muslim world.[12]"

This teaching of *jihad* is the primary theme driving the Palestinians in the present conflict, and it's all done and justified in the name of Allah, as indicated by this excerpt from a live Palestinian television broadcast by Sheikh Ibrahim Madhi from the Sheikh 'Ijlin Mosque in Gaza (the Palestinian Authority headquarters). These words were spoken on June 8, 2001, a week after the suicide bombing that killed 20 young Israelis outside the Dolphiarium nightclub in Tel Aviv, and are revealing of how *jihad* is an inseparable part of the final predetermined purpose of Islam:

Allah is almighty. Had He wanted, He would have beaten them. But He tests you in suffering. We must prepare the ground for the army of Allah that is coming according to the [divine] predetermination. We must prepare a foothold for them. Allah is willing, this unjust state will be erased—Israel, will be erased; this unjust state—the United States, will be erased; this unjust state—Britain, will be erased—they who caused this people's *Nakbah* [the "Catastrophe" of the establishment of the State of Israel in 1948]....Blessings to whoever waged *Jihad* for the sake of Allah; blessings to whoever raided for the sake of Allah; blessings to whoever put a belt of explosives on his body or on his sons' and plunged into the midst of the Jews, crying, "*Allahu akbar,* praise to Allah, there is no God but Allah and Muhammad is His messenger."[13]

On one Islamic website we read this: "And when it is said to them, do not make mischief on the earth, they say, we are peacemakers, surely they are the mischief makers but they know not." This is cited as a prediction of the United States and its Western allies being enemies of the Muslim world.

Thus, the Arab-Israeli or Palestinian-Israeli conflict is being interpreted by Islamic leaders and many Orthodox Jews as a righteous war whose outcome has been predetermined by prophecy. In like manner, what Muslims have called "World War III against Islam" (by the United States) is being cast in apocalyptic terms: "The final hour will not come until the Muslims conquer the White House" (Tabarani).[14] The ultimate goal is to vindicate either the God of the Jews or Allah of the Muslims. Furthermore, there is no human negotiation that can resolve a religious war. For this reason, as the conflict intensifies and sermons to the faithful multiply, so do the fears of anxious observers. Egyptian Hani Shukrallah, writing for the Al-Aharam Organization, represents such fears when he says,

"The notion of an apocalypse kept at bay underpinned the peace process from the start....How long can it go on before an apocalypse? Looking for signs and portents, soothsaying or standing before this or that oracle is no help at all. The most absurd prophecy can be self-fulfilling if people believe in it sufficiently."[15]

As the unholy war stretches on, those who are religious on both sides will be staking their lives on their beliefs that their interpretation is the correct one. However, the problem is not one of fundamentalism per se, as Gershom Gorenberg has suggested, but which fundamentalism has the correct scenario of the future. Someone will be right, and someone will be wrong. To be sure, as the quote above states, strong belief will generate strong action, regardless of whether it is wrong belief. For this reason the war on terrorism must consider Islamic belief seriously and understand that if it wages war against terrorists who are Muslims, it fights a battle against their beliefs. Certainly, a study of our own faith in light of historical evidences that support its tenets and a comparison with other faiths that compete for our worldview is basic to our convictions, which motivate our conduct. The comparison presented in this chapter will hopefully provide a start to examining the prophetic component in these religions and help us see why there is much to fear about faith if it is not centered in an evidential context and it is lived out in a way that threatens other humans. We must judge well, for in prophetic terms, the future depends on it.

Similarities in Muslim, Jewish, and Christian Eschatology

	Islam	Judaism	Christianity
Eschatological view of time	Linear	Linear	Linear
Purpose of Christ's coming	Defeat Antichrist, live 40 days, then die (He didn't die in A.D. 33 but has been in state of "suspended animation" since)	Defeat Armilus and Gentile nations, restore the kingdom of Israel, return of Jewish exiles, who rule in age of spiritual harmony	Rescue Israel, defeat Antichrist (Rev. 19:11-21), judge the nations (Matt. 25:31-46) and wicked in Israel (Ezek. 20:33-38), and rule over messianic kingdom (Matt.19:28; Rev. 20:1-6).
Resurrection of the body	Yes	Yes	Yes (1 Corinthians 15:4-7,12-23)
Destruction of present world	Yes (includes angels, earth will "spill out all its contents")	Yes (but excludes angels)	Yes (but excludes angels)
Signs preceding Judgment Day	Yes	Yes	Yes (Matthew 24:4-28)
Judgment announced with the trumpet of an archangel	Yes ("siren" or "horn"; cf. Qur'an 56:15-56; cf. 36:51)	Yes (shofar will announce beginning of messianic era, gather the scattered exiles, and serve as a summons to the heavenly court on the Day of Judgment)	Yes (Matthew 24:31;1 Thessalonians 4:16)
Who must experience death?	All people	All people	All people (except those living when Christ returns)
Basis for eternal life	Works (which results in attaining the mercy of Allah)	Works (by keeping God's commandments in the Torah)	Work of Christ (applied to sinner by grace through faith)

Similarities in Muslim, Jewish, and Christian Eschatology

	Islam	Judaism	Christianity
Levels of reward	Yes (seven levels)	Yes (three levels)	Yes (but degrees, not levels)
Hell as a place of eternal torment	Yes ("destruction by fire"; cf. Qu'ran 56, in eight levels of torment (Sura 4:56, 14:49-50; 22:21; 74:27-29) eternally (47:15; 87:13)	Yes (Gehinnon, where bodies burn eternally in fiery pit)	Yes

Differences in Muslim, Jewish, and Christian Eschatology

	Islam	Judaism	Christianity
Nature of man	Basically good (Sura 7:23)	Good/bad (two inclinations within man)	Depraved (Romans 9-20; Ephesians 2:1-3)
"Purgatory" taught	Yes called Barzakh	No	No (evangelicals); yes (Catholics)
Assurance of salvation	Impossible in this life	Yes (but only for observant Jews)	Yes (1 John 5:11-13), but some no (Colossians 1:23)
Nature of God as Judge	Allah is arbitrary	YHWH is just (Genesis 18:25)	God is just (Romans 3:26)
Double predestination	Yes (Sura 35:8)	No	No (2 Peter 3:9), but some yes (Romans 9:21-22)
Those experiencing the Tribulation	Believers of Allah hidden with the prophet, followed by "wind of destruction" which will kill all people	Whole world (Daniel 12:1), but Israel to be "delivered out of it" (Jeremiah 30:7)	Various views: only unbelievers (pre-Trib), all but believers only for 3 1/2 years (mid-Trib), all but believers protected throughout most or entire seven years (pre-Wrath & post-Trib)

Differences in Muslim, Jewish, and Christian Eschatology

	Islam	Judaism	Christianity
Christ will come again	Yes ("to break the cross and kill the swine" followed by an "eruption of a fire in Eden")	No, Messiah's (first) coming is yet future	Yes (John 14:3; Titus 2:13; Revelation 22:20)
End-time signs	Major and minor signs reveal the last days have arrived (Sura 21:96; 27:82; 43:61) *Major Signs* 1) Gross materialism ("beast of the earth"; cf. Rev. 13:11-18) 2) Women outnumber men 3) Muslims defeat Jews in battle; Muslims and Christians battle unbelievers together, then Muslims defeat Christians in battle *Minor Signs* 1) Increase in bloodshed and war 2) Contraction of time 3) Religious knowledge decreases 4) Prevalence of the ungodly	*Ten signs* will accompany the Messianic "birth pangs" of the end times (Sanhedrin 97b). They are: 1) The world is either all righteous or guilty 2) Truth is in short supply 3) Inflation will soar 4) Israel begins to be repopulated 5) Wise people will be scarce 6) Jews will despair of redemption 7) The young will despise the old 8) Scholarship will be rejected 9) Piety will be held in disgust 10) Jews will turn against Jews	Beginning of *birth pangs:* 1) Wars between nations (Matthew 24:6-7a) 2) Famines & earthquakes (Matthew 24:7b) 3) False christs (Matthew 24:5) 4) Israel reestablished (Isaiah 11:11-12) *Birth pangs:* 1) Temple worship restored & abomination of desolation (Daniel 9:27; Matthew 25:15; 2 Thessalonians 2:4; Revelation 11:1-2) 2) Jews persecuted (Matthew 24:9-10, 16-20) 3) False christs & prophets (Matthew 24:11,24) 4) Global preaching of kingdom (Matthew 24:14) 5) Celestial disturbances (Matthew 24:29; Revelation 6–19)
Result of end-time battle(s)	"Great Destruction," which destroys all but God, then a resurrection/recreation	War of Gog and Magog, in which God defeats Gentiles and establishes Israel in its kingdom over all the earth	After Armageddon, Satan bound, believers enter Millennium; after Gog and Magog battle (Revelation 20:7-9) destruction of cosmos (2 Peter 3:10-13) and recreation (Revelation 21:1)

Differences in Muslim, Jewish, and Christian Eschatology

	Islam	Judaism	Christianity
End-time rule	Gog and Magog led by Darius, the king of Persia (Sura 21:96)	King Messiah as God's regent rules over the earth until time of re-creation	Christ
Length of judgment	50,000 years (?)	World will exist for 6,000 years (2,000 Desolation; 2,000 Torah; 2,000 days of Messiah. The last 1,000 years (the Great Sabbath) will be a time of renewal (Sanhedrin 97a)	Eternal (Mark 9:43-48)
Temporal dwelling for dead	Most scholars say both good and evil with Allah, but some say "Alam Bazar" for all or for only the wicked	*She'ol* (place of departed spirits equivalent to the Netherworld)	Christ's presence for Christians (2 Corinthians 5:8) Hades for non-Christians (Luke 16:23; Revelation 20:13)
Eternal dwelling for believers	*Janab* ("Paradise")	*Gan 'eden* (Heavenly Abode)	Heaven/New Jerusalem (Revelation 21:2-3)
Nature of eternal life	*Mutashibir*—(sensual pleasure in sex with virgins (Sura 55:56), eating (Sura 56:15-22), and happiness (Sura 47)	Enjoying the radiance of the divine presence (Berakhot 17a)	Fellowship (Revelation 21:3, 7; 22:4) Service (Revelation 7:15; 22:3) Worship (Revelation 6:9-12) Praise (Revelation 19:1-6)
View of Israel	Eternally destroyed	Eternally restored (Jeremiah 31:35-37)	Eternally restored (Jeremiah 31:35-37)
Difficulty in understanding	Simple (unified views)	Complex (various views)	Complex (many views)

CHAPTER 17

Why Can't They All Just Get Along?

Peace for us means the destruction of Israel. We are preparing for an all-out war that will last for generations. …We shall not rest until the day when we return to our home, and until we destroy Israel.[1]
—YASSER ARAFAT

There is no solution. We want the country to be ours. They want the country to be theirs.[2]
—DAVID BEN-GURION

States do not make peace with enemies. They defeat them.[3]
—SIR WINSTON CHURCHILL

In March 1991, television stations in the United States broadcast an amateur videotape of four white LAPD officers kicking and clubbing a black motorist named Rodney King. On April 29, 1992 the trial ended, and the police officers were declared innocent. That very evening in Los Angeles, rioting broke out, and by the time order was restored, 54 people had been killed, 2,000 had been injured, and damages were estimated at $900 million.

During the rioting, Rodney King delivered a television appeal to the rioters and made the now-famous statement that has been parodied endlessly by comedians: "Can't we all just get along?" King, of course, did not mean his words to be humorous, but the sheer naïveté of this statement in the context of the racial rampage made it perfect for comic relief. Yet today, as people watch the evening news and see the angry crowds of Muslims shouting "death to the United States," Israeli tanks pushing into West Bank villages, and see the Palestinian rioting and the death tolls rising, they may find themselves asking the very same question: Why can't they all just get along?

In the case of the Israelis and Palestinians, many people who don't understand the complex issues involved in this conflict sincerely believe that all that is really needed is for both sides to apologize to one another, shake hands, and make peace. However, we must remember that before the 1992 riots in Los Angeles there were the Watts riots in 1965. Though the people involved in those riots may have symbolically shaken hands afterward and agreed to be peaceful, an unabated anger continued to fester inside a generation, only to burst out again in 1992. Superficial peace, or a peace on paper but not in practice—like most of the peace agreements concluded in the Middle East—only hides a hatred that's ready to make war when the opportunity exists.

Like all delusions, if the appearance is proper, the words are right, and the audience has displaced normal reservations in light of necessary (and expected) results, even seasoned statesmen can be deceived. On September 30, 1938, a day after British prime minister Neville Chamberlain met in Munich with German chancellor Adolf Hitler to sign an armistice, Chamberlain made this announcement to the British public in front of 10 Downing Street:

> We regard the agreement signed last night and the Anglo-German Naval Agreement as symbolic of the

desire of our two peoples never to go to war with one another again. We are resolved that the method of consultation shall be the method adopted to deal with any other questions that may concern our two countries....
My good friends, for the second time in our history, a British prime minister has returned from Germany bringing peace with honour. I believe it is peace for our time....Go home and get a nice quiet sleep.

That sleep was soon shattered, as well as the "peace" Chamberlain had negotiated. Less than a year later, Germany launched the Second World War, in which 52 million people perished and Chamberlain's city of London was bombed by the Germans into ruins. All the British could think of at that moment was that they had been deceived.

The same deception has colored the Oslo peace process from its inception. This was revealed when the Jerusalem administrator for the Palestinian Authority Faisal Husseini gave what would be a final interview before his death (May 31, 2001) to the Egyptian newspaper *Al-Arabi*. Husseini, who always appeared in public as the picture of peaceful coexistence, stated to the Egyptian reporter, "We are ambushing the Israelis and cheating them....our ultimate goal is the liberation of all historic Palestine from the [Jordan] River to the [Mediterranean] Sea....We distinguish the strategic, long-term goals from the political phased goals, which we are compelled to temporarily accept due to international pressure."[4]

In the war on terrorism, deceptions abound. One deception, made more pernicious due to the source, has been fostered by the United Nations. It argues that the cause of global terrorism is poverty. Hungry and frustrated people do desparate things...like highjacking airliners. Of course, these terrorists were living comfortably in Middle America before blowing themselves and 5,000 others to oblivion. It is not poverty that causes global terrorism; rather, global terrorism causes poverty. Wherever radical Islam has taken control, it has kept populations under control through poverty. Yet people who want simple solutions will accept such silly statements.

Our age has become intoxicated at the prospect of global peace. Weary of wars, and believing that technology can rescue the future, there is an unparalleled longing for "peace at any price" (so long as *our* country does not have to pay for it!). Yet, despite appearances to the contrary (since the nature of man and the conditions that foment wars have not changed), our planet is ready to pursue any process that may promise the coveted peace. While one-third of our world is at war at any time and at present the world is choosing sides as the search for terrorism continues, international anxiety is again heightened by the one supposed obstacle to "peace in our time"—the Israeli-Palestinian conflict. Regardless of the irreconcilable religious agendas that precipitated and continue to provoke their conflict, the international community is driven by a desire to resolve the political problem of "Palestine."

Amazingly, even though Israel was once willing to give up the historic divisions of its country—Judea and Samaria, and half of Jerusalem with the Temple Mount— as the price of peace, the Palestinians walked away from the negotiating table and renewed their local war of attrition. Even shortly after the peace process was initiated, it soon became apparent to many Israelis that it was doomed to fail. This conviction grew along with the statistics that revealed more Israelis and Palestinians were being killed *during* the peace process than before it was started! Today, the Palestinians have committed far greater acts of terror and have dramatically increased the Israeli death toll. In spite of all this, the world continues to urge that the peace process be renewed with the same naive ambition expressed by Chamberlain in 1938. That leads us to an important question many have asked:

If the Palestinians Get Their Land Back, Won't There Be Peace?

It is popularly believed that Israeli aggression and the unjust "occupation" of Palestinian land is the problem preventing peace. If so, the "simple solution" is for the Israelis to simply "unoccupy" the Palestinian land. But the issues involved are much more complex than people realize, as we saw in the previous chapters. Both the Israelis and Palestinians have certain claims regarding the land. Given the Palestinian claims, we know that to "unoccupy" the "Palestinian land" means the eradication of Israel. What's more, Israel could never offer enough concessions to satisfy the ultimate objectives of the Palestinian Authority, since to do so would mean moving from the Land of Israel and into the Mediterranean Sea! This statement may seem extreme, but we must remember that at the Camp David II Summit, Barak offered 90 to 91 percent of the territories as well as the dismantling of the Israeli settlements located in them. But Arafat refused this, demanding "more." Six months later, in the negotiations at Taba (just across the Egyptian Sinai border shared with Israel), Arafat refused the "more"—an Israeli withdrawal from 95 percent of the territories, with an additional offer to compensate the remaining five percent with *Israeli* territory! If land and settlements were *really* the problem to peace, then why did the Palestinians reject this "simple" solution? The answer is that the land-for-peace formula has never been acceptable to the Palestinians. Proof of this may be seen in the fact that prior to 1948, when the Arabs in Palestine *had* the land they now seek to possess, they didn't seek to live in peace with Israel, but *attacked* Israel along with neighboring Arab nations in an attempt to remove it from the Middle East.

Prior to 1967 when Gaza, the West Bank, and East Jerusalem were under Palestinian control (Jordan being 80 percent of the original Palestinian state created under the British Mandate, with its population primarily Palestinian), the Palestinians again attacked Israel and sought its destruction. The fact that the PLO (whose goal is "the liberation of all of Palestine") was founded in 1964 (before the 1967 Six-Day War), when the land presently contested *was* Palestinian land, reveals that the "Palestine" the PLO seeks to "liberate" can only be *the land in which the State of Israel was established*. Again, when the PLO was established, the Gaza Strip and the West Bank *belonged to the Arabs*. Therefore, the PLO was not set up to "liberate" these territories but the *rest* of the land, including the Jewish "settlements" in Haifa, Acre, Jaffa, and Tel Aviv (which are, of course, some of Israel's major cities). The Arab League Charter as well is based on the liberation of land "occupied" in 1948—i.e., from the founding of the State of Israel. In other words, PLO really ought to stand for "Palestinian Lands Only." Tragically, the true intentions of the PLO seem to be unknown or to have been forgotten by the international media, which, in turn, means that few people are aware of the PLO's goals.

The popular depiction of the Palestinians has been that of an unarmed people trying to defend themselves until they can find peace again in their ancestral land. However, the PLO charter adopted in 1968 declares, "Armed struggle is the only way to liberate Palestine. This is the overall strategy, not merely a tactical phase," and, "The partition of Palestine in 1947 and the establishment of the state of Israel are entirely illegal, regardless of the passage of time." In other words, the objective is not a peace with Israel nor a piece of Israel, but to take the place of Israel.

In addition, Palestinian leaders have continually assured their own peoples throughout the peace talks that nothing has changed in the stated PLO plan. For instance, George Habash, leader of the Popular Front for the Liberation of Palestine, the second-largest PLO faction, has revealed the real motive behind accepting limited land grants from Israel. In his organization's paper *Al-Hadaf*, he declared, "We seek to establish a state that we can use in order to liberate the other part of the Palestinian soil."[5] The PLO plan he has in view is the *gradual* acquisition of Israeli territory (the "other part" of the Palestinian soil). This will be accomplished through what Salah Khalaf Abu Iyad, Arafat's principal deputy, called the dual means of "rifle and diplomacy." He stated this plan plainly when, at a Fatah Day celebration in Amman on January 1, 1991, he said, "Now we accept the formation of the Palestinian state in part of Palestine, in the Gaza Strip, and West Bank. We will start from that part and we will liberate Palestine, inch by inch."[6] This "phased program" was originally adopted at the twelfth session of the Palestinian National Council in June of 1974, reconfirmed in 1988, and again stated by Arafat to 19 Arab ministers assembled in Cairo on September 19, 1993, less than a week *after* signing the Declaration of Principles with Israel on international television in Washington, D.C.!

In light of this, one writer summed up Israel's concessions to the Palestinian Authority as trading land for time: "But let us also be under no illusion as to what has happened, or what will happen hereafter. The Palestinian Arabs as a whole have not changed their minds one iota about what they regard as a great historic wrong [the existence of the State of Israel], nor have they abandoned their hope of rectifying it."[7]

Joan Peters addresses these facts in her 1984 book *From Time Immemorial* and gives the reason for the original and continued Palestinian nationalist uprising: "The Arabs believe that by creating an Arab Palestinian identity, at the sacrifice of the well-being and the very lives of the 'Arab refugees,' they will accomplish politically and through 'guerilla warfare' what they failed to achieve in military combat: the destruction of Israel—the unacceptable independent *dhimmi* state. That is the heart of the matter."[8] And that is exactly what Yasser Arafat has plainly stated: "Peace for us means the destruction of Israel. We are preparing for an all-out war which will last for generations....We shall not rest until the day when we return to our home, and until we destroy Israel."[9] Even with such direct statements about the PLO's intent, the American administration has repeatedly refused to identify Arafat as a terrorist and the PLO as a terrorist organization, going so far as to believe that he can be a partner in the war against terrorism—a belief he has taken pains to promote, although *not* among his Palestinian people or the Arab Muslim world!

Israel was once duped into making concessions to Arafat in the belief that he would control terrorism against Israel. Now Israel claims (credibly so) that he directly controls the terrorists. After a lifetime as a terrorist leader, to act otherwise would be an uncharacteristic comedown. The same deceptive demeanor can be seen in Arafat's lieutenants, such as Faisal Husseini, the late administrator for Jerusalem Affairs, who summed up the Palestinian strategy when he declared, "We may win or lose, but our eyes will continue to aspire to the strategic goal—namely, to establish Palestine from the river to the sea." Husseini in this statement described a Palestinian state whose boundaries will stretch from the River Jordan to the Mediterranean Sea—with no Israel in between! Interestingly, Husseini was routinely described as a moderate. With "moderates" like him, the Palestinians need no extremists. And even though he's now gone, the strategy lives on.

Have Israeli and Palestinian Attitudes Toward Peace Changed Since the Second Intifada?

Yasser Arafat's new Intifada to destroy Israel has brought not only the deaths of hundreds of Israelis and

Palestinians through the endless cycles of attack and counterattack initiated by Palestinian terrorism, but also the death of the Israeli peace movement. When Yitzhak Rabin was assassinated by a nationalist religious Jew, a radical split developed in the country between secular and religious Israelis. Many nationalist religious organizations were banned by the government as militant, and secular Israelis widely sponsored peace rallies, such as those by the Peace Now organization in Tel Aviv, where hundreds of thousands of Jews gathered. However, since the renewal of the Intifada, all of that has ended. "These days," as one Israeli writer put it, "all those Israelis who still believe Yasser Arafat wants peace could meet in a phone booth. 'Peace Now' might better be called 'Peace Where?' The Israelis have had their eyes opened at last, and it is difficult to find anybody in that country who can say peace process without smirking."[10] The entire nation has unified against Arafat and the Palestinians, and the nationalist religious groups have reemerged and gained secular support.

The attitude of Israel's leadership has also changed. Israeli prime minister Ariel Sharon stated his administration's changed position with regard to future negotiations with the Palestinian Authority to President Bush after the war on terrorism was announced:

> I've said it very clearly. Israel will not negotiate under fire and under terror. We've said it because if we will do that, we'll never reach peace. That is the point....what I'm saying is not an obstacle, not a barrier against peace. On the contrary, if we'll be very strict, then the Palestinians will understand they cannot gain anything by terror. Therefore, we have to be very strict in order to reach peace, which all of us would like to have.[11]

A similar change occurred with the American public after September 11, 2001, bringing a renewed show of patriotism with a 95 percent approval rating for President Bush's retaliation militarily against terrorism. Today, left-wing university political-science professors who blame American policies for terrorist attacks are themselves being criticized by the patriotic public.

Former president George Bush, Sr., when he was president, explained the principle Sharon has adopted: "Radical forces do not respect weakness, they prey on it. History has taught us that much." In fact, that lesson should have been learned after the Munich Conference of 1938, when countries capitulated to German chancellor Adolf Hitler, sold out Czechoslovakia, and paid the price of his greater aggression. As American Jew Yehuda Sherman has pointed out, "Hitler taught us that if you try to appease an aggressor by making concessions to his demands, he will perceive this as weakness on your part, and it will encourage him to make even greater demands, and eventually resort to violence."[12]

Between July 5 and 11, 2001, a joint survey was conducted by the Palestinian Center for Policy and Survey Research and the Harry S. Truman Institute for Peace at the Hebrew University. The study surveyed 1,318 Palestinians and 1,019 Israelis (519 Jews and 500 Arabs), and showed some definite changes in attitude that have taken place since the inception of the new Intifada. The results reveal that 41 percent of Israelis and 46 percent of Palestinians believe there is no chance of reaching a peace agreement in the foreseeable future. By contrast, a similar poll published a year ago after the failure of the Camp David peace summit, revealed that only 19 percent of Israelis and 23 percent of Palestinians felt there was no chance of peace.

In the more recent survey, a full 92 percent of Palestinians also said they supported armed attacks against Israeli soldiers in the West Bank and Gaza Strip, territories that have been occupied by the Jewish state since 1967. Another 58 percent said they supported armed attacks against civilians inside Israel. On the Israeli side, 44 percent support continued "moderate military measures," while 37 percent advocate the use of full force to remove Palestinian President Yasser Arafat from power. Only 16 percent support a unilateral cease fire. In addition, the survey found that 59 percent of Palestinians and 46 percent of Israelis characterize their relations five to ten years from now as "conflictual and violent." Consequently, the Palestinians are determined to continue their armed struggle, while Israelis, with each new terrorist act in their midst, call for Sharon to "go to war"!

A Palestinian poll conducted a month earlier by the Jerusalem Media Center, shows even more startling changes in attitudes among the West Bank populations. It reveals that 80 percent of Palestinians want to continue the Intifada, a rise from 70.1 percent in December 2000. Furthermore, 68.6 percent say they now support suicide attacks against Israelis, compared with 66.2 percent in April 2001, and only 26.1 percent in March 1999. But most troubling is the way in which the Palestinians polled see the *goals* of the current Intifada. One could assume that a vast majority would have replied that the aim of the current conflict is to end "the Israeli occupation" and set up a Palestinian state, as declared by the Palestinian leadership. However, only 45.6 percent gave that answer, while 41.2 percent said that the goal of the current Intifada is a "complete liberation of Palestinian land"—in other words, the destruction of Israel.

Furthermore, Palestinians no longer view the Jewish settlers in their territories as "a tolerable presence," but as an extension of the Israeli army. As Palestinian Authority cabinet secretary-general Ahmed Abdel Rahman stated on June 21, 2001, "The Jewish settlers in the territories are not civilians, but are an armed militia that need to be fought." The more moderate Palestinians, however, concerned more with their livelihoods than politics, have left the West Bank and Gaza Strip. According to Jordan's interior minister Awad Halifat, since the outbreak of Arafat's war, some 150,000 Palestinians have entered Jordan and have not left.[13] An additional 40,000 have fled for the United States, South America, or Egypt. Out of a population of only 3 million people, this is a sizable loss. But the real problem is that the more militant Palestinians remain at the core of an economically impoverished and desperate society. Having suffered for the cause of liberation, these people believe they have nothing more to lose and are not motivated to make peace, as an interview with a Palestinian in Bethlehem recently revealed:

> The frenzy of the Palestinian people will not allow any peaceful outcome. They believe that Jews and Christians must be driven out, and if not, the Palestinians will wage all-out war on Israel...."Arafat has been so successful in poisoning the minds of the entire Palestinian people, making them believe that Israel is rightfully theirs and that they will achieve eternal joy if they are willing to die for their beliefs, that there is only shame in turning back....They also believe that they will do so with the support of all the Arab nations in the area....that is what the leaders say at every meeting, every mosque, and every television broadcast. They are calling for a holy war against the infidel.[14]

As the aforementioned statements and statistics show, rather than a move toward "getting along," attitudes have atrophied and are worse than ever before.

Hasn't the Palestinian Authority Been Willing to Make Peace?

In the past, the media carefully cultivated the impression that the Palestinians were war weary and passionate to make peace. However, while Arafat has continually talked about peace to the English-language media and the Western world, he has never addressed the subject of peace in Arabic to his own Islamic world. The organizations that monitor all the Arab broadcasts and publications with Palestinian Authority spokesmen report they have yet to find a single one that speaks of peace in the context of a relationship with the Israelis. Rather, in both the Arab press and in Muslim mosques, Palestinian leaders have continually called for Israel's destruction. Furthermore, the Palestinian Authority has never amended its PLO charter to recognize Israel's right to exist, as required by the Declaration of Principles signed with Israel in 1993.

Arafat did write a *letter* to Yitzhak Rabin on September 9, 1993 that stated, "The PLO recognizes the right of the State of Israel to exist in peace and security," but he left the PLO *charter* unchanged, still calling for "the elimination of the Jewish state." When questioned about this seeming contradiction, Arafat stated that when a Palestinian state is set up (according to the terms of the Palestinians), a new charter would be made that includes the recognition of Israel. However, if the Palestinians' stated goals are achieved, there will be no Israel to recognize!

The Declaration of Principles also required the Palestinians to *renounce terrorism*. But statistics kept since the day of the handshake on the White House lawn—when the United States removed the PLO from its list of terrorist organizations—reveal that PLO terrorism has actually *increased*. Between the signing of the Israeli-Palestinian Declaration of Principles in 1993 and September 2001, more than 400 Israelis were killed in terrorist violence—more than in the seven years before the declaration. For example, during the first few years of this "peace" period, when terrorism was to have been controlled by the Palestinian Authority, there were 32 Israeli civilians murdered, 438 Israeli civilians

Burned-out bus along a road. Hamas terrorism has launched suicide bombers at city buses in Jerusalem, causing terrible fatalities.
Photo by Paul Streber

Anti-Arab demonstration in downtown Jerusalem in response to multiple bus and city bombings in May 1997.
Photo courtesy of Israel Government Press Office

injured, 21 Israeli soldiers murdered, 527 Israeli soldiers injured, 239 Israelis stabbed, 88 bombings, 1,220 petrol bombs thrown, 210 shootings, and 51 hand-grenade attacks.[15] At the height of the peace negotiations from 1996-97 there were 286 attacks (from firebombs to suicide bombings) in 1996, and there were 521 such attacks in 1997, and in 1998 (for which we do not have numbers yet) there were more extensive and intensive attacks such as the suicide bombings at a Tel Aviv restaurant and at

Jerusalem's crowded outdoor market, Mahane Yehuda.[16] In addition, during this time over 100 planned attacks were prevented on such places as Jerusalem's largest mall, its amphitheater, railroads, and Tel Aviv's Diamond Exchange. Kidnapping attempts on Jerusalem's mayors were prevented as well. And since the return to Intifada conditions, things have gotten even worse. For example, there were the two young Israelis who, seeking protection from a violent Palestinian mob, entered a Palestinian police station for help. They were stabbed, thrown from the police station window, and lynched by the mob.

In light of these conditions, chief of staff Shaul Mofaz reported to the Knesset's Foreign Affairs and Defense Committee that the Palestinian Authority has become a "terrorist entity." Of course, the PLO never stopped being a terrorist organization, but when the Palestinian Authority was established, it was to be a legitimate interim "democracy" leading

Aftermath of Israeli retaliation at a Palestinian police station in Nablus after two Israeli soldiers were lynched there by a Palestinian mob.
Photo by Binyamin Lalizou

A young Palestinian during a riot against Israeli rule.
Photo by Binyamin Lalizou

to nationhood. That it has become a "terrorist entity" indicates that it has either moved backward or never intended to move forward.

What About an Enforceable Kind of Peace?

There are only two types of peace possible in the world today. The first kind is that which exists between democracies. The peace between the United States and its neighboring countries of Canada and Mexico is an example of this type of peace. Even though Canada may protest the fact that the United States is poisoning its environment with acid rain, and the United States may oppose the trafficking of drugs from Mexico, these countries do not go to war with each other over these issues. Democracies generally resolve their differences through nonviolent negotiations that do not require guarantees, since there is no threat to their respective national security.

The second kind of peace that exists is that between democracies and nondemocracies. When the nature of the regime changes, so must the nature of the peace. When political philosophies are inherently different, the type of peace expected will follow suit. In this case, agreements must be accompanied by guarantees of security and a balance of power that promotes détente. This is the type of peace that is being negotiated between Israel (the sole democracy in the Middle East) and its nondemocratic Arab neighbors.

When dealing with the Palestinian Authority, we need to keep in mind that the founders and leaders of the Palestinian Authority were once at the top of the United States' list of terrorists because they employed terrorism as the means of achieving political ends. PLO factions used the terrorist tactic of "uprising" (Intifada) against Israel *before* the Oslo Accord, and it continued to call for a *jihad* throughout the peace process and still promotes this as its present cause today. The Palestinian Authority has also continued to openly embrace and support terrorist organizations such as Hamas, Islamic Jihad, Hizbullah, and others, and it has called for and implemented the death penalty for so-called "Israeli Collaborators," such as Palestinians who sell family-owned land to Jews. Such use of terror is the way of nondemocracies, but is totally unacceptable when it comes to negotiating with democracies.

This may help to explain why peace between democratic and nondemocratic parties cannot be achieved on the basis of handshakes and nonviolent negotiations. It is the reason the United States does not attempt to negotiate with terrorists or states that support terrorism, but gives ultimatums to "be with us or against us." The only possibility that a manageable peace could exist between such parties is if it exists with enforceable guarantees of security and a balance of military armaments. Paul Greenberg explains the options available to the Israelis:

> As for the Israelis, they now have a choice between grim alternatives: They can continue to pretend that they have a negotiating partner and resign themselves to a peace process that is really a long, slow war of attrition, which has already begun. Or they can try to impose their borders by force and wage a real war with no hope of establishing anything like a real peace. The best they could achieve would be an armed separation, which would have to be maintained at the price of unending vigilance. Even then the occasional suicide bomber would get through.[17]

There are some who continue to believe that peace can come by a return to the negotiating table, as former U.S. Assistant Secretary of State William Burns once stated: "It's obvious that there can be no military solution to this problem. It's only through a political process that security can be re-established."[18] However, the best efforts to achieve peace by this process have failed, and the renewal of the Intifada has only served to unite secular and religious Israelis against further negotiations with the Palestinians. Does that mean war is the only option left? That's what we'll explore in the next chapter.

CHAPTER 18

Will There Be Another War?

Things won't be the same as they were
before. We will raise the level of reaction
against the Palestinian Authority.
—ISRAELI PRIME MINISTER ARIEL SHARON
TO THE ISRAELI CABINET AFTER THE
ASSASSINATION OF CABINET MEMBER
REHOVAM ZE'EVI BY THE POPULAR FRONT
FOR THE LIBERATION OF PALESTINE

Our choice is the military option.
We must put an end to the despicable
negotiations. The time has come for jihad
and martyrdom.[1]
—SHIEKH HAMED BITAWI, CHAIRMAN OF THE
PALESTINE RELIGIOUS SCHOLARS ASSOCIATION
AND HEAD OF THE PALESTINIAN AUTHORITY'S
SHARIA COURT OF APPEALS IN NABLUS

Israel is not going to sit on its backside
waiting for life to turn into hell.
If the Palestinians want all-out war…
Israel's response will be strategic; it will
fight this war to win.[2]
—HIRSH GOODMAN, FOUNDING EDITOR,
THE JERUSALEM REPORT

As I prepared to write this chapter, I decided its serious nature required a more pastoral setting. So I took my laptop computer outside to work on the patio. But no sooner had I began addressing the subject of war than I began to experience a "war" of my own with an overly aggressive wasp. Every time I drove it away it disappeared, only to return again as soon as I took my seat. Finally, I looked underneath my chair, and discovered the wasp had built its nest there. From the perspective of the wasp I was the aggressor, an intruder who had occupied its territory and forced a fight. How could I explain to the wasp that the chair was mine and not his—that I had purchased and possessed it long before the wasp's arrival? With no common ground to negotiate the matter, knowing that by nature a wasp can only go to war, my only recourse was to end the conflict so I could fulfill my purpose. Of course the irony of this interruption didn't escape me as my thoughts returned to the question of Middle East hostilities. With no common ground left for the Israelis and Palestinians to negotiate their conflicting claims, a war on terrorism in progress, and the surrounding Islamic world pressing the West with *jihad*, can there be any recourse for these peoples already engaged in a limited war but to wage an all-out war? That's the question we'll examine in this chapter.

How Serious Is the Present Political Impasse?

Oslo had offered the prospect of peace, but from its inception it was clear to many that the one-sided peace it offered was one Israel could ill afford. This "pseudopeace" seemed to offer the possibility of peace, but in fact it only made war more probable. An agreement with the Palestinians would have effectively turned back the calendar to 1947, when Israel was contained within its least-defensible boundaries, only nine miles wide in some places. It would have removed the buffer zone that's necessary between Israel and its hostile Arab neighbors, and it would have made it possible for the Palestinians to use their newly acquired territories to establish (or host) an enemy army that could invade Israel.

While the world hoped the Oslo meeting would bring peace in the Middle East, insiders feared just the opposite would happen. When the PLO and Israel signed the Oslo Accord in 1994, Benjamin Netanyahu explained that Palestinian leader Yasser Arafat could not have negotiated unless the Israelis were considered a part of the PLO's "phased plan" (first developed in 1974). This document proposed that "any portion of land liberated from the Zionist occupiers, whether by peaceful or military means, will be used *as a staging ground for the complete destruction of Israel*" (emphasis added). Arafat's intentions, especially concerning his promised conquest of Jerusalem, were never concealed in the speeches he made to his people. In one secretly recorded speech made in a mosque in Johannesburg, South Africa, Arafat called for faithful Muslims to "come and to fight and start the *jihad* to liberate Jerusalem," comparing the agreement signed with Israel to Muhammad's deceitful peace pact with his own Quraysh tribe. This ten-year peace pact was made because the Quraysh tribe was too strong for Muhammad to defeat. But only two years later, when Muhammad's forces had grown stronger, he violated the treaty and slaughtered the Quraysh tribe. Arafat then asked his Arab audience to join him "to continue our way to Jerusalem" as "*mujaheddin* [warriors of *jihad*],"[3] the very term the Taliban and all radical Muslims use for themselves.

Even former prime minister Ehud Barak, who took part in the final series of peace negotiations with Arafat, now concludes that he was duped and agrees that the peace process was only a part of the phased plan devised to weaken Israel as a prelude to the next Arab-Israeli war. One writer, comparing the situation to a similar situation in the past, stated: "Weakening Israel territorially or spiritually...will soon force it to face the choice Chamberlain faced when appeasement failed and Hitler invaded Poland: fight a desperate war or perish."[4] One Palestinian in Bethlehem put it this way:

> Arafat doesn't want peace. He is a warhorse who wants Muslims to fill Israel to throw the Jews and Christians out....the leaders of Hamas, Islamic Jihad, Hezbollah, and the PLO within the Palestinian Authority...will stop at nothing, killing and maiming anything that moves and has the title Jew....They are calling for a holy war against the infidel. My personal opinion is that unless the Europeans and the Americans wake up to the truth very, very soon, we will all die.[5]

Such rhetoric can easily give the impression that the present political impasse is permanent. The Israeli government will not negotiate under fire, and the Palestinians, having walked away from the negotiation process, will not cease firing until all of their demands are met. Today, Israelis and Israeli settlements are continually being fired upon and Israelis are firing back with less and less defined restraint. The borders between Israel and the Palestinian areas of the West Bank remain closed, and a permanent seam to separate the two populations has been considered, but a similar plan in South Lebanon failed, and had to be abandoned. Meanwhile, hate continues to flow over Arab radio and television, in the Arab press, and in fiery sermons delivered in mosques each Friday across the Arab world—sermons that call for the destruction of Israel and America.

What's more, the rhetoric is not new. Even Anwar Sadat, the Egyptian president, who negotiated peace with Israel, expressed the Palestinian mindset 30 years ago: "Jerusalem is the property of the Muslim nation.... Nobody can ever decide the fate of Jerusalem. We shall retake it with the help of Allah out of the hands of those of whom the Qur'an said: 'It was written of them that they shall be demeaned and made wretched.'...We are getting ready for them, O brethren!"[6] And the Palestinians have not stopped at mere words; they are putting their hatred into action. Recently, Palestinian extremists held a meeting at Jerusalem at which they recruited some 250 volunteer suicide bombers who will help initiate a campaign of terror.[7] In July 2001 this campaign affected one of my good friends, an Israeli pastor. He and his family live in the Jerusalem suburb of Pisgat Ze'ev, where a car bomb exploded below their apartment complex. Evidently the intent was to get the building to collapse; fortunately, it didn't. Many of the bomb attacks around Israel are unsuccessful or do only a minimum of damage because the bombs explode prematurely or not at all due to the inexperience of the terrorists. However, there is no question that the number of attacks has increased, with the clear aim of provoking a war.

For this reason, on July 26, 2001, former prime minister Benjamin Netanyahu, in a speech at the Likud central committee meeting, declared war on the Palestinian entity, calling Arafat "the head of the largest terrorist concern in the world." Prime Minister Sharon has also spoken of "the continuation of the 1948 War of Independence" with reference to the current situation, a war that includes broad-scale commando-type battles against terrorism. In like manner, Moshe Arens, addressing a Likud faction meeting in Ariel, Samaria, said that the Israel Defense Forces must be deployed to stop the violence in the territories. Referring to the policy of restraint then required by the government, he stated, "It is a policy based on the mistaken assumption that the problem is also a diplomatic problem, [one] that cannot be solved by military means. I say only by military means."[8] It is only a matter of time before the next shooting, the next suicide bombing, the next explosion in a crowded Israeli market or teenage nightspot—and the next response from the Israeli side.

With all that in mind, let's now consider the response that has come from the U.S. side. When America declared it was at war with terrorism, every Arab Muslim regime in the Middle East panicked. On the one hand, they believed that the United States would aid Israel in going after the Palestinians (which they knew fit the U.S. definition of terrorism) as well as other Arab states that supported the Palestinians. And Israelis expected a new sympathy from Americans for their long war with terrorism—a sympathy that would enable them to finally put down the Palestinian Authority.

However, the U.S.-built Coalition—which includes Arab states—prevented this. Nevertheless, the risky U.S. partnership with Arab Muslim states may contribute ultimately to the very regional war it has sought to avoid by keeping Israel at bay. As the pro-government *Egyptian Gazette* warned: "American jingoistic militarism, unleashed on mere suspicion, is set to radicalize moderate Muslims and earn (the) country more enemies."[9]

Worse, as the United States promised increased arsenal sales to Coalition partners in the Middle East, a congressional aide told *Defense News*, "God help us if [Egyptian President Hosni] Mubarak falls or gets shot, because every weapon we ever sold to him will be used against us."[10] And, if America attacks any Arab Muslim state (other than the Taliban), the Coalition threatens to break apart, with the Arab states siding with their fellow Muslims. Thus, whatever the United States may do, its efforts in the Middle East are sure to draw Israel (and the Palestinians) into the conflict—whether or not intended.

How Likely Is the Threat of War?

All-out war between Israel and the Palestinians (if not a regional war) is not merely likely, but inevitable. Israel is well aware that the conditions of Intifada constitute a war of attrition that is unwinnable. As *New York Times* reporter and former Middle East Bureau Chief Chris Hedges notes, "Rather than defeating the Palestinians, Israel may be slowly defeating itself....Unlike the wars of 1967 and 1973, Israel today is fighting not against armies but against a subject people."[11] The Israeli government is aware, having endured the previous Intifada from 1987–1993, of the emotional drain to Israeli society and the heavy financial and political costs of a prolonged bout with terrorism.

At the same time, Palestinians have been told that Israeli society is weak and divided, and have been led to believe their Intifada is weakening and dividing Israel to the point where it will either have no heart to fight or will fight a war with itself. They've also been told that international condemnation of Israel will cause it to back down from war. But the opposite has actually occurred: The Intifada has united all of Israel and enraged it as never before, making Israelis willing to go to war regardless of international opinion. Hirsh Goodman, the founding editor of *The Jerusalem Report* magazine, tells us, "Israel is not going to sit on its backside waiting for life to turn into hell. If the Palestinians want all-out war using in-depth terrorist bombing as a strategy, Israel's response will be strategic; it will fight this war to win."[12] The only solution they see is a resolution, and thereby the inevitability of war.

This inevitability is also reflected in the irreconcilable religious and nationalistic convictions that govern today's Palestinians and Israelis. For example, Abu Alli, a Hamas Brigade spokesman, has stated the usual radical Muslim justification for continued terrorist attacks against Israelis: "We in Hamas see the killing of Jews as an act that brings us closer to Allah."[13] On the Israeli side, similar impassioned rhetoric once came from the late Chief Rabbi Shlomo Goren: "Arafat is responsible for thousands of murders. Therefore, everyone in Israel who meets him in the streets has the right to kill him."[14] It was just such a belief that drove Orthodox Jew Yigael Amir to assassinate Yitzhak Rabin for initiating the Oslo peace process with the terrorist Arafat. However, even if Yasser Arafat dies or is assassinated, the inevitability of war will not be averted. The range of potential replacements for the leadership of the Palestinian Authority consists only of Islamic fundamentalists and local warlords. The Palestinian Authority of today that offers some semblance of "order" will most likely be replaced by either fanaticism or chaos.

Because of the ongoing terrorist attacks instigated by the Palestinians, many of the Jewish settlers who reside in what have become Palestinian-controlled areas have felt especially vulnerable during the land-for-peace negotiations, distrusting the Israeli government's "desire" to protect them in the midst of enemy territory. They have called the government's orders for them to evacuate their homes (as in previous withdrawals from areas of Judea and Samaria) "traitorous," and the order to turn in their army-issued rifles "insane." The late Benny Kahane, leader of Kach (assassinated by a Palestinian terrorist, like his brother Meir) went further, calling the orders "illegal" and "criminal."[15] Nevertheless, these settlers will gladly support the government in the call for an all-out war, although they are not willing to wait much longer. Settlers have already openly attacked Palestinians (who also openly attack them) and have plotted counterterrorism against Palestinian villages.

Given the increased violence between Palestinians and Israelis, Arab writer Hani Shukrallah, writing before the events of September 11, 2001 and following, believes the whole of the Arab world may be on the brink of war: "Sharon is fighting Israel's War of Independence all over again. Peres is speaking of a battle for Israel's existence, describing the current situation as an existential dilemma the likes of which he's never seen before (and he's seen a lot)....More ominous still, references to the possibility of all-out regional war have become commonplace."[16] For the first time in years, the Israeli military has reentered territories conceded to Arafat in order to control terrorist attacks launched from these areas (e.g., Jennin, Bethlehem/Beit-Jala, Hebron, Gaza Strip). Even though such acts have been considered temporary punative or preventative measures "until Arafat controls the terrorism" in these areas, just as the Israeli Defense Forces previously maintained a presence in major Palestinian population centers for safety purposes, Israel may have to remain in these areas to root out the terrorist infrastructures within them. Of course, taking such a

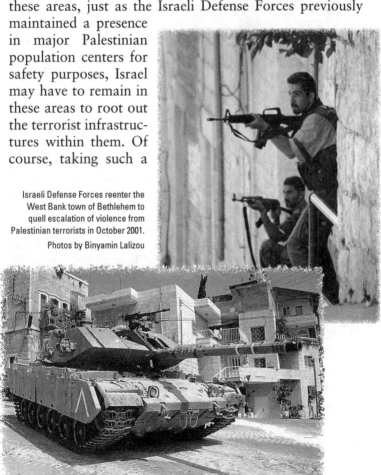

Israeli Defense Forces reenter the West Bank town of Bethlehem to quell escalation of violence from Palestinian terrorists in October 2001.

Photos by Binyamin Lalizou

step risks precipitating a full-scale war that's greater in magnitude than any that has transpired so far between the two sides.

What hasn't helped matters is the so-called Palestinian "police" force, now numbering more than 40,000, which, under the Oslo agreement, was to *restore* order among the civilian population and to *protect* the borders between the Palestinian territories and Israel against terrorism. As it now stands, the police commit terrorist acts, fire on Israeli Defense Forces, and are arming civilians who want to murder Jewish soldiers and citizens. One PLO recruit for the Palestinian police declared, "As a Palestinian police officer, I will not hesitate to give my gun to anyone who approaches me and tells me he is going to commit an attack against the army or the settlers. I will even kiss the gun before and after the operation."[17] And the Palestinian police are only part of other Palestinian armed forces (such as the Tanzim and Force 17). The presence of such forces assure that another war will break out soon.

Israeli posters protesting Yitzhak Rubin's agreement with Yasser Arafat to allow Palestinian "police" to bear arms. The sign reads, "Don't give them rifles!"

Photo by Dr. Karl DeRouen II

When Will the Next War Occur?

When the United States began its war on terrorism, former Israeli prime minister Benjamin Netanyahu advised a swift and severe retaliation because, as he stated, "any sign of weakness will only strengthen the terrorist determination to attack."[18] But will Israel implement its own advice? CIA director George Tenet, who was part of an unsuccessful attempt to negotiate a cease-fire between the

Palestinians and Israelis, believes Israel's prime minister Ariel Sharon will eventually launch a retaliatory full-scale attack on Palestinian-controlled territories with the intent of driving Arafat into exile and destroying the Palestinian Authority. Because of the international political impact such a move would have, Israel must time its response carefully so that it can justify its actions before a watching world.

Before September 11 and the attack on America, Israel was waiting for a suicide bombing to kill a significant number of Israeli civilians because, as one official put it, "You'll have public outrage, you'll have high morale among the Israeli military—it's the perfect time."[19] In fact, after the suicide bomb attack that killed over 20 young people at the Dolphanarium near Tel Aviv, United Press International reported on June 12, 2001 that Israel's military was poised to carry out a huge, full-force invasion that would involve two infantry and paratroop divisions, an armored force, large numbers of U.S.-supplied F-15 and F-16 fighter jets, and Apache helicopter gunships that would attack the West Bank and Gaza, including the major Palestinian cities of Ramallah, Qualqilya, Jericho, Tulkarm, Nablus, Jenin, and Bethlehem. Portions of the West Bank and the Gaza Strip would be captured and held for an indeterminate length of time. Under that plan, the Israeli forces would also capture and kill any members of Hamas, Hizbullah, the Islamic Jihad, or any other organizations defined by Israel as terrorist. Israel never moved ahead with its plans because the Bush administration urged restraint. Such restraint is urged because the United States wants to keep Israel out of war until its own agenda in the war on terrorism and against Islamic states that support terrorism (such as Syria and Iraq) can be realized (see chapter 3). Aware of this "restraint" on Israel, yet wary of being labeled as terrorists by the United States, the Palestinian leadership has sought to restrict its suicide attacks, but continue other forms of attacks (shootings, assassinations). But Israeli public opinion is pressing its leadership to stop the Palestinian violence. In fact, a Gallup Poll of 596 Israelis (including Israeli-Arabs) conducted September 23, 2001, revealed that some 50 percent believed a regional war was imminent. To stop the violence (which is adversely affecting the Israeli economy), Israel wants to implement a short battle plan that will destroy the Palestinian Authority and then offer assistance to resident Arabs who have suffered as a result of the Palestinian conflict. Even though the United States and its international allies in the Coalition would condemn such an action, the Israeli government does not feel it needs to continue suffering casualties in order to exercise "restraint." Public opinion at home is more significant than public opinion abroad, and if Palestinian violence continues to escalate, Israel will surely retaliate with a final assault, regardless of foreign objections.

How soon the next war will erupt depends on a number of factors (including the U.S. plans to attack terrorism in Iraq), but it is clear that both Israeli and Palestinian forces are now actively preparing for the unavoidable conflict to come. The Israelis have issued gas masks to the public (fearing chemical and biological warfare), built up their armor at strategic points, and plowed up roads that link to the West Bank, splitting the territory into eight blockaded zones and isolating the Palestinian towns from one another. Fuel supplies in the Gaza Strip have been cut off to reduce Palestinian mobility. The Israel Defense Forces has also set up recruitment bureaus in nine major cities throughout the world so as to be ready to call up reservists for military duty in case of war. In case of an emergency, the national airline, El Al, is willing to carry out an airlift operation that will transport reservists from these nine cities and take them to Israel. The Palestinians have worked to increase their armed forces to 100,000 men and have smuggled huge caches of weapons from Egypt, Syria, Jordan, Iraq, and Iran. Arafat, too, has already engaged in talks with Syria about relocating Palestinian leaders to that country when such an invasion occurs. In addition, an Iraqi "liberation army" has been promised to the Palestinians and is supposedly waiting for marching orders to join them in a war with Israel.

Couldn't the Israelis Easily Defeat the Palestinians?

If the Palestinians and the Israelis engaged in a local war, as matters stand today, no one doubts that the Israelis would most certainly defeat the Palestinians. This fact is well understood by the Palestinians, as the official Palestinian news agency Wafa has reported: "We have to admit that no matter how many casualties we may cause the Israelis, we will not be able to win the war against them."[20] It is for this reason that the Palestinians have not yet sought a full-scale war. However, the Palestinian forces are still growing, and with the war on terrorism in part blamed on the Israelis, radical Muslims are rallying to join in a massive battle between Islam and the West (which includes Israel). The official estimates of armed military and paramilitary forces operating within the Palestinian Authority's boundaries now stands at about 85,000 men, with a goal of 100,000.[21] Under the Oslo agreement, that number was not to exceed 24,000!

The armed military force of about 45,000 men consists of eight main security units, divided into three types: army (national security), intelligence, and police. Most of the personnel come from units of the Palestine Liberation Army and from other countries such as Egypt, Jordan, Libya, Iraq, Sudan, and Algeria. The military forces are engaged to some extent in terrorist activities, but most terrorist attacks are governed by a special unit known as Force 17, which also acts as Arafat's personal guard. In

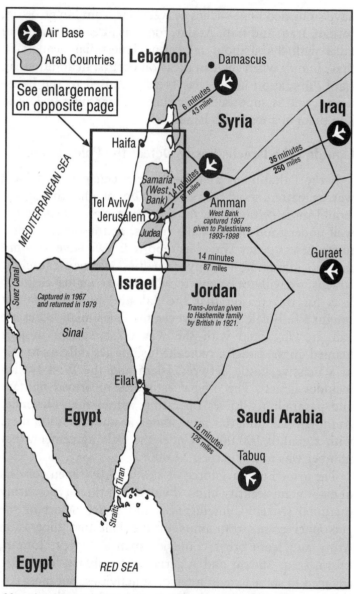

Map showing proximity of Israel's enemies to the State with respect to military engagement.

Close-up map showing vulnerability of major Israeli cities to attack from Palestinian Authority in West Bank and access for other enemy nations.

addition, there is a force headed by Tawfik Tirawi in the Gaza Strip.

The paramilitary force of some 40,000 men make up what is known as the *Tanzim* (Arabic, "organization"). They make up the field activity wing of Fatah, and its members (aged 20-35) have largely been drafted from the ranks of student demonstrators, predominately from Bethlehem (Bir Zeit University) and Nablus (An-Najah University), as well as terrorists once imprisoned in Israeli detention centers such as Ansar and Ketziot. Many who serve in this force act as policemen by day and soldiers by night.

The arsenal of this army can only be conjectured. It is thought that the Palestinian police (and civilians) are holding some 40,000 illegal weapons—which goes well beyond the 11,000 Kalashnikov rifles, 4,000 pistols, and 240 mortars allowed under the terms of the Oslo Accord. In May 2001, the Israeli Navy confiscated weaponry from one of four gun-running boats carrying heavy arsenals for Arafat's forces, and the confiscated items can give us some idea of the kinds of weapons in Palestinian hand. On board this single craft were RPG rockets, Katyusha rockets, and SA-7 Strella anti-aircraft missiles. The SA-7 Strella anti-aircraft missiles have a range that allows Palestinians to shoot down Israeli aircraft over Israeli airspace from inside the Palestinian Autonomy. The anti-tank weapons are able to pierce the armor being used by Israel in the conflict with the Palestinians, and the range of the Katyusha rockets would bring much of the Sharon Plain (greater Tel Aviv area) within striking distance from within the Palestinian Autonomy. In addition, it is certain that terrorist states with chemical weapons have, or will, supply the Palestinian Authority with these weapons to carry out bioterrorism against Israel.

Even with this considerable force and arsenal, the Palestinians would still lose in an all-out war, although such a war would be extremely costly to Israel in terms of loss of life to both the soldier and civilian populations. Too, after a military victory, Israel would still find itself facing a hostile subject population of three million Palestinians who would go on producing guerrilla squads while demanding from the United Nations various kinds of compensation from the Israeli government. This is one of the reasons Israel has not yet moved in a final assault to remove the Palestinian Authority and quash the Intifada. Israel also knows that under the present Coalition and with the demands of the United States and Great Britain to refrain from violence, to launch an attack would isolate it from its Western allies and bring world condemnation. This would cost Israel economic and military support from the United States—support on which it is vitally dependent.

As we saw in chapter 17, the greatest threat (which the United States hopes to prevent at all costs) is that a local war between Israel and the Palestinians could become a regional war. The other Arab nations in the region (both moderate and radical) have already pledged themselves to the Islamic cause of "liberating holy Jerusalem"—a cause presently being led by the Palestinians. If the United States attacks Iraq, and Saddam Hussein attacks Israel in an attempt to separate America's Arab allies (as in the Gulf War), it is highly doubtful Israel would restrain itself again (and has said so). Such a retaliation by Israel on Iraq would surely put Israel and the United States alone as allies against the Muslim world, and would stir a battle of international proportion, making the Gulf War pale by comparison.

Should that happen, it appears that Israel hopes it can expand the war efforts to include some of the terrorist regimes that have long plagued it. A Global Intelligence Update report suggested just this when it stated:

> The chances are high for a major military explosion in the Middle East....In the absence of external constraints against Israel by the United States and regional neighbors, there is a chance Israel may apply this option [of full-scale military assault] to two other longstanding problems: Syrian control over Lebanon and the potential Iraqi military threat to Israel....From Israel's standpoint, a broader strike would carry minimal additional cost.[22]

A call for such a widespread end to Israel's conflicts in the region has been voiced by Martin Sherman, a political science professor at Tel Aviv University who served seven years in Israel's defense establishment:

> It is time for this embattled nation to arise, to cry "havoc" and let slip the dogs of war....Only a dramatic change of policy can turn back the inevitable tide of events relentlessly washing away the awe-inspiring achievements of the Zionist revolution and eroding the very foundations upon which the nation-state of the Jews were founded. The Arab attack must now be met with a response of ferocity and force that will leave a traumatic scar on the collective national consciousness of the Arabs. Israel must now unleash upon its assailants a fury akin to that which the democratic powers unleashed in World War II on those who dared threaten their survival.[23]

Before September 11, 2001, I was asked on a national talk show if I thought there would be another war between Israel and the Arabs. My reply then was, "There will *always* be another war!" So long as the Arab nations want to destroy the Jews and the Jews want to survive, there will continue to be "wars and rumors of wars." That is part of the human condition—especially so in the Middle East.

Today, after September 11, I would only revise my statement to say, "There will always be another war—I just didn't think it would be here so soon!" Never before has the prospect of a regional war in the Middle East been so real or so close. The powers leading the surgically precise war on terrorism are very much aware of this, and are treading as carefully as possible to avoid political "unintended consequences." However, in order to root out and eradicate terrorism, one must root out the radical elements in the Middle East who have sworn to destroy Israel, and that requires letting Israel get involved in the effort against terrorism. That, of course, would be condemned by the Arab world—and possibly incite a war that would engulf all of the Holy Land!

If such a pessimistic prognosis is the case, then what hope is there for the permanent peace for which our planet longs? My optimistic answer is that just as there will one day come a war to end all wars, so there will come a peace so perfect that it will prevail. Come join me in the next chapter as we explore this peace.

CHAPTER 19

Will There Ever Be Peace?

*I believe that there is a morning to open
yet for the Jews in heaven's good time, and
that if that opening shall be in any way
commensurate with the darkness of the
night through which they have passed,
it will be the brightest that ever
dawned upon a faithful people.*[1]
—SENATOR ZEBULON BAIRD VANCE

*Let us not forget that the State of Israel is
one of the most amazing success stories
of the twentieth century. And I am
convinced that this is only the beginning."*[2]
—FORMER ISRAELI PRIME MINISTER
BENJAMIN NETANYAHU

One of the prayers of the Bible, familiar to Jews and Christians alike, is a prayer for the peace of Jerusalem as a symbol of God's peaceful rule over the world: "Pray for the peace of Jerusalem....May peace be within your palaces [places of rule]" (Psalm 122:6-7). This hope of permanent peace is expressed each week by Jewish families as they recite the Sabbath *Kedusha* in the Daily Prayer Book: "From Thine abode, our King, appear and rule over us, for we await Thee. When wilt Thou again reign in

Zion? Soon in our day Thou shalt dwell there forever. Thou shalt be magnified and sanctified in Jerusalem, Thy city, for all generations, forever and ever. And our eyes shall behold Thy kingdom...." By contrast, there is no such prayer in the Qur'an or in the daily prayers of Muslims. Nevertheless, all people want peace, however they perceive it. Throughout this book we have heard a great many words that indicate that the hostilities will not end soon, but are there any words that promise peace? I believe there are, for the Bible declares, "For everything there is a season...a time for war and a time for *peace*" (Ecclesiastes 3:8b, emphasis added). In this chapter it is time for peace, for America, the Middle East, and all the earth.

What Must Be Done to Achieve Peace in Jerusalem and the Middle East?

What is the hope for achieving peace in the Middle East? One writer pessimistically put it this way: "The dream of perfect peace is also the enemy of peace....Is there any hope for the future? Yes, but only if all sides abandon messianic dreams and remember Isaiah Berlin's message that we cannot resolve great ideological problems. We can only make pragmatic arrangements that bring some calm to the world."[3] In other words, this writer believes only a temporary and relative peace can be enjoyed from time to time. This is the only kind of "peace" permitted in Islam with a superior enemy (for a period of ten years). Longer peace is possible only if Islam is able to subdue their enemy and keep him in subjugation to Muslim law. However, this is not peace, but imprisonment, and a far cry from that for which a peaceless world longs and the Promised Land awaits.

However, it *is* possible to formulate what would need to be accomplished in order for lasting peace to come to

Jerusalem and the Middle East. Political experts agree that at least three conditions must be met. The first condition relates to the actual root of the Middle East conflict itself, namely, the peoples in conflict with one another. As we have seen, the conflict is not simply between Israeli Zionists and Palestinian-Arabs fighting over a place to live. If it were, then the international proposals to create an independent Palestinian state in the biblical territories of Judea (with Jerusalem), Samaria, and the Gaza Strip would settle the issue. Yet, even when Israel has willingly given up some of its heartland, there has still been continued unrest, and the Palestinians have persisted in their call for war against the Israeli state. Surely, then, this conflict is not rooted in Palestinian nationalism but in the greater objective of the Arab Muslim world: the destruction of Israel and the creation of an Islamic state.

Still, peace between Israel and the Palestinians would not bring peace to the region, any more than Israel's peace with Egypt and Jordan has done. The reason for this is that regardless of the Palestinian problem, most of the Arab states exist in a declared state of war with Israel. Therefore, the first condition that must be met for permanent peace is one that can be established between Israel and *all* of the Arab League nations and the Islamic world, with an unconditional guarantee of complete security for Israel. Yet even then peace would not prevail. Conflicts between Arab regimes are endemic to the region, and occurred before there was a State of Israel or a Palestinian conflict.

The second condition has to do with the religious factor—the danger of militant Islamic fundamentalism. That the religious factor is paramount to peace can be seen from the following facts: The Arab countries surrounding Israel are populated by some 300 million people on five million square miles of land. By contrast, there are less than six million Jews inhabiting some 10,000 square miles. Israel is like a tiny island in a sea of Islam. Given that the Arabs have such immense territory, if a group of Arabs are homeless and stateless, there are 21 other Arab countries that can absorb them. But if Israel were to lose her land, her people would again be homeless. For these reasons Israel cannot pose a demographic or political threat to the Arab world. Also, the Arab states control most of the oil reserves of the world, while Israel has none. So Israel does not constitute an economic threat to them.

The only threat Israel poses is to the religion of Islam, which warns Muslims against agreements with Jews and strictly forbids non-Muslim people from holding land that was previously conquered by Islam. From the Islamic perspective, the very existence of Israel as an independent and sovereign state is an insult to Allah and all Muslims. In order for real peace to become possible, either the menace of Islamic fundamentalism must be radically removed, or a complete change must take place in the religious principles and political policies that govern these Arab states.

If the war against terrorism succeeds in its ultimate objectives—to rid the world of terrorism (half of which is Islamic)—then the Arab states would be left with moderate Muslim or secular governments. If these would then recognize Israel's right to exist in secure borders, the second condition for peace would be partly realized.

The third condition understands that the Middle East conflict is not just a local or a regional conflict but a *global* one. The conflict, which is between Muslims and non-Muslims, and especially between Arabs and Jews, encompasses every country where these people live or have influence. That's not simply because these people are a part of the populations of other nations, but because the Middle East itself is strategic to the nations of the world. Israel's democratic government and advanced intelligence gathering arsenal are critical to the democratic superpowers that are concerned about the threat of Islamic fundamentalism. The Arab states possess large quantities of oil, and they can easily cut off its flow to the West. Thus, the world powers have continually been engaged in the Middle East to protect their own global standing and standard of living. In light of the volatile state of Middle Eastern politics—as well as the nuclear capability of both Israelis and Arabs—foreign powers have continued to intervene in order to prevent these nations from self-destruction and spreading that destruction to the West. Therefore, any permanent peace for the Middle East would have to be made on a global scale, with all nations involved. This idea of global peace of course, has been the goal of organizations like the United Nations, the Peace Corps, etc., but has always been unachievable because wars continue to disrupt plans for peace.

Ironically, before a lasting peace can come to the Middle East, the ultimate condition that must be met is that there must come a war to end all wars. According to the Bible, war is not an alien imposition, but a by-product of our own passions—the selfish, insatiable ambitions of human nature (James 4:1-2) that we extend beyond ourselves to our cities, states, nations, and the world. For this reason war becomes the rod of God's judgment against rebellious peoples and the staff of His salvation to those who are oppressed. Thus, the only way to resolve present conflicts, be they personal or global, is to resolve the source of strife and the need for judgment. To do this would require the imposition of a peaceful power over all other powers that would radically regulate human nature on a global scale! This, however, is what the Bible presents as the final chapter in God's plan for man: "Nation will not lift up sword against nation, and never again will they *learn* war" (Isaiah 2:4, emphasis added).

War has always been a part of our world, and in Isaiah 2:4 the prophet promises a different world than that which we have ever known—a world where war will not be taught and mankind will be beyond the need to learn. This new world of peace will begin, strangely enough, with a great climatic conflict of international proportions. This battle will not be as much a war between nations as it will be a war between the nations and God. According to the biblical account of this last war, the rebellious are the nations, the oppressed is Israel, and the crisis of conflict will be ended by the twofold application of God's rod (against the nations) and staff (delivering Israel). The Bible also makes it clear that this war will take place on the same Middle-Eastern stage upon which the present conflict is being played out. And, like the present conflict, this final battle will be settled in Jerusalem: "I will gather all the nations against Jerusalem to battle..." (Zechariah 14:2; cf. 12:1-2).

Although the global dimensions of the war on terrorism have the potential to take us down the road to Armageddon, I do not believe that these events will lead to this end-time climax. However, they may be setting the stage for that yet-future drama which will end one age in war and begin another in peace. Whether or not today's events will bring peace or provoke more war, the Bible makes it clear that war will one day have run its course, God will have arrived, human nature will have been changed, and, afterward, peace will finally prevail.

When this perfect peace comes, what will it look like? Perhaps the place to best see this is the Middle East, since the contrast will appear greatest where peace has been most elusive.

What Does the Bible Say About Peace in the Middle East?

According to the Bible, a perfect peace *will* eventually come to the Middle East—but in order to obtain it we must *not* do as Isaiah Berlin has suggested and "abandon our messianic dreams." In harmony with the conditions we discussed earlier, this perfect peace will be imposed by a peaceful foreign power—God—and it will be imposed on a universal scale—the whole earth. It will resolve the religious differences that now divide: " 'They will not teach again, each man his neighbor and each man his brother, saying "Know the LORD," for they will all know Me, from the least of them to the greatest of them,' declares the LORD, 'for I will forgive their iniquity, and their sin I will remember no more'" (Jeremiah 31:34). Also, this peace will be a *permanent* peace: "There will be no end to the increase of His government or of peace" (Isaiah 9:7a).

This peace has been promised to all the nations of the world: "He will judge between the nations, and will render decisions for many peoples; and they will hammer their swords into plowshares and their spears into pruning hooks. Nation will not lift up sword against nation, and never again will they learn war" (Isaiah 2:4). It is also promised to Israel and the Jewish people: "I will make a covenant of peace with them; it will be an everlasting covenant with them. And I will place them and multiply them, and will set My sanctuary in their midst forever" (Ezekiel 37:26). This peace will extend to Jerusalem— "Speak kindly to Jerusalem; and call out to her, that her warfare has ended" (Isaiah 40:2a)—and the Temple Mount: "'The latter glory of this house will be greater than the former,' says the LORD of hosts, 'and in this place I will give peace,' declares the LORD of hosts" (Haggai 2:9). And in harmony with what we've learned in this book, it will be Jerusalem that tells the world of this perfect peace that attends God's return: "Get yourself up on a high mountain, O Zion, bearer of good news, lift up your voice mightily, O Jerusalem, bearer of good news; lift it up, do not fear. Say to the cities of Judah, 'Here is your

God!' Behold, the Lord GOD will come with might, with His arm ruling for Him" (Isaiah 40:9-10).

The prophetic details of this perfect peace are given chiefly by the prophets Isaiah, Jeremiah, and Ezekiel. They refer to a "covenant of peace" (Ezekiel 34:25; 37:26) made between the Lord and the "sons of Israel," with several provisions: 1) it will involve a secure lifestyle in the Land of Israel (Ezekiel 34:25); 2) it will create a new spiritual nature in mankind that will obey God and be at peace with other men (Isaiah 11:6-9; 65:25; Ezekiel 36:25-27); 3) it will abolish all forms of warfare and enforce the destruction of all implements of war (Isaiah 2:4); 4) it will be everlasting (Ezekiel 37:26b); 5) it will establish and increase the Israeli population in the Land (Ezekiel 37:26c; cf. verses 25 and 36:24,28); and 6) it will secure the rebuilding of the Temple and return of the Divine Presence (Ezekiel 37:26d-27; see also chapters 40–48).

Isaiah, building upon these guarantees, adds in Isaiah chapter 2 that this peace will also be universal and pervasive (verse 2), spiritual (verse 3; see also 11:9b), unparalleled (verse 4), and will emanate from Jerusalem (verses 2-3; see also 27:13). Isaiah also depicts this peace as extending beyond the political realm to the natural order (Isaiah 11:6-9a; Ezekiel 34:25), and as being inclusive of Gentiles as well as Jews (Isaiah 56:6-7), so the Arabs have a future in this program of peace (see also Isaiah 19:24-25).

Jeremiah's details of this period of promised peace focus on its unconditional and spiritual nature. He calls it the "new covenant" because it differs from the conditional and strictly legal nature of the Mosaic Covenant, which it supersedes. This covenant promises a national spiritual regeneration and restoration (Jeremiah 31:33-34) and guarantees Israel's existence as a national entity.[4] This national existence is designated in Jeremiah 31:36 by the use of the stronger Hebrew term for a corporate body, *goi*

("nation"), rather than the weaker *'am* ("a people").
Thus, Israel will be preserved as a recognizable national
entity, not simply as a distinguishable people. Although
the Jews have been known for the past 2,000 years as a
distinct people, their national distinction was only
returned to them in May 1948 when the State of Israel was
established. It is for this reason that those who seriously
regard the biblical prophecies of Israel's return and
restoration see this historical event as significant.

The prophet Zechariah also says that peace will be the
hallmark of the coming age, in contrast with the former
time, in which "there was no peace because of his enemies"
(Zechariah 8:10). The millennial kingdom is described as a
time of promised refreshing (Acts 3:19), and there will be
peace for agricultural activity, peace for Israel among the
nations, and peace within every Israeli city (Zechariah
8:12-19). According to the Christian New Testament (Revelation 20:1-9), this period of peace on earth will persist
for 1,000 years before becoming the permanent possession
of the saints in the eternal state (Revelation 21:4,24-26;
22:2-3).

In addition, Israel's return to blessing will include the
spiritual instruction and blessing of the nations, who will
join with them in the annual celebration of the Feast of
Tabernacles, or *Succot* (Zechariah 14:16-19). It is perhaps
significant that the Scripture passage read in Jewish synagogues on the Sabbath during the Feast of Tabernacles is
Ezekiel chapter 38, which deals with the future battle of
Gog and Magog, in which the Lord miraculously preserves
Israel in an end-time war. Having been brought through
this great end-time war, those who formerly were enemies
will worship together as friends, and more, as family. The
connection with "tabernacle" also recalls the famous
prophecy of the restoration of the Davidic kingdom ("the
tabernacle of David") given in Amos 9:11-12: "In that day

I will raise up the fallen booth [tabernacle] of David, and wall up its breaches; I will also raise up its ruins and rebuild it as in the days of old; that they may possess the remnant of Edom, and all the nations who are called by My name." The fulfillment of this prophecy, as explained in the New Testament (Acts 15:14-18), will take place after the full number of Gentiles has been grafted onto Israel, "the olive tree" (in keeping with the blessing of the Gentiles in the Abrahamic covenant) "through faith" (Romans 11:25) at the completion of the church age. These redeemed Gentiles will join with redeemed Israelites in the true worship of God.

In addition, in the New Testament the apostle John specifically used the imagery of the Feast of Tabernacles in relation to the end-time "Tribulation" martyrs from among the nations. He depicted these Gentiles as having "palm branches" and "serving in His Temple" while God "spreads His tabernacle over them" and Jesus "guides them to springs of living water" (Revelation 7:9-17). Such Gentile inclusion was anticipated by the alternate name for the feast, "the Feast of Ingathering" (Exodus 23:15-16), a reality demonstrated during the feast in Second Temple times as Jewish men took part in a Temple ritual where 70 sacrifices were offered in atonement for the sins of the 70 nations that had come from the sons of Noah. The prophets cited this future inclusion of Gentile nations as one of the evidences of the changed conditions under the new covenant (Jeremiah 31:31-34). For example, Zechariah states that "many nations will join themselves to the LORD in that day and will become My people." (Zechariah 2:11), while Isaiah describes the Temple of this peaceful age as "a house of prayer for all the peoples" (Isaiah 56:7; cf. Matthew 21:12; Mark 11:17; Luke 19:46) to which all the nations of the earth will come to learn the ways of the Lord (Isaiah 2:2-3; 60:3; 62:2), behold God's glory (Isaiah 60:3; 62:2; 66:18), offer sacrifices (Isaiah 56:6; 66:20) and pay material tribute (Isaiah 60:5; 66:18-19; cf. Haggai 2:7-8; Zechariah 8:22; cf. Revelation 21:24).

In covenantal terms, these nations who become "vassals" of the Lord will be called "His people," just as He, as their "suzerain," will rightly be called "their God." Although this language of identification ("My people") is absent in Zechariah's presentation of the restored Gentile nations, it is found elsewhere (see Jeremiah 24:7; 30:22; 31:33; 32:38). Isaiah also elevates some of Israel's most prominent historical enemies, the nations of Egypt and Syria, to special status, making them co-participants in both the obligations and benefits of the future Temple (Isaiah 19:21; 27:13; 56:6-8; 60:3,21; 66:20), and calling them equally "My people" (Isaiah 19:24-25).

Indeed, all these promises of longtime intractable enemies coming alongside Israel in intimate worship and fellowship would indicate that the old order of national conflict has ended and a new order of peace for the people of God has begun.

How Can This Peace Be Ours?

This has been a book about unholy conflict, but I would like it to end with holy consolation. It has been said that there are two ways to handle difficulties: "change the situation, or change yourself." Neither you nor I can change the situation in the Middle East, but we can change *ourselves*. One of the first inspirational placards I was ever given read, "God changes things." If the entire world is to experience peace someday, it must be changed—and God promises that He can and will do it. And if it is possible one day for the entire planet to be changed and have peace, then it's also possible *today* for you to have peace. To take the first step we need only to listen: "I will hear what God the LORD will say; for He will speak peace to His people..." (Psalm 85:8a). Just as the way of war must end before peace can prevail, so too must the strife in our souls be ended before His peace can rule in us. The Israeli prophet Isaiah explained this when he wrote more than 2,650 years ago, "There is no peace, says my God, for the wicked" (Isaiah 57:21).

According to the Scripture, "wickedness" is being away from God. It is the condition of the human heart that wants its way rather than His, that prefers war with men rather than peace with God. And regardless of how reasonable it may seem, there are no negotiations with our fellow men (or nations) that can ever achieve the peace of God: "They have healed the brokenness of My people superficially, saying, 'Peace, peace,' but there is no peace" (Jeremiah 6:14; 8:11). Yet, without peace, we have no part with the God of peace: "Pursue peace with all men, and the sanctification without which no one will see the Lord" (Hebrews 12:14).

The peace we seek can only be found in a Person, the One known as the Prince of Peace (Isaiah 9:6). According to the Israeli prophet Micah, that Person is the Messiah: "He will arise and shepherd His flock in the strength of the LORD, in the majesty of the name of the LORD His God. And they will remain, because at that time He will be great to the ends of the earth. This One will be our peace" (Micah 5:4-5). The New Testament records that when this One first came to earth, He said, "My peace I give to you; not as the world gives do I give to you. Do not let your heart be troubled, nor let it be fearful" (John 14:27), and, "These things I have spoken to you, that in Me you may have peace. In the world you have tribulation, but take courage; I have overcome the world" (John 16:33).

This promise of peace in His Person can only become ours as He becomes ours (or rather, as we become His).

Such a relationship can be ours only through believing: "Having been justified by faith, we have peace with God through our Lord Jesus Christ" (Romans 5:1). By simple faith we walk away from our sin and to Jesus the Messiah, who died for our sins. We must trust Him who made peace with God for us by His death in our place: "through Him to reconcile all things to Himself, having made peace through the blood of His cross..." (Colossians 1:20). And if we trust Him for time and for eternity, we have the promise of peace, "for He Himself is our peace" (Ephesians 2:14).

Despite the conflicts that presently rage in America and the Middle East, and the troubles they may bring to our weary planet, we have the word of Him who works all things according to His will that when He comes again as the Prince of Peace, there will be peace—*real* peace. It is my prayer that you will come to Him even now and find in Him, for yourself, that peace which He alone has promised. "Now may the God of hope fill you with all joy and peace in believing, so that you will abound in hope by the power of the Holy Spirit" (Romans 15:13).

CHAPTER 20

What Should We Do?

*For Zion's sake I will not keep silent, and
for Jerusalem's sake I will not rest, until
her righteousness will shine forth as the
morning star and her salvation as a torch
that is burning (Isaiah 62:1).*

I took a morning off from writing this book to visit a local used book sale. Amid stacks of colorful titles there was one that particularly caught my eye, considering the topic still consuming my thoughts. The title was *Holy Terror*. Opening to the first chapter, I was amused to read, "As Americans, we don't worry much about terror. Not the way people do in the Middle East or Northern Ireland, where terrorism has become a way of life, or in the Soviet Union, where it has been an instrument of government policy for decades. In the United States, we have seen relatively little organized violence for political ends."[1] That was written way back in 1984. Times have sure changed! In 1984 the drug of demand was cocaine; in the days following September 11, 2001 it was Cipro, the antibiotic regimen used to treat anthrax! And in 1984 the concern of the book *Holy Terror* was a Christian fundamentalism that repressed our right to lust, while today it is Islamic fundamentalism that threatens our right to life.

Yes, things have changed, and as we come to this concluding chapter, it's appropriate for us to consider how we can best respond to our current circumstances by asking the question, "What should we do?" While the opinions offered are mine, I hope that you will seriously consider each with a resolution to revise your own attitudes and actions in light of our changed and still changing world.

We Should Be Sure We Have the Facts

Action follows attitude. Thus, we will only be as effective in *doing* as we are accurate in *knowing*. Today, we must all be careful to guard against media misinformation and political propaganda that abounds with regards to the Middle East. Many media elite are more concerned about selling a story than about presenting facts objectively. The old news adage "If it bleeds, it leads" warns us that unbiased coverage is not a high priority. Therefore, "seeing *may not* be believing" when images are set in a controlled context and interpreted by a politically correct script.

For example, the prestigious *New York Times*, one of America's most trusted newspapers, recently published an Associated Press photo of an enraged Israeli officer with his nightstick raised menacingly above a fallen young man who was bleeding profusely from the head. Seen behind the officer was a sign in Hebrew swathed in the smoke and flames of an ongoing riot. The caption accompanying the photo read "An Israeli policeman and a Palestinian on the Temple Mount." To every reader who saw this dramatic photo and read the supposedly factual caption, it appeared to offer irrefutable evidence of Israel's use of excessive violence against Palestinians, and especially its provocative presence at an Islamic holy site. However, two days later, the editor of the *New York Times* received the following letter from Aaron Grossman, M.D.:

Regarding your picture on page A5 (Sept. 30) of the Israeli soldier and the Palestinian on the Temple Mount—that Palestinian is actually my son, Tuvia Grossman, a Jewish student from Chicago. He, and two of his friends, were pulled from their taxicab while traveling in Jerusalem, by a mob of Palestinian Arabs and were severely beaten and stabbed. That picture could not have been taken on the Temple Mount because there are no gas stations on the Temple Mount and certainly none with Hebrew lettering, like the one clearly seen behind the Israeli soldier attempting to protect my son from the mob.

Yes, a picture is worth a thousand words, but only a few words can change the meaning of a picture! As Tuvia Grossman's uncle would later write, "The *Times* wishes to convey the belief that the Palestinians are all innocent lambs being tormented by an aggressive oppressor; it cannot conceive that the wounded and injured are *not* Palestinians."

However, on September 11, 2001 neither the media nor a watching world could misconstrue the pictures of Palestinians by the thousands celebrating—with shouting, rounds of rifle salutes, and gifts of candy—the attack on America. Even though Yasser Arafat attempted to censor the images by confiscating media footage and threatening those who might yet release more, for once our televisions told the truth! The rarity of such moments reminds us that we need to buttress our beliefs with more than merely the media, even though news programs are now dispensing 24-hour-a-day updates by videophone.

Nevertheless, we are blessed to have a freedom of information unparalleled in the entire world. After all, the Syrian press is still reporting that Zionists perpetrated the attack on America because thousands of Jews had not turned up for work at the World Trade Center on that fateful day, and the official station of the Taliban,

Al-Jazeera, has broadcasted to its viewers that the United States poisoned the tons of food it dropped to the Afghanistan refugees! In light of this misinformation, how should we regard the statement of British prime minister Tony Blair, who declared, "This war has nothing to do with Islam"? Or, what do we make of the October 25, 2001 edition of the *New York Times,* which ran two locator maps depicting the city of Jerusalem divided by a heavy black line with one side labeled "Jerusalem" and the other labeled "East Jerusalem"? With no map key included to explain what the black line represents, it looks like an attempt to show the border that divided Jerusalem from 1948 to 1967. However, this would be as anachronistic as depicting today's city of Berlin divided as "West Berlin" and "East Berlin." The reality is that Jerusalem has been a single united city since 1967, regardless of the political correctness of that fact.

Israel knows well the ways of deception. It is suffering today because a path it thought was taking it toward peace has increasingly led toward destruction. While the international media had pressured Israel to accept Oslo's paper peace, Israel's alternative source of time-tested truth, the Bible, held a different message. On the eve of destruction Israel's prophets had warned, "They have healed the brokenness of My people superficially, saying, 'Peace, peace,' but there is no peace" (Jeremiah 6:14; see also 8:11); and, "They have misled My people by saying, 'Peace!' when there is no peace" (Ezekiel 13:10). In ancient times Israel made unwise alliances with enemies whose ultimate aims were to destroy her. Israel's past reveals that its downward path resulted from its politicians heeding the advice of other governments rather than God (see Isaiah 7:1-9). Unfortunately, Israel's past prophets and present-day politicians have not had much communication. Responding to the international call for

Israel to make concessions with respect to Jerusalem and the Temple Mount, Jan Willem van der Hoeven, director of the International Christian Zionist Center in Jerusalem, spoke of his concern over deception when he wrote,

> How did this all come to pass? Would the Muslims, for peace's sake, surrender Mecca and the *Ka'aba* stone to the Jews? Would Catholics, for peace's sake, surrender the Vatican and St. Peter's Cathedral? Would any nation in the world, after praying for 2,000 years to return to its holiest place on earth, forfeit it for a peace which will not even be a real peace but a stage for further concessions till Israel, according to the deep-seated wish of many of her Muslim enemies, is dissolved and is no more?[2]

Wanting peace at any price may cost much more than we ever dreamed, and as we have seen, in Israel's present plight, it may cost the future! Our own country must avoid being so deceived as it makes new resolutions about its old relations with Israel.

Deception is difficult to discern when it comes in the form of revisionist history from trademarked sources. Still, the facts are out there, and we must attempt to find them. We must be careful about accepting the images we see on television as the whole picture. We can't passively believe every statement we read in the papers that seems one-sided. We need to ask questions, examine the evidence, and try to get the uncut and unbiased version of the truth, if possible, remembering always that there is, as Paul Harvey says, "the rest of the story."

We Should Become Familiar with the Middle East

One of the surprising revelations I had while I was living in Israel was learning that every child in Israeli public schools memorizes the states and capital cities of the United States. Of course every American child does this, too (don't they?), but this was not America, it was a country on the other side of the world! And I thought at the time, *How many children in America even know where Israel is on the map?* I might guess, especially after watching one of Jay Leno's on-the-street quiz encounters, that Americans are geographically challenged. I do not discount the fact that the United States is more prominent and therefore more important in international education, but I cannot help but feeling that the Land of the Bible, from which our Judeo-Christian culture came, should matter to us more.

Undoubtedly, one of the contributing factors to our lack of concern has been our social self-sufficiency. In Middle Eastern countries, where many languages are learned in school, there is a joke often told that goes like this: "What do you call someone who speaks *three* languages?" Answer: "A trilinguist." "What do you call someone who speaks *two* languages?" Answer: "A bilinguist." "What do call someone who speaks one language?" Answer: "An American."

We have not learned more because we have not needed to. And until the events of the Gulf War, and now America's war against terrorism, the map of the Middle East never much mattered. However, since September 11, Americans have become much more aware of places like Kabul, although most would still be hard-pressed to find Afghanistan on a map, much less Kabul! And, as the West's involvement in the Middle East continues, Western people's acquaintance with the region must grow.

However, why wait until a place makes the front pages to get familiar with the facts? We, and especially our children, are growing up in a new world in which the map of the Middle East does matter. This region affects vital aspects of our economy, our security, and our faith, and not only should we know what the people there believe, but also why. We must understand what the religion of Islam is and why it acts as it does. Even if the problem is said to be with radical Islam only, which, we are told, comprises a mere one percent of the religion, that is still 18 million Muslims! We must understand why the Israeli-Palestinian conflict is at the center of the problems in the Middle East and how its future is tied to the future of the world. The events of September 11 made it clear that we in the West can no longer live in isolation from the East. So, let us find ways to familiarize ourselves with our foreign friends and foes alike.

We Should Support Israel

The headlines reveal that a major rift is growing between the United States and Israel, its only dependable ally in the Middle East. Our State Department "demands" that Israel end its forays into West Bank terrorist centers and promise to never again respond punitively. Israel "rebuffs" this angry order and "defies" the U.S. spokesman. Then Colin Powell brushes aside President Bush's cautious "as quickly as possible" request and escalates the call for withdrawal to "immediate."[3]

Today the United States is raising up a coalition of its worst enemies while rejecting its best friend. Is that wrong? How could it be right? Perhaps not being privy to the secrets of this most secretive war, I am overreacting to what I see as double standards and reversals of position in our relations with Israel. I understand that the good guys have to partner with the bad guys in order to get "the evil-doers." I understand that Israel needs to be restrained from far-reaching acts that could inflame the Muslim world and make the achievement of our stated goal to eradicate terrorism more difficult, if not impossible. I understand that we want to show the Arab "street" that the United States is not pro-Israel, that we can be evenhanded brokers of

Palestinian peace. But in the same Texas tradition that backed Colonel Travis and his paltry defenders of the Alamo against Santa Ana and his Mexican hoards, I think America should stick with defenders of democracy, not despots in the desert. Israeli prime minister Sharon has declared from the beginning: "The war against terrorism was, and continues to be, the State of Israel's war. Israel has provided, and will continue to provide, assistance to the nations of the free world in any way they may require in the struggle against terrorism."[4] The reason we should stop our political posturing and show solidarity with Israel, who has been fighting terrorism for more than half a century, has been well stated by columnist William Safire:

> All this diplomacy by deflection is too clever by three-quarters. Just as corrupt Arab potentates try to protect themselves from the fury of their downtrodden subjects by fanning hatred of the U.S. and the West, we are trying, through our charade of selective antiterrorism, to deflect that hatred over to Israel exclusively. (Don't blame us, it goes—see how we're pressuring the Jews on your behalf?) Such buck-passing won't work. With logic, followers of Osama bin Laden will say, "By killing thousands of Americans, we got the U.S. to put pressure on Israel. In the same way, by panicking Americans with the threat of germ warfare, we will force the infidels to abandon their Jewish ally. And then..." The consequence of our misbegotten diplomacy of deflection would be intensified attacks on America.[5]

This is a very good reason to stay steady with our friend Israel, for on the sea of Islam, in which the course of our ship is set, Israel alone is the island of safety and security.

However, the ultimate battle for support of Israel will be won or lost over the issue of Jerusalem. On the afternoon of May 14, 1948, David Ben-Gurion signed the proclamation of Israel's independence, but he did not stay for further ceremonies. He left with his wife Paula and headed straight for his headquarters feeling, he said, "like the mourner at the feast." The Arabs had sworn that if a Jewish state were established they would immediately launch an all-out attack to destroy the infant nation. For months the 100,000 Jews of Jerusalem had been under siege as the Arabs had controlled the countryside and cut off all access to the city. Frenzied Arab mobs had attacked and killed or taken prisoner the Jews there who had surrendered. Therefore, when Ben-Gurion finally reached his headquarters, his first question was, "What news of Jerusalem?" That question is again today the concern of the hour, and in concert with this story, the players and the predicament are the same.

The Islamic world demands that Jerusalem be divided again and that the West Bank return to its pre-1967 borders. Should we wonder why this should *not* be supported, please listen to the words of one of Israel's past prime ministers, Mrs. Golda Meir:

> Most of all I wanted the world to know what would have happened to us had we withdrawn before the war to pre-Six-Day War lines of 1967—the very lines, incidentally, that had not prevented the Six-Day War itself from breaking out, although no one seems to remember that. I have never doubted for an instant that the true aim of the Arab states has always been, and still is, that even if we had gone back far beyond the 1967 lines to some miniature enclave, they would not still have tried to eradicate it and us.[6]

In like manner, Israeli Prime Minister Benjamin Netanyahu once observed that Israel's survival in the almost disastrous 1973 Yom Kippur War depended on its secure boundaries. He said, "There was an important lesson here for both Israelis and Arabs. On both the Egyptian and Syrian fronts, the Arabs had managed to penetrate as much as 20 miles before Israeli forces finally checked them. If the war had begun not on post-1967 lines, but on the *pre*-1967 lines, and if the Arab armies had advanced the same distances, Israel would have ceased to exist."[7]

Today, Israel is again being pressured by not only its foes, but also by its friends, and chiefly by the United States, to cease from defending itself and to withdraw to indefensible lines. Today, Israel, as the only outpost of the free world in the Middle East, is battling for its survival in a sea of hostile dictatorships while Jerusalem is under siege by Islamists who would convert it to a Muslim enclave and its Temple Mount to a Mecca-like mosque.

What's more, Israel should be supported not only because it is fighting terrorism and it is indispensable to our fight with terrorism, but because the Jews are still God's Chosen People and the Land of Israel is still His Promised Land. According to Prime Minister Sharon, no less a figure than the Pope admitted this (in spite of his church's adherence to replacement theology). At Israel's thirty-eighth Annual International Bible Contest for high-school students, Sharon related that in a recent conversation with the Pope, the Pontiff said, "The land is holy to the three religions of Judaism, Christianity, and Islam, *but the Land is promised only to the Jews!*" (emphasis added). On the Protestant side, the Reverend J.C. Ryle, Bishop of Liverpool, once explained, long before the First Zionist Congress and its dream of a Jewish state, why Christians should support Israel. He wrote in 1867, "Is there anyone that desires God's special blessing? Then let him labor in the cause of Israel and he shall not fail to find it."

This, of course, does not require that we "love Israel right or wrong" and ignore bigotry, brutality, harassment, and use of excessive force when and where it is fully documented and censure deserved. In the worsening conditions in which open hostilities and violence exists, where suicide bombers and terrorist organizations are settled next to private homes, hospitals, orphanages, and mosques, and West Bank areas must be reentered and resecured, human rights will be violated on both sides and on both sides, innocent civilians will suffer and die.

The positions taken in this book have not meant to trivialize such suffering in any way or to ignore the need to decry legitimate violations as defined in the Geneva Convention. While Christians especially are commanded, "If possible, so far as it depends on you, be at peace with all men" (Romans 12:18), they are not asked to sacrifice discernment or ignore justice. But "laboring in the cause of Israel," as Ryle suggests, does require us to do this while still recognizing the biblical promises to the Jewish people and supporting every means to their fulfillment.

The problem today with Christianity and its view of Israel is not a want of justice, but of a proper recognition of what God has done and yet will do with His Chosen People. One Christian who has been awakened to this recognition said this:

> Are Gentile believers in Jesus expected to be involved in what God is doing with Israel and the Jewish people? If the Jewish people are truly the Lord's brethren, then they are our brethren as well. Most well-balanced people are involved with their natural family, particularly if a member of the family is about to give birth. In these days we will see Israel go into labor, preparing to bring forth the Messianic kingdom. We have seen a nation born in one day, we have seen the miraculous restoration of the Hebrew language, and now we are witnessing that great final exodus of the Jewish people, returning to Israel from the four corners of the world. What a privilege to be involved in what God is doing. Imagine if we lived in the days of the first exodus, when Moses brought the

children of Israel out of Egypt and through the Red Sea. Would we want to be involved in such a spectacular event? Yet the Bible says that this second exodus is so much greater than the first, that the first will not even be remembered! And yet, how few Christians want to be involved.[8]

We can get involved by educating ourselves about Israel and the Jewish People, what they believe (and believe about Christians) and why, getting to know Jewish people on friendly terms, and seeking to show our gratitude for their having given us our Bible, our heritage, and our Messiah. But above all, we must be a people of prayer, praying specifically for "the peace of Jerusalem" (Psalm 122:6). When we pray for the peace of Jerusalem, we are praying for the fulfillment of God's program on earth, which ultimately means peace for all the world. This day of fulfillment may be coming soon; but until that day our responsibility is clear: "You will arise and have compassion on Zion; for it is time to be gracious to her; for the appointed time has come....For the LORD has built up Zion; He has appeared in His glory" (Psalm 102:13,16).

We Should Not Fear the Future

To turn on the news these days has become an act of self-masochism. It seems that every report is designed to maximize the fear factor and, like the adrenaline rush from a horror flick, somehow keep us coming back for more. People are saying things like, "This is World War III," or "This is the beginning of the end of the world!"[9] In this vein, under a title banner reading "The New Age of Terror," *Time* magazine reminds us: "There is one inescapable fact we must all take away from the events of September 11: if something can be thought of, it can be done."[10] And so, we are assured, the worst is yet to come: bioterrorism in the form of anthrax, smallpox, and a hundred more untamed viruses. A prolonged war is likely to create more enemies, and incite further attacks on America. So said Colonel Stanislav Lunev, the highest-ranking military spy ever to defect from Russia, and now serving as a security consultant to the U.S. government:

> International terrorists are still targeting the U.S. and the American people as never before....After such an elaborate and coordinated attack...isn't it reasonable to think that terrorist groups, backed by powerful nations, might already have plans for an escalation of such attacks now seeing the vulnerability of the U.S. and be encouraged to launch additional attacks?...From now on, we know that there are hundreds if not thousands of terrorists who are living among us in America. They are preparing to continue the war against the countries that provide them hospitality, including dozens of so-called "sleepers" or specially-trained terrorists who pretend to be U.S. citizens and residents. Twenty-four hours a day, every day, they are waiting for the wake-up call from their organization leaders for a new attack against American people. The next attack may be more severe. According to Western intelligence estimations, the most powerful international terrorist organizations already have access to weapons of mass destruction, including chemical, biological, and nuclear weapons and materials. There is no doubt that the leaders of terrorist organizations already have their own combat groups in America....The war against America declared by international terrorism is REAL, PRESENT, and DANGEROUS[11] (emphasis in the original).

In addition, we are told that the recession will deepen and jobs will be lost in even greater numbers. In America, the armed forces and National Guard armories are on full alert, as is Israel, where the government, in the days following September 11, was dispensing gas masks to its citizens. Are these not reasons to fear?

Yes, not fearing the future does not mean we do not fear anything at all. Fear has a function, psychologists tell us—it prepares us to fight or for flight, whichever is most necessary for our survival. Fear also comes in two forms. One is called *intrepidation*, which is a fear that does not prevent us from following through with action. The other is called *panic* and it is a paralyzing fear that keeps us locked within its grip and incapable of response. It is intrepidation we should have as we hear about the reports of the day, and not panic.

A proper look at the future unveils the hand of God moving the pieces of the puzzle into place. With respect to Israel, these are dark days, but the Jewish people have come through dark days before. When World War I came, the Land of Israel had been, for hundreds of years, under Muslim Turkish dominion. But that ended as a result of the war. When World War II came, the Jewish people were scattered all over the earth, but that too ended as a result of the war. Out of the evil of these wars, God brought good. He used World War I to prepare the Land for the people, and He used World War II to prepare the people for the Land. In like manner, we can only speculate about the outcome of the present situation whose epicenter is the Middle East. The Christian author Arthur Pink, though writing about the First World War when he wrote these words, has said best what we need to remember about the future and He who holds it:

> Without a doubt a world-crisis is at hand, and everywhere men are alarmed. But God is not! He is never taken by surprise. It is no unexpected emergency which now confronts Him, for He is the One who "worketh all things after the counsel of His own will"

(Eph. 1:11). Hence, though the world is panic-stricken, the word to the believer is, "Fear not"! "All things" are subject to His immediate control: "all things" are moving in accord with His eternal purpose, and therefore, "all things" are "working together for good to them that love God, to them who are the called according to His purpose" (Rom. 8:28). It must be so, for "of Him, and through Him, and to Him are all things" (Rom. 11:36).[12]

We are all now engaged in a new world crisis, but nothing is new to God, for He "is the same yesterday and today and forever" (Hebrews 13:8). This is indeed an unholy war, but as we face the future in "the fear of the Lord," we will discover that the fear of Him casts out every other fear, for the fear of (faith in) God removes from us the fear of man.

This book began with the fearful words of the American president that "our world has changed forever." It should end with the faith-filled words of the psalmist, who said, "God is our refuge and strength, a very present help in trouble. Therefore we will not fear, though the earth should change....The LORD of hosts is with us; the God of Jacob is our stronghold" (Psalm 46:1-2,7). To this promise of security we must also add the promise of the Savior: "These things I [Jesus] have spoken to you, so that in Me you may have peace. In the world you will have tribulation, but take courage; I have overcome the world" (John 16:33).

Those who started this unholy war want to fill us with fear. Those who have attacked believe they will win—if not today, then tomorrow. But the last day belongs not to the West nor the East, but to those who have faith today and trust their tomorrow to the Overcomer. The future of holy peace that He has won, which can never be altered by the events of our days, is the unfailing assurance of victory in this unholy war. May your future be as bright as the promises of God!

Chronology of the
Middle-East Conflict

B.C.

1976 Jewish immigration to Canaan begins under Patriarch Abraham.

1926 Abraham offers Isaac on Mount Moriah in Jerusalem (future site of the Temple Mount).

1406 Jews under Joshua begin military conquest of Canaan.

996 King David captures Jerusalem from Jebusites and makes it the capital of Israel (2 Samuel 5:6-10).

996– Jews establish independent kingdom with

A.D. 636 Jerusalem as capital.

Despite being conquered and ruled by various peoples (Assyrians, Babylonians, Persians, Greeks, Egyptians, and Romans), the Jewish people remained the dominant population in the Land (especially in the four "holy cities" of Judaism: Jerusalem, Hebron, Tiberias, and Safed) with various interim periods of independence.

A.D.

70 Roman destruction of Jewish Second Temple.

135 Roman emperor Hadrian changes name of country to Palestine and Jerusalem to Aelia Capitolina.

614 Persian King Chosroes II favors Jews and offers opportunity to rebuild the Temple.

637 Arab Muslim invasion and conquest of Palestine (Muslim Caliph entered Jerusalem in 638).

1099– Arab and non-Arab Muslim rule in Palestine.

1500– Period of Jewish expulsions from Spain, Portugal, France, Germany, Italy, England, Austria, Hungary, Lithuania, Silesia, and the Crimea.

1291–   Periods of Crusader rule in Palestine.

1516–   Muslim rule returns under Egyptian Mameluks, who allow Jews to live within walls of Jerusalem and visit the Western Wall.

1517–   Ottoman Turkish Muslim rule under Suleiman, who writes a firman recognizing right of Jews to the Western Wall and designates it as the Jews' place of worship.

1845–1933 Period of European Anti-Semitism.

1862   Publication of *Rome and Jerusalem* by Moses Hess.

1869   First Jewish quarter of Nahlat Shiva built outside walls of Jerusalem's Old City.

1881   Assassination of Tsar Alexander II followed by persecution of Russian Jews.

1882–1903 First *Aliyah* (mass Jewish immigration to Jewish national home—*Eretz-Yisrael*).

1891   Arab protests against Jewish settlers in Palestine.

1894–95   Anti-Semitism revealed in Alfred Dreyfus trial (falsely charged with espionage).

1896   Publication of *The Jewish State* by Theodor Herzl.

1897   First International Zionist Congress.

1903   Publication and distribution of *The Protocols of Zion* (anti-Semitic propaganda).

Persecution of Jews in Kishinev.

1904   Beginning of second *Aliyah*.

1905   Seventh Zionist Congress rejects alternative to Palestine as aim of Zionism.

1908–09   Arab opposition to Zionist settlements intensifies.

1914–18   First World War (Arabs and Jews aid British to overthrow Turkish control of Palestine).

1915–16   Sykes-Picot agreement.

1917   Balfour Declaration advocating a Jewish national home in Palestine. Arab Revolt: Lawrence of

Arabia takes Aqaba and British General Allenby enters Jerusalem.

1919   Chaim Weizmann leads Zionist delegation at Paris Peace Conference.

1919–23   Third *Aliyah*.

1920–21   Arab anti-Jewish riots in Jerusalem over holy places.

1924–32   Fourth *Aliyah*.

1929   Arab riots in Jerusalem, and massacre of Jews in Hebron and Safed.

1930   Passfield White Paper seeks British disengagement from Jewish national home, aspects of Balfour Declaration and Palestine Mandate.

1931   Irgun (Jewish Resistance) established.

1933–45   Jews search for safety as anti-Semitism, pogroms, and persecutions force the Jewish population from Europe.

1935   Fifth *Aliyah*.

1937   Peel Commission recommends partition of Palestine into separate Arab (Palestinian) and Jewish states.

1937–38   Arab-Jewish conflict over British allowance of Jewish immigration.

1938   White Paper repudiates partition and restricts Jewish immigration.

1941   Muslim Mufti of Jerusalem Haj Amin al-Husseini relocated to Berlin, meets with German Chancellor Adolf Hitler and offers to assist in his campaign to exterminate world Jewry by creating a fascist Arab state.

1941–45   Holocaust occurs with orchestrated German extermination of Jews of Europe.

1945   President Truman supports Jewish refugee immigration to Palestine.

1946   British block Jewish refugee immigration and Jewish sabotage operations begin throughout Palestine.

Truman endorses partition of Palestine and creation of a Jewish state.

1947   British Foreign Secretary Ernest Bevin declares intention to refer the Palestine Mandate back to the United Nations.

1948   General Assembly votes for partition of Palestine into a Palestinian and a Jewish state.

Ben-Gurion declares the State of Israel.

Arab states declare war on the new State of Israel.

Termination of the British Mandate.

Mass Arab exodus from Palestine begins in wake of Arab forces and Arab-Israeli war.

1948–49   Arab-Israel war fought.

1949   Israel concludes armistice agreements with Jordan, Egypt, Lebanon, and Syria. Jordan controls the eastern section of Jerusalem and violates armistace by denying Jews access to the Western Wall.

Ben-Gurion declares Jerusalem the capital of Israel.

U.N. Resolution 194 issued.

1949–67   Jerusalem divided city.

Arab refugees in refugee camps and Jordan.

1950   Beginning of immigration to Israel of Jews from Arab countries.

King Abdullah of Jordan formally annexes the West Bank.

Jewish Law of Return gives the right to all Jews to settle in Israel.

King Abdullah assassinated by Palestinian in Jerusalem at Al-Aqsa Mosque.

Israeli Nahal settlements established in areas exposed to continued Arab attacks.

1951–56	Fedayeen (Palestinian terrorist group) raids and attacks Israel.
1955	Egyptian blockade of Gulf of Aqaba and sealing off of Israeli port of Eilat (considered act of war by Israel).
1956	Sinai Campaign (Israel at war with Egypt; captures Sinai).
1957	Israel withdrawal from Sinai due to U.S. pressure.
	Palestinian Liberation Party (Fatah) founded.
1964	Palestine Liberation Organization (PLO) founded.
1967	Fedayeen activity against Israel increased.
	Syrians bombard Jewish settlements around the Sea of Galilee (Kinneret).
	Egyptian President Nasser sends troops into Sinai and closes Strait of Tiran to Israeli shipping.
	On May 25 Syrian, Iraqi, Jordanian, and Saudi Arabian troops move to Israel's borders. Six-Day War is fought between Israel and Arab nations from June 5–10. Israel captures the Golan Heights, West Bank (including East Jerusalem), the Gaza Strip, and Sinai; Temple Mount in Israeli hands.
	In August, Moshe Dayan returns jurisdiction of the Temple Mount to the Islamic Waqf.
	Summit at Khartoum.
	U.N. Security Council Resolution 242 issued.
1968–70	Egypt commences war of attrition against Israel.
	Yasser Arafat elected chairman of the executive committee of the PLO.
1970–73	Soviet Union supplies arms to Egypt, Syria, and Iraq for next attack on Israel.
1970	Black September attack by Jordanian army to remove PLO guerrillas from Jordan.
1971	PLO guerrillas leave Jordan for Syria and south Lebanon.

1972   Black September organization under Yasser Arafat seizes Israeli athletes at Munich Olympics.

1973   Yom Kippur War (October 6-24), in which Egypt and Syria launch full-scale war against Israel.

1974   Summit meeting of Arab leaders in Rabat declares the PLO the only legitimate representative of the Palestinian people. U.N. General Assembly accepts PLO as representatives of Arab Palestinians.

1976–84   Civil war breaks out in Lebanon. Palestinian guerrillas fight alongside Lebanese leftists and Muslims against Maronite Christians.

1976   U.N. resolution condemning "Zionism as racism" is approved by 17 Arab states, 13 Communist states, 22 African states, and 20 other states.

1977   Egyptian President Anwar Sadat goes to Jerusalem and speaks at Israeli Knesset as part of peace plan.

1978   Israel invades south Lebanon and attacks Palestinian guerrilla bases.

Camp David Accords signed by Egypt, Israel, and United States.

1979   Egypt and Israel sign peace treaty.

1980   Israel returns Sinai to Egypt and Egyptian Embassy opens in Tel Aviv.

East Jerusalem is officially annexed to western part of city as Israel's capital.

1981   Katyusha war between the PLO and Israel in Lebanon.

Sadat assassinated by Egyptian militants.

1982   Israel invades Lebanon again in an all-out offensive against the PLO. Israeli forces reach outskirts of Beirut.

PLO leaves Lebanon and establishes headquarters in Tunis.

Mass murders of Palestinans at the Sabra and Chatila refugee camps in Lebanon by Christian Phalangists (September 16-17).

1985   Israeli Air Force attack on PLO headquarters in Tunis.

Palestinian Liberation Front hijacks Achile Lauro in the Mediterranean and kills Jews aboard.

1987   Palestinian Intifada begins in the Israeli-occupied Gaza Strip and the West Bank.

1988   Jordanian disengagement from the West Bank to allow for it becoming Palestinian state. Palestinian National Council declares an independent Palestinian state.

The Temple Mount and Land of Israel Faithful Movement, directed by Gershon Salomon, attempt to lay a cornerstone for the Third Temple on the Temple Mount but are turned away by Israeli police.

1989–91   Mass immigration of Soviet Jews to Israel. Iraq invades Kuwait.

Temple Mount Faithful attempts a second laying of their cornerstone for the Third Temple. Rioting occurs on the Temple Mount, leaving 19 Palestinians dead.

The Middle-East Peace Conference convenes in Madrid, Spain on October 31.

1993   On January 20, Yitzhak Rabin and Yasser Arafat meet secretly in Oslo, Norway in talks that lead in August to the Oslo Accords.

1994   On September 13 the Israeli Labour Party, under Prime Minister Yitzhak Rabin, signs Declaration of Principles on PLO interim self-government.

1995   Israel begins withdrawal from Gaza Strip and Jericho in accordance with first phase of the Declaration of Principles.

Jewish settler Baruch Goldstein murders Palestinian Muslims worshiping at Hebron Mosque.

Cairo Agreement between Israel and PLO.

On October 26, peace treaty signed between Israel and Jordan.

Yitzhak Rabin, Shimon Peres, and Yasser Arafat are jointly awarded the Nobel Peace Prize.

On November 2 Rabin is assassinated by a nationalist religious Jew at a peace rally in Tel Aviv.

1996   Benjamin Netanyahu becomes prime minister, promising to keep Jerusalem "united forever."

Israel withdraws from Hebron in further compliance with the Declaration of Principles.

Jerusalem celebrates its 3,000th anniversary as the capital of Israel; Arabs boycott the celebration and claim that Israel is trying to "create a history" in the Palestinian city.

On September 25 Israel opens exit for Western Wall Tunnel in Jerusalem and Palestinians riot, resulting in 58 deaths.

1998   Wye River agreement between Netanyahu and Arafat.

1999   Ehud Barak wins Israeli election with expectations of preserving Israel's security in negotiations.

King Hussein of Jordan dies and is succeeded by his eldest son Abdullah II, who pledges to continue his father's policies and preserve the peace treaty with Israel.

In December the Palestinian Mufti moves his offices to the Temple Mount.

2000   Israel withdraws from Lebanon.

The Camp David II Summit ends when Arafat abandons the talks even though offered significant concessions by Ehud Barak.

Death of President Hafez al-Asad of Syria.

Border skirmishes and shooting of an Israeli police officer by Palestinians renew Palestinian uprising.

Islamic Waqf begins construction on Marawami Mosque below Al-Aqsa Mosque, Solomon's Stables, and at the Eastern Gate, destroying remains from the First and Second Temple periods.

On September 28, Ariel Sharon visited the Temple Mount with a delegation from the Israeli Knesset and police escort to inspect the degree of destruction caused by the Waqf's construction activity at the site. A small riot followed Sharon's departure.

On September 29 Palestinians throw stones down upon Jews praying at the Western Wall and another riot ensues. The Palestinian Authority cites "Israeli provocation" at the Al-Aqsa Mosque the previous day and declares the beginning of the Al-Aqsa Intifada, which intends to liberate Jerusalem and the Muslim holy places.

2001   February 6—Ariel Sharon elected prime minister of Israel with expectations that he will take a firm hand with Palestinians.

July—Repeated terrorism and suicide bombings of Jewish civilians cause Israeli politicians to jointly declare an end of the Oslo Accords and begin targeted assassinations of Palestinian leaders and the destruction of PLO bases of operation through-out the West Bank.

Israeli closure and seizure of Palestinian Authority administrative buildings, such as the Orient House in Jerusalem, initiate new policy of reentering Palestinian-controlled areas in the West Bank.

August—Iraqi "Jerusalem Liberation Army" is formed, and 10,000 troops enter Jordan with infiltration into Palestinian areas of the West Bank.

September 11—Radical Islamic terrorists attack United States, destroying the twin towers of the World Trade Center, sections of the Pentagon, and crashing an airliner (meant for the White House) in Pennsylvania, killing all aboard. Total loss of life reaches approximately 5,000.

September 12— United States declares war on terrorism and the states that harbor terrorism, begins building coalition of Western allies (excluding Israel) and Islamic states.

October 1-6—United States pressures Israel to renew peace negotiations with Palestinians; Ariel Sharon warns United States to not abandon Israel as the United Kingdom did Czechoslovakia in the 1930s; United States returns warning and announces its support for establishment of an independent Palestinian state.

October 7—United States and United Kingdom forces launch first strike against terrorist targets in Kabul, Afghanistan, while crowds of Palestinians in Gaza and other West Bank towns publically protest the United States and show support for terrorist Osama bin Laden.

October 14—First reports of biologically engineered anthrax virus mailed by terrorists to U.S. address in Florida, later to media and political figures in New York and Washington, D.C., and then other Western countries (e.g., Great Britain and Kenya).

Glossary

Note: source language of foreign terms marked as follows: A (Arabic), G (Greek), H (Hebrew), L (Latin), R (Russian).

Abbasid(ian) (A): caliphate (dynasty) at Bagdad from the eighth through thirteenth centuries that claimed descent from Abbas, the uncle of Muhammad.

Abomination of Desolation (H): the expression used to describe the act of setting up an idolatrous image in the holy place in the Temple, thus defiling or "making desolate" the Temple, and ending the offering of all sacrifices. This was done in the past by Antiochus Epiphanes (Daniel 11:31), whose act reflects the future defilement by the Antichrist (Daniel 9:27). Both Daniel and Jesus indicated that this future act would signal the start of the Great Tribulation (Daniel 12:11; Matthew 24:15; Mark 13:14).

Abrahamic Covenant: the covenant made by God with Abraham that unconditionally promised his descendants a land (the Land of Israel), a seed (the Jewish people), and a blessing (to the nations), Geneis 12:1-3; see restatements in Genesis 13:14-17; 15:1-7. The Land's boundaries were given as from the "river of Egypt" (wadi el-Arish) to the river Euphrates (Genesis 15:18).

Abu Bakr (A): name of one of Muhammad's first converts in Mecca and the first caliph in Medina.

Aggadah (H): name given to those sections of Talmud and Midrash containing homiletic expositions of the Bible, stories, legends, folklore, anecdotes, or maxims. In contradistinction to halakhah.

Al-Aqsa (A) "the farther": term used for the farther mosque in Sura 17 of the Qur'an. It originally indicated a site in the northern corner of Mecca which later tradition moved to Jerusalem; the name of the mosque built at the southern end of the Temple Mount in A.D. 691 by Caliph al-Walid.

Alawites (A): a minority offshoot of Islam that neither Orthodox Sunnis nor Shi'ite Muslims consider Muslim. It is the religion of the Assad dynasty which presently rules Syria and represents less than 10 percent of the Syrian population.

Aliyah (H): 1) being called to Reading of the Law in synagogue; 2) immigration to 'Eretz Yisrael; 3) one of the waves of immigration to 'Eretz Yisrael from the early 1880s.

Allah (A) *al-liah* ("the god"): personal name of a vague astral deity (corresponding to the Babylonian Bel) who served as head of a pre-Islamic pantheon associated with the moon. Although a misnomer, it is commonly used as a synonym for "God" equivalent to the deity of Judaism and Christianity. Today, it is also the normal Arabic word for "God" used in Arabic translations of the Old and New Testament.

Allahu Akbar (A) "Allah is Great!" or "Great(er) is God!": exclamation used by Muslims (and especially by jihadic "martyrs" such as suicide bombers before detonation) to demonstrate their commitment (or call) to holy war (see *jihad*).

Al-Quds (A) "the holy": Arabic term used for the city of Jerusalem in the later period of the Muslim conquest.

Amidah (H) "standing": the series of benedictions that constitute the central part of the synagogue service.

Anti-Semitism: the term applied to the hostile attitude of non-Jews toward Jews, individually and collectively. The actions of anti-Semitists have ranged from imposing restrictive laws against Jews and requiring the social isolation of Jewish groups to instituting pogroms and widespread genocide (as in the Nazi holocaust). *Christian* anti-Semitism has historically resulted from adopting a view known as *replacement theology*.

Apocalyptic (G) *apocalypsis* ("unveiling"): pertaining to a genre of literature that divulges otherwise unknown secrets about the nature of God and the heavens and the end of days. Especially prominent is the concept of divine intervention and the dualistic idea of a cosmic/earthly conflict between evil angels, their agents and God, His Messiah, and His holy angels. The term is also used to describe the imminent messianism that is often part of these texts.

Armageddon (H) *har-Megiddo* ("mount of Megiddo"): The place to which the armies of the world are gathered together for one of the central battles at the end of the Tribulation period (Revelation 16:16). In popular usage, the term is used to refer to the end of the world.

Av (H): fifth month of the Jewish religious year, eleventh of the civil calendar, approximating to July/August.

Ayatollah (A): highest-ranking religious leader among Shi'ite Muslims.

Babylonian exile: the deportation of the Jewish people from Judea during three periods of invasion (605–586 B.C.) that lasted for 70 years (Jeremiah 25:11-13; Daniel 9:2).

Basilica (L) "portico, colonnaded building": a long, rectangular building with two rows of pillars or columns dividing it into a central nave and two aisles. Common to Roman administrative architecture, its design influenced both that of the royal portico on the Temple Mount and that of synagogues and churches of the period.

Byzantine: the period of Roman Christian rule in Jerusalem (A.D. 313–638), during which Christianity was made the official religion of the Roman Empire, and the center of imperial power was moved to Byzantium. The Byzantine Period is divided into the early period (313–491), the great Christian architectural period, and the late period (491-638), which saw a temporary conquest by the Persians and ended with the Islamic invasion under Caliph Omar Ibn el-Khattab.

Caliph (A) "successor": the title of an official successor of Muhammad who serves as the head of the community of Muslims; *Imam* (see later in glossary) is the preferred Shi'ite term to describe the same office.

Canaanites (from Hurrian) "belonging to the land of red-purple": the original inhabitants of the land of Canaan, the ancient name of the Land of Israel west of the Jordan (Numbers 34:3-12), which include a lengthly list of various nationalities (Genesis 10:6; 15:8).

Constantinople: the capital of the Byzantine (Christian) Empire, named after its Roman conqueror, the emperor Constantine I (c. A.D. 324), and located on the European shore at the southern end of the narrow straits of the Bosporus that connect the Black Sea with the Sea of Mamara (present-day Istanbul, Turkey). Because legend attributes its founding to a Megarian captain by the name of Byzas (c. 667 B.C.), it was later called Byzantium.

Crusaders (L): medieval army comprised of western European "Christians" who waged holy wars, at the order of the papacy, to recapture the Church of the Holy Sepulcher from the Muslims.

Dar al Harb (A) "House of war": the areas of the world not yet subdued by Islam (non-Muslim lands); the geographical realm of infidels and *dhimmi,* which must be brought under Islam by surrender or warfare.

Dar al Islam (A) "House of Islam": the areas of the world subdued by Islam (Muslim lands); the geographical realm in which Islam is in complete devotional, political, and legal actuality.

Dawah (A): a "call" to missionary activity or organization for the propagation of Islam in the world.

Dhimmi (A): a non-Muslim subject under Islamic rule in one of the tolerated minorities (Jews and Christians), who must pay the *jizya* (tax) in place of *zakat* (alms) that is required of all Muslims.

Diaspora (G) "dispersion": the Jewish communities outside of *'Eretz Yisrael.*

Eastern Gate: term for the present-day gate within the eastern retaining wall of the Temple Mount compound. Also referred to as the Golden Gate and Gate of Mercy.

East Jerusalem: the term used by most non-Jewish media and sources for the eastern section of the Old City (including the

Temple Mount), which was shared by Jews and Arabs before 1948, came under Jordanian control from 1948–1967, and which since 1967 has continued to be inhabited by an Arab population. Israel officially annexed East Jerusalem in 1980, uniting the whole city as Israel's capital.

End of days/end time (H) *qetz ha-yammim:* a biblical term that Jewish and Christian tradition has understood to refer to the eschatological Messianic era. It is inclusive of both *Yom YHWH* ("the Day of the Lord"), in which God's judgment falls upon Israel's adversaries, as well as *Yemot ha-Mashiach* ("the days of Messiah"), the period preceding the judgment. It is followed by *'olam ha-ba* ("the world to come"), the eschatological future world.

'Eretz Yisrael (H) "the Land of Israel": the land promised to the Israelites in the Abrahamic Covenant; in law, Palestine and adjacent areas where the *halakhot* had to be strictly observed.

Eschatology (G) "study of last things": the study of things relating to the end of the world, the final judgment, and the life and world to come.

Fatah (A): a reverse mnemonic for *Hizb al-Tahrir al-Filastini* ("the Palestinian Liberation Party"), a terrorist group founded by Yasser Arafat in 1958.

Fatwa(h) (A): an advisory judgment on a case of Islamic law rendered by a competent authority; a legal opinion issued by a mufti (Sunni) or ayatollah (Shi'ite) in which the *Shari'ah* is applied to cases or issues so that its authority may be upheld. For example, the Taliban issued fatwah to permit the murder of U.S. civilians under *jihad*.

Foundation Stone (H) *'Even Ha'shtiyah:* the stone which, according to ancient sources, existed within the Holy of Holies in the Temple, and upon which the Ark of the Covenant rested in First Temple times. According to tradition, this stone is identified with the rock inside the Muslim Dome of the Rock.

Gush Emunim (H) "Block of the faithful": the movement to foster Jewish settlements in the West Bank in order to continue the national stream of Zionism. Activist by definition, members of this movement have been involved in attempting to blow up the Dome of the Rock and anti-Arab attacks and demonstrations.

Hadith (A) "Tradition": (purported) reports of the words, deeds, and attitudes of Muhammad on the authority of his contemporaries, which constitutes a body of literature second only to the Qur'an in authority.

Haganah (H): the underground Jewish organization for armed self-defense under the British Mandate period in Israel, which became the basis for the Israeli army.

Hajj (A): pilgrimage, especially the pilgrimage to Mecca incumbent upon all Muslims.

Halakha/halakhot (H): a binding legal enactment of the rabbis that was either derived from Scripture by exegetical means or appealed for its authority to the "tradition of the Fathers."

Hamas: a terrorist organization with ties to the PLO. This group follows the Palestinian Covenant, which calls for the eradication of the State of Israel. They employ terrorist tactics against Israel, especially suicide bombings, for which they promise suicide bombers immediate entrance into Islamic paradise.

Haram (A) "enclosure": the present platform upon which the Dome of the Rock is built and which is thought to approximate the original Herodian Temple platform. The full title used by the Muslims is *Haram es-Sharif* ("The Noble Enclosure").

Hegira, hijrah (A) "immigration": Muhammad's immigration from Mecca to Medina in A.D. 622, which became the date marking the beginning of the Muslim era.

Hezbollah or **Hizbullah** (A): "Party of Allah"; a Shi'ite Muslim "Palestinian" terrorist organization headquartered in the Bekaa Valley, a mini-Shi'ite Islamic state in Lebanon.

Holocaust (H) *shoah* ("a burnt offering or sacrifice"): term applied to the organized mass persecution and annihilation of European Jewry by the Nazis during the Second World War

(1933–1945). In all the Holocaust, many millions of people were killed, including more than six million Jewish men, women, and children, who were systematically exterminated in this sacrifice of Jewish lives.

Imam (A): leader; prayer-leader; the charismatic leader of the Muslim community; in the Shi'ite view, a descendant of Ali who is so designated by his predecessor.

Intifada (A) "shake off, uprising, strike": the Palestinian revolt against Israeli rule in the so-called "occupied territories" that began in December 1987 and was reinstituted in September 2000.

Islam (A) "submission" (to the will of Allah): a monotheistic religion whose deity is Allah ("God"), and whose prophet is Muhammad; the faith, obedience, and practice of peoples who follow the teachings of Muhammad. See *Muslim*.

Jahiliyyah (A) "ignorance": the period in Saudi Arabia before Muhammad's ascendancy and the teaching of Islam.

Jebusite: the original Canaanite inhabitants of Jerusalem at the time of the first conquest of Jerusalem (by Joshua—Joshua 10:23; 12:10).

Jihad (A) "striving": the term used in Muslim religious law for the holy war waged against all infidels until the end of time.

Jizya (A) "tribute": poll tax levied on the *dhimmis* by Muslim rulers in Muslim lands.

Ka'aba (A): the name of a cube-shaped structure in the southeast corner of the city of Mecca that enshrines a large black meteor found in the Arabian desert. This meteor is believed to have been sent by astral deities. Every Muslim is required to make a pilgrimage (see *hajj*) to Mecca to visit the *Ka'aba* once in his lifetime.

Kach (H) "thus": the name of the Israeli party created by the late Rabbi Meir Kahane, which advocates the deportation of all Arabs from the Land of Israel after due compensation was paid.

Members of Kach have attempted to take over the Temple Mount in the past.

Kafir (A): an unbeliever; one who has not submitted to the will of Allah; a pagan.

Kingdom of God: the manifestation of God's dominion and of divine justice on earth in a spiritual sense, and especially the literal period of God's restoration of His divine plan in history at the end of days.

Knesset (H): parliament of the State of Israel.

Latter days/last days (H) *'Acharit ha-yamim:* a biblical term that can indicate a final period in history climaxed by severe judgments ("latter days"), or the final days of history prior to the end time or end of days.

Likud (H) "union, alignment": the right-wing bloc or political party in the Israeli system of political representation.

Mandate, Palestine: responsibility for the administration of Palestine conferred on Britain by the League of Nations in 1922.

Masjid (A) "place of prostration": shrine, mosque.

Mecca: Islam's most holy city; birthplace of Muhammad and site of the Great Mosque, which contains the sacred *Ka'aba* and which is believed to have been built by Abraham and Ishmael; direction of prayer for Muslims and place of required pilgrimage (*hajj*).

Medina(h): the second holiest city of Islam after Mecca; Muhammad fled to Medina in A.D. 622 to escape persecution in Mecca and first established the religion of Islam there; place of Muhammad's tomb.

Messiah (H) *Mashiah* (lit. "anointed [one]"): equivalent to the Greek term *Christos,* from which is derived the English "Christ." In traditional Orthodox Jewish definition this is a human political-military deliverer who is sent by God to usher in the age of redemption for Israel as promised by the biblical prophets. In historic Orthodox Christian definition it is God the

Son who was sent to fulfill this role. Thus, Christians accept a divine Messiah whom they identify with the Jewish man Jesus of Nazareth.

Messianic age or Messianic era: the Era of Redemption, the period that spans the beginning of redemption for the Jewish people in the Land of Israel (interpreted by some as 1948) through the coming and rule of King Messiah at the end of 6,000 years of history to bring a reign of universal peace, moral justice, and spiritual life.

Mibrab (A): a niche in the mosque wall indicating the direction of Mecca and thus the orientation of prayer; see *qiblah*.

Midrash/midrashim (H) "study": the study of Scripture, exegesis, and the words devoted to such.

Millennium (L) "thousand": the final period of Jewish history, lasting 1,000 years (Revelation 20:1), which follows the Tribulation and the second advent of Christ. It is characterized by a restoration of the Jewish nation and the reign of Christ on earth. See also *Kingdom of God*.

Minaret (A): the spiral column or columns of a mosque that houses stairs within, and from which, at the top, the prayer leader may call Muslims to prayer.

Mishnah (H) "learning, repetition": the earliest written collection of Jewish Oral Law (i.e., Jewish religious and legal teachings handed down orally). It was compiled about A.D. 200 by Rabbi Judah ha-Nasi ("the Prince"). It comprises the first part of the Talmud and appears in the form of homiletical discourses by the Jewish sages.

Mufti (A): one who is competent to render an opinion on a case of Islamic law; see *fatwa*.

Muhammad or Mohammed (A) "to praise": the founder and prophet of Islam, who was born in A.D. 570 and died at Medina in A.D. 632.

Mujahideen (Arabic, "warriors of Jihad"): the term used by Islamic terrorists for those who join in the fight to annihilate the

State of Israel and the Jewish people in the holy war commanded in the Qur'an.

Murtad Harbi (A): a military apostate (*murtad*—"apostate" + *harbi*—"military").

Muslim or **Moslem** (A) *'aslama:* one who has submitted, converted to the will of Allah; a believer or follower of Islam.

Muslim Brotherhood: an Egyptian puritanical organization founded in 1928 by Hasan Brotherhoodal-Banna.

New Covenant: the covenant made with Israel that enlarges the blessing promise of the Abrahamic Covenant, which includes the realization of the boundaries of the Promised Land in the future kingdom (Jeremiah 31:31-34; Ezekiel 37:24-28).

Orthodox (G) "straight": those holding to religious views that have been traditionally accepted and taught. *Orthodox Jews* are those accepting the *Tanakh* (Old Testament) as divine revelation, and the *Talmud* as divine direction for the interpretation of the *Tanakh*, and are observant (practitioners) of Jewish law. Orthodox Christians are those who accept the cardinal doctrines of the historic faith, whether as formulated by various creeds or by personal affirmation to the basic scriptural tenents of the triune nature of the One God (Father, Son, and Holy Spirit), the deity, virgin birth, and mediatorial work of Christ as an atoning Savior, and salvation by grace through personal faith in Christ apart from works. Today, there are many different divisions within both Orthodox Judaism and Christianity.

Ottoman (Empire): the empire of Ottoman Turks who converted to Islam and ruled from A.D. 1453–1918 in the Middle East (and "Palestine"). It supported Sunni Islam and was dismantled after World War II.

Palestine (G/L): A perjorative term for the country west of the Jordan River, first coined by the Greeks and Romans after the word *Philistine*, which refers to the enemies of Israel who inhabited the Mediterranean Coastal Plain. The Bible refers to the same territory as *Canaan*, after its pre-Israelite inhabitants, though Jews have always called it *'Eretz Yisrael*, the Land of Israel.

Palestinian: A mixed ethnic group of immigrant workers who arrived in "Palestine" in the nineteenth century to work land under the Ottoman Turkish empire and who settled there with the native Jews and Jewish immigrants. The name *Palestinian* was used of them primarily after the partitioning of Palestine, at which time "Palestinian Jews" took on the name "Israeli Jews," and "Palestinian Arabs" took on the name "Israeli-Arabs" as citizens of the State of Israel. Most Palestinians are Sunni Muslims (as is Yasser Arafat), but some are also Shi'ite and Christian.

Palmah (H): abbreviation for Hebrew *peluggot mahaz*, "shock companies"—striking arm of the Haganah.

PLO: The abbreviation for Palestine Liberation Organization, the terrorist group established in 1964 to represent the Palestinian people in their nationalism.

Pogrom (R) "devastation": An organized persecution, massacre, or attack on the Jewish people in the *Diaspora*.

Polemics, polemical (G) "to make war": an argument or refutation, usually of an idea or practice and/or the group that holds the idea or practice. In the case of the scrolls, the manner in which other sectarian groups may be described (i.e., by example in order to refute the group).

Premillennialism (L) "before millennium": the theological view that Christ and His saints will reign on the earth for 1,000 years *after* His final return.

Qiblah (A) "orientation," especially for prayer: the direction toward Mecca marked in the mosque by the mibrab.

Qur'an or **Koran** (A) "recitation": the collected revelations (114 chapters) given by God to Muhammad through the agency of the angel Gabriel at Mecca and Medina and the text in which they are written down.

Quraysh: the Meccan Arabian tribe to which Muhammad's family belonged and which he attacked after establishing Islam in Medina.

Rabbi (H) "master": derived from the Hebrew verb *rabab* "to be great," the term was an honorable title for an ordained Jewish teacher of the law or the leader of a Jewish community. Roughly equivalent to Christian term *pastor* or *bishop*.

Ramadan (A): the ninth month of the Muslim year, in which it is required of Muslims to fast during the day. It corresponds on the Gregorian calendar to October/November. The fast concludes on the 27th of Ramadan.

Reform Judaism (H): trend in Judaism advocating modification of Orthodoxy in conformity with the exigencies of contemporary life and thought.

Replacement Theology: a theological perspective that teaches that the Jews have been rejected by God and are no longer God's Chosen People. Those who hold to this view disavow any ethnic future for the Jewish people in connection with the biblical covenants, believing that their spiritual destiny is either to perish or become a part of the new religion that superseded Judaism (whether Christianity or Islam).

S.a.a.w. (A): abbreviation for the Arabic phrase *Salla Allah Alaihi Wasallam* (literally, "God prayed and gave peace upon him," or "May God bless him and grant him peace").

Second advent: the eschatological designation for the final messianic return of Jesus. In premillennialism it consists of two phases: the *rapture*, being the return of Christ "in the air" (1 Thessalonians 4:13-17), and the *revelation*, being the return of Christ "to the earth," which, according to Zechariah 14:4, will be to Jerusalem.

Second Commonwealth: the political organization of the Jewish people in the Land of Israel beginning with the return from exile in the sixth century B.C. and ending with the final dismantling of the Herodian dynasty in the first century A.D.

Second Temple: the Temple that was constructed in Jerusalem in 515 B.C. by Zerubbabel, reconstructed by Herod the Great (beginning circa 20 B.C.), and lasted until its destruction by the

Romans in A.D. 70. The term can also designate the period during which this Temple stood.

Shari'ah (A): the Islamic law in general; in particular those enactments whose authority is derived from 1) the Qur'an, or 2) the sunnah of the Prophet, or 3) the consensus of the community of Muslims, or 4) the legal reasoning of jurisprudence. Sacred and canonical law given in the Qur'an, Hadith, Qiyas, and Ijma; the path of duty both ritual and general for Muslims, and the only rule of government for a true Islamic state.

Sheikh (A) "elder, chief": a Muslim ruler or head of an Arab tribe or family.

Shekinah (H): the Divine Presence manifested in glorious form (e.g., cloud or pillar of fire), usually within the Jewish Tabernacle or Temple. Also "dwelling, resting": a term developed by the rabbis and used for the Divine Presence of God that was manifested by "dwelling" between the wings of the cherubim on the Ark (1 Chronicles 13:6). It represented the immanence of God with the Israelites, first in the Tabernacle and later in the First Temple.

Shi'ite (A) "Partisan": the minority branch in Islam made up of the followers of Ali (Muhammad's son-in-law and husband of Fatima) who accept him as the legitimate successor to Muhammad and whose descendants should rule the Umma (Islamic community). Iran is the primary Shi'ite Muslim nation. See *Sunnah*.

Shirk (A) "association": the sinful act of regarding anything as equal to Allah, including idolatry, polytheism, or attributing divinity to anyone (as in the Christian doctrine of the Trinity).

Shofar (H): horn of the ram (or any other ritually lean animal except the cow) sounded for the memorial blowing on Rosh Hashanah, and other occasions.

Siloam (H) *Shiloah* ("the one sent"): the pool located at the end of the water tunnel of King Hezekiah, which collected water from the Gihon Spring on the eastern slope of the Ophel. During the ancient *Hoshana Rabba,* water was drawn from this source for the libation poured on the altar in the Temple.

Six-Day War: the war that occurred June 5-10, 1967, when Israel reacted to Arab threats and a blockade by defeating the Egyptian, Jordanian, and Syrian forces. The Sinai Peninsula, the West Bank, and the Golan Heights fell to Israel in this conflict. The Sinai was returned to Egypt in 1979 as a condition of the Camp David Peace Treaty. For Jerusalem, the war was a three-day conflict on June 5-7 that resulted in the liberation of East Jerusalem and the Temple Mount from Jordan.

Sukkot (H) "booths": the one-week Feast of Tabernacles or Booths; the last of the three pilgrim festivals that begins on the fifteenth of Tishri (approximately September/October on the Julian or Christian calendar). The word *sukkot* is the plural of *sukkah*, a booth or tabernacle that the Israelites dwelt in during their time of wandering in the wilderness (Leviticus 23:42).

Sunnah (A): custom, customary practice, especially the customary practice of the Prophet as reported in the hadith; English, *Sunni*. The majority branch in Islam, which relies on the authority of the Qur'an and the Hadith and differs from the Shi'ites, who rely on the authority of the Imams.

Sura(h) (A): a chapter of the Qur'an. There a total of 114 suras.

Synagogue (G) "gathering together": an institution that was developed by Jews in the *Diaspora,* after the destruction of the First Temple, for worship and study of the Bible. In Hellenistic usage, the term also referred to a Jewish community.

Tafsir (A): an "explanation" or "exegesis" of the Qur'an.

Talmud (H): the Hebrew Mishnah of Rabbi Judah ha-Nasi accompanied by either its Palestinian (Jerusalem Talmud) or its Babylonian (Babylonian Talmud) Aramaic commentary (gemara).

Tawhid (A): the doctrine of the divine unity of Allah.

Temple Mount (H) *Har-Habayit:* the elevated enclosed platform built on top of Mount Moriah in Jerusalem as a support for the

Jewish Temples. Although having increased in size from the time of Solomon (First Temple) to the Herodian period (Second Temple), it remains essentially the same since the destruction of the Temple in A.D. 70.

Times of the Gentiles: the period of Gentile domination over Jerusalem, which began in 586 B.C. and will end with the final battle of the Armageddon campaign at the second advent of Christ and His destruction of the armies of the Antichrist (as recorded in Zechariah 14 and Revelation 19).

Tisha B'Av (H) "Ninth of Av": a fast day commemorating the destruction of the First and Second Temples. This occurs on the ninth day of *Av*, the first month of the Jewish religious year, approximating July/August on the Julian (Christian) calendar.

Torah (H): the law; a term used generically of Jewish religious law or specifically of the first five books (the Pentateuch) of the Bible, where the terms of the covenant between God and the Israelites are set forth within the narrative framework of early Jewish history.

Tribulation: the New Testament term for that period of time, according to the biblical prophets, during which Israel as a nation will experience unparalleled distress as a part of the "Day of the Lord." In Jewish theology it is the time of "messianic woes" or "messianic birthpangs," which will occur prior to the coming of the Messiah. In the dispensational premillennial interpretation of prophecy it is the period that follows the rapture of the church and lasts for seven years, the first three-and-one-half years being a time of peace during which the Antichrist will rise and the Jewish Temple will be rebuilt. The last three-and-one-half years are a time of divine judgment known in the Old Testament as "the time of Jacob's trouble." At the end of this period, climaxed by the Battle of Armageddon, Christ returns to rescue Israel and set up His millennial kingdom.

Ulama (A): "the learned"; the Islamic "rabbinate" whose prestige derived from their mastery of the religious sciences.

Ummah (A): "nation," "people," "community": this word is used only in the singular (never the plural) because in Islamic thinking there are not "nations" or "peoples," but only one unified community under Islam and its *Shari'ah* (regardless of ethnic or racial backgrounds or geographical or national boundaries).

Valley of Jehoshophat: a name given by tradition to the valley situated between Jerusalem and the Mount of Olives, also known as the Kidron Valley. It was in this valley that the Judean king Jehoshophat overthrew the united enemies of Israel (2 Chronicles 20:26), and which in biblical prophecy will be the place where God will destroy the armies that will attack Jerusalem in the last days (Joel 3:2,12).

Wahhabi (A): the puritanical Islamic movement founded by al-Wahhab of Arabia (A.D. 1703–92), which accepts only the authority of the Qur'an and Sunnah Islam; the predominant religious influence in Saudi Arabia.

Waqf (A): land or property whose income was inalienably deeded to the support of pious causes, such as the construction of a mosque or madrash and the support of its faculty and students. Title of the body of Muslim clerics and administrators that oversee the *Haram* (Temple Mount).

West Bank: the term originally employed to describe the land occupied by Jordan from 1948–1967 (west bank of Jordan), and continued in use by non-Jewish media and sources to refer to the territory of biblical Judea and Samaria (including East Jerusalem), captured by Israel in the Six-Day War of 1967 and the Yom Kippur War of 1973.

Western Wall (H) *kotel* ("wall"): the name given to the ancient remnant of the Herodian retaining wall on the western side of the Temple Mount platform. It was not the western wall of the Temple itself, but since the destruction of the Temple in A.D. 70 it has become the focus of Jewish prayer as the only (at that time) known portion of the Temple complex. Today it is still the only portion of the area accessible to Jews, the Temple Mount being under the jurisdiction of Arab Muslims. Orthodox

Judaism believes that the presence of God "hides behind" the wall and that prayers made or directed to this spot have a special efficacy.

World to Come (H) *'olam ha-ba'*: the final period in Jewish eschatology, in which the heavenly blessings are realized.

Yeshiva/Yeshivot (H): academy; school for the study of the Torah and Talmud.

Yom Kippur (H) "Day of Atonement": The most solemn day of the Jewish year, celebrated on the ninth day of Tishri (September/October on the Julian or Christian calendar), ten days after the Jewish New Year. Considered a day of judgment and reckoning, it is a time when the Jews—individually and as a nation—are cleansed of sin and granted atonement. It was on this day alone that the high priest was permitted to enter the Holy of Holies in the Temple. In postbiblical tradition, the theme of the day is human repentance, which leads to divine forgiveness. The 1973 war with the Arab states took place at this time, which is why it's called the Yom Kippur War.

Zion (H): originally the hill area north of the City of David, the Ophel, where the Tabernacle resided. Through poetic usage it became a synonym for the City of Jerusalem and Israel itself, and spiritually it became a synonym for the eschatological ideal of God's chosen place on earth.

Zionism: the movement to establish an autonomous Jewish national home in the Land of Israel, so called because of the historical desire of Jews to return to Zion. Zionism as a political movement of world Jewry (The World Zionist Organization) began with the first Zionist Congress (1897), convened by Theodor Herzl. With the establishment of the State of Israel, the political aspirations were attained, and the organization now assists in development of the State and as a bridge between Israel and Jewish communities in the *Diaspora*.

Recommended Reading

Andrews, Richard. *Blood on the Mountain: A History of the Temple Mount from the Ark to the Third Millennium*. London: Weidenfeld & Nicolson/The Orion Publishing Group, 1999. (Traces the history of conflict over the Temple Mount in Jerusalem and provides interesting archaeological details.)

Bennett, Ramon. *When Day and Night Cease*. Jerusalem: Arm of Salvation, 1993. (A study of the biblical promises to Israel and the political challenges to survival it has faced in modern times.)

————. *The Great Deception Philistine*. Jerusalem: Arm of Salvation, 1995. (Documents and critiques the attempt by Palestinians to create a history and claim rights to the Land of Israel.)

Chertoff, Mordecai S. *Zionism: A Basic Reader*. New York: Herzl Press, 1975. (A simplified guide to understanding the meaning of Zionism, its historical claims, and documentation on the same.)

Cohen, Richard I., ed. *Vision and Conflict in the Holy Land*. Jerusalem: Yad Izhak Ben-Zvi, 1985.

Cohn-Sherbok, Dan, & Dawoud El-Alami. *The Palestine-Israeli Conflict: A Beginner's Guide*. Oxford: Oneworld Publications, 2001. (Contains both Israeli moderate and Palestinian nationalist viewpoints.)

Dennis, Anthony, J. *The Rise of the Islamic Empire and the Threat to the West*. Wyndham Hall Press, 1996. (Explains how Islamic fundamentalism will threaten the world by the beginning of the twenty-first century.)

Dixon, Murray. *Whose Promised Land: Conflict in Palestine-Israel*. Heinemann History Project (new edition). Auckland: Heinemann Education/Octopus Publishing Group, 1996. (A manual that provides pictorial and documentary overviews of crucial events and issues in the historical struggle for survival of the Jewish people.)

Dolan, David. *Israel at the Crossroads: Fifty Years and Counting*. Grand Rapids: Baker Book House, 1998. (A reporter living in Israel details the political issues that have faced the formation and fulfillment of the Jewish state and how the present conflict affects its future.)

Dyer, Charles, ed. *Storm Clouds on the Horizon: Bible Prophecy and the Current Middle East Crises*. Chicago: Moody Press, 2001. (A brief compilation of essays on Israel in prophecy in light of the modern conflict.)

Fregosi, Paul. *Jihad in the West: Muslim Conquests from the 7th to the 21st Centuries*. Prometheus Books, 1998. (Traces the development of Islamic imperialism through "holy war" from attacks on Byzantium to the modern conflict in Kosovo.)

Gefen, Aba. *Israel at a Crossroads.* Jerusalem: Gefen Publishing House, 2001. (A former Israeli statesman gives an insider's view of where Israel has come from and where it must go in the future.)

Gilbert, Martin. *The Routledge Atlas of the Arab-Israeli Conflict.* London: Routledge, 1996. (One of the most helpful and detailed set of historical maps providing essential facts on the conflict from its beginning to the present.)

Gorenberg, Gershom. *The End of Days: Fundamentalism and the Struggle for the Temple Mount.* New York: Free Press, 2000. (A study of religious fundamentalism in the three world religions and how this ideology threatens world peace.)

Grant, George. *The Blood of the Moon: The Roots of the Middle East Crisis.* Tennessee: Wolgemuth & Hyatt, 1991. (A popular study of the origins and beliefs of Islam and its role in the Middle East conflict.)

Green, D.F., ed. *Arab Theologians on Jews and Israel.* Geneva: Editions de l'Avenir, 1976. (A compilation of quotes by Arab clerics, academics, and political figures concerning the Jewish people and the State of Israel.)

Gulston, Charles. *Jerusalem: The Tragedy and the Triumph.* Grand Rapids: Zondervan, 1978. (A succinct treatment of the history of Jerusalem from a biblical and historical perspective.)

Hagee, John. *The Battle for Jerusalem.* Nashville: Thomas Nelson Publishers, 2001. (A popular presentation of the Israeli-Palestinian conflict within the context of present politics and Bible prophecy.)

Harkabi, Y. *Arab Attitudes to Israel.* Jerusalem: Keter Publishing House, 1972. (A massive compilation of quotes, treatises, documents, and other writings by Arabs that display their true intentions toward Jews and the State of Israel.)

Harkness, Georgia, & Charles F. Kraft. *Biblical Backgrounds of the Middle East Conflict.* Nashville: Abingdon Press, 1976. (A helpful academic study of the early historical origins and interactions of the peoples whose descendants are presently involved in conflict.)

Idinopulos, Thomas A. *Jerusalem Blessed, Jerusalem Cursed: Jews and Muslims in the Holy City from David's Time to Our Own.* Chicago: Ivan R. Dee, 1991. (A historical and political overview of Jerusalem's history of conflict.)

Israeli, Raphael. *Muslim Fundamentalism in Israel.* London: Brassey's, 1993. (A study of Islamic fundamentalist organizations within Israel and their objectives and operations in the modern conflict.)

Kac, Arthur W., M.D. *The Rebirth of the State of Israel: Is It of God or of Men?* Chicago: Moody Press, 1958. (A dated but useful historical study of the formation of the Jewish State as part of God's prophetic purpose and plan.)

Kushner, Harvey W. *Terrorism in America: A Structured Approach to Understanding the Terrorist Threat.* Springfield, IL: Charles C. Thomas Publisher, Ltd., 1998. (Predicts attack on World Trade Center.)

Lewis, David Allen, with Jim Fletcher. *The Last War.* Arkansas: New Leaf Press, 2001. (A brief overview of the current Israeli-Palestinian conflict including an extensive interview with Israeli prime minister Ariel Sharon.)

Marshall, Paul, with Lela Gilbert. *Their Blood Cries Out: The Worldwide Tragedy of Modern Christians Who Are Dying for Their Faith.* Dallas: Word Publishing, 1977. (Documents the oppression and persecution of Christians in Islamic countries, including Sudan, Iran, Saudi Arabia, Pakistan, and Egypt, as well as explains the threat of Islam to Christianity in many other Middle Eastern and Asian countries.)

Miller, Judith. *God Has Ninety-Nine Names.* New York: Simon & Shuster, 1996. (An excellent and well-documented book explaining radical Islam.)

Mordecai, Victor. *Is Fanatic Islam a Global Threat?* South Carolina, 1997. (Traces and documents the recent rise of Muslim terrorism and how it threatens to dominate Israel, the West, and the world.)

Netanyahu, Benjamin. *A place Among the Nations: Israel and the World.* New York: Bantam Books, 1993. (Defends the role Israel must play internationally and how its struggles affect the security of all nations.)

Norval, Morgan. *Triumph of Disorder: Islamic Fundamentalism, the New Face of War.* Siligo Press, 1999. (Describes the violent aspects of Islamic fundamentalism and why and how it sponsors international terrorism.)

Olsen, Arnold. *Inside Jerusalem, City of Destiny.* Glendale, CA: Gospel Light/Regal Books, 1969. (A dated but still useful summary of how God has prepared Jerusalem to fulfill its ultimate destiny.)

Peters, Joan. *From Time Immemorial: The Origins of the Arab-Jewish Conflict over Palestine*. Chicago: JKAP Publications, 1984. (The best single documented book for the facts on this issue.)

Price, Randall. *Jerusalem in Prophecy: God's Stage for the Final Drama*. Eugene, OR: Harvest House Publishers, 1998. (Traces the significance of Jerusalem historically, politically, and prophetically in the context of the modern Middle East conflict.)

_____. *The Coming Last Days Temple*. Eugene, OR: Harvest House Publishers, 2000. (Documents the biblical and historical hope of the Jews to rebuild the Temple on the Temple Mount in Jerusalem and the conflict over this issue with Islam.)

Rabinovich, Abraham. *Jerusalem on Earth: People, Passions, and Politics in the Holy City*. New York: The Free Press, 1988. (A Jewish writer's perspective on life and its struggles in the holy city.)

Ravitzky, Aviezer. *Messianism, Zionism, and Jewish Religions Radicalism*. Trans. by Michael Swirsky and Jonathan Chipman. Chicago: University of Chicago, 1996. (A well-documented study of Jewish nationalist organizations and the threat they pose to the stability of Israel and the Middle East.)

Shorrosh, Anis A. *Islam Revealed: A Christian Arab's View of Islam*. Nashville: Thomas Nelson, 1988. (A Christian-Palestinian Arab raised in Nazareth explains Islam and its dangers to civilization in popular language.)

Tal, Eliyahu. *Whose Jerusalem?* Tel Aviv: International Forum for a United Jerusalem, 1994. (The best single study on the question of dividing the city. Profusely illustrated with numerous helpful sidebars, charts, and appendices.)

Wagner, Clarence, Jr. *365 Fascinating Facts about the Holy Land*. Arkansas: New Leaf Press, 1999. (A popular summary of facts about all aspects of Israel, including historical and political details on the Middle East conflict.)

Wasserstein, Bernard. *Divided Jerusalem: The Struggle for the Holy City*. London: Profile Books, 2001. (The most up to date and detailed documentary account of the historical attempts to divide Jerusalem and its consequences.)

Ye'or, Bat. *The Dhimmi: Jews and Christians Under Islam*. Trans. by David Maisel, Paul Fenton, and David Littman. London and Toronto: Associated University Presses, 1985. (The definitive documented study of the historical treatment of Jews and Christians under Muslim rule.)

Notes

The Day the World Changed

1. From a transcript of a translation of the videotaped remarks of Osama bin Laden broadcast on Al-Jazeera television, October 7, 2001.

2. Al-Muhajiroun: The Voice, the Eyes, and the Ears of the Muslims website (wwww.almuhajiroun.com), September 16, 2001.

3. Louis Rene Beres, "The Meaning of Coming Violence Against Israel," Internet publication (June 10, 1999), pp. 1-2.

4. See the *International Jerusalem Post* (June 8, 2001), p. 16.

5. As cited in Walter B. Knight, *Knight's Treasury of Illustrations* (Grand Rapids: Wm. B. Eerdmans Publishing Co., 1963), p. 349.

Chapter 1—Why Are We at War?

1. Statement of Osama bin Laden, Hindukush Mountains, Khurasan, Afghanistan, Friday September 4, 1996.

2. All of these expressions were used by President Bush in his speech to the Department of Labor on October 4, 2001.

3. As cited in the AFP article "Israel slams Syria joining U.N. Security Council as 'bad joke' (October 9, 2001).

4. The president made this remark on September 16, 2001, but later explained this reference carried no historical implications.

5. Interview with Sheikh Khalil Al Alami with *Palestine Report Online*, October 3, 2001.

6. As cited in "Bin Laden denies terror attacks and points finger at Jews" (September 28, 2001), at http://www.ananova.com/news/story/sm 410936.html?menu=news.latestheadlines.

7. From the text of the Al-Qaeda statement, delivered by Osama bin Laden aide Suleiman Abu Ghaith and broadcast by Qatar-based Al-Jazeera television, October 14, 2001.

8. Saad G. Hattar, "Defendant accuses Sharon of attacks on the U.S.," *Jordan Times* (October 3, 2001).

9. As cited in the *Jordan Times* (October 1, 2001).

10. Interview with Hosni Mubarak on ANN-TV (September 24, 2001).

11. Interview with Sheikh Yussuf Al-Qaradhawi on Al-Jazeera Television (Qatar), September 16, 2001.

12. As reported in iNews-only@yahoogroups.com (September 17, 2001).

13. As cited by Naomi Ragen, "Praying Towards Mecca," iNews-only@yahoogroups.com (September 17, 2001).

14. From the text of the Al-Qaeda statement, delivered by Osama bin Laden aide Suleiman Abu Ghaith and broadcast by Qatar-based Al-Jazeera television, October 14, 2001.

15. Results of a CNN/USA Today/Gallup poll of 1,032 Americans taken on September 14-15, 2001 as reported by Sharon Samber, "Israel rates high marks in polls in wake of terror attacks on U.S.," *Jewish Telegraph Agency, Inc.* (September 25, 2001), p. 1.

16. Yoram Ettinger, "Islamic Terrorism Targeting the United States," *Ynet* (www.ynet.co.il-Hebrew), September 30, 2001.

17. Itamar Marcus and Ruthie Blum, "Western civilization will become a pile of rubble," *Palestinian Media Watch Special Bulletin* (September 17, 2001).

18. Larry Derfner, "Terror on the Beach, a suicide bomber strikes amid Tel Aviv's night life," *U.S. News & World Report* (June 11, 2001), p. 38.

19. As cited in "Hizbollah: Arabs, Muslims target of U.S. war," *Jordan Times* (October 3, 2001).

20. Ibid.

Chapter 2—What's Israel Got to Do with It?

1. As cited in the "Periscope" section, *Newsweek* magazine (July 30, 2001), p. 6.

2. As reported in an interview with John Miller on ABC News (September 27, 2001).

3. Ariel Sharon, press briefing statement from a communiqué by the prime minister's media adviser, October 7, 2001.

4. Rabbi Chaim Richman, "Garments of Salvation," www.templeinstitute.org (September 17, 2001).

5. Richar A. Serrano, "Officials deny report of Israel warning," *Los Angeles Times* (September 21, 2001).

6. See Douglas Davis, "Mossad warned CIA of attacks—report," *Jerusalem Post Internet Edition* (September 19, 2001).

7. Translation of videotaped speech by Osama bin Laden broadcast on Al-Jazeera television (Qatar), October 7, 2001.

8. From the text of the *fatwah* published in *Al-Quds al-Arabi* (February 23, 1998).

9. Cited on A&E channel program "Biography" (September 22, 2001).

10. As cited by Lee Hockstader and Daniel Williams, "Israel Says It Won't 'Pay Price' of Coalition," *Washington Post Foreign Service* (September 18, 2001), p. A14.

11. As cited by Ewen MacAskill, "Palestine state essential for peace, says Blair," *The Guardian* (October 16, 2001).

12. Interview with Shimon Peres on CNBC (October 10, 2001).

13. Remarks of Prime Minister Ariel Sharon at a press conference at Beit Sokolov in Tel Aviv (October 4, 2001).

14. As cited by Alan Philips, "Bush fails to pacify Palestinians," *London Telegraph* (October 13, 2001).

15. From the report of the statements of King Fahd at the eightieth session of the Gulf Cooperation Council in Jeddah, Saudi Press Agency (September 21, 2001).

16. As cited by Muawia E. Ibrahim, "Muslim world call for U.N. meeting on terrorism," *Khaleej Times Online* (October 11, 2001), pp. 1-2.

17. Prime Minister Ariel Sharon, speech to the opening of the fifteenth Knesset winter session, October 15, 2001, communicated by the prime minister's media adviser in Jerusalem.

18. President George W. Bush, speech before the U.S. Congress, September 20, 2001.

19. Tarwq Y. Ismael, *The Arab Left* (New York: Syracuse University Press, 1976), pp. 12-13.

20. As cited by Nina Gilbert, "Knesset backs U.S. decision to wage war on terror," *Jerusalem Post Internet Edition* (September 17, 2001).

21. Eugene Narret, "If the Jews Left Israel," iNews-only@yahoogroups.com (September 12, 2001).

22. As cited by Mubeer Rizeq, "Coming days will be harder—Military Intelligence Chief on the future of the Intifada," *The Jerusalem Times* (September 14, 2001).

23. Marc Berley, "Why Can't Israel Be 'With Us'?" www.jewishworldreview.com (September 25, 2001).

24. As cited in an article in *Gamla* (September 17, 2001) and reported in *Bridges for Peace Update* (September 21, 2001), pp. 1-2.

25. As cited in a press release from the American Muslims for Jerusalem and distributed by Aaron Lerner, director of Independent Media Research and Analysis (October 16, 2001).

26. As cited by Gil Hoffman, "Palestinian state issue pits Sharon against Likud," *Jerusalem Post* (October 15, 2001).

27. As cited by Karin Laub, "U.S. creating new plan for a Palestinian state," *Sun Times* (October 14, 2001).

28. The report of the meeting and the citations included are from *The Jordan Times* (October 1, 2001).

29. *The Jordan Times* (October 1, 2001).

30. Islamic Resistance Movement (Hamas) communiqué issued on the first anniversary of the Al-Aqsa Intifada (September 28, 2001).

31. See the final program of action of the World Conference on Racism, Racial Discrimination, Xenophobia and Related Intolerance posted at ww.unhchr.ch/html/racism.

32. As cited in the film *Israel, Islam and Armageddon* (Bend, OR: The Berean Call, 2001).

33. Ibid.

34. Paul Eidelberg, "PLO Terrorism and Grand Strategy," www.freeman.org/m_online/apr01/eidelberg.htm (April 2001).

35. As cited by Andrea Levin, "Is American support for Israel to blame?" *International Jerusalem Post* (October 5, 2001), p. 12.

36. Ibid.

37. As cited in "Arabs pledge to eradicate terrorism, demand independence for Palestinians," *Jordan Times* (October 3, 2001).

38. Words of a Palestinian cleric at the Gaza mosque broadcast on Palestinian-controlled television and reported by Robert Tracinski, "We are all Israelis now," on iNews-only@yahoogroups.com (September 21, 2001).

39. Palestinian Authority Mufti Ikrama Sabri in his weekly Friday prayer sermon at the Al-Aqsa Mosque, Jerusalem, July 11, 1997 as published by Independent Media Research and Analysis (September 20, 2001).

Chapter 3—What Are Jews and Arabs Fighting About?

1. As cited in "Fear of Sharon," *The Economist* (February 10, 2001), p. 49.

2. John L. Lyons, "Jerusalem: Besieged by the Sacred," *The World & I* (March 1997), p. 60.

3. As cited by Matt Rees in "The Bloody Mountain," *Time* (October 16, 2000), p. 70.

4. For the full report by Lamia Lahoud see *Jerusalem Post* (March 4, 2001).

5. See Leslie Susser, "Which Way Forward Now?" *The Jerusalem Report* (November 6, 2000), p. 18.

Chapter 4—Why Should Their Fight Matter to Me?

1. Cardinal Carlo Maria Martini of Milan (1892) as cited by Eliyahu Tal, *Whose Jerusalem?* (Tel Aviv: The International Forum for a United Jerusalem, 1994), p. 290.

2. James G. McDonald, *My Mission in Israel (1948-1951)* (New York: Simon & Schuster, 1951), p. xiii.

3. Joan Comay, *Ben-Gurion and the Birth of Israel* (New York: Random House, 1967), p. 158.

4. David Ben-Gurion, *Rebirth and Destiny of Israel* (New York: Philosophical Library, 1954), pp. 360, 397, 399, 437.

5. Edward Gibbon, *The History of the Decline and Fall of the Roman Empire*, ed. J.B. Bury (London: Meuthen & Co., 1909), vol. 5, ch. 58.

6. For a discussion of these factors and the theological views of the church, see Peter Walker, "Jerusalem in the Early Christian Centuries," *Jerusalem Past and Present in the Purposes of God*, ed. P.W.L. Walker (Grand Rapids: Baker Book House, 1994), pp. 79-97.

7. The edict placed "circumcised persons" under penalty of death for staying within the area of Aelia Capitolina (Hadrianic Jerusalem); however, it is unclear how much this edict was enforced by the Roman authorities. For the edict itself see Michael Avi-Yonah, *The Jews of Palestine* (Oxford: University Press, 1976), and for a discussion on it, see Peter Walker, *Holy City, Holy Places? Christian Attitudes to Jerusalem and the Holy Land in the Fourth Century* (Oxford: University Press), p. 8, n. 12.

8. An exception to this was the proposal of Cyril, bishop of Jerusalem (A.D. 320-386), which stated that since Jerusalem was now a Christian Jerusalem, it was not the same city as that Jewish one judged by God. Furthermore, since the Christian Jerusalem worshiped Christ, it was now a "holy city," and deserved to be at the center of the new Christian world that was being formed. Even though Cyril's positive view of Jerusalem is distinct from the negative view of Eusebius, it nevertheless is based on the same theological premises, which are against a future reestablishment of a Jewish Jerusalem.

9. An example of this thinking in Luther is his famous statement: "A Jew or a Jewish heart is so wood, stone, iron, devil-hardened, that it can in no way be moved."

10. For a good discussion of why and how this took place, see Pinchas LaPaide, *Hebrew in the Church* (Grand Rapids: Eerdmans Publishing Co., 1987).

11. As cited in Peter Toon, ed., *Puritans, the Millennium, and the Future of Israel: Puritan Eschatology 1600 to 1660* (Cambridge: James Clarke, 1970).

12. Salo W. Baron, *A Social and Religious History of the Jews* (New York: 1952), 2:329.

13. David L. Larsen, *Jews, Gentiles & the Church: A New Perspective on History and Prophecy* (Nashville: Discovery House Publishers, 1995), p. 130. The original citation is in M.M. Noah, *Discourse on the Restoration of the Jews*, pp. 1-55.

14. For the details of Truman's leadership in support of Jewish nationalism, see Abba Eban, *My People* (New York: Random House, 1968), pp. 453-58.

15. James G. McDonald, *My Mission in Israel (1948-1951)* (New York: Simon & Schuster, 1951), p. 273.

16. Edwin A. Locke, "The Palestinian Choice" as cited by Shoshanna Walker (rosewalk@concentric.net), June 22, 2001.

17. Rabbi Chaim Richman, Temple Institute newsletter (January 16, 2000).

18. Peretz Smolenskin, *Nekam Brit* (1842-85), as cited by Eliyahu Tal, *Whose Jerusalem?* (Tel Aviv: International Forum for a United Jerusalem, 1994), p. 299.

Chapter 5—Why Is Jerusalem So Important?

1. Gerald M. Steinberg, "This Year and Next—in Jerusalem," opinion section of the *Jerusalem Post* website http://www.jpost.com (April 6, 2001).

2. As cited by Etgar Lefkovits, "Three Hundred Thousand Rally for Jerusalem," *Jerusalem Post Online News* (January 9, 2001).

3. Ibid.

4. Chaim Hazaz, *The Right of Redemption* (1977), as cited by Eliyahu Tal, *Whose Jerusalem?* (Tel Aviv: International Forum for a United Jerusalem, 1994), pp. 297-98.

5. Menachem Mendel Ussiskin, *Last Words* (1947), as cited by Eliyahu Tal, *Whose Jerusalem?* (Tel Aviv: International Forum for a United Jerusalem, 1994), p. 288.

6. Ariel Sharon, "Towards a National Agenda of Peace and Security," address to AIPAC Policy Conference (Washington, D.C., March 19, 2001), p. 1.

7. Nadia Matar, Women for Israel's Tomorrow (Women in Green), cited on Monday, August 14, 2000 at the organization's website: http://www.womeningreen.org.

8. David Bar-Illan, "Errors in Arabizing Jerusalem," *International Jerusalem Post*, November 27, 1993, p. 13.

9. Abdul Hadi Palazzi, "No Authentic Theological Reason Why Moslems Should Not Recognize Jerusalem as the Capital of the Jewish State of Israel," Root & Branch Association, Ltd. (July 10, 1998).

10. See Nasir I, *Khursau's Travelogue* (A.D. 1047), as cited in Eliyahu Tal, *Whose Jerusalem?* (Tel Aviv: International Forum for a United Jerusalem, 1994), p. 285.

11. Shelomo Dov Goitein, "The Historical Background of the Erection of the Dome of the Rock," *Journal of the American Oriental Society* 70:2 (April-June, 1950), p. 107.

12. According to the Arab historian Ibn Asakir, quoting a twelfth-century Hadith, as cited in Tal, *Whose Jerusalem?* p. 284.

13. Correspondence between Wickley in the Jerusalem office to Rose in the Foreign Office, April 7, 1955, Public Record Office, Foreign Office 371/121850.

14. As cited in Bernard Wassertein, *Divided Jerusalem: The Struggle for the Holy City* (London: Profile Books Ltd., 2001), p. 189.

15. Nadav Shragai as cited in *Ha'aretz*, Israel Line, *Arutz 7*, and *Tsemach News* (March 28, 1999).

16. Abdullah Yusuf Ali on Sura 2. 126, *The Holy Qur'an* (Beirut: Dar al Arabia Publishers), p. 53, n. 127.

17. Shmuel Katz, author of the biography of Ze'ev Jabotinsky, *International Jerusalem Post*, August 1996.

18. "Holy Sites Are First Targets," an interview with Yasser Arafat by Christiane Amanpour of CNN, Thursday, September 7, 2000.

19. As cited by Yasser Arafat in Amman, Jordan and reported by *Washington Post* service (September 27, 1993).

20. As cited in the article "Sheik: 'Jerusalem is ours and not yours,' " in *Watch: Jerusalem*, 2:7 (April 14, 1998), p. 1. Original source: MEMRI's Media Review of April 6, 1998.

21. As cited in Lisa Beyer and Dean Fischer, "Men of the Year: Yitzhak Rabin & Yasser Arafat," *Time* (January 3, 1994), p. 49.

22. Mayor Ehud Olmert, interview by Randall Price at Mayor's office, Jerusalem (November 1998).

Chapter 6—How Did the Conflict Begin?

1. See Sidney Zion, "The Palestinian Problem: It's All in a Name," *New York* magazine (March 13, 1978), pp. 42-45.

2. Quoted in the article "Is Jordan Palestine or Not?" *Dispatch from Jerusalem* (Fall 1993).

3. Yasser Arafat speaking to Orina Fallacei and quoted in *The New Republic; International Jerusalem Post* (Friday, September 11, 1992).

4. However, Arabs in Palestine, most of whom came from Egypt, Syria, and Jordan, shunned the name "Palestinian Arabs." So the British were careful to refer to the Jews only as "Palestinian Jews," while referring to the Arabs as simply "Arabs."

5. See Feisal al-Husseini, The Land, Its People and History, a PLO version of Arab history as reported in the article "The Gospel According to Husseini," *International Jerusalem Post* (December 12, 1992).

6. For a presentation of these facts and documentation see Ramon Bennet, *When Day and Night Cease* (Jerusalem: Arm of Salvation, 1993), pp. 193-202, and quotations throughout George Grant's *The Blood of the Moon* (Nashville: Wolgemuth & Hyatt, 1991).

7. Mordecai Gur, *The Temple Mount Is in Our Hands* (Tel Aviv: Defense Ministry Publishing House, 1968) as cited in Abraham E. Millgram, *Jerusalem Curiosities* (Philadelphia: The Jewish Publication Society, 1990), p. 291.

8. As cited by Martin Gilbert, *Jerusalem in the Twentieth Century* (New York: John Wiley & Sons, Inc., 1996), p. 287.

9. Lawrence Wright, "Forcing the End," *The New Yorker* (July 20, 1998), p. 46.

10. Anwar el-Sadat, April 25, 1972, as cited in *Zionism: A Basic Reader,* ed. Mordecai S. Chertoff (New York: Herzl Press, 1975), p. 14.

11. Herb Keinon, "Barak: We'll never have a peace agreement with Arafat," *Jerusalem Post* (July 16, 2001), p. 2.

12. Ibid.

13. Ibid.

Chapter 7—Who Are the Palestinians?

1. The actual count was 2,895,683. The census was taken in early December 1998 (as reported by Reuters, December 14, 1998).

2. David Jacobson, "When Palestine Meant Israel," *Biblical Archaeology Review* 27:3 (May/June 2001), pp. 43-47.

3. Josephus, *Antiquities* 20.259.

4. "Palestine" in *Calmert's Dictionary of the Holy Bible,* ed. Edward Robinson (Boston: Crocker and Brewster, 1843), p. 91.

5. Ovid, *Art of Love* 1.416 in Menachem Stern, *Greek and Latin Authors on Jews and Judaism* (Jerusalem: Israel Academy of Sciences and Humanities, 1974), 1:348-349.

6. Statius, who never uses the term *Judea,* refers to the "juices of Palestine" and to "Palestinian and Hebrew essences." See Silvae 2.1.161; 3.2.105; 5.1.213 in Stern, *Greek and Latin Authors on Jews and Judaism*, 1:515-520. Dio Chrysostom, as quoted by Synesius, refers to the Dead Sea as being "in the interior of Palestine." See H. Lamar Crosby, *Dio Chrysostom* (Cambridge: Loeb Classical Library, 1951), 5:378-379.

7. "Palestine" by Immanuel Benzinger in *The Jewish Encyclopedia* (London: Funk and Wagnalls Co., 1905), 9:479.

8. As cited by Eliyahu Tal, *Whose Jerusalem?* (Tel Aviv: International Forum for a United Jerusalem, 1994), pp. 100-01.

9. David George Hogarth, "Arabs and Turks," *The Arab Bulletin* 48 (April 21, 1917).

10. As recorded in the Minutes of the Supreme Council and cited by D.H. Miller, *My Diary at the Conference of Paris* (New York: 1924), 14:405.

11. As cited by Eliyahu Tal, *Whose Jerusalem?* (Tel Aviv: International Forum for a United Jerusalem, 1994), p. 93.

12. As cited by Clarence Wagner, "40 Significant Facts About Israel's History," *Bridges for Peace Teaching Letter* (October 2000), 3:3.

13. For this list see DeHass, *History,* p. 258, and John of Wuzburg in Reinhold Rohricht edition, pp. 41, 69.

14. Ernst Frankenstine, *Justice for My People* (London: Nicholson & Watson, 1943), p. 127.

15. Daniel Pipes, "The Origins of the Palestinian Arabs," at www.us-israel.org/jsource/History/palarabs.html.

16. As cited by Abba Eban, *Heritage* (1984), p. 330.

17. As cited in the *Jerusalem Post* (November 2, 1991) and by Clarence Wagner, "40 Significant Facts About Israel's History" (Jerusalem: October 2000), 3:3.

18. Quoted in the newspaper *Al-Nahar Al-Arabi* (December 26, 1981) and 1984, as cited by Benjamin Netanyahu, *A Place Among the Nations,* p. 147.

19. Quoted in *New Republic* (1974) as cited by Ramon Bennett, *When Day and Night Cease,* p. 211.

20. Roger David Carasso, "Palestinians (Western Palestinian Arabs)," 1994 at www.carasso.com/roger/Israel/palestine.html.

Chapter 8—What Is the Palestinian Claim to the Land?

1. Tad Szulc, "Who are the Palestinians?" *National Geographic* (June 1992).

2. As cited in "The Arab Case of Palestine: Evidence Submitted by the Arab Office, Jerusalem, to the Anglo-American Committee of Inquiry, March 1946," in *The Israel-Arab Reader*, ed. Walter Laqueur (New York: Bantam Books, 1969), p. 92.

3. This publication was part of an appointment calendar and was cited in "The Gospel According to Husseini," *International Jerusalem Post* (December 12, 1992). Note: For the sake of readability, in my citation I have corrected numerous spelling errors that appeared in the original.

4. Quoted in *Ha Ubal Or* (Jerusalem edition, January 3, 1991), as cited in George Grant, *The Blood of the Moon* (Nashville: Wolgemuth & Hyatt, 1991), p. 47.

5. As cited by Moshe Kohn in his column "View from Nov," in *International Jerusalem Post* (February 19, 1999), p. 30.

6. See E.A. Knauf, *Ismael.* 2nd ed. *Abhandlungen des Deutschen Palästina-Vereins* (Wiesbaden, 1989), pp. 5-9, 45.

7. For a summary of the historical evidence see *The Anchor Bible Dictionary*, s.v. "Ishmaelites," by Ernst Axel Knauf (New York: Doubleday, 1992), 3:513-520, and *Encyclopedia Judaica*, s.v. "Ishmaelites," by L. Nemoy (Jerusalem: Keter Publishing House, 1992), 9:87-90.

8. Rabbi Bachya, citing Rabbi Chananel's comment on Genesis 17:20.

9. Rabbi Meir Zlotowitz, *Bereishis (Genesis),* Artscroll Tanach Series (New York: Mesorah Publications, Ltd., 1995), 1:582.

10. For this argument see Speiser, *Interpreter's Dictionary of the Bible,* 3:235-42.

11. Trude Dothan, "The 'Sea Peoples' and the Philistines of Ancient Palestine," *Civilizations of the Ancient Near East,* ed. Jack M. Sasson (Peabody, MA: Hendrickson Publishers, 2000), 1:1271.

12. Shem was the father of the Semitic peoples, while "the children of Japheth" are identified with the nations of the Mediterranean islands (Gen. 10:2,4-5). See "Canaan, Curse of," in *Encyclopedia Judaica* (Jerusalem: Keter Publishing House, Ltd., 1972), 5:98.

13. See Jonathan N. Tubb, *Canaanites*, Peoples of the Past series (Norman: University of Oklahoma Press, 1998), pp. 145-46. Tubb sees a Neo-Punic artistic tradition continuing until A.D. 200, but agrees that the Canaanite influence ended at Carthage.

14. Philip K. Hitti, *The Arabs, A Short History* (Princeton: University Press, 1943), p. 83.

15. Prominent networks and news publications where an Arab-revisionist position has been assumed in reporting include CNN, ABC, NBC, CBS, and NSBC, *Time*, *Newsweek*, *U.S. News & World Report*, *National Geographic*, and *The Webster New World Encyclopedia* (1992), as well as anti-Semitic publications such as *Spotlight*.

16. As cited in Benjamin Netanyahu, *A Place Among the Nations*, p. 37.

17. See "The Origins of Modern Palestine" in Dan Cohn-Sherbok and Dawoud El-Alami, *The Palestine-Israeli Conflict* (Oxford: Oneworld Publications, 2001), pp. 91-95.

18. As cited by Gil Hoffman, "Netanyahu: Palestinians are 'foreign workers,'" *Jerusalem Post* (July 15, 2001), p. 3.

19. Carl Hermann Voss, *The Palestine Problem Today, Israel and Its Neighbors* (Boston: 1953), p. 13, as cited in Ramon Bennett, *Philistine*, p. 147.

20. Pierre Loti, *La Galilee* (Paris: 1895), cited in Joan Peters, *From Time Immemorial* (London: Michael Joseph, 1984), p. 161.

21. Joan Peters, *From Time Immemorial: The Origins of the Arab-Jewish Conflict over Palestine* (London: Michael Joseph, 1984), p. 152.

22. As cited by Moshe Aumann, "Arab Immigration into Palestine," *Zionism: A Basic Reader* (New York: Herzl Press, 1975), p. 29.

Chapter 9—What Is the Palestinian Right to Return?

1. As cited in Khaled Amayreh, "No Waiving the Right of Return," *Al-Ahram*, no. 518 (January 25-31, 2001).

2. "Who Were the 1948 Refugees?" Ariel Center for Policy Research (February 4, 2001), as cited in *A Time to Speak* (speak@actcom.co.il) 1:9 (September 16, 2001).

3. Aref el-Aref, *Al-Mufassal fi Tarikh al-Quds* (Jerusalem: 1961).

4. The material answering this question has been adapted and edited from legal material presented by Ruth Lapidoth, Professor of International Law at the Hebrew University of Jerusalem.

5. As cited in Herb Keinon, "Barak: 'We'll Never Have a Peace Agreement with Arafat,'" *Jerusalem Post* (July 16, 2001), p. 2.

6. As reported by Yated Neeman, July 13, 2001 and cited in endtimes-news-events@egroups.com.

7. As cited in "Peace Watch," *Dispatch from Jerusalem* (July/August, 2001), p. 8.

8. Yasser Arafat, as reported to the Norwegian Daily *Dagen*, February 6, 1996 and cited by Arutz 7 (February 7, 1996).

9. As cited in *Al-Misri*, October 11, 1949.

10. As cited in Murray Dixon, *Whose Promised Land: Conflict in Palestine-Israel*. Heinemann History Project (Octopus Publishing Group, 1996), p. 88.

11. As cited in *The Jerusalem Report* (June 27, 1991).

12. Cited by Joseph Farah, World Net Daily (April 2001).

Chapter 10—What Is Islam's Role in the Conflict?

1. Jacques Ellul in the preface to Bat Ye'or, *The Dhimmi: Jews and Christians Under Islam*, trans. David Maisel, Paul Fenton, and David Littman (London and Toronto: Associated University Presses, 1985), p. 31.

2. Ikrama Sabri, *Al-Bilad*, July 31, 1997.

3. The Supreme Islamic Research Council, February, 1970 as cited in Yvonne Haddad, "The Arab-Israeli Wars, Nasserism, and the Affirmation of Islamic Identity," ed. Andrew C. Kimmens, in *Islamic Politics and the Modern World* (New York: The H.W. Wilson Co., 1991), p. 61.

4. Based on a world religion survey conducted by and reported in *Christianity Today* (January 8, 1985), p. 61.

5. Karen Armstrong, "Islam's Stake: Why Jerusalem Was Central to Muhammad," www.time.com/time/2001/jerusalem/islam.html.

6. George W. Braswell, Jr., *Islam: Its Prophet, Peoples, Politics and Power* (Nashville: Broadman & Holman Publishers, 1996), p. 44.

7. For a discussion of the historical events between Muhammad and the Meccans, see W. Montgomery Watt, *What Is Islam?* Arab Background Series (New York: Frederick A. Praeger, 1968), pp. 97-101.

8. For the tradition concerning David, see Fannie Fern Andrews, *The Holy Land Under Mandate* (Boston and New York: 1931), 1:165; for Jesus, see Ermete Pierotti, *Customs and Traditions of Palestine* (Cambridge: 1864), pp. 70-72.

9. Jonathan Riley-Smith, ed., *The Oxford Illustrated History of the Crusades* (Oxford: University Press, 1995), p. 227.

10. As cited in Samuel M. Zwemer, *Islam: A Challenge to Faith* (New York: Laymen's Missionary Movement, 1907), pp. 94-95.

11. Video clips of this kind of indoctrination of children in *jihad* can be seen on the program.

12. As cited by Mustafa, former lecturer of Islamic history at Al-Azhar University, Cairo in *The Falling of Islam*, p. 64.

13. Personal correspondence with missionary to Muslims (September 25, 2001), identity withheld by request.

14. Andrew Greeley, "Religion Is Key in Any Mideast Deal," *Chicago Sun Times* commentary (June 10, 2001).

15. Al-Muhajiroun, "Jihad the Only Solution for Palestine" (September 22, 2000).

16. As cited in an advertisement by Al-Muhajiroun, the radical Muslim organization claiming to be the "ears, eyes, and voice of Islam" (September 20, 2001) at their website www.almuhajiroun.com.

17. Dr. Kamel el Baker as cited in D.F. Green, ed., *Arab Theologians on Jews and Israel: Extracts from the Proceedings of the Fourth Conference of the Academy of Islamic Research*, 3rd ed. (Geneva: Editions de l'Avenir, 1976), p. 59.

18. As cited by Hannah Bloch and Sayed Talat Hussein, "On the Edge: A Nation with Nukes," *Time* (October 1, 2001), p. 43.

19. As cited in the onine article "Call to Kill All Jews," endtimes-news-events@egroups.com (October 5, 2000).

20. A.B. Davidson, *Biblical and Literary Essays,* ed. J.A. Peterson (London: Hodder and Stoughton, 1902), p. 228.

21. Sermon at Al-Aqsa Mosque, Friday, June 22, 2001.

22. Sheikh Muhammad Abu Zahra, as cited in D.F. Green, ed., *Arab Theologians on Jews and Israel: Extracts from the Proceedings of the Fourth Conference of the Academy of Islamic Research,* 3rd ed. (Geneva: Editions de l'Avenir, 1976), p. 62.

23. A similar statement was made by Yasser Arafat on *Voice of Palestine* radio, Algiers, October 24, 1993.

24. This excerpt was taken from the contents of the recorded speech first reported by the offshore radio station Arutz Sheva, February 7, 1996, and published in the *Jerusalem Post,* February 23, 1996.

25. As cited by Cal Thomas, "Preaching hate OK for one side," syndicated column for Monday, July 28, 1997.

26. As quoted in an interview with Faisal Al-Husseini in the Jordanian newspaper *Al-Aswak.*

27. As cited in Yotam Felder, "The Debate over the Religions Legitimacy of Suicide Bombings," *Independant Media Review and Analysis* (May 2, 2001).

Chapter 11—What Makes a Muslim Militant?

1. Address before the convention of the Islamic Society of North America, Columbus, Ohio, September 11, 1995.

2. Translation of videotaped speech by Osama bin Laden broadcast on Al-Jazeera television (Qatar), October 7, 2001.

3. Ray Takeyh, "Why They Hate Us," *National Review Online* (October 9, 2001), p. 1.

4. As cited by M. Rafiqul-Haqq and P. Newton, "Tolerance in Islam," online copy (1996), pp. 1-2.

5. Daniel Pipes, "Islamists are not who they say they are," *Jerusalem Post* (May 9, 2001).

6. Personal correspondence received September 24, 2001. The author was asked to protect the source's identity.

7. Rabbi Yossi Markel, iNews-only@yahoogroups.com (September 17, 2001).

8. Jeffery L. Sheler, "Of faith, fear, and fanatics," *U.S. News & World Report* (September 24, 2001), p. 56.

9. Thomas Friedman, "Understanding the Next Conflict," *New York Times* (September 15, 2001).

10. The show was taped live on October 4, 2001, but was aired on October 5 in my area. The comments are from my own notes from the program.

11. Jeffery L. Sheler, "Of faith, fear, and fanatics," *U.S. News & World Report* (September 24, 2001), p. 56.

12. As cited in the transcript of the videotape presented by Rita Cosby, Fox News senior correspondent on "Special Report" with Brit Hume, Fox News (September 28, 2001).

13. Ibid.

14. As cited by Paul Eidelberg, "PLO Terrorism and Grand Strategy" at www.freeman.org/ m_online/apr001/eidelberg.htm (October 11, 2001).

15. Comment of Paul Eidelberg posted at iNews-only (Islam) at iNews-only-owner@ yahoogroups.com (September 17, 2001).

16. Paul Johnson, "Relentlessly and Thoroughly," *National Review* (October 15, 2001).

17. Compiled from a more detailed list by Abdullah Al Araby, "Islam: The Façade and the Facts," www.IslamReview.com (September 14, 2001), pp. 1-2.

18. See Judith Miller, Benjamin Weiser, and Ralph Blumenthal, "Mass-destruction weapons feared in one-two punch," *New York Times* (September 16, 2001).

19. John Leo, "The Terrorist Next Door," *U.S. News & World Report* (October 1, 2001), p. 43.

20. Translated from Osama bin Laden's speech broadcast on Al-Jazeera television (Qatar), October 7, 2001.

21. As cited by Fred Siegel, "Radical Islam at War with America," Fox News Channel Views (September 18, 2001).

Chapter 12—Why Can't They Share Jerusalem?

1. Wes Gallagher, *Lightning Out of Israel: The Six-Day War in the Middle East* (The Associated Press, 1967), p. 5.

2. Interview with Ehud Olmert, Mayor's office, Jerusalem, November 1996.

3. As reported by Arutz 7 news, July 26, 2000.

4. As cited by Matthew Seriphs, "Present Tense, Past Imperfect," *Israel Scene* magazine, *International Jerusalem Post* (May 23, 1992), p. 14.

5. From the Friday, May 15, 1998 broadcast as cited in *Dispatch from Jerusalem* (July-August 1998), p. 19.

6. Remarks of Prime Minister Benjamin Netanyahu at the National Unity Coalition for Israel, Washington, D.C., December 7, 1996.

7. Benjamin Netanyahu in a question/answer session following a scheduled speech on Israeli economic cooperation and prospects for foreign investment to the Foreign Correspondent's Club of Japan, Tokyo, Tuesday, August 26, 1997.

8. James Parks, *Whose Land?* (1949) as cited in Eliyahu Tal, *Whose Jerusalem?* (Tel Aviv: Forum for a United Jerusalem, 1984), p. 153.

9. As cited in "Let Them Speak for Themselves!" *Dispatch from Jerusalem* 18:4 (November/December 1993), p. 8.

10. As cited by John Wheeler, Jr., in the *Christian American* 5:2 (February 1994), p. 4.

11. Voice of Palestine broadcast, September 26, 1997.

12. Yasser Arafat to Arab ambassadors in Stockholm, January 30, 1996. This excerpt was taken from the contents of a recorded speech first reported by the offshore radio station Arutz Sheva, February 7, 1996, and published in the *Jerusalem Post* (February 23, 1996).

13. Faisal Al-Husseini, December 26, 1997. Quoted from an interview with Faisal Al-Husseini that was published in *Al-Quds,* the official newspaper of the Palestinian Press.

14. As cited in the sidebar in Nancy Gibbs article (reported by Lisa Beyer and Dean Fischer), "Yitzhak Rabin and Yasser Arafat," *Time* (January 3, 1994), pp. 44, 49.

15. As cited in the *San Antonio Express-News* (September 27, 1993), p. 3A.

16. *Eternal Jerusalem: A Reader and Teaching Manual,* ed. Ariel Eisenberg (New York: Jewish Education Press, 1971), p. 125.

17. Ehud Olmert as cited in "Jerusalem's Mayor Blasts Peace Initiative," interview with Chris Mitchell, CBN News (September 14, 2000).

18. As cited in API story "Temple Mount Control Hot Issue," by Dan Perry, *San Antonio Express-News* (December 26, 2000), p. 6A.

19. Ibid.

20. See *The Omega Code,* which depicts the destruction of the Dome of the Rock and its rebuilding along with the Temple and the palace of the Antichrist on the Temple Mount.

21. Interview with Jeries Soudah by Irwin Baxter in "Arafat and Jerusalem," *Endtime* magazine (September/October 1997), pp. 11-12.

Chapter 13—What Is the Trouble with the Temple Mount?

1. Yasser Arafat, speech to the Organization of Islamic Conference Summit in Teheran, Iran, December 9, 1997.

2. As cited in an article in *Ha'aretz,* March 12, 1997.

3. Statement issued by Hamas as cited by Saud Abu Ramadan, "No Israeli Jews in Holy Site," United Press International (April 7, 2000).

4. As cited in D.F. Green, ed., *Arab Theologians on Jews and Israel: Extracts from the Proceedings of the Fourth Conference of the Academy of Islamic Research,* 3rd ed. (Geneva: Editions de l'Avenir, 1976), p. 50.

5. Statement issued by Hamas as cited by Saud Abdu Ramadan, "No Israeli Jews in Holy Site," United Press International (April 7, 2000).

6. As cited in *The Jerusalem Report* (December 16, 1993).

7. Interview by Etgar Lefkovits, "Mufti again denies Wall's Jewish link," February 21, 2001.

8. As cited by Jeffrey Goldberg, "Israel's Y2K Problem," *New York Times* magazine (October 3, 1999), p. 52.

9. Interview with Jeris Soudah by Irwin Baxter, "Arafat and Jerusalem from a Palestinian Perspective," *Endtimes* magazine 7:5 (September/October 1997), pp. 9-10.

10. PA Information Ministry press release, December 10, 1997.

11. Interview with Adnan Husseini by Ulf Carmesund, September 1991.

12. As cited in Ulf Carmesund's book *Two Faces of the Expanding Jewish State: A Study on How Religious Motives Can Legitimate Two Jewish Groups Trying to Dominate Mount Moriah in Jerusalem* (Uppsala, Sweden: Uppsala University, 1992), pp. 86-87.

13. Cited in a posting (no longer available) from an Islamic professor in the Department of Religious Studies at Stiring University, Scotland at http://www.stir.ac.uk/Departments/Art/ReligiousStudies/afa/jerusalem/News.htm.

14. Islamic Relations Department of Islamic Resistance Movement (Hamas), July 29, 2001, as reported by endtimes-news-events@egroups.com.

Chapter 14—What Is the Truth About the Temple Mount?

1. Stated in an interview in January 2000 with the German paper *Die Welt* and reported in the *Jerusalem Post* (January 26, 2000).

2. As cited by Etgar Lefkovits, "1930 Moslem Council: Jewish Temple Mount ties 'beyond dispute,'" *Jerusalem Post* (January 26, 2000).

3. As cited by Melissa Radler, "*New York Times* ad: Temple Mount central to Jews," endtimes-news-events (May 21, 2001).

4. Gaalya Cornfield, *The Mystery of the Temple Mount,* p. 10.

5. See Israel Finkelstein and Asher Silberman, *The Bible Unearthed* (New York: The Free Press, 2001).

6. See the Palestinian statements in Netty C. Gross, "Demolishing David," *The Jerusalem Report* (September 11, 2000), pp. 41-42.

7. John Michell, *The Temple at Jerusalem—A New Revelation* (The Academy of Jerusalem: Gospels of the Temple, 1999), p. 5.

8. Interview with Ikrama Sabri, office of the Grand Mufti, Jerusalem (November 1998).

9. Quoted from *Palestine: History, Case and Solution* as cited in the newspaper *Al Qaida,* June 21, 2001.

10. Miriam Ayalon, "Islamic Monuments in Jerusalem," in *Jerusalem: City of the Ages,* p. 82.

11. This explanation was offered by the historian Ya'qubi in A.D. 874, cf. G. Le Strange, *Palestine Under the Moslems,* reprint of the 1890 edition (Beirut: Khayats, 1965), p. 116. While repeated by later Muslim authors and accepted by most Western historians, the account suffers by virtue of the fact that no other contemporary historians are aware of Ya'qubi's story, but instead offer entirely different explanations.

12. Gershon Salomon, "Arabs Destroy Remains of First and Second Temples," *Voice of the Temple Mount* (May 3, 1998).

13. *Al-Muqaddasi: Description of Syria, including Palestine,* translated from the Arabic and annotated by G. Le Strange, Palestine Pilgrims Text Society 3, reprint of 1896 edition (New York: AMS Press, 1971), pp. 22-23, as cited in F.E. Peters, *Jerusalem,* p. 198.

14. For some of these Islamic associations from folklore see Abraham E. Millgram, *Jerusalem Curiosities* (Philadelphia and New York: The Jewish Publication Society, 1990), pp. 185-216.

15. For the quote by Yakut see Eliyahu Tal, *Whose Jerusalem?* (Tel Aviv: International Forum for a United Jerusalem, 1994), p. 69.

16. As discussed by Professor Hava Lazarus [Yafeh] in her book *Some Religious Aspects of Islam* (Leiden: E.J. Brill, 1981).

17. As cited by Etgar Lefkovits, "1930 Moslem Council: Jewish Temple Mount ties 'beyond dispute,'" *The Jerusalem Post* (January 26, 2000).

18. Abdul Hadi Palazzi, "No Authentic Theological Reason Why Moslems Should Not Recognize Jerusalem as the Capital of the Jewish State of Israel," Root & Branch Association, note 1. (July 10, 1998), note 1.

19. Karen Armstrong, "Islam's Stake: Why Jerusalem Was Central to Muhammad," at www.time.com/time/2001/jerusalem/islam.html.

20. As cited in the *Palestinian Encyclopedia* (Beirut: 1978), 2:667.

21. Sari Nusseibeh, "Islam's Jerusalem," Seminar on Jerusalem—Religious Aspects, Milan, Italy, May 9-11, 1995 (Jerusalem: Palestinian Academic Society for the Study of International Affairs, May 2001), p. 4.

22. Interview with Elwood McQuaid at the Lawrence Welk Resort in Escondido, California, September 22, 1998.

Chapter 15—What Is Happening on the Temple Mount?

1. Nadav Shragai, "A cause for lament—situation on Temple Mount," *Ha'aretz* (July 29, 2001).

2. Cited in Nadav Shragai, "Settlement rabbis mull ending the ban on Jews on Temple Mount," endtimes-news-events@egroups.com (July 18, 2001).

3. Aaron Lerner, "Museum Exhibit That Sums It All Up," *Jerusalem Post* (February 17, 1997).

4. As cited in "Conflicting Claims," *Artifax* (Winter 2000), pp. 1, 3.

5. Ariel Sharon, "Towards a National Agenda of Peace and Security," address to Palestinian Authority Policy Conference in Washington, D.C. (March 19, 2001), p. 1.

6. As cited in a *Baltimore Sun Service* and Associated Press report, "Israel Closes Holy Site Fearing Reprisal Attack" (March 5, 1994).

7. As cited by Saud Abu Ramadan, "No Israeli Jews in Holy Site," United Press International (April 7, 2000).

8. As cited by Etgar Lefkovits, "Wakf 'Did not coordinate with police' Temple Mount workers evicted," *The Jewish Press* (September 14, 2001), p. 10.

9. Report on CNN from mayor's office, September 25, 1996.

10. Much of this report is based on a personal conversation with Gershon Salomon and details he published on the website of the Temple Mount Faithful in October 1998.

11. Rabbi Chaim Richman, *Newsletter of the Temple Institute* (January 16, 2000), p. 2.

12. Ronny Reich as cited in Netty C. Gross, "Demolishing David," *The Jerusalem Report* (September 11, 2000), p. 42.

13. Dr. Eilat Mazar, member of the Committee Against the Destruction of Antiquities, as cited in Etgar Lefkovits, "Illegal Waqf construction destroying Temple Period artifacts on Temple Mount," *Jerusalem Post* (March 1, 2001).

14. Arutz Sheva News Service, Thursday, December 26, 1996.

15. Avraham Shmuel Lewin, "Fear Collapse of Temple Mount Wall," *The Jewish Press* (August 24, 2001), p. 82.

16. Ibid.

17. As cited in "Temple Mount in Congress: Bill Seeks to Halt Construction" (September 26, 2001).

18. Cited in Nadav Shragai, "Settlement rabbis mull ending the ban on Jews on Temple Mount," endtimes-news-events (July 18, 2001).

19. Nadav Shragai, "A cause for lament—situation on Temple Mount," *Ha'aretz* (July 29, 2001).

20. As cited in the press briefing "Cantor Introduces Temple Mount Preservation Act (VA-07)" (July 19, 2001), p. 2.

21. Cited by Avraham and Judith in Ramot endtimes-news-events@egroups.com (July 30, 2001).

22. Ibid.

23. Saud Abu Ramadan, "No Israeli Jews in holy site," United Press International (April 7, 2001).

24. Ibid.

25. Gerald M. Steinberg, "Playing out a familiar script," *Jerusalem Post* (July 29, 2001).

26. Joseph Farah, "Destruction of Holy Places," *Worldnet Daily* (August 2, 2001).

Chapter 16—Does Prophecy Affect Politics?

1. As cited by Arthur Kac, *The Rebirth of the State of Israel* (Chicago: Moody Press, 1958), p. 86.

2. Arthur Hertzberg, "A Small Peace for the Middle East," *Foreign Affairs* 80:1 (January/February 2001), p. 139.

3. Joseph Heller, "Zionism and the Jewish Problem," symposium on *The Future of the Jews*, edited by J.J. Lynz (London: Lindsay Drummond, 1945), p. 72.

4. As cited by Arnold Olson, *Inside Jerusalem, City of Destiny* (Glendale, CA: Gospel Light Publications, 1968), pp. 179-80.

5. Harold Foos, "Jerusalem in Biblical Prophecy," *Dictionary of Premillennial Theology*, ed. Mal Couch (Grand Rapids: Kregel Publications, 1996), pp. 209-10.

6. Gershon Salomon, *The Voice of the Temple Mount* online newsletter (July 26, 2001).

7. Ibid.

8. Sheikh Nadim Al-Jisr as cited in D.F. Green, ed., *Arab Theologians on Jews and Israel: Extracts from the Proceedings of the Fourth Conference of the Academy of Islamic Research,* 3d ed. (Geneva: Editions de l'Avenir, 1976), p. 51.

9. Ibid., p. 52.

10. As cited in D.F. Green, ed., *Arab Theologians on Jews and Israel: Extracts from the Proceedings of the Fourth Conference of the Academy of Islamic Research,* 3d ed. (Geneva: Editions de l'Avenir, 1976), p. 51.

11. Ibid.

12. Ibid.

13. As cited in *Dispatch from Jerusalem* 26:4 (July-August, 2001), p. 6.

14. As cited at the Al-Muhajiroun website (September 20, 2001).

15. Hani Shukrallah, "Apocalypse Deferred," *Al-Ahram Weekly Online,* issue no. 537 (June 7-13, 2001), pp. 1-2.

Chapter 17—Why Can't They All Just Get Along?

1. Yasser Arafat, *El Mundo* (Venezuela, February 11, 1980), as cited in Ramon Bennet, *The Great Deception: Philistine* (Jerusalem: Arm of Salvation, 1995), p. 100.

2. Niak Goldberg, "Setting the Stage for Conflict: A History of Palestine Under British Rule Shows How Little Has Changed in the Battle Between Arabs and Jews," *Newsday* (November 18, 2000).

3. *Oxford Dictionary of Quotations.*

4. Shafiq Ahmad Ali, *Al-Arabi* (June 24, 2001), translated by the Middle East Media Research Institute (Washington, D.C.) as cited by David Horovitz, "Infamous Last Words," *The Jerusalem Report* 12:7 (July 30, 2001), p. 4.

5. As cited by Clarence Wagner, Jr., "Israel's Defensible Borders," *Dispatch from Jerusalem* 15:4 (1990), p. 11.

6. Salah Khalaf Abu Iyad, in Amman, Jordan on January 5, 1991 at a Fatah Day celebration.

7. William Rusher, "No Peace in Store for Israel," *San Antonio Express-News* (September 21, 1993), p. 11A.

8. Joan Peters, *From Time Immemorial* (San Francisco: Harper & Row, 1984), pp. 391-92.

9. Yasser Arafat, *El Mundo* (Venezuela, February 11, 1980), as cited in Ramon Bennet, *The Great Deception: Philistine* (Jerusalem: Arm of Salvation, 1995), p. 100.

10. As cited in an article distributed by Shoshana Walker, iNews-only@yahoogroups.com (April 30, 2001).

11. Remarks with President George W. Bush and Israeli prime minister Ariel Sharon (White House Oval Office, Washington, D.C., Tuesday June 26, 2001).

12. Yehuda Sherman, "The Hitler-Arafat Comparison," *Jerusalem Post International Edition,* Letters section (May 18, 2001), p. 80

13. As cited by Tzemach News Service, June 16, 2001. See also, "When the Good Get Going, the Going Gets Tough," by Matt Rees and Jamil Hamad, *Time* (July 30, 2001), p. 10.

14. As cited in an interview with Hassan by Sheila Raviv, *Jerusalem Post* (June 15, 2001).

15. As reported by Stan Goodenough of the International Christian Embassy in Jerusalem News Service in Jerusalem, March 20, 1998.

16. *Jerusalem Post* (March 11, 1998).

17. Paul Greenberg, "The War Called Peace," http://www.Townhall.com (June 25, 2001).

18. As cited by Ibrahim Barzazk, "U.S. is attempting to preserve truce," Associated Press report (June 16, 2001).

Chapter 18—Will There Be Another War?

1. As reported on Al-Jazeera television, May 14, 1998 and quoted in *Dispatch from Jerusalem* (July-August 1998), p. 19.

2. Hirsh Goodman, "My Word: A Recipe for Palestinian Disaster," *The Jerusalem Report* (June 18, 2001), p. 8.

3. Recorded on May 10, 1994 and reported by Arutz Sheva offshore radio.

4. Grant Livingstone, "Israel's Integrity and the SLA," *International Jerusalem Post*.

5. As cited in an interview with Hassan by Sheila Raviv, *Jerusalem Post* (June 15, 2001).

6. Anwar El Sadat, speech at the El Hussein Mosque celebrating the birthday of the prophet Muhammad (April 25, 1972), as cited in D.F. Green, ed., *Arab Theologians on Jews and Israel: Extracts from the Proceedings of the Fourth Conference of the Academy of Islamic Research*, 3d ed. (Geneva: Editions de l'Avenir, 1976), pp. 89-90.

7. As cited in *Jerusalem Post* (May 21, 2001).

8. Moshe Arens as reported on Israel's Channel 1 television, July 26, 2001.

9. As cited by Peter King, *Jordan Times* (September 25, 2001).

10. As cited in article "Bush Opens Arsenal to Mideast" *Defense News* (September 24-30, 2001).

11. Chris Hedges, "The New Palestinian Revolt," *Foreign Affairs* 80:1 (January/February 2000), p. 137.

12. Hirsh Goodman, "My Word: A Recipe for Palestinian Disaster," *The Jerusalem Report* (June 18, 2001), p. 8.

13. As cited in an Associated Press report, "Militants Lash Out at Both Sides," December 11, 1993.

14. As cited by Marguerite Michaels and reported by Robert Slater, "Settlers: Violence to Do God's Work," *Time,* September 13, 1993.

15. As cited in Associated Press report "Riots Deepen Pessimism over Peace Talks in Mideast," March 3, 1994.

16. Hani Shukrallah, "Apocalypse Deferred," *Al-Ahram Weekly Online*, issue no. 537 (June 7-13, 2001), p. 1.

17. As cited in the newspaper *Iton Yerushalayim,* Jerusalem (December 10, 1993).

18. Benjamin Netanyahu, address before U.S. Congress (September 20, 2001).

19. As cited by United Press International terrorism correspondent Richard Sale, "U.S. Intelligence: 'Israel Will Attack' " (July 20, 2001).

20. As cited in "Palestinians Round Up Collaborators," BBC News (August 1, 2001).

21. See Khaled Abu Toameh, "Uniform Culture: Yasser Arafat secretly builds up an army of 100,000 men ahead of statehood," *The Jerusalem Report* (July 31, 2000), pp. 28-29.

22. As cited in "Israel's risk in major strike," *Stratford Global Intelligence Update*, WorldNetDaily (August 3, 2001).

23. Martin Sherman, "Unleash the dogs of war," endtimes-news-events@egroups.com (July 29, 2001).

Chapter 19—Will There Ever Be Peace?

1. Zebulon Baird Vance, *The Scattered Nation* (Raleigh, NC: Alfred Williams & Company, 1891), p. 57.

2. Speech by Benjamin Netanyahu at the general assembly of the American Council of Jewish Federations, November 16, 1997 (communicated by the prime minister's media advisor), p. 2.

3. Arthur Hertzberg, "A Small Peace for the Middle East," *Foreign Affairs* 80:1 (January/February 2001), pp. 139, 143.

4. The basis for this new covenant is the atoning death of the Messiah, and thus becomes the shared reality for Gentiles as well as Jews who, in the present dispensation of the church, have been included under its spiritual provisions through faith in Jesus (see Hebrews 8:6-13). Its provisions concerning the Land and outreach to the nations will be realized by the whole nation of Israel (as promised by Jeremiah in this chapter), not simply a remnant left by grace (Romans 11:5), when it is fulfilled after the second advent of Christ.

Chapter 20—What Should We Do?

1. Flo Conway and Jim Siegelman, *Holy Terror: The Fundamentalist War on America's Freedoms in Religion, Politics and Our Private Lives* (New York: Dell Publishing Co., Inc., 1984), p. 3.

2. Jan Willem van der Hoeven, director, "Two Thousand Years of Longing and Praying for Nothing?" (International Christian Zionist Center, June 22, 2001).

3. As cited in William Safire, "Bush's Mideast Charade" (October 25, 2001).

4. Ariel Sharon, press briefing statement communicated by the prime minister's media adviser (October 7, 2001).

5. William Safire, "Bush's Mideast Charade" (October 25, 2001).

6. Golda Meir, *My Life* (New York: Dell Publishing Co., Inc., 1975), pp. 417-18.

7. Benjamin Netanyahu, *A Place Among the Nations: Israel and the World* (New York: Bantam Books, 1993), p. 259.

8. New Jerusalem Ministries "SOS" website: "Frequently Asked Questions: The Christian's Obligation and Involvement" (http://www.fan.net.au/`sos/obli.htm).

9. Comments on the Israeli street as reported by David Dolan, personal report (September 11, 2001).

10. As cited in the "Letters" section, *Time* (October 29, 2001).

11. Col. Stanislav Lunev, "Attacks on America Are Not Over" (September 14, 2001), http://www.NewsMax.com.

12. As cited in personal correspondance to the author, October 12, 2001.

Person Index

Abdullah II (King of Jordan)	24, 96, 102, 141-42
Alami, Khalil al	17, 20
Alamoudi, Abdurahman	217-18
Allah	21, 31, 53, 85, 99, 100, 116, 179-96, 205-06, 216, 219, 223, 234, 241, 254, 263-64, 270, 310, 314-17, 343
Arafat, Yasser	29, 41, 53-4, 59, 62-8, 98, 100, 102, 108, 113, 119, 123-27, 142, 146, 155-56, 173, 197, 200, 223, 226, 229, 233-45, 252-54, 277, 281, 285, 294-95, 311-13, 323, 327-35, 343-51, 353, 356, 377
Balflour, Alfred James	75
Barak, Ehud	62-68, 102, 126, 172, 250, 291, 295, 312, 327, 343
Ben-Gurion, David	71, 171, 301, 304, 323, 382-83
Blair, Tony	24, 40, 378
Bush, George Sr.	331-32, 351
Bush, George W.	7, 17, 18, 20, 24, 38-44, 217, 303, 331-32
Churchill, Winston	175, 225, 323
Clinton, Bill	24, 48, 63, 217, 243, 312
Dayan, Moshe	117-18, 281
Durras, Mohammad al	12, 59
Eidelberg, Paul	51, 218
Goodman, Hirsh	341, 347
Goren, Shlomo	79, 118, 122, 347
Gorenberg, Gershom	302, 318
Grossman, Aaron M.D.	376
Gur, Mordecai	117, 281
Hattut, Hasan	211-15
Hitti, Philip	138, 154
Hoeven, Jan Willem van der	379
Hogarth, David George	136-37
Hussein, King (of Jordan)	101, 102, 108, 111, 142, 166, 213
Hussein, Saddam	19-20, 30, 51, 53, 65, 67, 124, 224, 299, 357
Husseini, Mufti Haj Amin el	229, 294
Jesus	21, 73, 99, 179-82, 219, 269, 271, 277, 306-07, 310, 370, 373, 385, 389
King, Rodney	323-24
Laden, Osama bin	9, 17-24, 30-41, 46-48, 51, 53, 65, 124, 190, 194, 199, 202, 204, 207, 210, 212, 217-18, 220-21, 224, 382
Landau, Uzi	298-99
McDonald, James G.	26, 69
McGuire, Barry	55-56
Mubarak, Hosni	23, 123, 346
Muhammad	21, 31, 39, 93-94, 123, 149, 179, 180, 181-88, 191, 196-97, 205-06, 210-11, 214, 245, 264, 266, 269-70, 276, 310, 314-17, 343

Nadim, Sheikh Al-Jisr	315-16
Netanyahu, Benjamin	4, 14, 35, 64, 101-02, 156, 225, 252, 343, 345, 350, 361, 383
Olmert, Ehud	87, 101, 223, 236, 252, 286, 291
Omen, Mullah Mohammad	40, 203
Palazzi, Abdul Hadi	94, 275
Pipes, Daniel	141, 206
Powell, Colin	39, 381
Rohan, Dennis	247-49
Sabri, Ikrama	113, 177, 240-45, 253, 259, 263, 291, 295
Sadat, Anwar	102, 122, 123, 146, 344
Salomon, Gershon	268, 311
Sharon, Ariel	23-4, 35, 38, 41, 44, 49, 57-68, 91, 102, 127, 226, 253-55, 282-83, 299, 312-13, 331-33, 341, 345, 348, 351, 382, 384
Shragai, Nadav	98, 281, 292, 295
Soudah, Jeris	239, 245
Steinberg, Gerald	86, 299
Truman, Harry S.	75, 323
Yitzhak, Rabin	4, 63, 101, 124-26, 252, 286, 331, 335, 348

Subject Index

Al-Aqsa

burning of	247-48
intifada of	61, 254
riots at	57-60, 283-84, 297

Al-Qaeda

nature of	207
threat of	18-19, 24, 37, 190

America

as Great Satan	30, 33, 36, 79, 208, 218
previous terrorist attack on	203-04
and radical Muslims	208-09

Christians

beliefs of	21-22, 73-76, 213, 306-07, 311, 369
challenge to	178-79
Islamic view of	12, 20-22, 39, 100, 115, 183, 193, 209, 210-11, 221-23, 269-70, 276, 303, 344
and Jews	13-14, 296, 302, 313, 319-21, 385-86

CIA   37, 350

Coalition   10, 38-50, 98, 127, 209, 224, 346, 352, 381

Crusades

period of rule	158
holy war terminology	184, 214
and states of Jerusalem	187

Dhimmis

description of	183, 198
fight against	21
history of Jews as	227-230, 269
Israel as state of	229-230
restrictions upon	226-227

Intifada

Al-Aqsa	61, 254
beginnings of	64
at Temple Mount	280-81

Iraq

and attack on U.S.	20, 204, 209
and declared war on Jews	67
and refusal of Palestinian refugees	174
independence of	155
Invasion of Kuwait and	31
Islam's holy sites and	93
Jewish communities in	107
new immigration from	175
Palestinian immigrants from	112
Palestinian soldiers from	353
students in U.S. from	220
ties with Osama bin Laden	46
U.S. Gulf War and	43, 203
U.S. plan to attack	45, 209, 351, 352, 357
U.S. support of	30
war with Iran and	184
weapons smuggling and	353

Islam

beliefs of	179-81
compared to the Bible	181-82
establishment of Khilafah	29, 197, 205
militant beliefs	205
moderate behavior	206, 216-20
origin of radicals	200-03
problems of shirk	183, 269
as religion of peace	193
sects of	199-200
spread of	178, 201-02

Israel

and coalition	38-40, 45
key to conflict	10
and Osama bin Laden	39
and terrorism	36, 44
U.S. support	32, 53

Jerusalem

in bin Laden's poem	40
capture in 1967	78, 232
center of conflict	28
end-time gathering	79
in history	99-101, 272
Jewish majority	159, 232
Palestinian statements about	197-98
problem of redivision	236-240

significance   76, 80-83, 87-97, 101-03, 225-26, 237-238, 271
and war on terrorism   47

Jihad
against Israel, U.S.   195-98, 204-05, 216, 225, 317, 339
against Jews, non-Muslims   47-48, 63-65, 127-28, 175, 195-98
Arab retaliation   45
call to   39, 45, 56, 59, 64-67, 213, 245, 298, 316-17, 341, 343
and coalition   46
concept of   184-85, 210
and deception   191, 200, 202, 205, 220, 222, 339
and foreign control   194-95
Islamic duty   179, 183-85
and Jerusalem Project   47
and peace   190-93, 198
recent causes of   28
reward for   188-89, 206
training for   189-90, 194-95
types of   186-88, 200-05, 220, 222, 339

Jordan
Al-Qaeda attacks in   23
Arab League and   113
armistice of 1949 and   230
assassination of Abdullah I of   102
attitude toward Jerusalem   96-97
attitude toward Jews of king of   218
creation of   108, 138, 142
East Jerusalem and   65, 96, 103, 231-32, 281
and identification with southern Syria   141
independence of   155
and Israeli war with Palestinians   23-24, 40
negotiations over Jerusalem and   101
new immigration from/to   175, 334
no Jewish citizenship in   112
Palestine as   108, 112, 142, 327-28
Palestinian population of   112, 168
Palestinian refugees and   163, 166-67, 170, 174
Palestinian soldiers from   353
Palestinian state and   116
and peace treaty with Israel   38, 101, 113, 170, 185, 363
PLO and   123, 142
Roman name of   137
Six-Day War and   138, 159-60, 166-67
Temple Mount and   113, 272
terrorists attack on   26
training for *jihad* in   194
weapons smuggling from   353
West Bank annexation and   109

Joseph's tomb
attack on   58

Judaism
beliefs of   102, 232, 239, 261, 303-06, 319-22
and the Temple   28, 57-58, 98, 271

Media
disinformation in   8, 378
errors in   376-77
objectivism of   8, 376

Muhammad
conquest of Mecca   182
corrupted by Satan   181
early life of   181-83
and Jews   179, 266
marriages   67
Mount of Olives (pilgrimage)   260
and terrorism   196-97

Palestine
and Haram   250-51
identity of   132-36, 139-41
immigrant workers   157-58
and independent state   49, 65
nationalism of   142-43
as refugees   161-67
revisionism   146, 152-56, 161, 192, 246
statements against America   53-54, 254

Peace
and Christians   385-86
future   92, 308-12, 359-74, 378-79
Islamic   99-101, 115-16, 132, 161, 185-86, 190-201, 209-10, 214-20, 301, 317, 323
negotiations   8, 36, 61-67, 70, 87, 98, 102, 108-09, 13, 118, 122-29, 141, 170-71, 209, 224, 226, 232-33, 236-37, 242, 318, 234-44
Oslo process   11, 36, 65-66, 99, 113, 115, 119, 122, 129, 143, 172, 192, 281, 325, 335, 342-48, 350, 353, 356, 378
prospects for   38-58, 92, 116
with God   389-90

Prophecy
in address of Ben-Gurion   304-05
aim of Zionism and   75, 302
and Antichrist   238, 307, 310
and burning of the Al-Aqsa Mosque   247
in comparison chart   319-22
and education in Israel   71
of end of warfare   365-66
of false peace   378
and Feast of Tabernacles   305-06, 370
and founding of Israel   71-72
of Gentile worship   370-71
Gershom Gorenberg and   302
of Gog and Magog   312
of Jerusalem (in Christianity)   306-09
of Jerusalem (in Islam)   309-10
of Jerusalem (in Judaism)   303-06
of Jerusalem as a peaceful center   368
of Jerusalem's destruction (Jesus)   73
of Jewish regathering   76, 314
of Jewish state (in Islam)   315
and millennium   308-09, 369
and Mount of Olives   309
of Muhammad   315
of the New Covenant   368-69
and political decisions   13, 301-18
of rebuilding Temple (Muslim)   272

and return to Zion 75, 78-79, 90
status of Jesus as (in Islam) 269
in symbolic interpretation 74
and terrorists 316-17
of United States (in Islam) 317
of universal peace 367-71

Radicalism
Arab nationalism and 44-46
beliefs of 32, 49, 70, 185, 205-07, 212, 303
and blame for terrorist attack on U.S. 19, 204
definition of Islam in 193, 222
and distinction from moderate Islam 209-15, 346
global objectives of 242, 353
groups in 203-04
and hatred of Jews 222, 347
immorality of 207-08
and Jews 254, 331
jihad in 189, 194, 203, 216, 220-21, 343
origin of 200-23
Oslo Accord and 125
percentage of Islam as 381
popularity of (in Mid-East) 218
poverty and 326
student associations and 220
support of Palestinian cause by 131-32
Taliban government as 191
U.S. support of 30-31
U.S. war with 221-22
view of Israel in 38
view of Jerusalem 28-29, 68, 102, 242, 357
view of U.S. in 208-09
World Trade Center and 212

Radicals
majority outside West are 218
perception of Muslims as 9-12

Rebuilding of the Temple
in Jewish prayers 76, 92
Muslim claim of Jewish desire to 242, 245, 251-52, 285, 294
prophecy of 313, 368, 370, 390
Six-Day War and 116-17, 272
Temple Mount Faithful and 252-53

Revisionism
distribution by 146
examples of 154-60, 226-28, 243-44, 263-64
media and 379, 390
Palestinian purpose of 143
Temple Mount and 244, 263-64

Settlers
dispute with 63, 186, 333, 350
Israeli and Arab 175, 348
removal of 66, 333

Syria
claim to Israel 163
religion of ruling dynasty 199-200
terrorism 19-20

Temple
ancient history of	88-89
antiquities of	289-91
archaeological evidence for	246, 260-61
burning model of	53
Camp David II and	239
Christians and	280
Ezekiel's future plan of	308
Foundation Stone of	94
Gentiles in	370-71
in replacement theology	276
Jesus prophecy and	73
Jewish prayers for	92
location of	239, 294
Muslim identification of	266, 273
Muslim prophecy of rebuilding	272
Muslim threat against	251
Palestinian denial of	239, 243-44, 246, 253, 259, 262-64
remembrance of destruction of	102
terms for	135
Western Wall and	58, 245

Temple Mount
biblical promise to	303
Christians and	314, 379
claim of Jewish plot against	257
closing of	283-84, 295-96
construction on	292-99
and conversion to mosque	384-85
danger of Southern Wall collapse	291-92
destruction of antiquities	62, 287-92
in Islamic history	266-71
Israeli raid on	299
and Israeli Supreme Court	62
in Jewish history	271-72
Jewish prayers on	239
Jewish sovereignty over	283-84, 287
Jordanian restrictions	280-81
lifting of ban on	299
Marawani Mosque and	288
Muslim burials on	310
Muslims' disregard for	267, 273-87
negotiations for	326
new war and	300
New York Times error about	376-77
Preservation Act of 2001 and	296
prophetic glory of	367
Rabbinic plan for visit to	298
right of access to	58, 62, 250, 282, 284
Sharon's visit to	283-84
status quo change	62, 279-87
struggle for	302, 311
Temple Mount Faithful and	311-13
why cannot be shared	238-40

Temple Mount Faithful
cornerstone ceremony of	253-54, 270-80

Terrorism

in America 23, 28-29, 32-36, 303, 386-87
countries of occurrence 26, 380, 375
ethics of 207-08, 318, 325-26
and Islam 9, 26-29, 214-21, 242, 318, 326, 375
in Israel 10-13, 18, 25-36, 130, 330-39, 356
and Jerusalem 14, 330-39
organizations 19, 130, 330-333
and Palestine 11, 13, 25
rejection of 9
and Syria 20
types of 13, 26, 207
view of U.S. 208-09, 303
war on 10, 26, 224, 296, 303, 314, 318, 326, 342-68,
                                        381-84

United Nations

censure of Israel 61, 248
deceptions of 323
partitioning of Arab states 54, 66, 108, 129, 166, 171, 230-31, 163
peace resolutions 40
recognition of Jewish state 109
refugee resolutions 167-74

War

against terrorism 10
Arabs and Israel (1948) 44
blame for 19-26, 30, 41, 52
Christians and 12, 20-23
comparison to Pearl Harbor 17-18
as a crusade 20-22
declaration of 17-19
nature of 9-12, 17-18
with Islam 9, 29, 221-22
with Israel at center 15, 39, 42-44

Weapons

Nuclear 14
Palestinian arsenals 356-57

Zionism

history of 72, 107, 129, 157, 302
Islamic view of 23-24, 39, 46-53, 66, 98, 142, 145, 160, 162, 193, 103,
                                        226, 242, 249, 257
leaders of 144, 277

Free Newsletter About the Unholy War

If you enjoyed the information in this book and would like to stay updated on current events in the Middle East, you can do so with our bimonthly newsletter *World of the Bible News & Views*. To receive a complimentary subscription, please make your request through our website or send it to our ministry address.

A catalog of our books, publications, videos, and CD products can be found online at our website www.worldofthebible.com, or you may request a printed copy from our office.

Dr. Randall Price is available as a speaker and also conducts annual tours to the Bible Lands. To contact him about speaking to your group or joining him on one of his tours, please call (512) 396-3799.

Dr. Randall Price is the founder and president of World of the Bible Ministries, Inc., a nonprofit corporation that seeks to provide accurate information about the past, present, and future of the biblical world. For information about our various ministries, please contact us at:

World of the Bible Ministries, Inc.
P.O. Box 827
San Marcos, TX 78667-0827

(512) 396-3799/Fax: (512) 392-9080
email: wbmrandl@itouch.net

Other Books by J. Randall Price

Secrets of the Dead Sea Scrolls
Discover the new technology that helps translators with previously unreadable Scrolls fragments, supposedly "secret" Scrolls, the debate about who owns the Scrolls, and the newest efforts to find more. Includes never-before-published photos.

The Stones Cry Out
Recently uncovered ancient artifacts shed light upon the lives of the patriarchs, the Ark of the Covenant, the fall of Jericho, and more. A fascinating survey of the latest finds in Bible lands, with more than 80 photographs affirming the incontrovertible facts that support biblical truth. (Video also available.)

Jerusalem in Prophecy
Jerusalem has an incredible future in store, and it's at the very center of Bible prophecy. This book reveals what will happen, who the key players will be, and what signs indicate we're drawing close. (Video also available.)

The Coming Last Days Temple
The Bible says there's a new Temple in Jerusalem's future, but the current Israeli-Arab conflict makes that seem unlikely. Some claim the prophecies of Jerusalem's future are merely symbolic—but are they? Does the Bible give evidence that we can expect a literal Temple? Dr. Price surveys the preparations now being made for the next Temple, and offers a fascinating perspective on how they fit with biblical prophecy. (Video also available.)